Kamisama Kiss

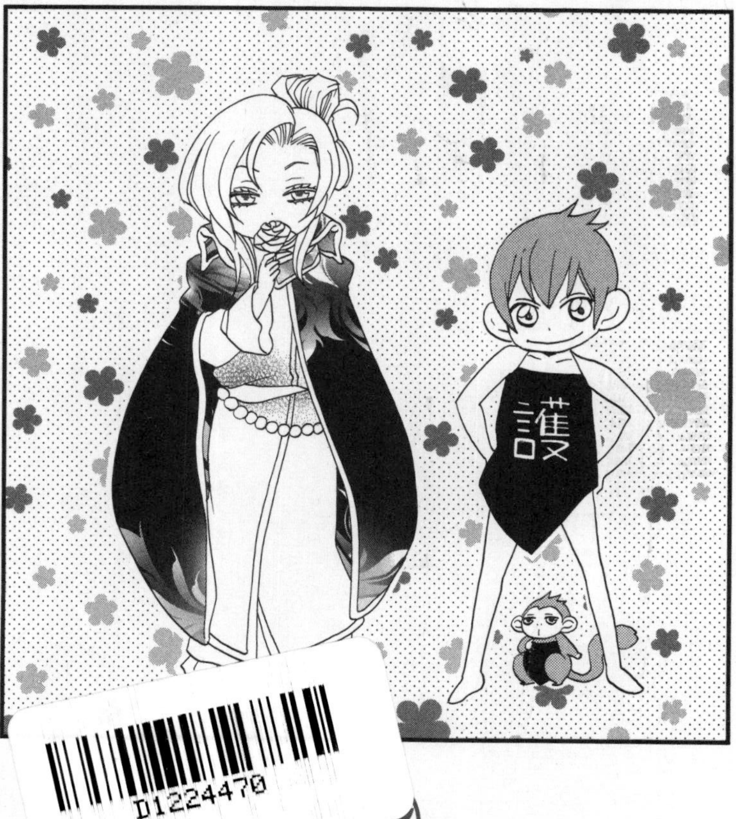
護

21

Story & Art by

Julietta Suzuki

Kamisama Kiss

Volume 21
CONTENTS

CHARACTERS

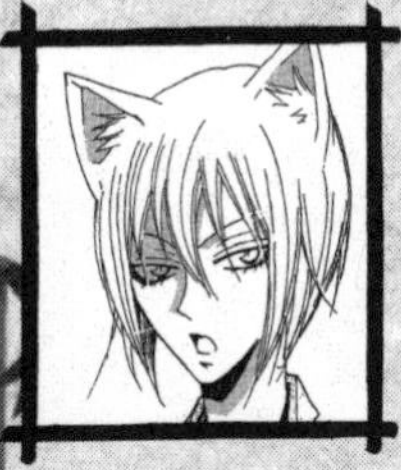

Tomoe

The shinshi who serves Nanami now that she's a tochigami. Originally a wild fox ayakashi.

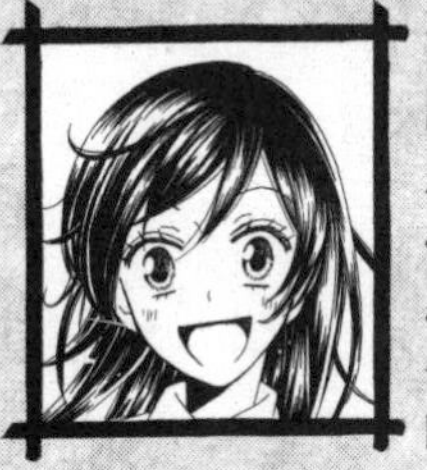

Nanami Momozono

A high school student who was turned into a kamisama by the tochigami Mikage. She likes Tomoe.

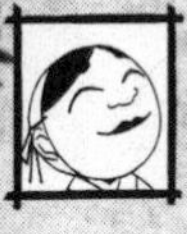

Onikiri

Onibi-warashi, spirits of the shrine.

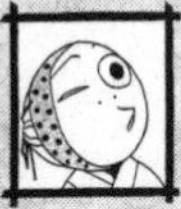

Kotetsu

Onibi-warashi, spirits of the shrine.

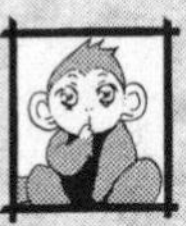

Mamoru

Nanami's shikigami. He can create a spiritual barrier to keep out evil.

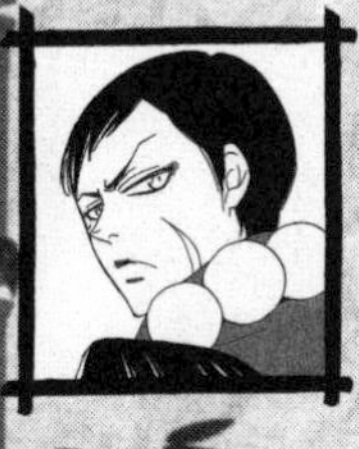

Jiro

A militant tengu from Mount Kurama. He's in love with Nanami.

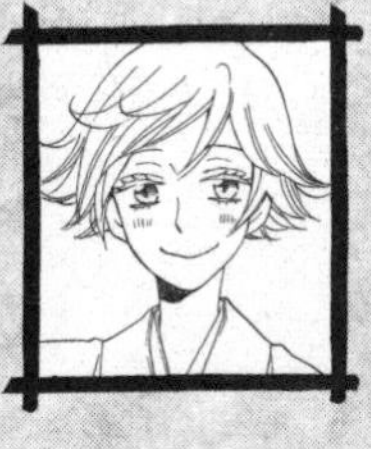

Mizuki

Nanami's second shinshi. The incarnation of a white snake. Used to be the shinshi of Yonomori shrine.

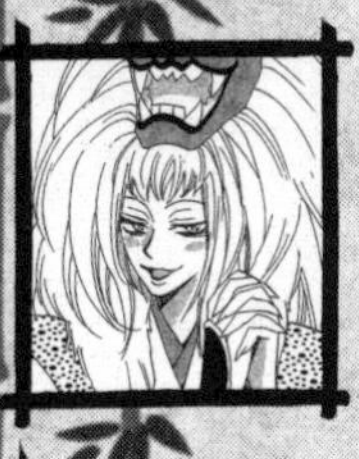

Yatori

A mysterious ayakashi who is cooperating with Kirihito. He yearns for Akura-oh's resurrection.

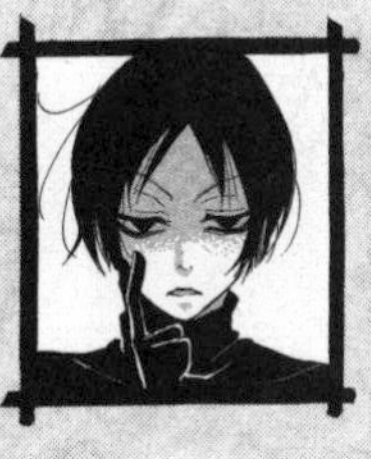

Kirihito

A human whose body was taken over by the great yokai Akura-oh, who committed every evil he possibly could.

Story so far

Nanami Momozono is a high school student who was evicted from her home when her dad skipped town.
She meets the tochigami Mikage in a park, and he leaves his shrine and his kami powers to her.
Now Nanami spends her days with Tomoe and Mizuki, her shinshi, and with Onikiri and Kotetsu, the onibi-warashi spirits of the shrine.
Nanami has been slowly gaining powers as kamisama by holding a festival at her shrine, attending a big kami conference, and all sorts of other adventures.
Nanami's and Tomoe's feelings for each other are finally out in the open and they have started to date!
After some unexpected excitement on the school trip to Okinawa, Tomoe realizes how fleeting human life spans are. So in order to live out his life with Nanami, he drinks the water of evolution to become human, but he's transformed into a fox instead...!

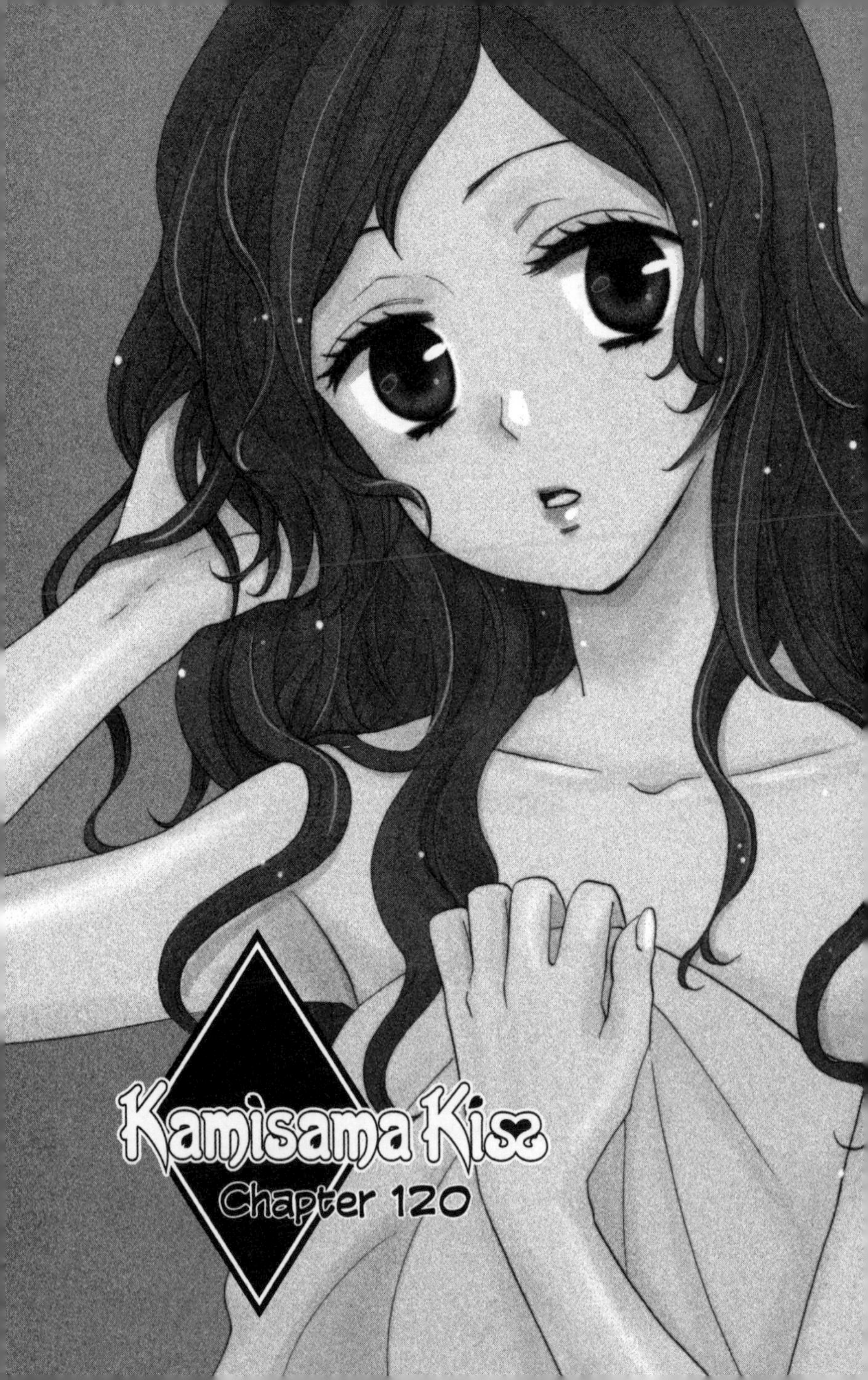
Kamisama Kiss
Chapter 120

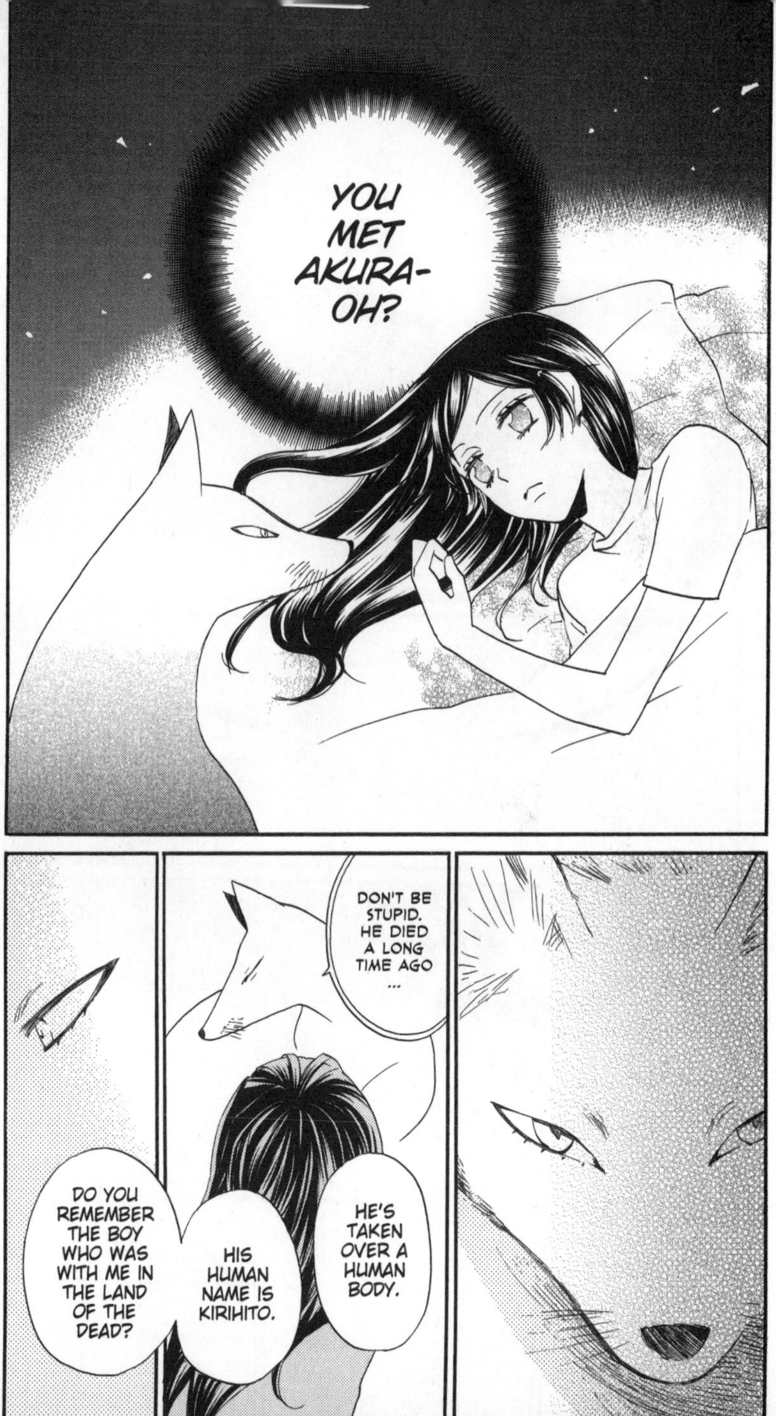
YOU MET AKURA-OH?
DON'T BE STUPID. HE DIED A LONG TIME AGO ...
HE'S TAKEN OVER A HUMAN BODY.
HIS HUMAN NAME IS KIRIHITO.
DO YOU REMEMBER THE BOY WHO WAS WITH ME IN THE LAND OF THE DEAD?

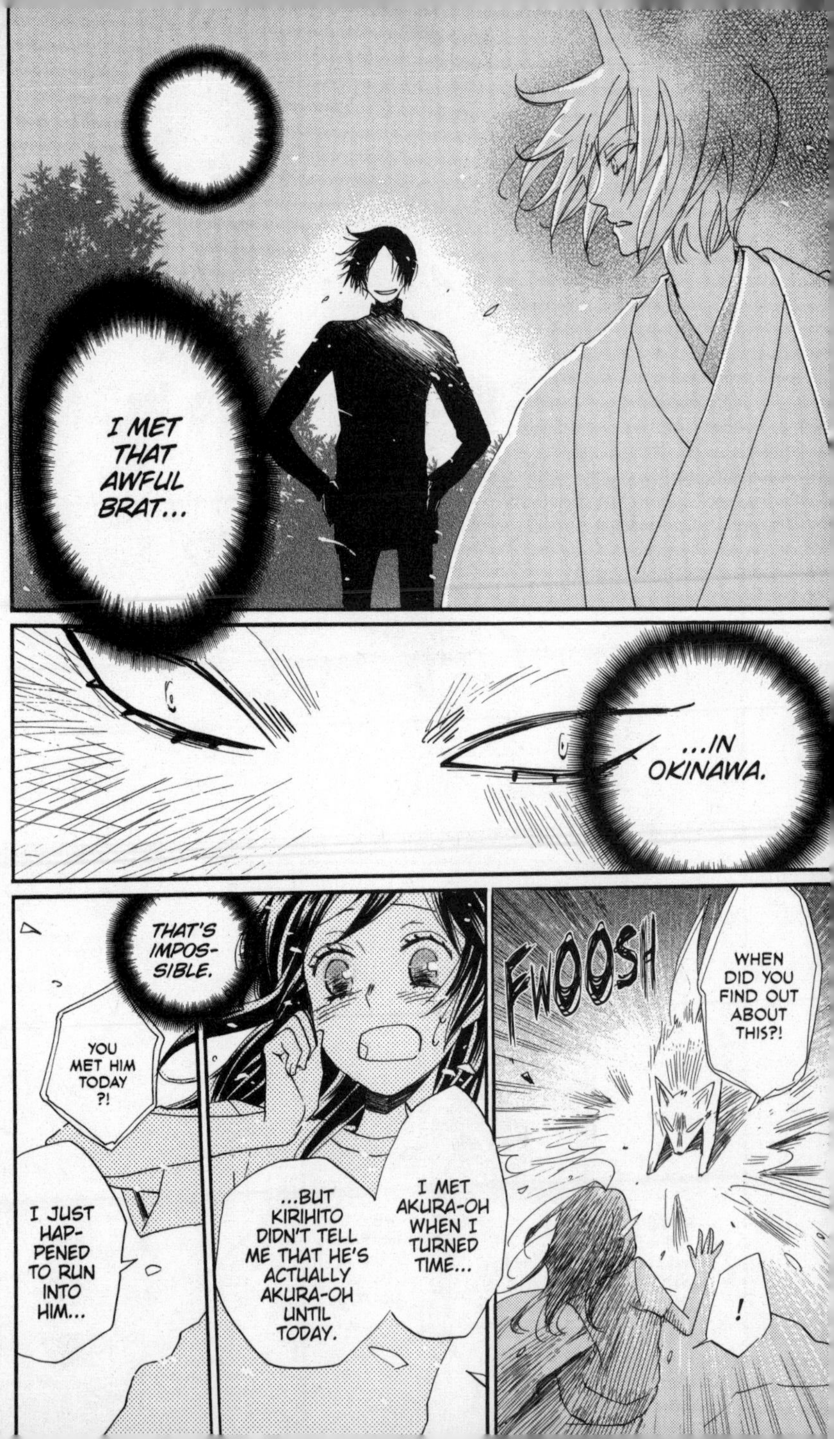
I MET THAT AWFUL BRAT...
...IN OKINAWA.
WHEN DID YOU FIND OUT ABOUT THIS?!
FWOOSH
!
THAT'S IMPOS-SIBLE.
YOU MET HIM TODAY?!
I MET AKURA-OH WHEN I TURNED TIME...
...BUT KIRIHITO DIDN'T TELL ME THAT HE'S ACTUALLY AKURA-OH UNTIL TODAY.
I JUST HAP-PENED TO RUN INTO HIM...

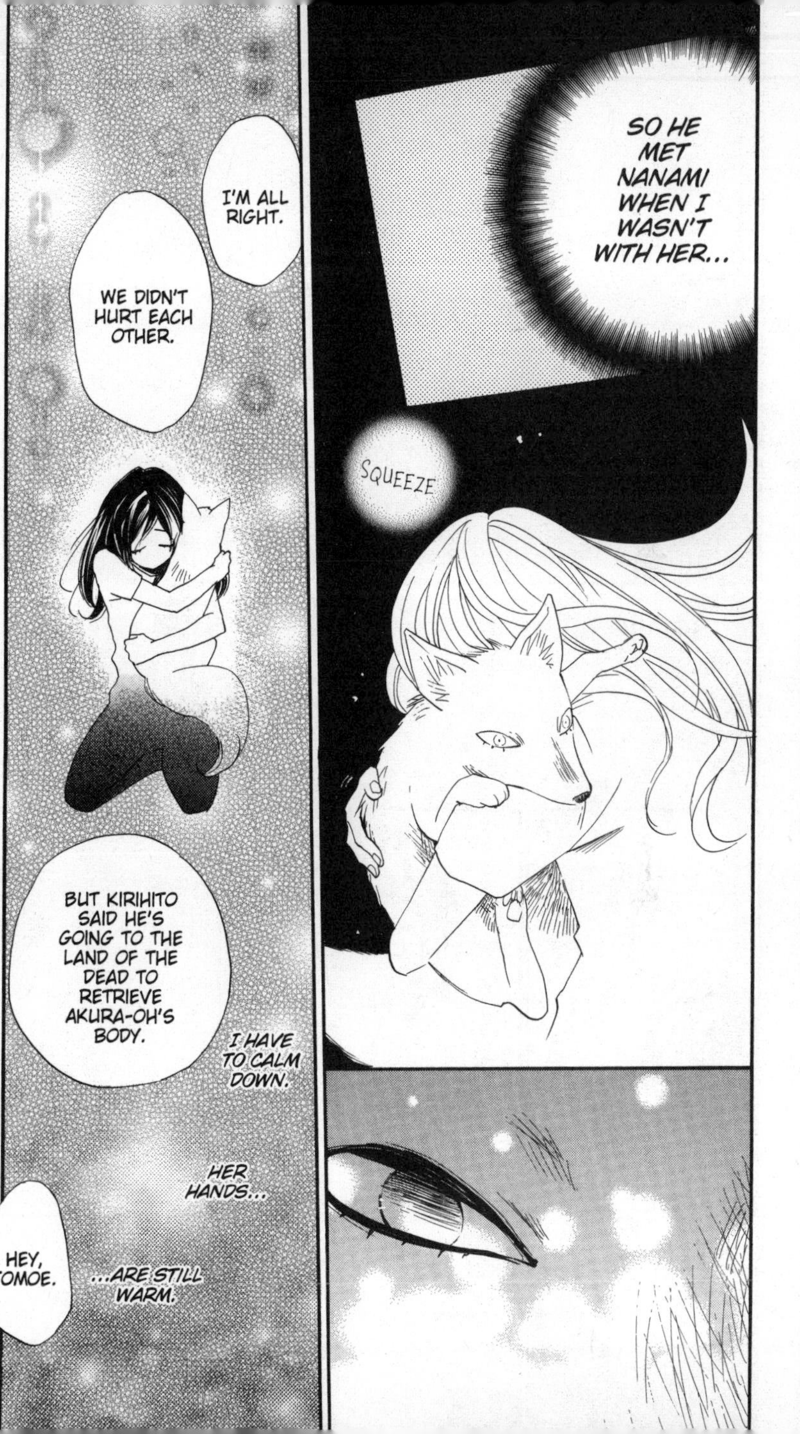
SO HE MET NANAMI WHEN I WASN'T WITH HER...
SQUEEZE
I'M ALL RIGHT.
WE DIDN'T HURT EACH OTHER.
BUT KIRIHITO SAID HE'S GOING TO THE LAND OF THE DEAD TO RETRIEVE AKURA-OH'S BODY.
I HAVE TO CALM DOWN.
HER HANDS...
...ARE STILL WARM.
HEY, TOMOE.

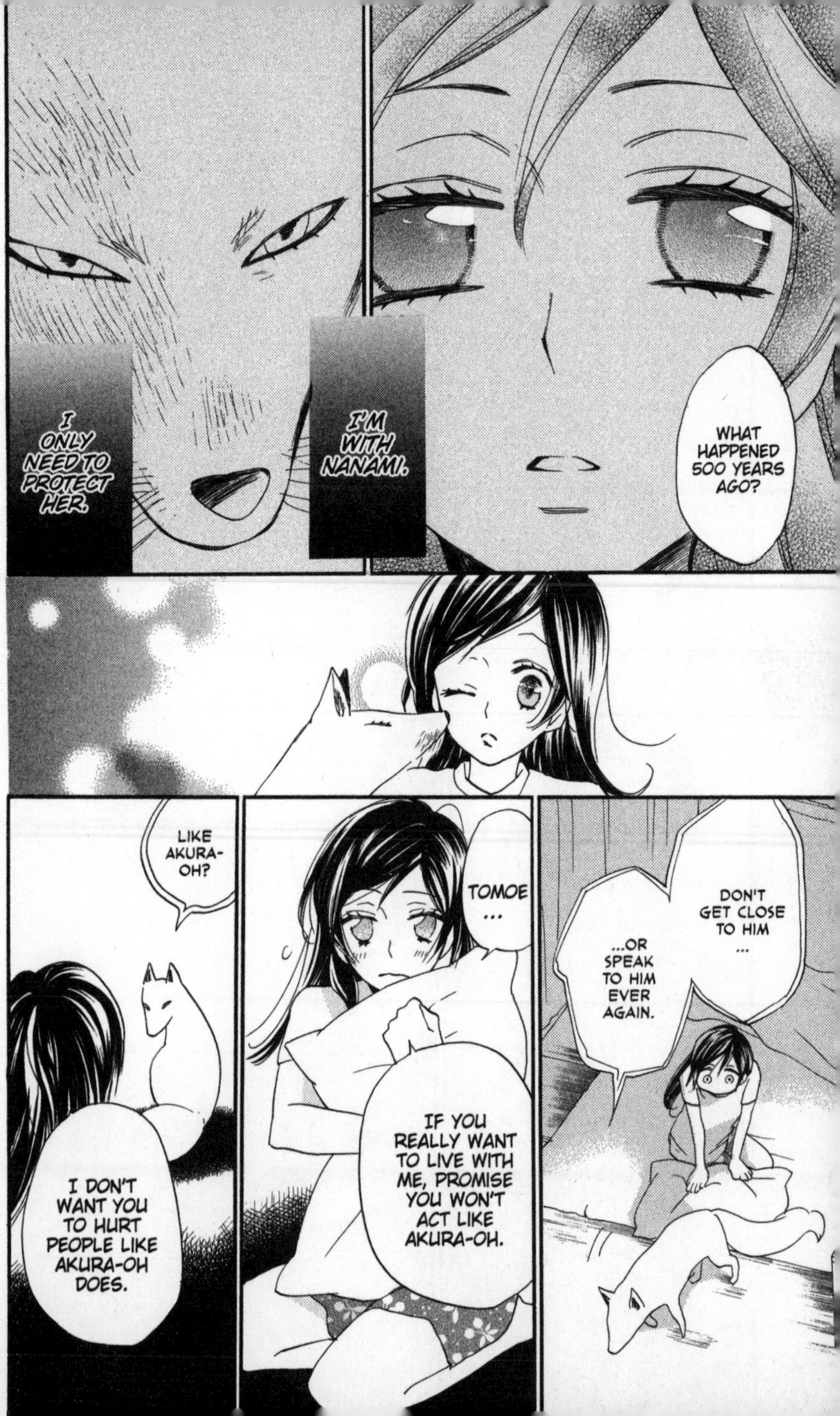
WHAT HAPPENED 500 YEARS AGO?
I'M WITH NANAMI.
I ONLY NEED TO PROTECT HER.
DON'T GET CLOSE TO HIM ...
...OR SPEAK TO HIM EVER AGAIN.
TOMOE ...
IF YOU REALLY WANT TO LIVE WITH ME, PROMISE YOU WON'T ACT LIKE AKURA-OH.
LIKE AKURA-OH?
I DON'T WANT YOU TO HURT PEOPLE LIKE AKURA-OH DOES.

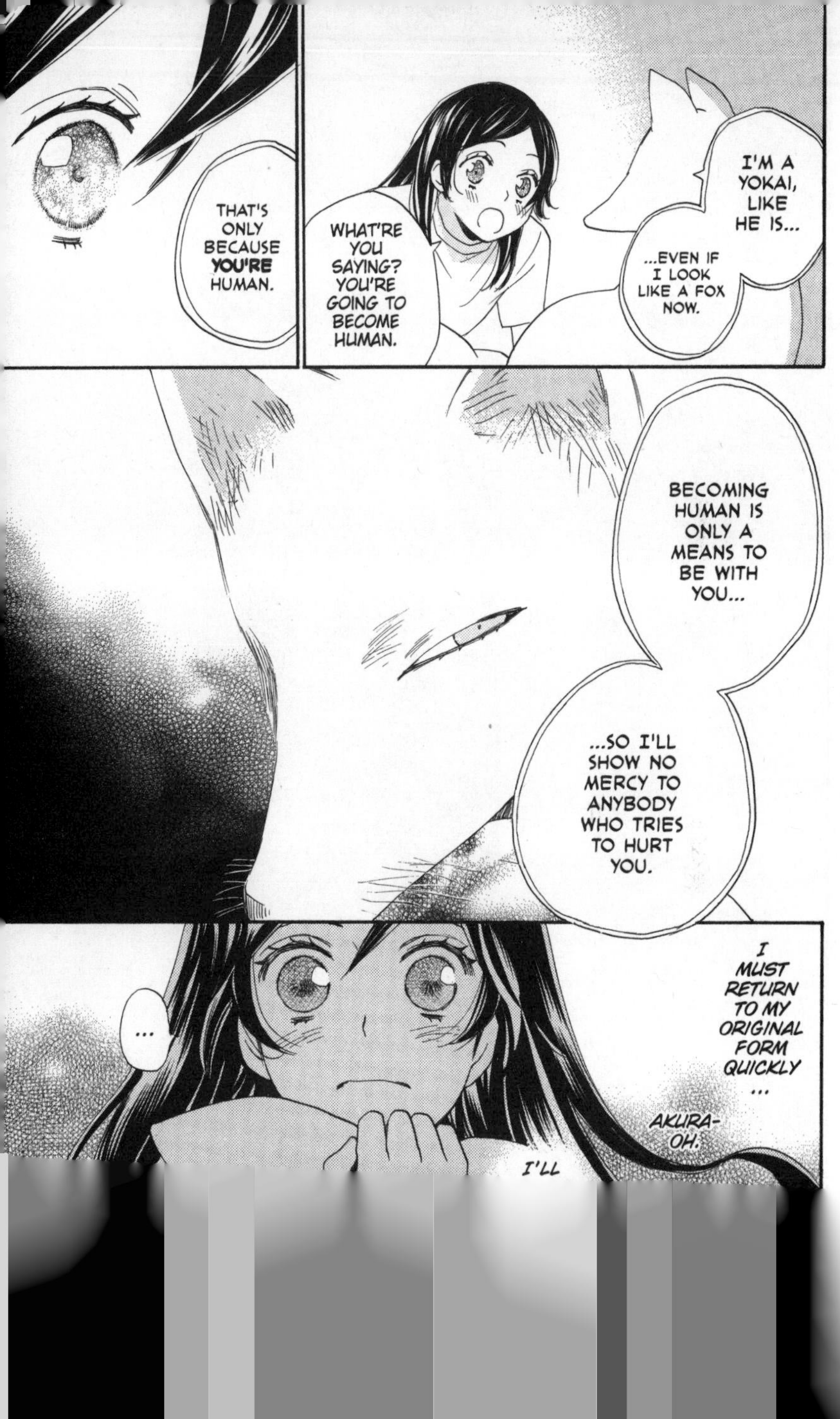
I'M A YOKAI, LIKE HE IS...
...EVEN IF I LOOK LIKE A FOX NOW.
WHAT'RE YOU SAYING? YOU'RE GOING TO BECOME HUMAN.
THAT'S ONLY BECAUSE **YOU'RE** HUMAN.
BECOMING HUMAN IS ONLY A MEANS TO BE WITH YOU...
...SO I'LL SHOW NO MERCY TO ANYBODY WHO TRIES TO HURT YOU.
I MUST RETURN TO MY ORIGINAL FORM QUICKLY ...
AKURA-OH.
...
I'LL

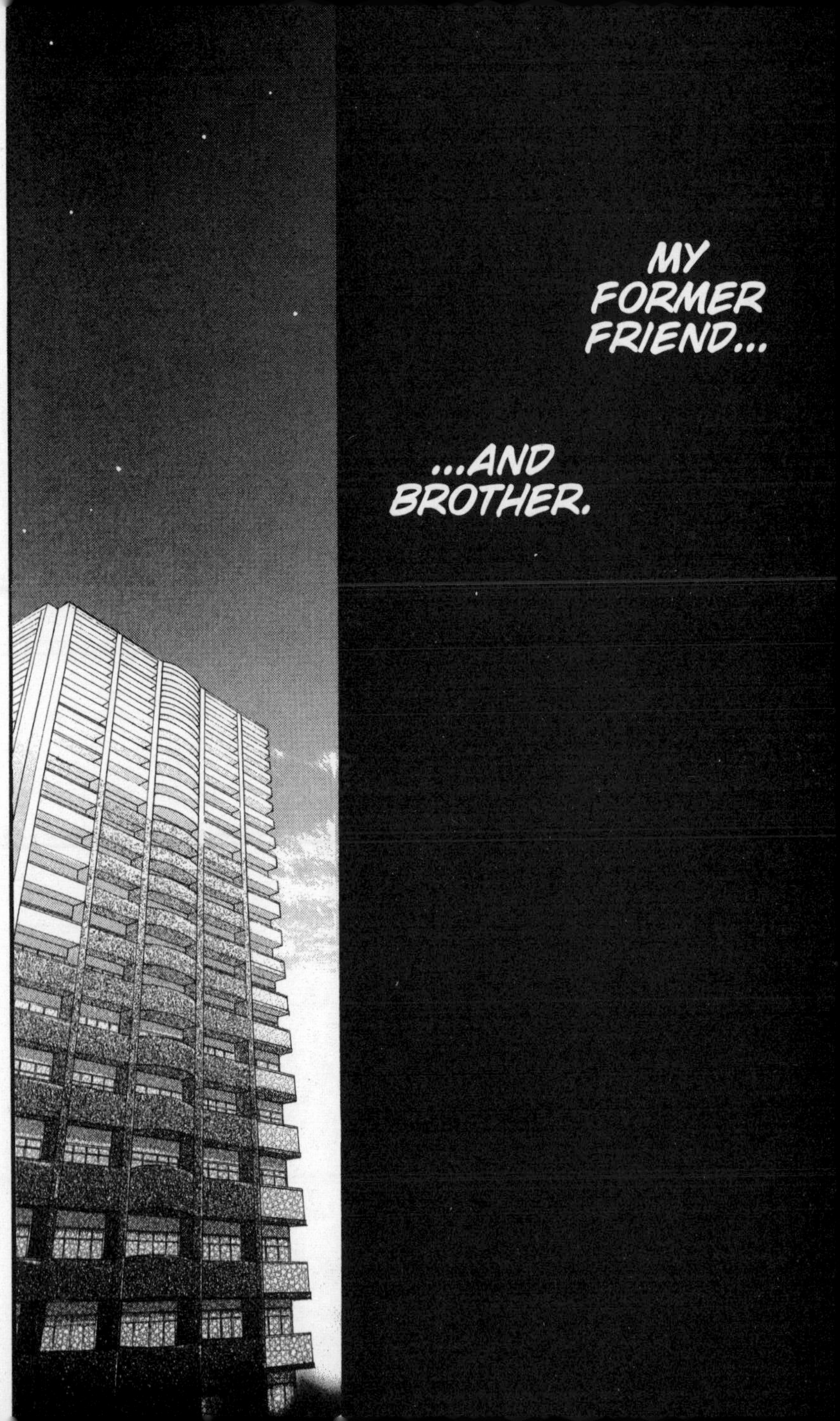
MY FORMER FRIEND...
...AND BROTHER.

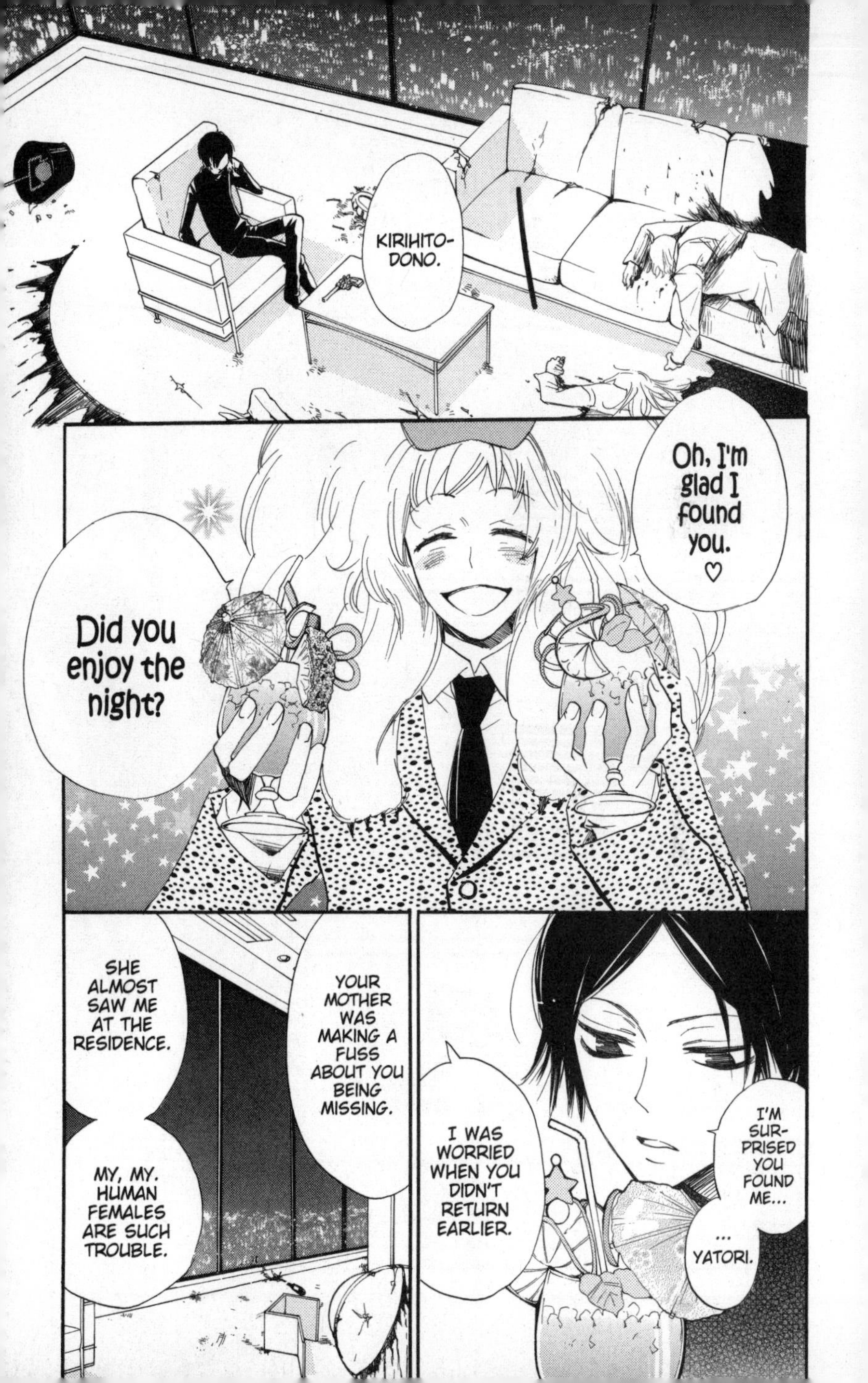
KIRIHITO-DONO.
Oh, I'm glad I found you. ♡
Did you enjoy the night?
I'M SURPRISED YOU FOUND ME... ...YATORI.
I WAS WORRIED WHEN YOU DIDN'T RETURN EARLIER.
YOUR MOTHER WAS MAKING A FUSS ABOUT YOU BEING MISSING.
SHE ALMOST SAW ME AT THE RESIDENCE.
MY, MY. HUMAN FEMALES ARE SUCH TROUBLE.

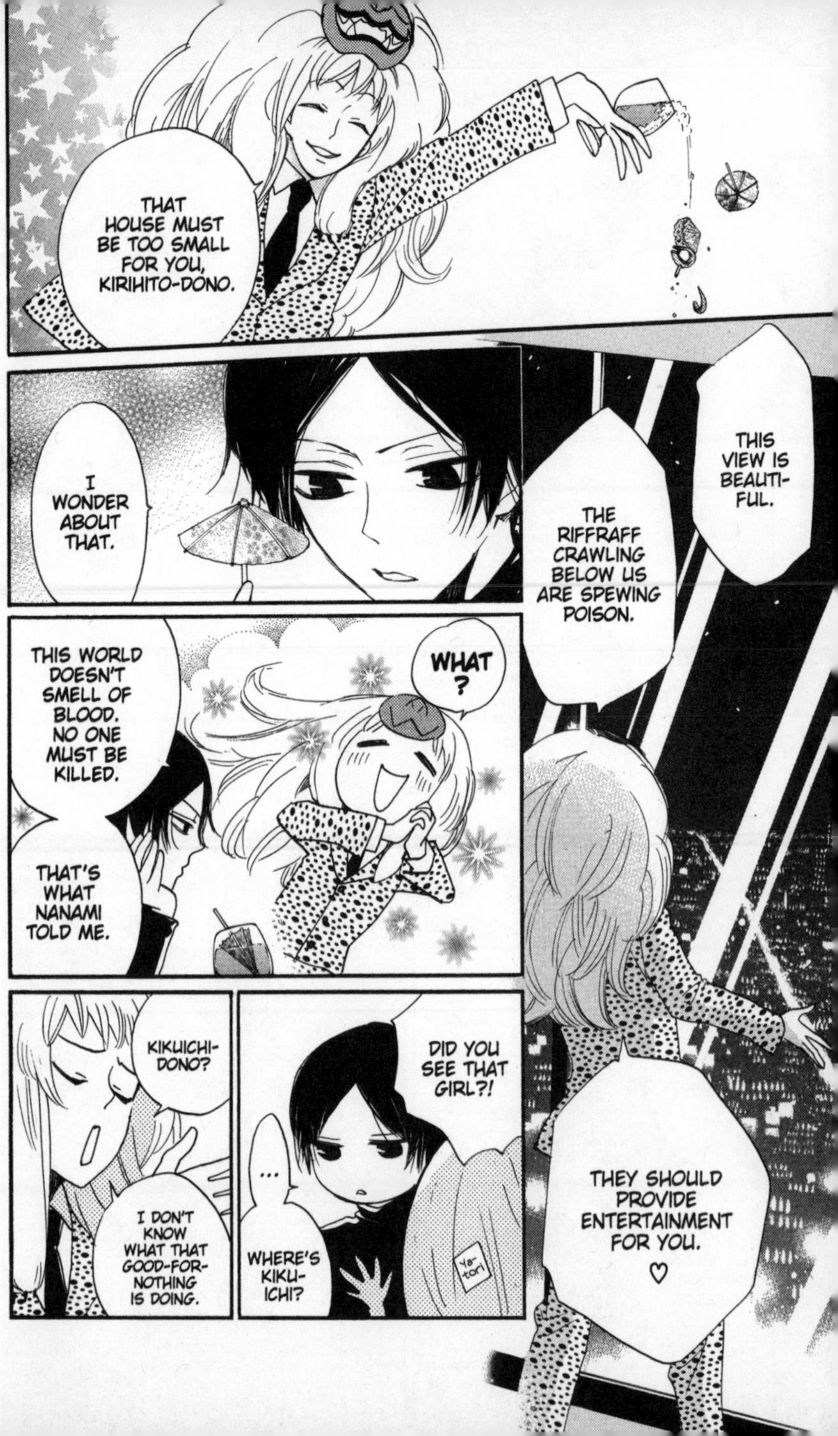
THAT HOUSE MUST BE TOO SMALL FOR YOU, KIRIHITO-DONO.
THIS VIEW IS BEAUTIFUL.
THE RIFFRAFF CRAWLING BELOW US ARE SPEWING POISON.
THEY SHOULD PROVIDE ENTERTAINMENT FOR YOU. ♡
I WONDER ABOUT THAT.
WHAT?
THIS WORLD DOESN'T SMELL OF BLOOD. NO ONE MUST BE KILLED.
THAT'S WHAT NANAMI TOLD ME.
DID YOU SEE THAT GIRL?!
...
WHERE'S KIKUICHI?
ya-tori
KIKUICHI-DONO?
I DON'T KNOW WHAT THAT GOOD-FOR-NOTHING IS DOING.

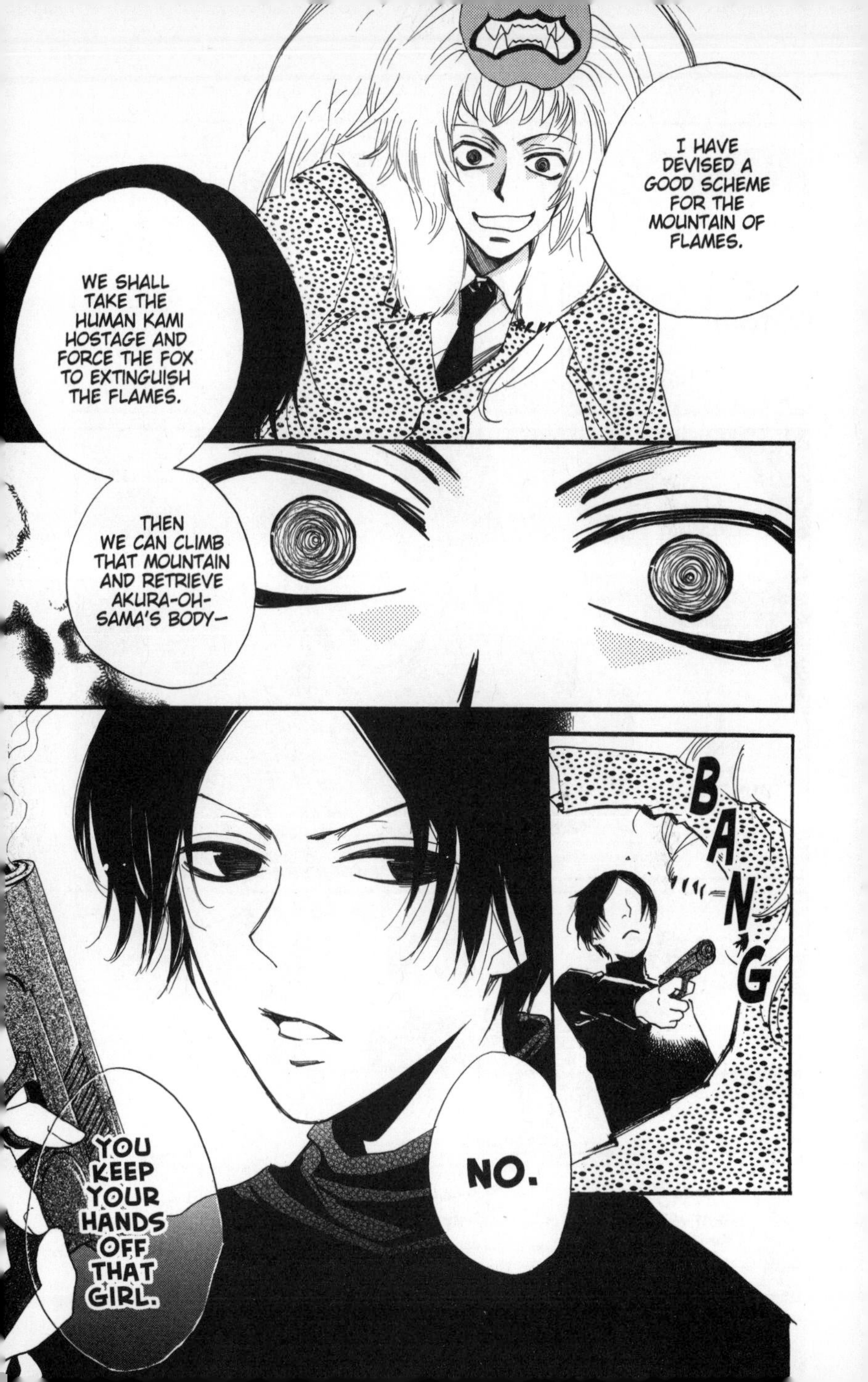
I HAVE DEVISED A GOOD SCHEME FOR THE MOUNTAIN OF FLAMES.
WE SHALL TAKE THE HUMAN KAMI HOSTAGE AND FORCE THE FOX TO EXTINGUISH THE FLAMES.
THEN WE CAN CLIMB THAT MOUNTAIN AND RETRIEVE AKURA-OH-SAMA'S BODY-
BANG
NO.
YOU KEEP YOUR HANDS OFF THAT GIRL.

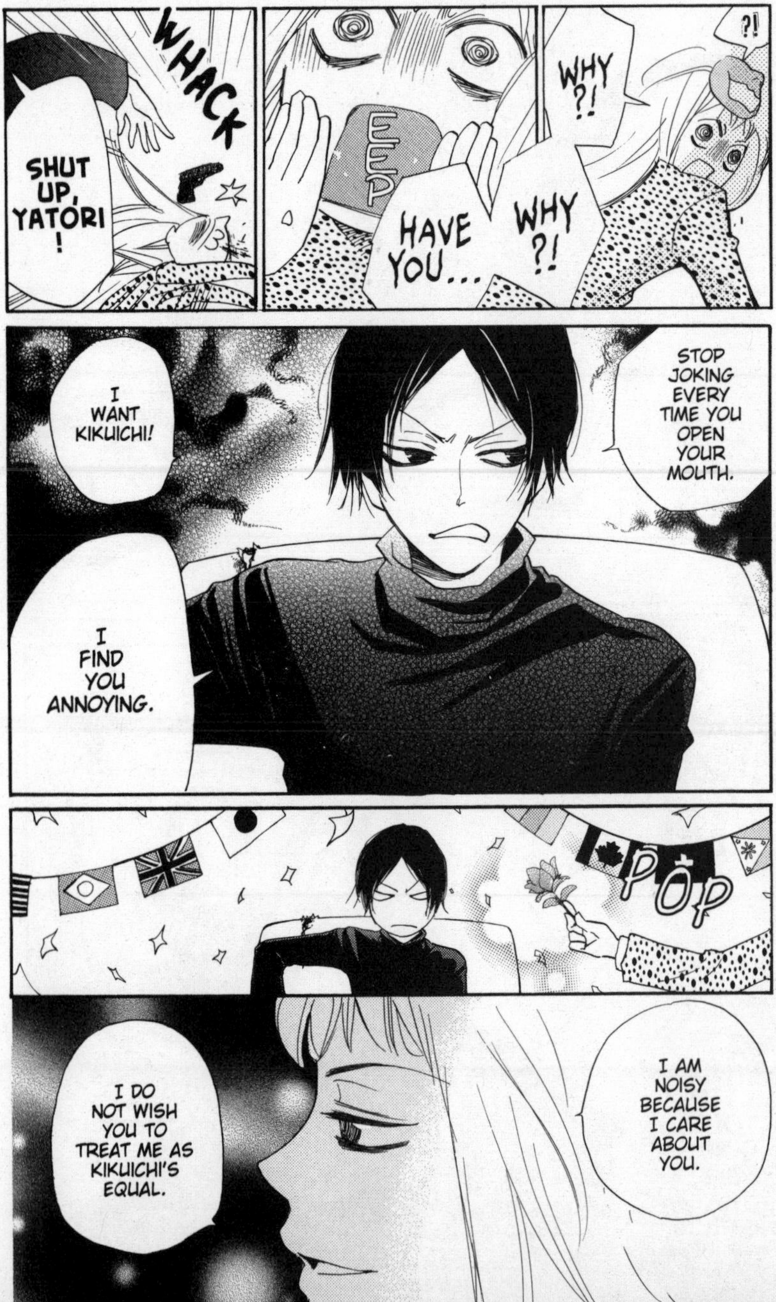
?!
WHY ?!
WHY ?!
HAVE YOU...
EEP
WHACK
SHUT UP, YATORI!
STOP JOKING EVERY TIME YOU OPEN YOUR MOUTH.
I WANT KIKUICHI!
I FIND YOU ANNOYING.
POP
I AM NOISY BECAUSE I CARE ABOUT YOU.
I DO NOT WISH YOU TO TREAT ME AS KIKUICHI'S EQUAL.

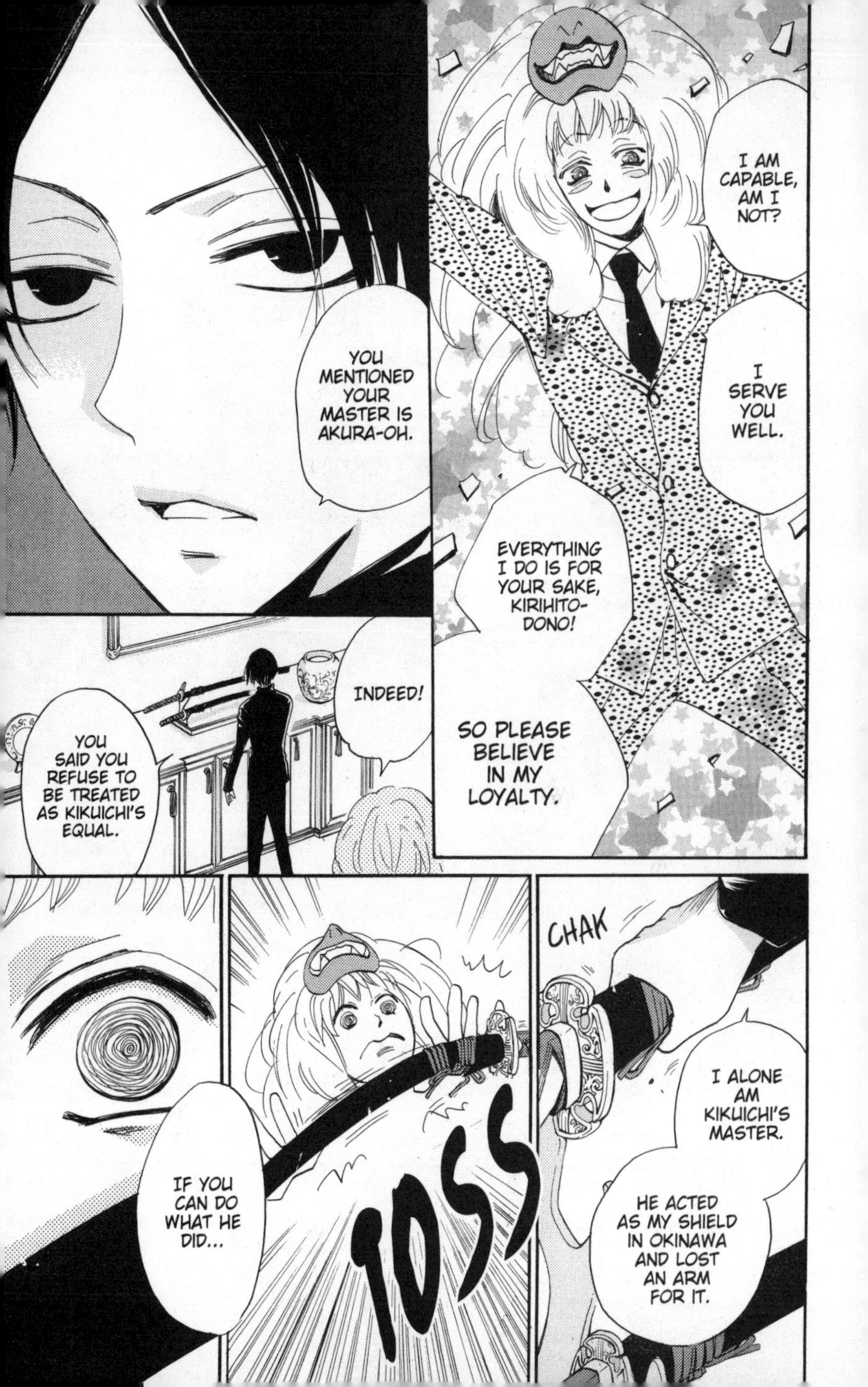
I AM CAPABLE, AM I NOT?
I SERVE YOU WELL.
EVERYTHING I DO IS FOR YOUR SAKE, KIRIHITO-DONO!
SO PLEASE BELIEVE IN MY LOYALTY.
YOU MENTIONED YOUR MASTER IS AKURA-OH.
INDEED!
YOU SAID YOU REFUSE TO BE TREATED AS KIKUICHI'S EQUAL.
CHAK
I ALONE AM KIKUICHI'S MASTER.
HE ACTED AS MY SHIELD IN OKINAWA AND LOST AN ARM FOR IT.
TOSS
IF YOU CAN DO WHAT HE DID...

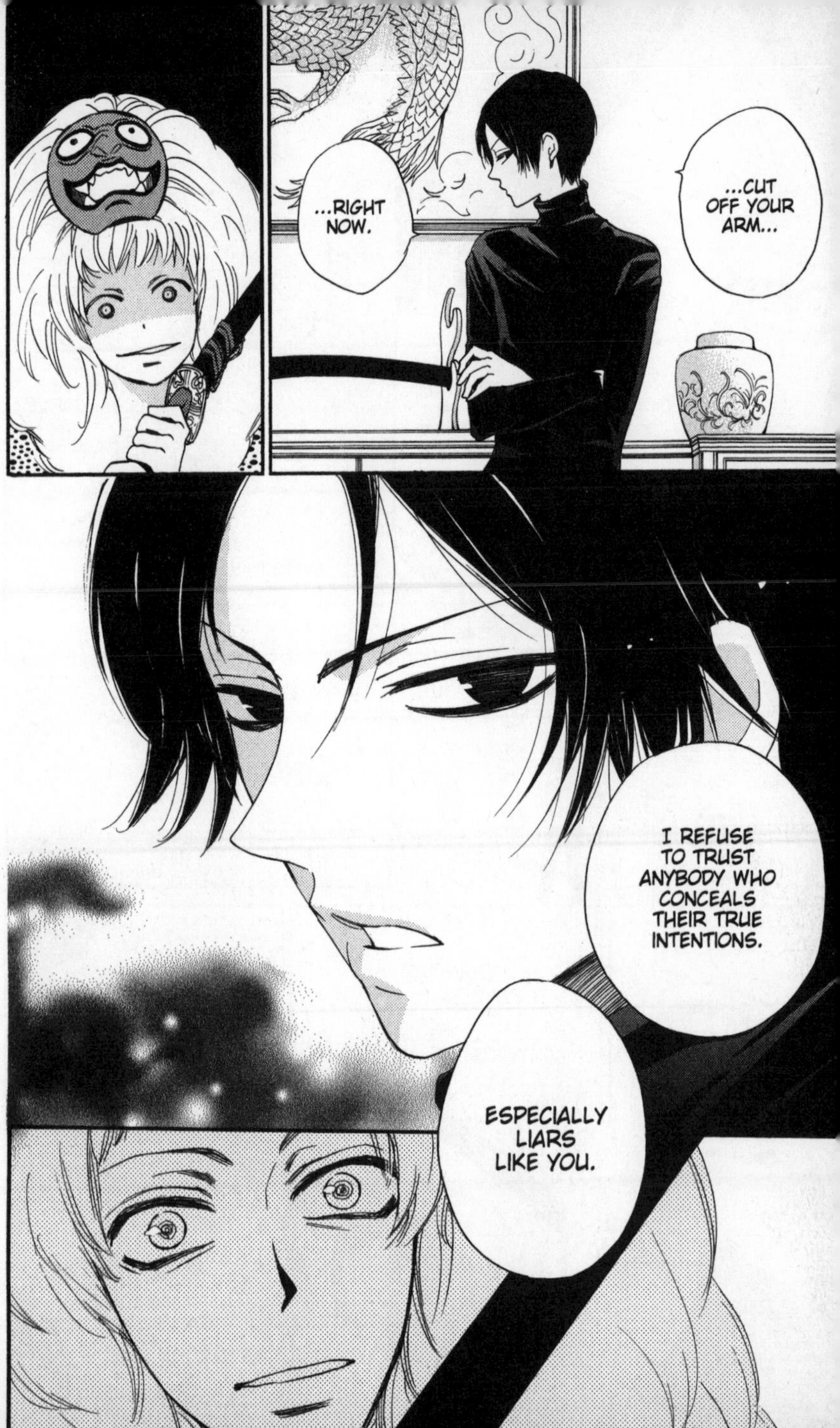
...CUT OFF YOUR ARM...
...RIGHT NOW.
I REFUSE TO TRUST ANYBODY WHO CONCEALS THEIR TRUE INTENTIONS.
ESPECIALLY LIARS LIKE YOU.

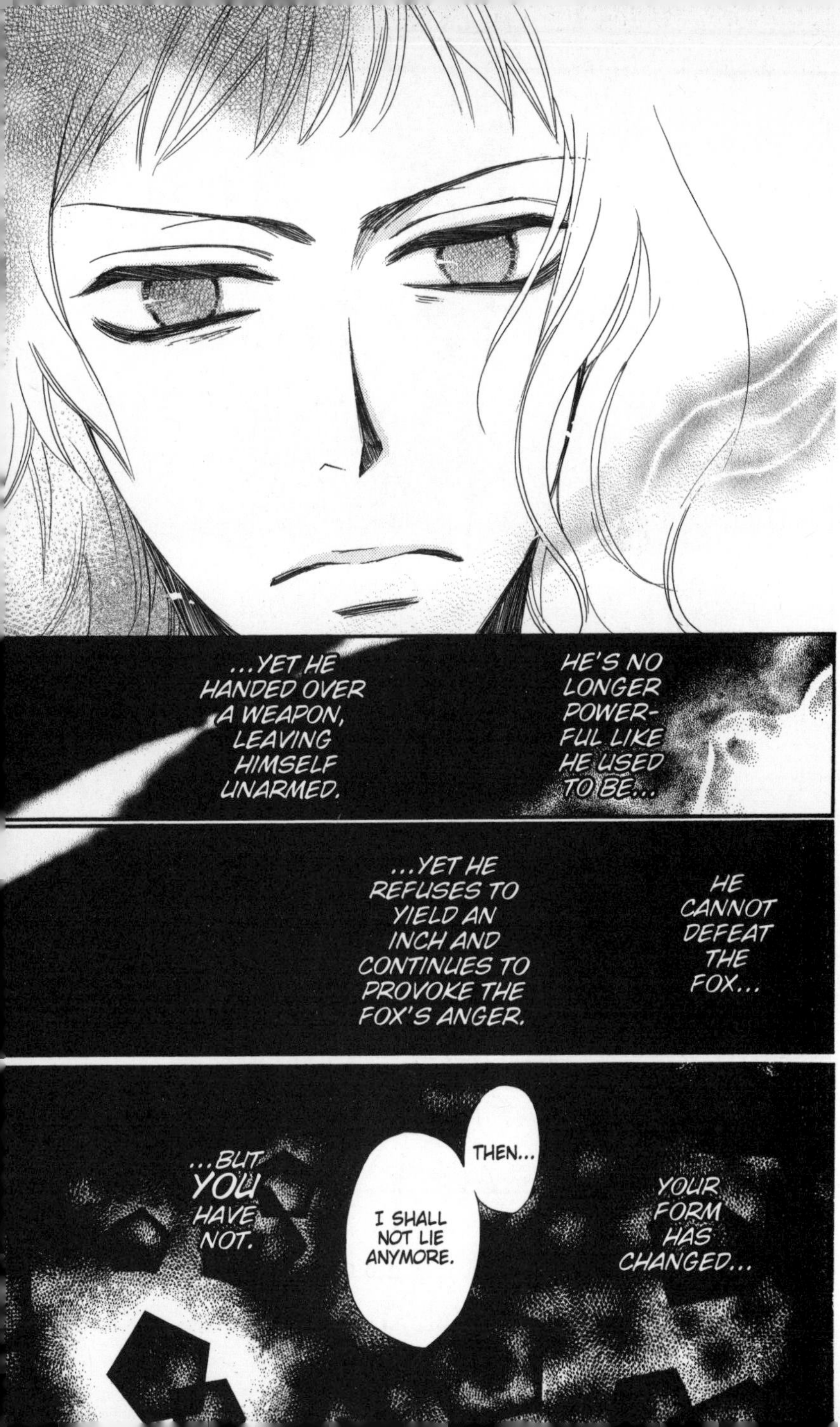
HE'S NO LONGER POWERFUL LIKE HE USED TO BE...
...YET HE HANDED OVER A WEAPON, LEAVING HIMSELF UNARMED.
HE CANNOT DEFEAT THE FOX...
...YET HE REFUSES TO YIELD AN INCH AND CONTINUES TO PROVOKE THE FOX'S ANGER.
YOUR FORM HAS CHANGED...
...BUT YOU HAVE NOT.
THEN...
I SHALL NOT LIE ANYMORE.

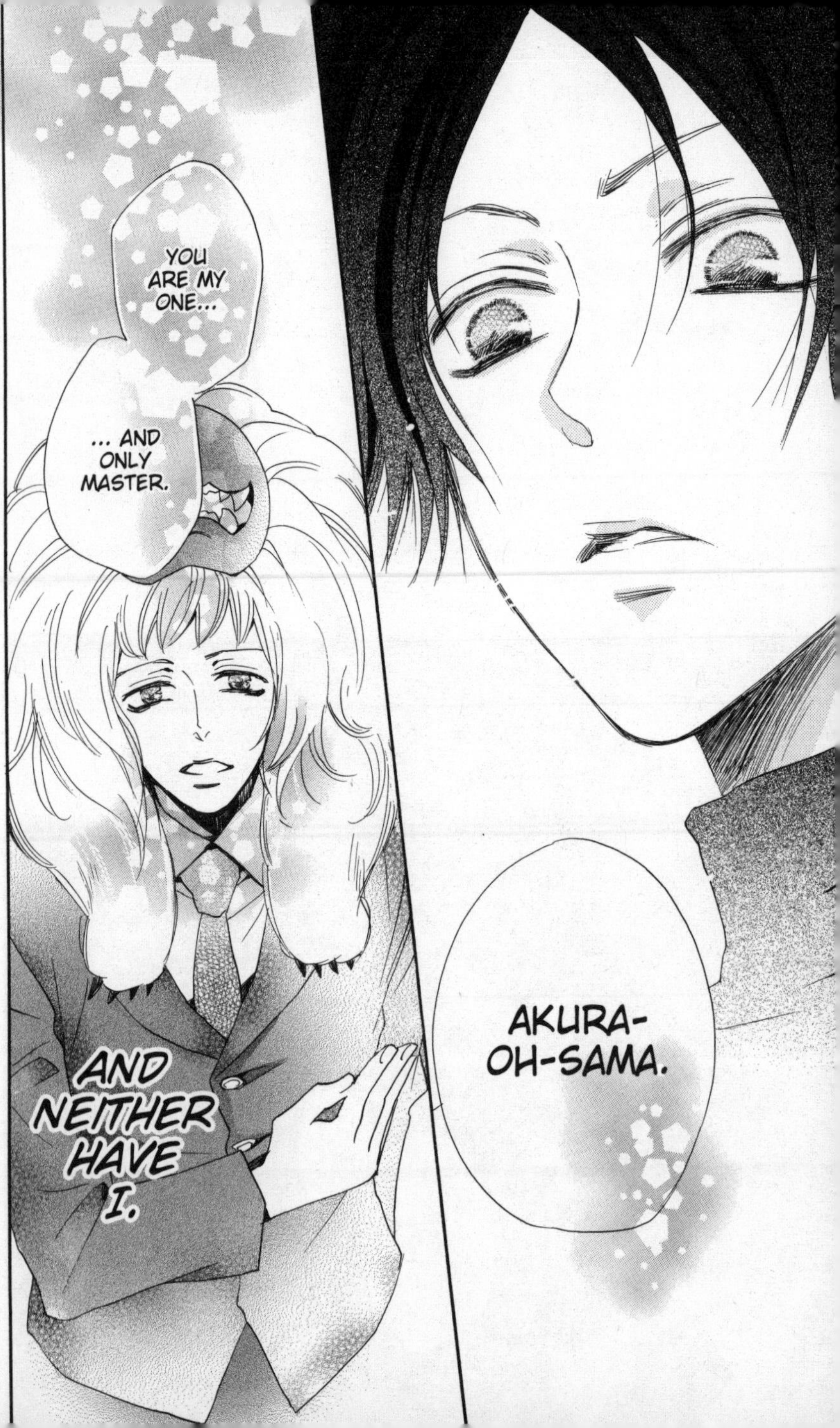
AKURA-OH-SAMA.
YOU ARE MY ONE...
... AND ONLY MASTER.
AND NEITHER HAVE I.

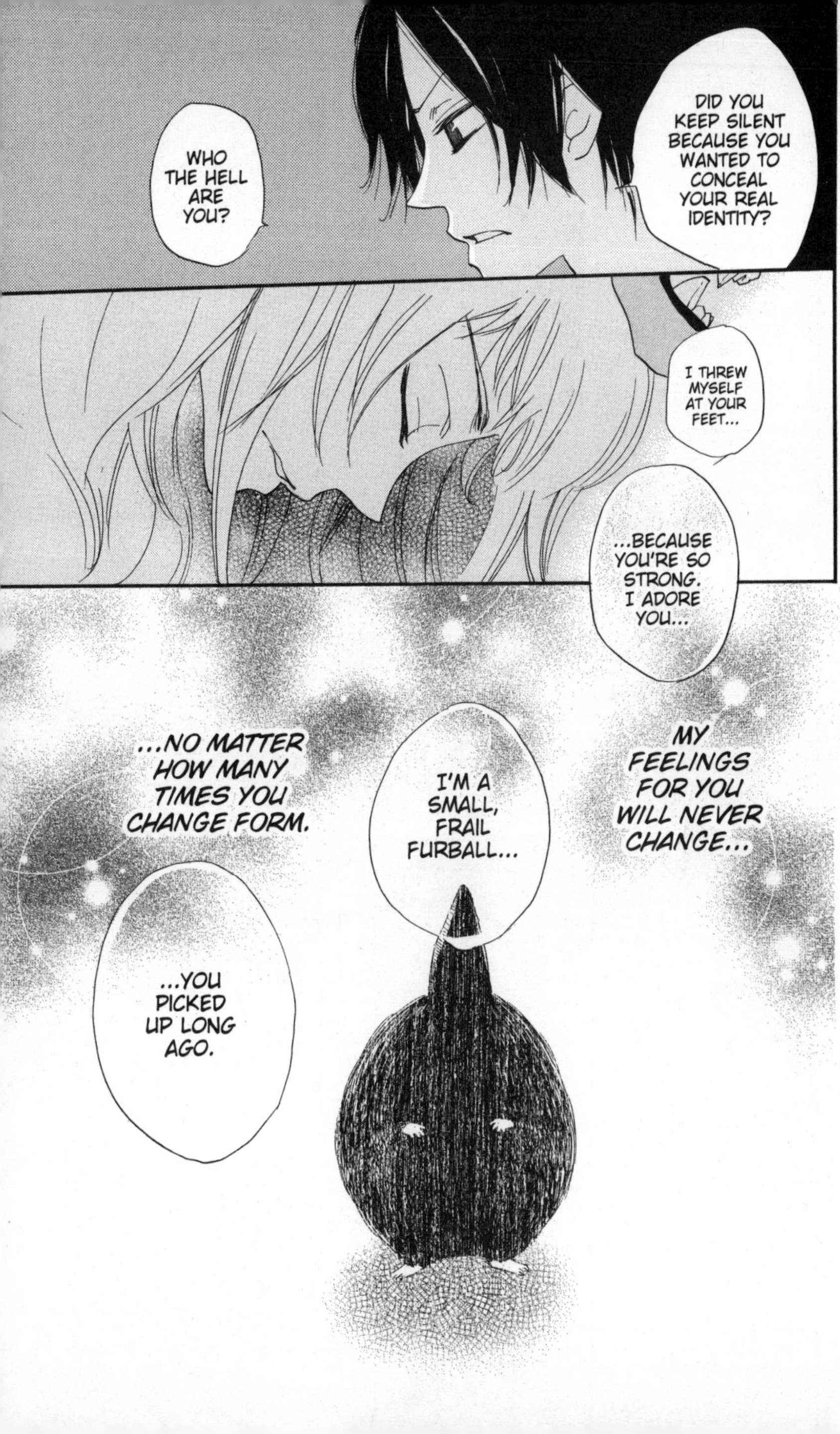
DID YOU KEEP SILENT BECAUSE YOU WANTED TO CONCEAL YOUR REAL IDENTITY?
WHO THE HELL ARE YOU?
I THREW MYSELF AT YOUR FEET...
...BECAUSE YOU'RE SO STRONG. I ADORE YOU...
MY FEELINGS FOR YOU WILL NEVER CHANGE...
...NO MATTER HOW MANY TIMES YOU CHANGE FORM.
I'M A SMALL, FRAIL FURBALL...
...YOU PICKED UP LONG AGO.

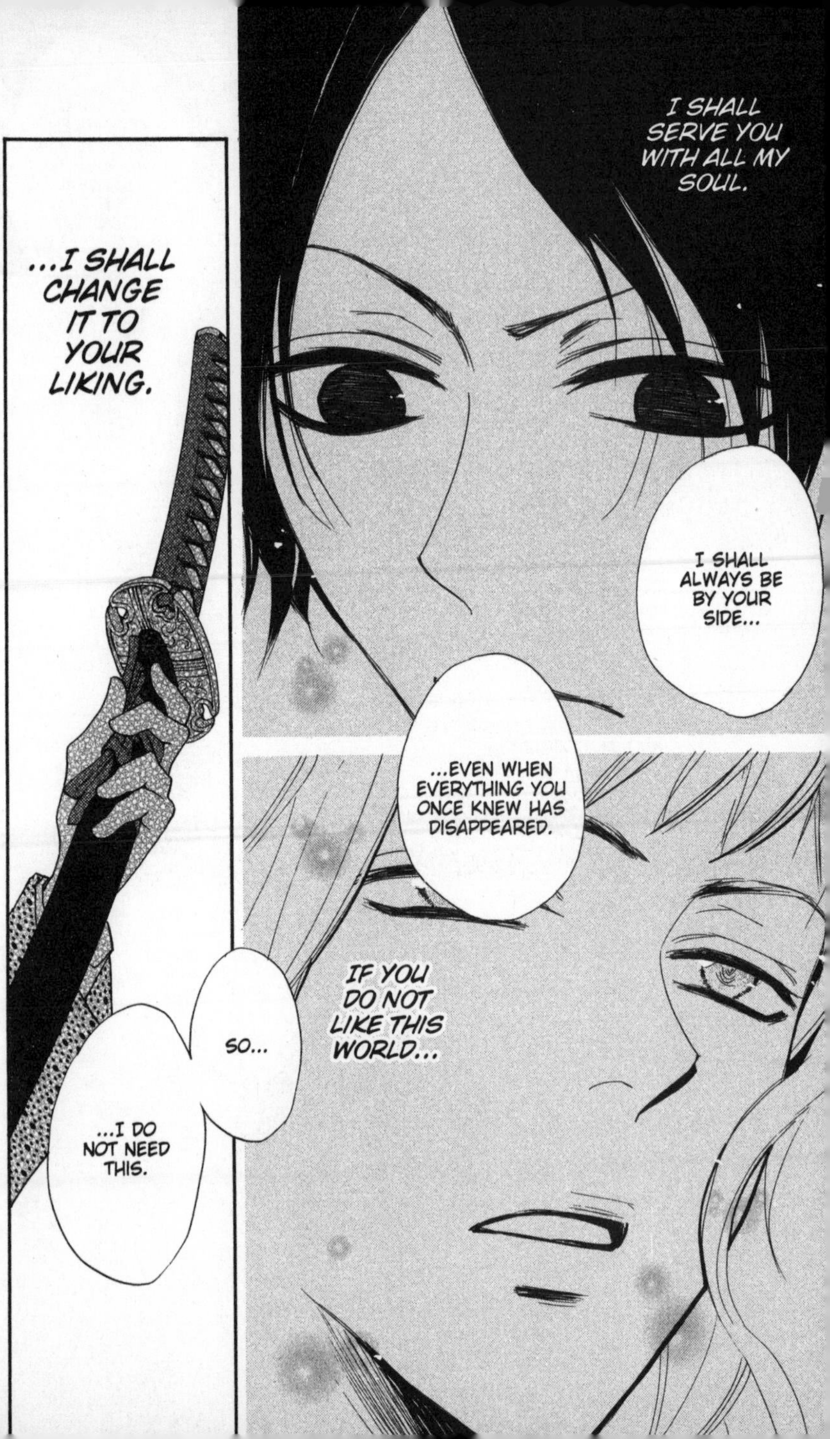

I SHALL SERVE YOU WITH ALL MY SOUL.
I SHALL ALWAYS BE BY YOUR SIDE...
...EVEN WHEN EVERYTHING YOU ONCE KNEW HAS DISAPPEARED.
IF YOU DO NOT LIKE THIS WORLD...
SO...
...I DO NOT NEED THIS.
...I SHALL CHANGE IT TO YOUR LIKING.

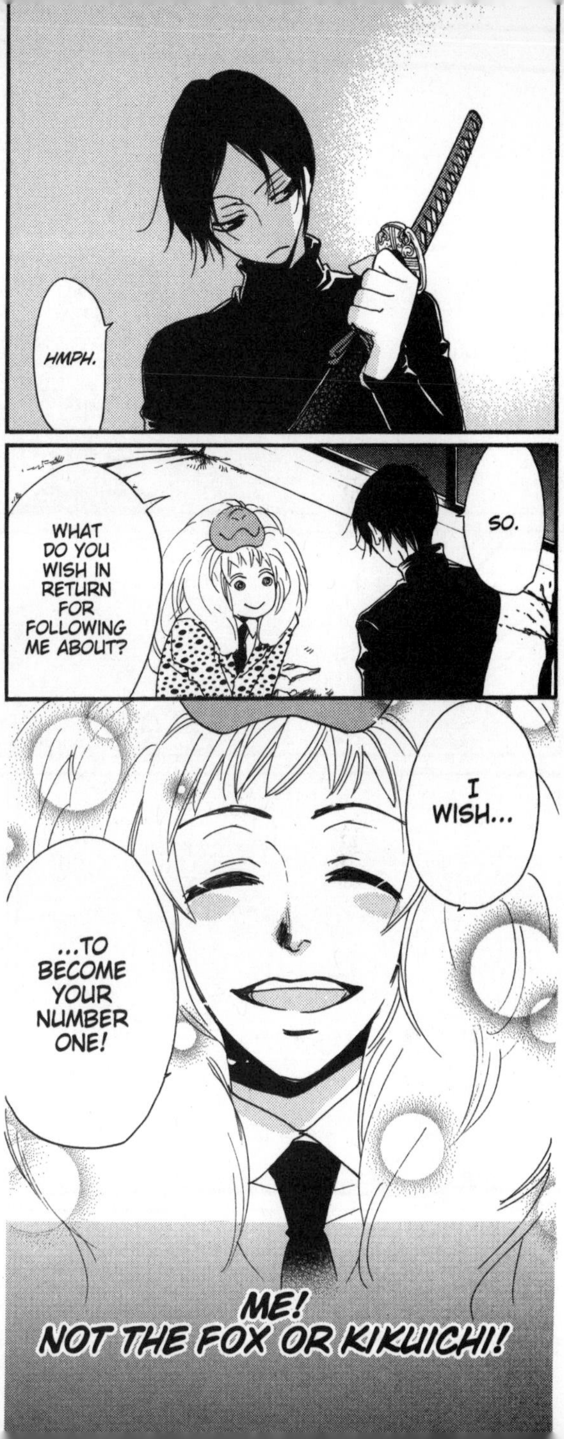
HMPH.
SO.
WHAT DO YOU WISH IN RETURN FOR FOLLOWING ME ABOUT?
I WISH...
...TO BECOME YOUR NUMBER ONE!
ME! NOT THE FOX OR KIKUICHI!

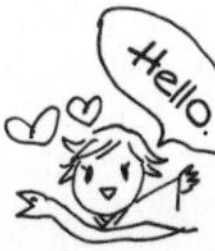
Hello.

Thank you for picking up volume 21 of Kamisama Kiss!! I hope you enjoy reading this volume.

I had my assistant O-san draw a sidebar. Thank you for the cute cats, O-san.

Do enjoy reading.

-Juli

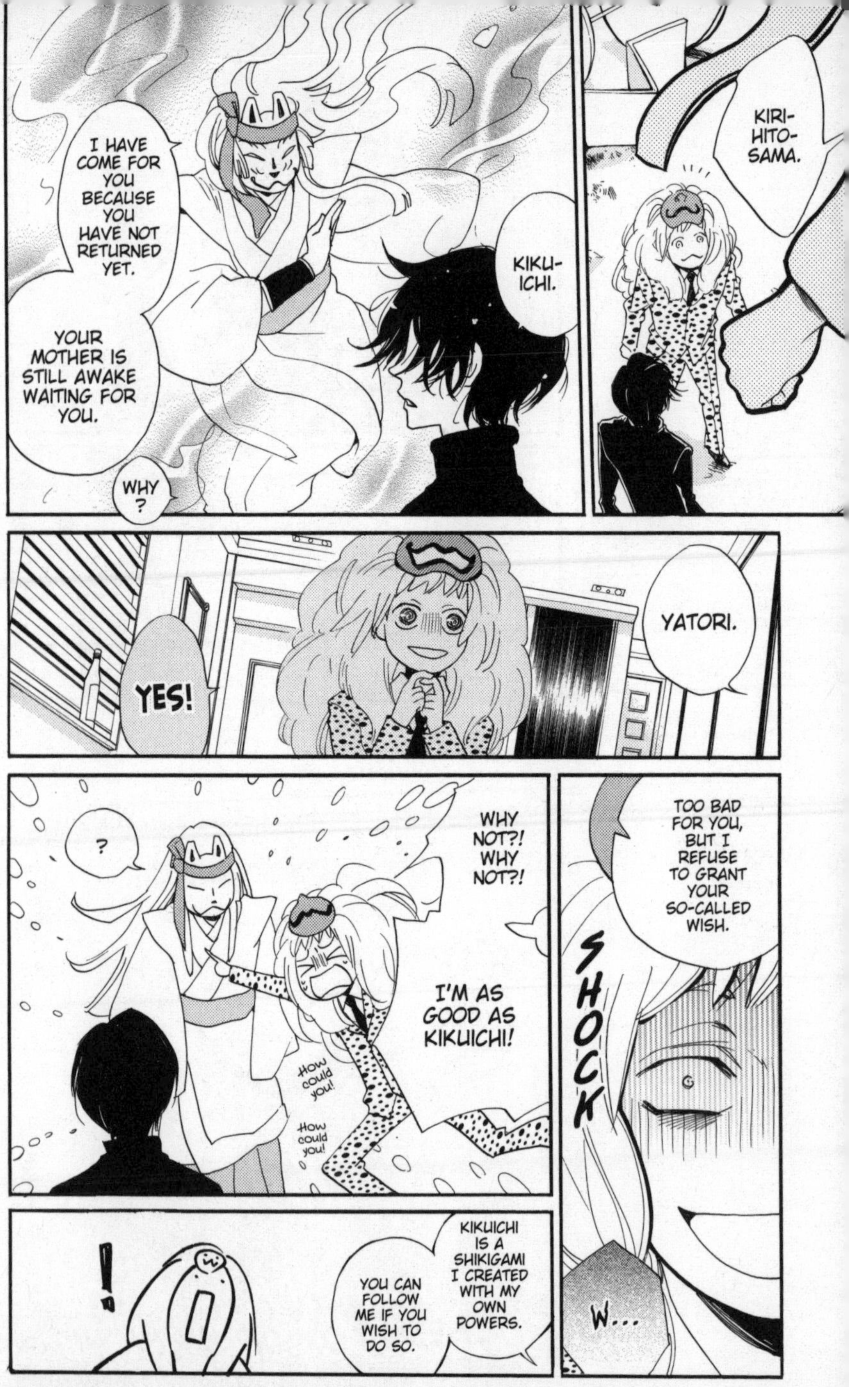
KIRI-HITO-SAMA.
KIKU-ICHI.
I HAVE COME FOR YOU BECAUSE YOU HAVE NOT RETURNED YET.
YOUR MOTHER IS STILL AWAKE WAITING FOR YOU.
WHY?
YATORI.
YES!
TOO BAD FOR YOU, BUT I REFUSE TO GRANT YOUR SO-CALLED WISH.
SHOCK
W...
WHY NOT?! WHY NOT?!
I'M AS GOOD AS KIKUICHI!
How could you!
How could you!
?
KIKUICHI IS A SHIKIGAMI I CREATED WITH MY OWN POWERS.
YOU CAN FOLLOW ME IF YOU WISH TO DO SO.
!

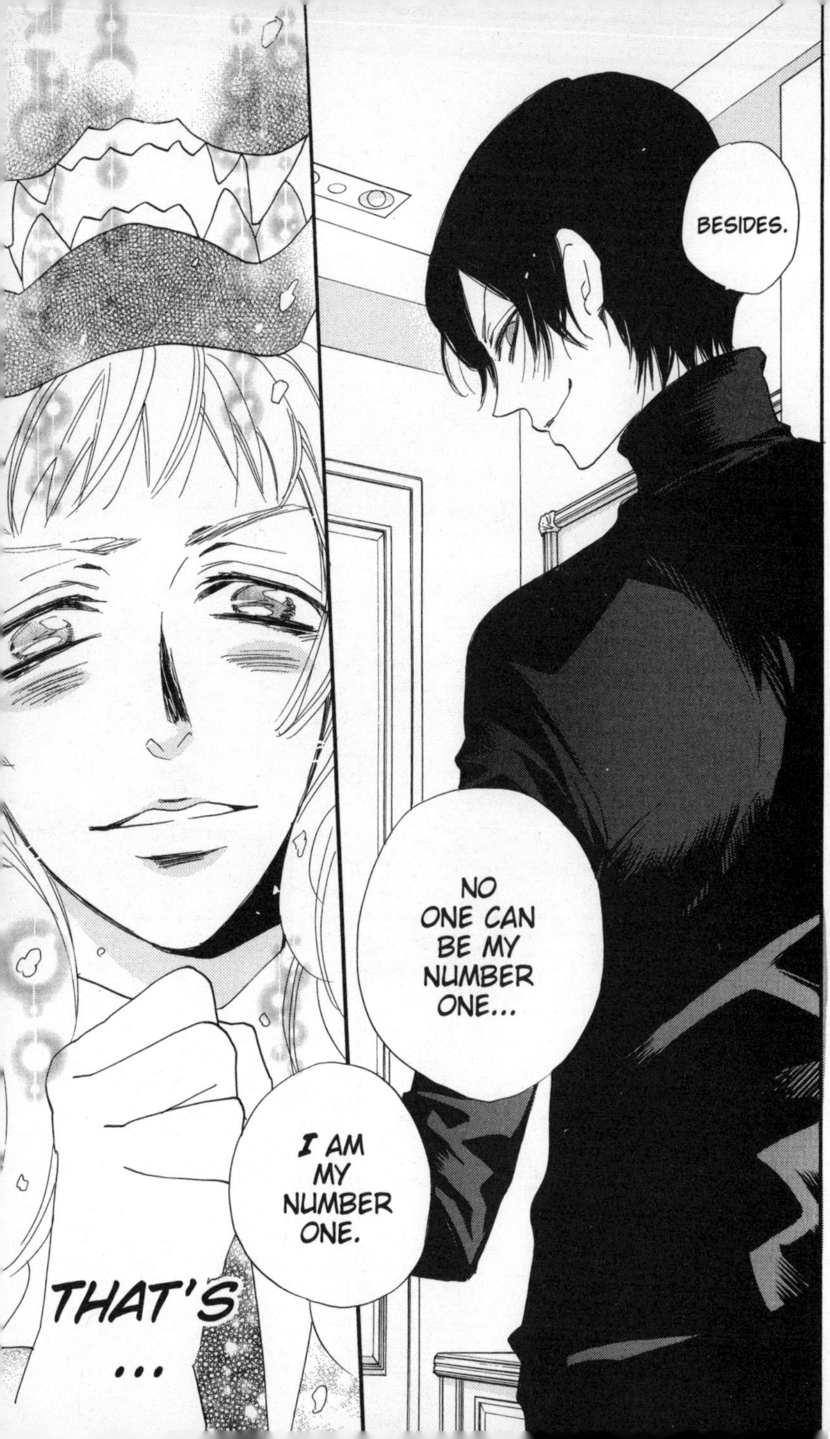
BESIDES.
NO ONE CAN BE MY NUMBER ONE...
I AM MY NUMBER ONE.
THAT'S ...

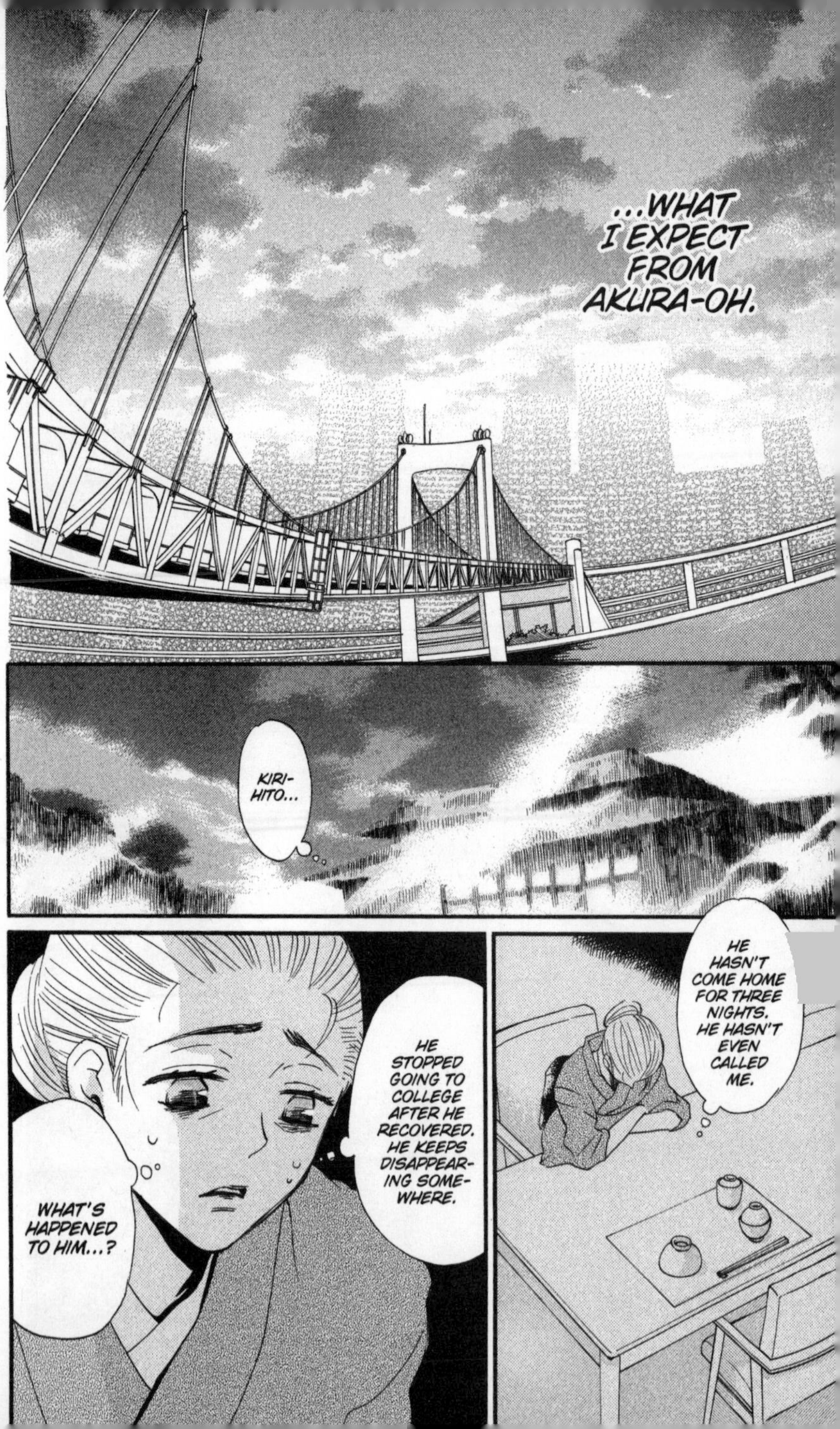
...WHAT I EXPECT FROM AKURA-OH.
KIRI-HITO...
HE HASN'T COME HOME FOR THREE NIGHTS. HE HASN'T EVEN CALLED ME.
HE STOPPED GOING TO COLLEGE AFTER HE RECOVERED. HE KEEPS DISAPPEAR-ING SOME-WHERE.
WHAT'S HAPPENED TO HIM...?

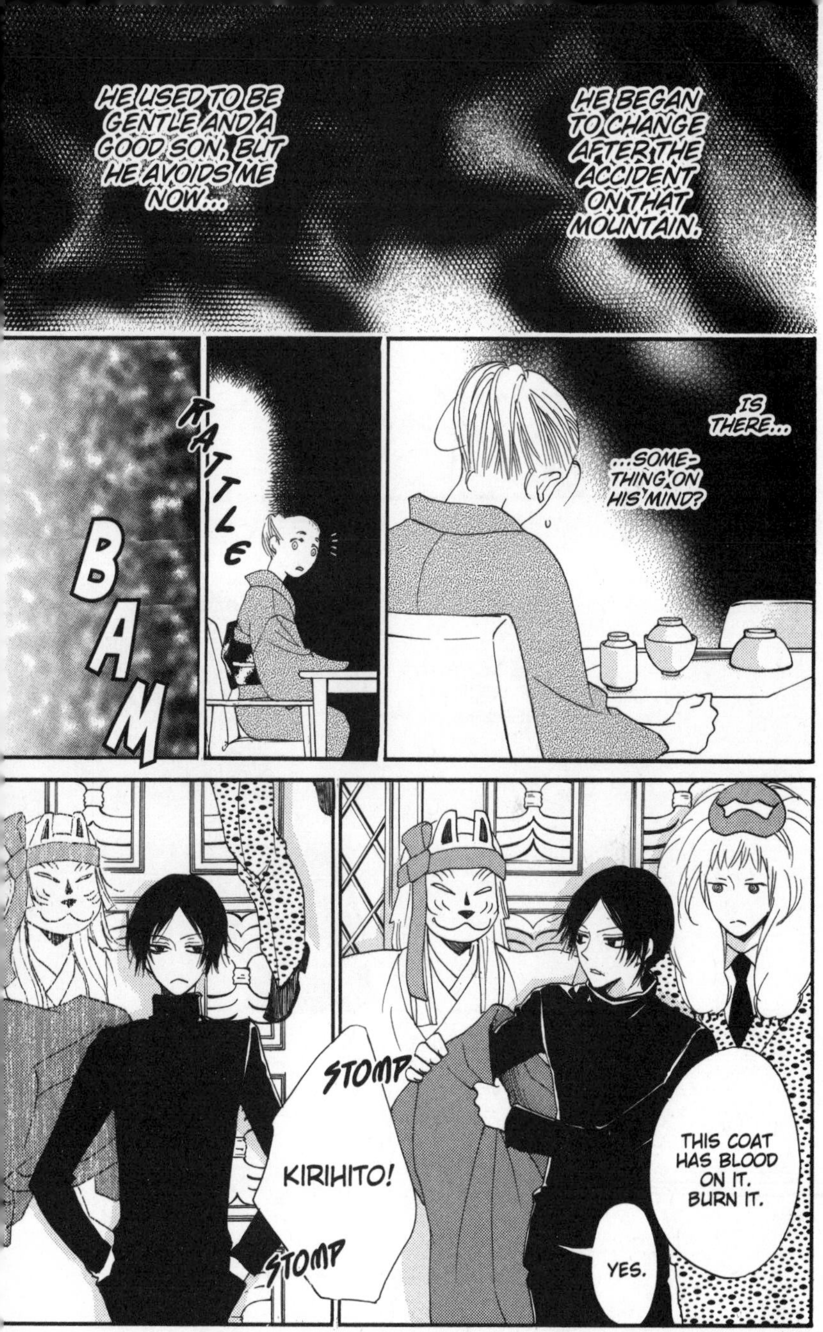
HE BEGAN TO CHANGE AFTER THE ACCIDENT ON THAT MOUNTAIN.
HE USED TO BE GENTLE AND A GOOD SON, BUT HE AVOIDS ME NOW...
IS THERE...
...SOME-THING ON HIS MIND?
RATTLE
BAM
THIS COAT HAS BLOOD ON IT. BURN IT.
YES.
STOMP
KIRIHITO!
STOMP

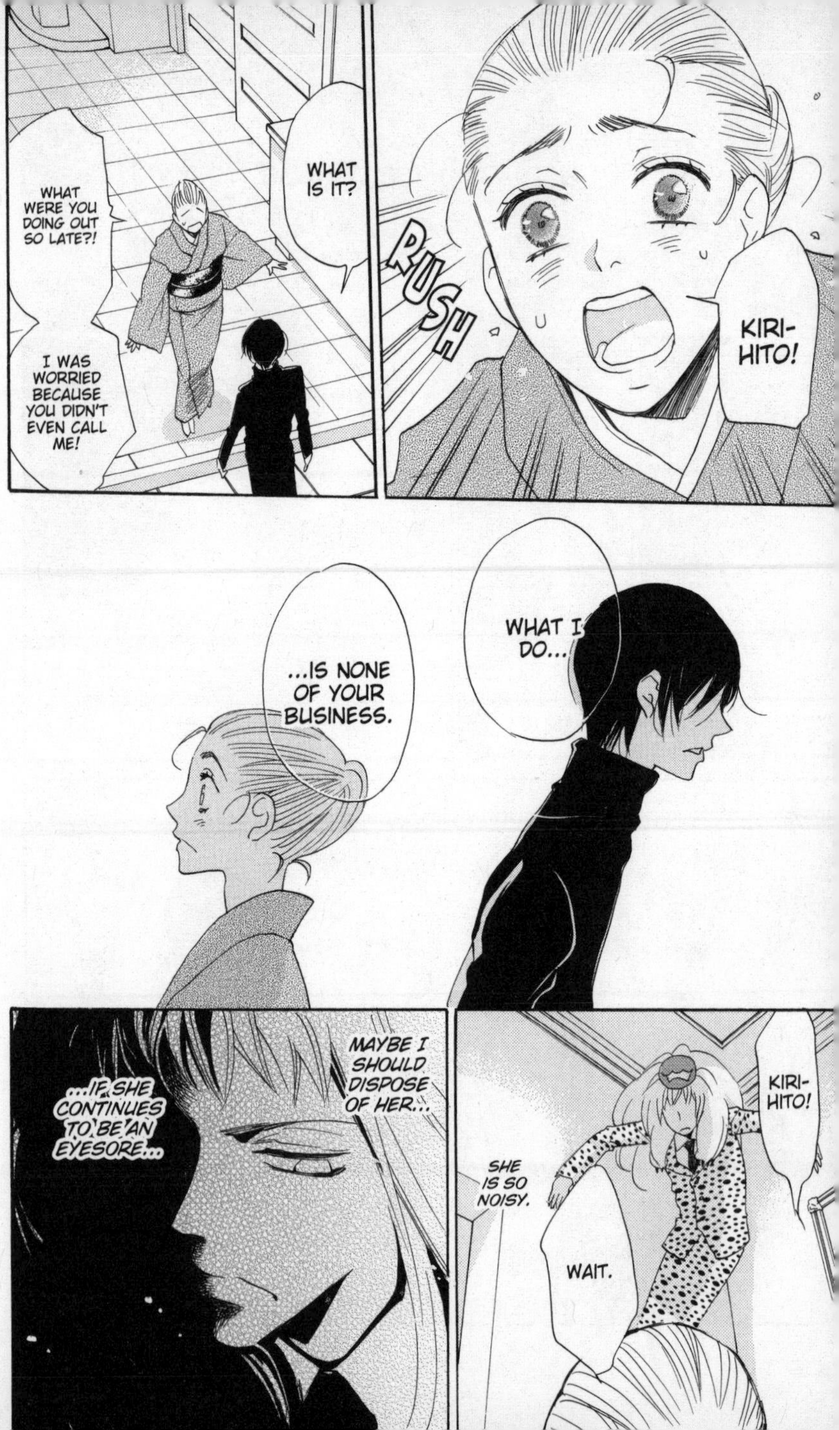
RUSH
KIRI-HITO!
WHAT IS IT?
WHAT WERE YOU DOING OUT SO LATE?!
I WAS WORRIED BECAUSE YOU DIDN'T EVEN CALL ME!
WHAT I DO...
...IS NONE OF YOUR BUSINESS.
KIRI-HITO!
SHE IS SO NOISY.
WAIT.
MAYBE I SHOULD DISPOSE OF HER...
...IF SHE CONTINUES TO BE AN EYESORE...

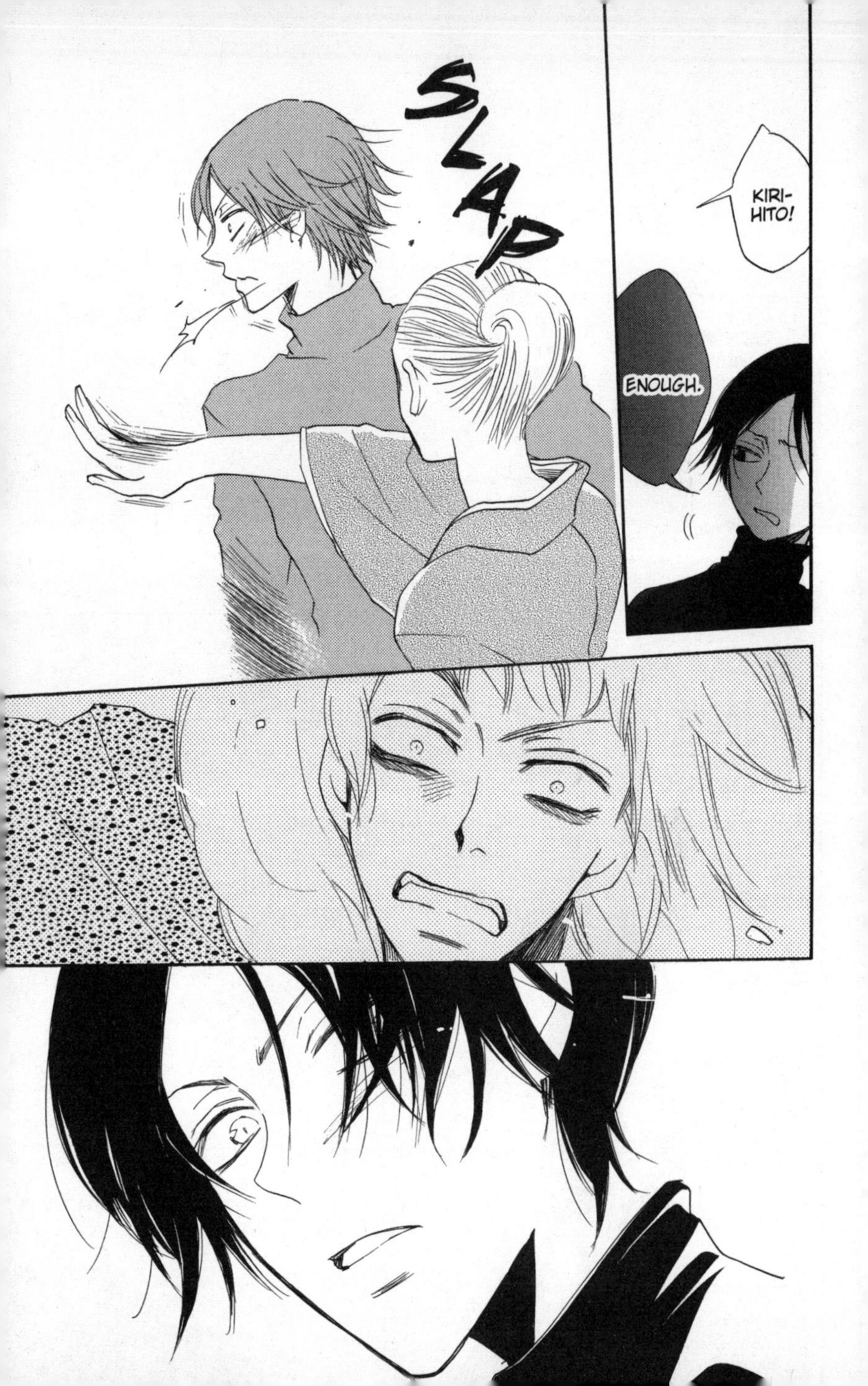
KIRI-HITO!
ENOUGH.
SLAP

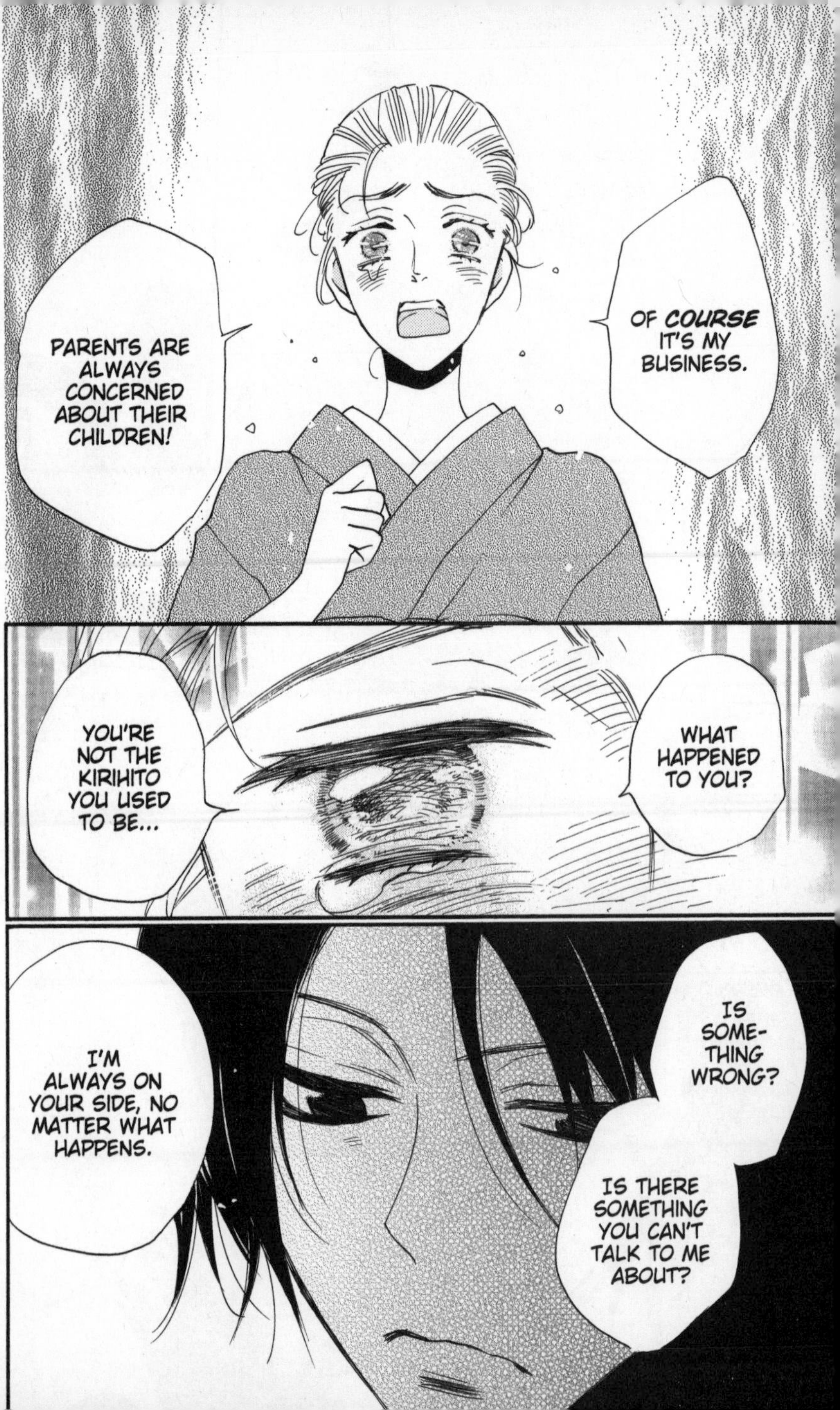
OF COURSE IT'S MY BUSINESS.
PARENTS ARE ALWAYS CONCERNED ABOUT THEIR CHILDREN!
WHAT HAPPENED TO YOU?
YOU'RE NOT THE KIRIHITO YOU USED TO BE...
IS SOME-THING WRONG?
IS THERE SOMETHING YOU CAN'T TALK TO ME ABOUT?
I'M ALWAYS ON YOUR SIDE, NO MATTER WHAT HAPPENS.

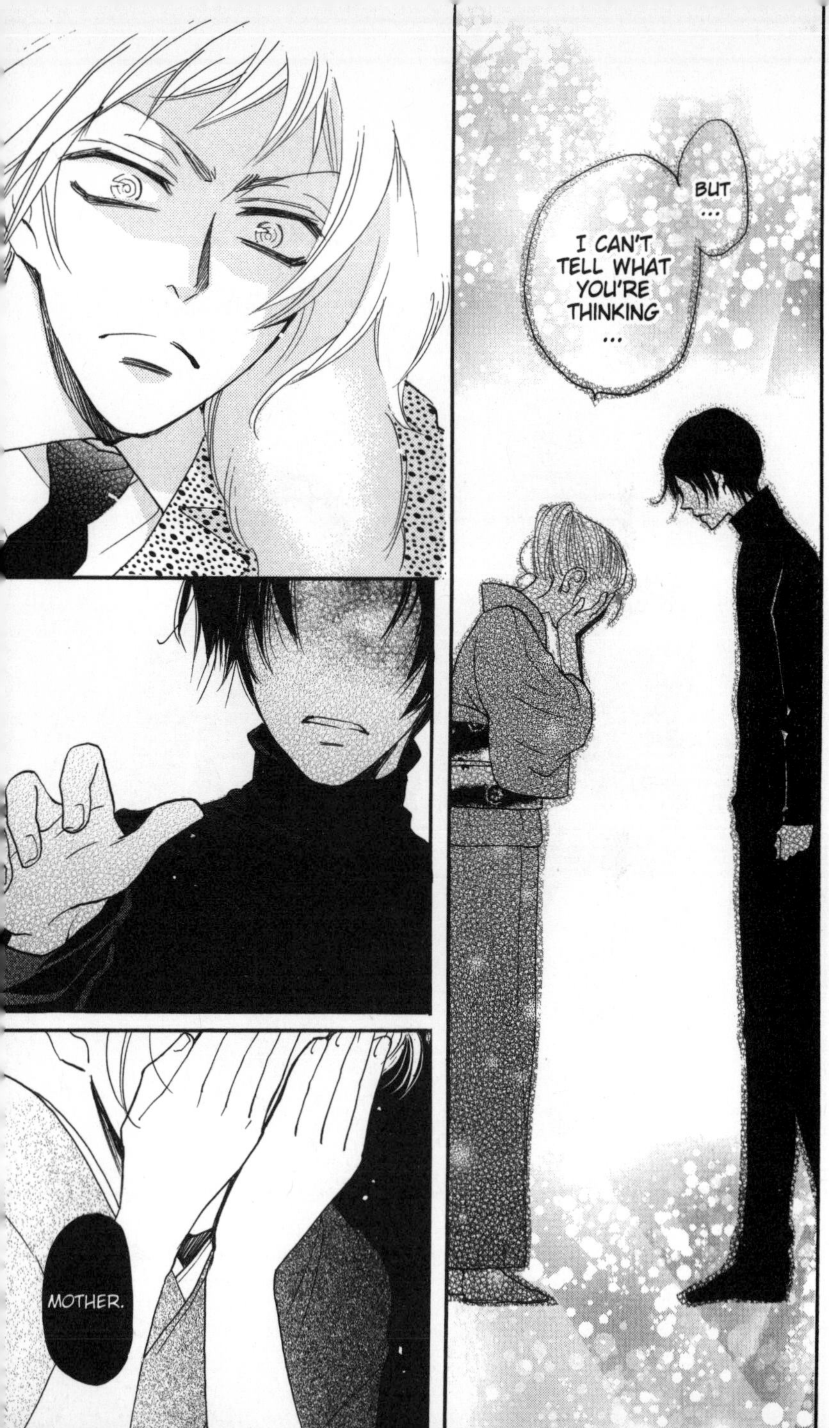
BUT ...
I CAN'T TELL WHAT YOU'RE THINKING ...
MOTHER.

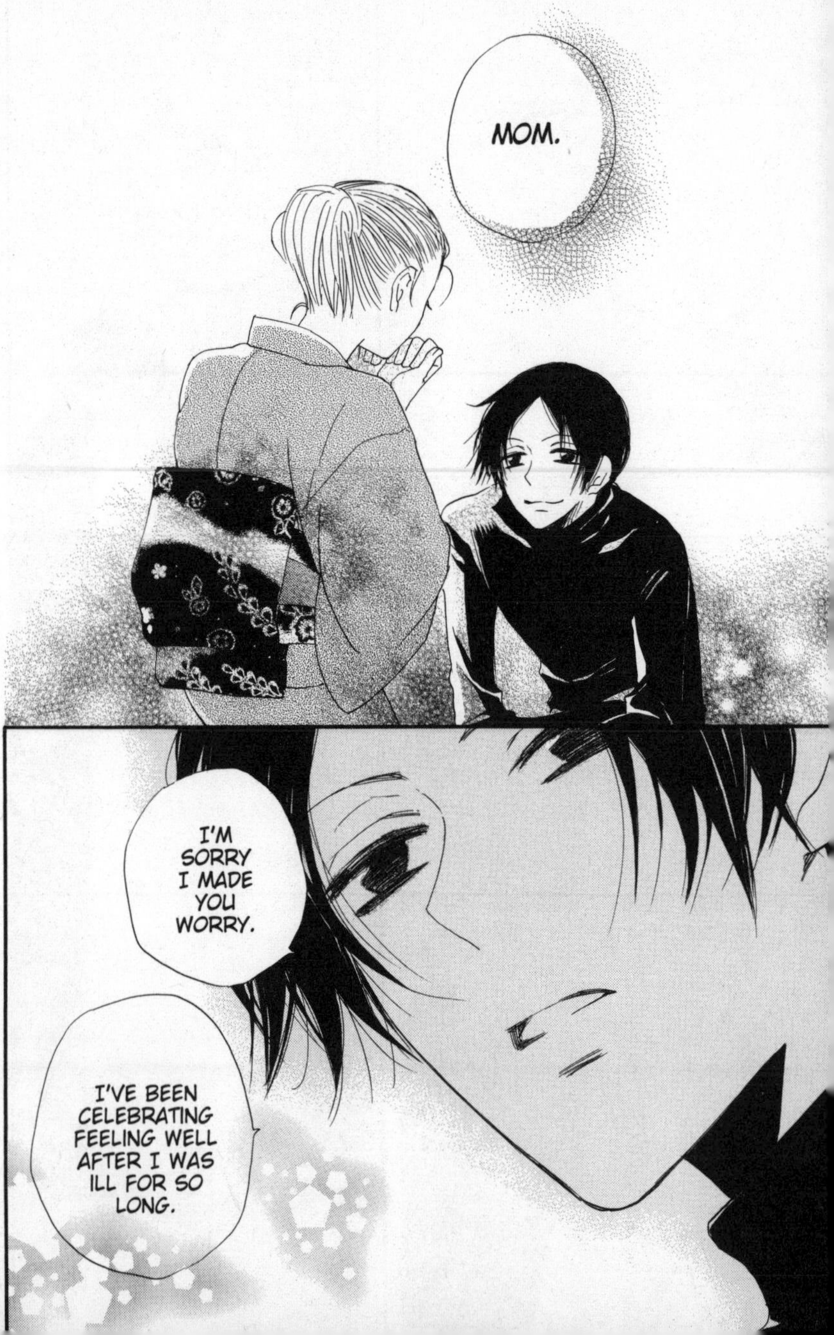
MOM.
I'M SORRY I MADE YOU WORRY.
I'VE BEEN CELEBRATING FEELING WELL AFTER I WAS ILL FOR SO LONG.

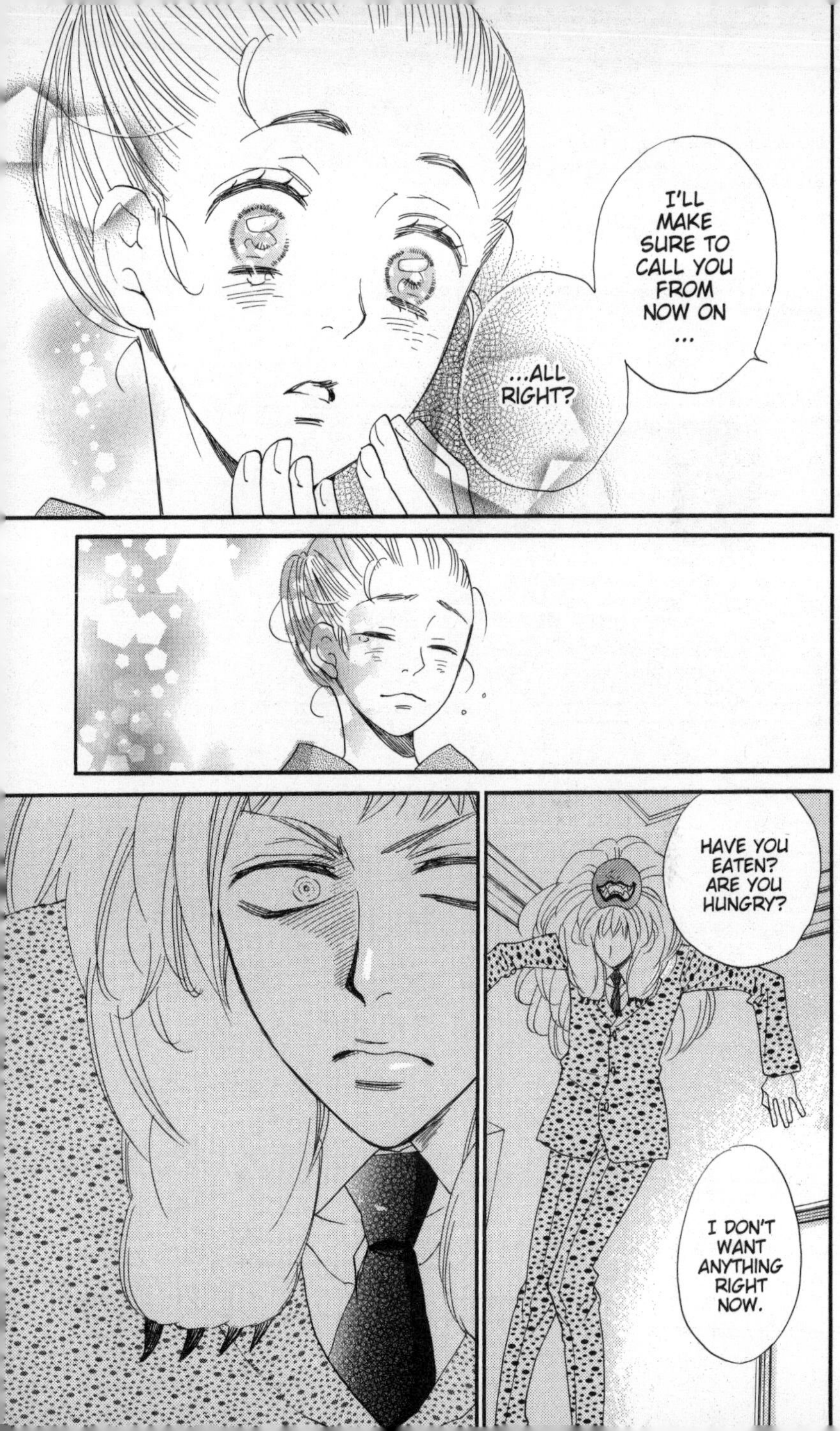
I'LL MAKE SURE TO CALL YOU FROM NOW ON ...
...ALL RIGHT?
HAVE YOU EATEN? ARE YOU HUNGRY?
I DON'T WANT ANYTHING RIGHT NOW.

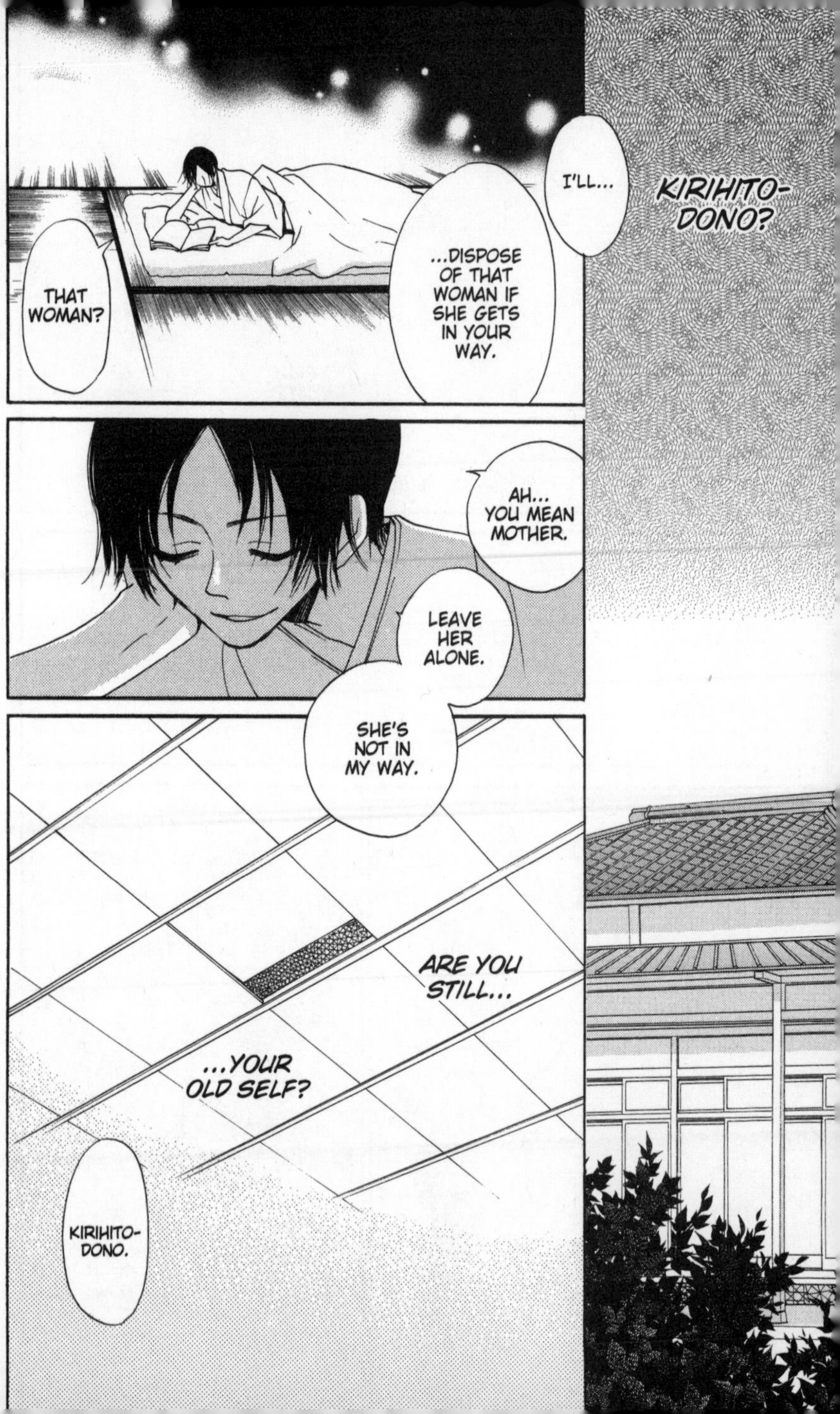
KIRIHITO-DONO?
I'LL...
...DISPOSE OF THAT WOMAN IF SHE GETS IN YOUR WAY.
THAT WOMAN?
AH... YOU MEAN MOTHER.
LEAVE HER ALONE.
SHE'S NOT IN MY WAY.
ARE YOU STILL...
...YOUR OLD SELF?
KIRIHITO-DONO.

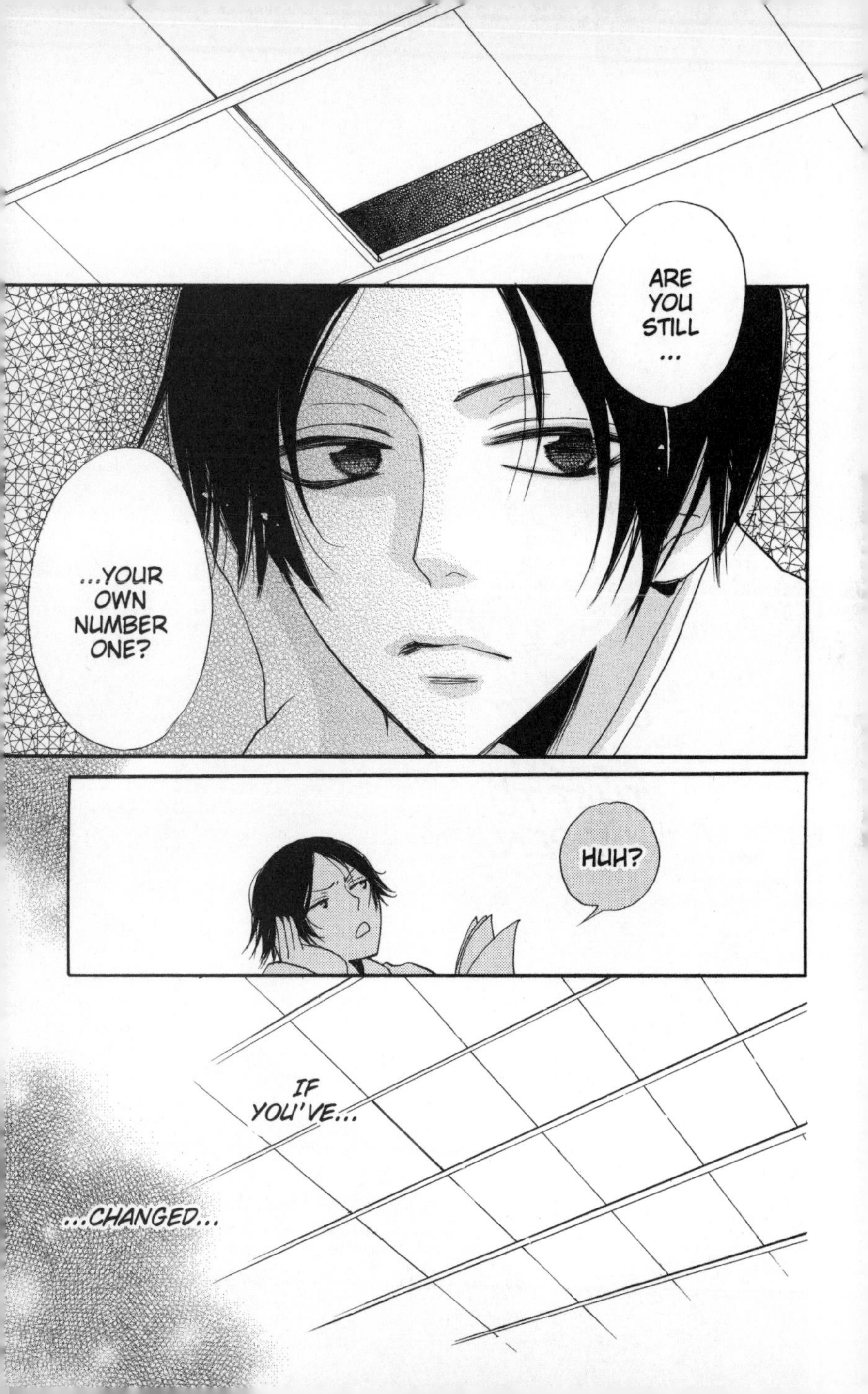
ARE YOU STILL ...
...YOUR OWN NUMBER ONE?
HUH?
IF YOU'VE...
...CHANGED...

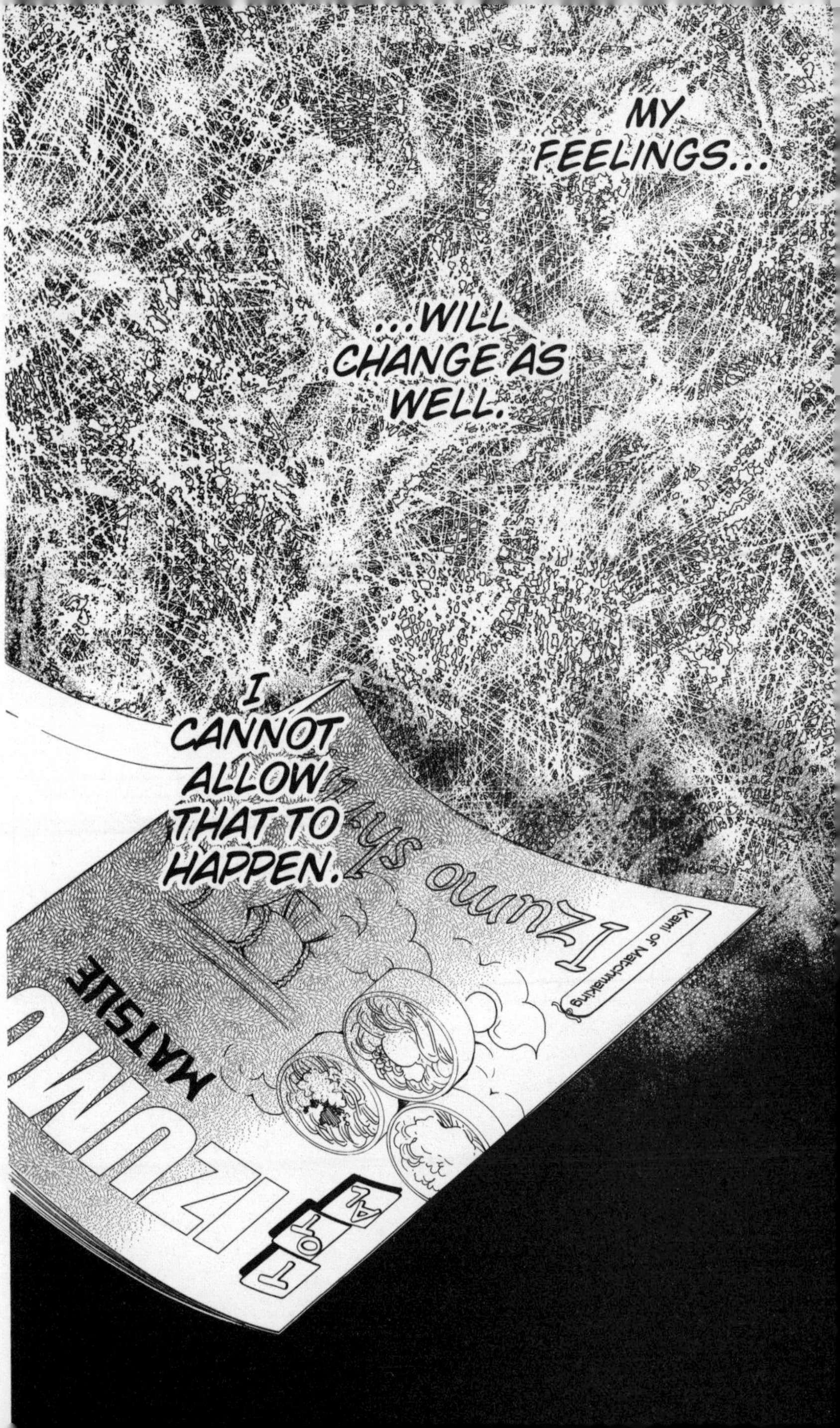
MY FEELINGS...
...WILL CHANGE AS WELL.
I CANNOT ALLOW THAT TO HAPPEN.

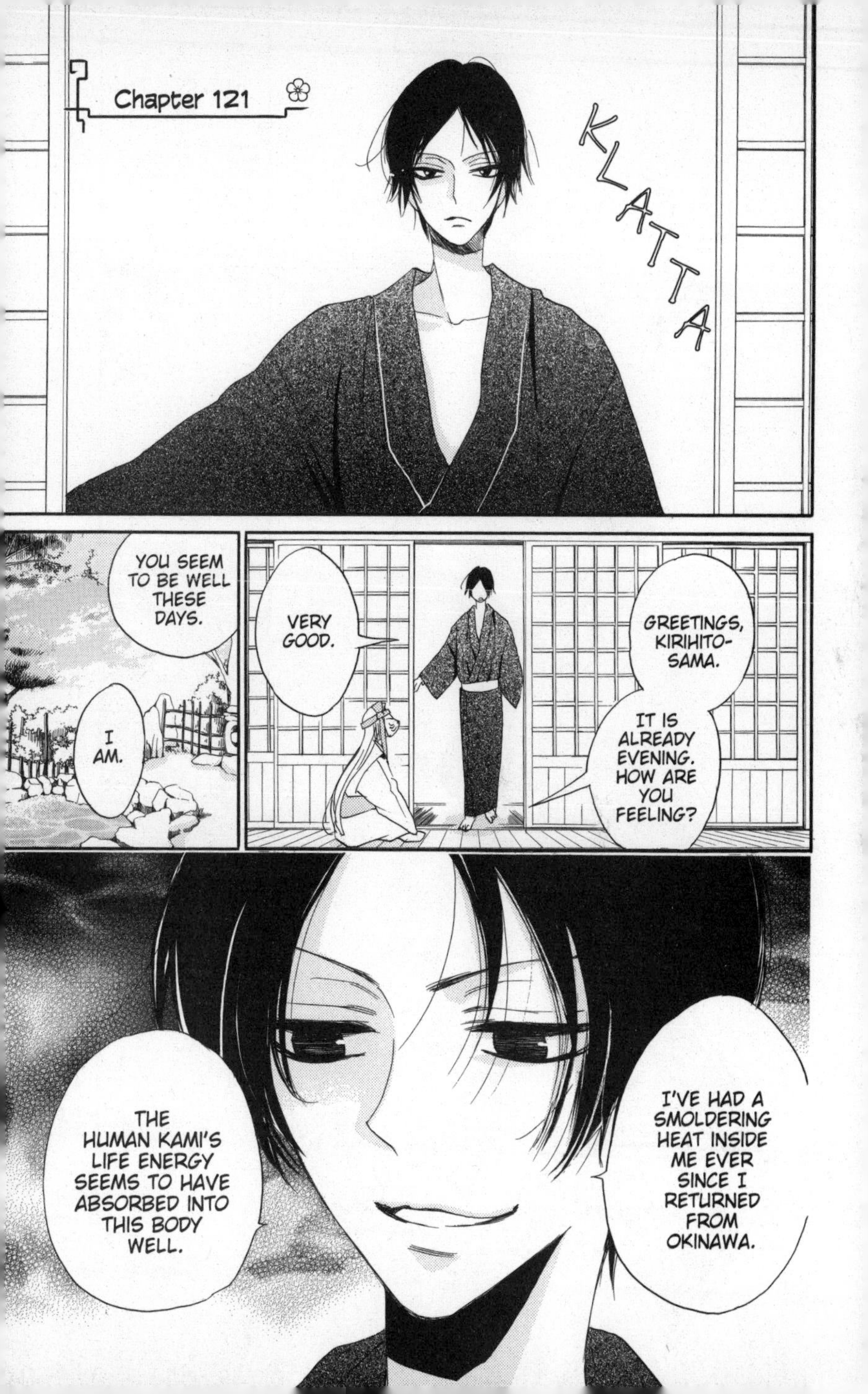
Chapter 121
KLATTA
GREETINGS, KIRIHITO-SAMA.
IT IS ALREADY EVENING. HOW ARE YOU FEELING?
VERY GOOD.
YOU SEEM TO BE WELL THESE DAYS.
I AM.
I'VE HAD A SMOLDERING HEAT INSIDE ME EVER SINCE I RETURNED FROM OKINAWA.
THE HUMAN KAMI'S LIFE ENERGY SEEMS TO HAVE ABSORBED INTO THIS BODY WELL.

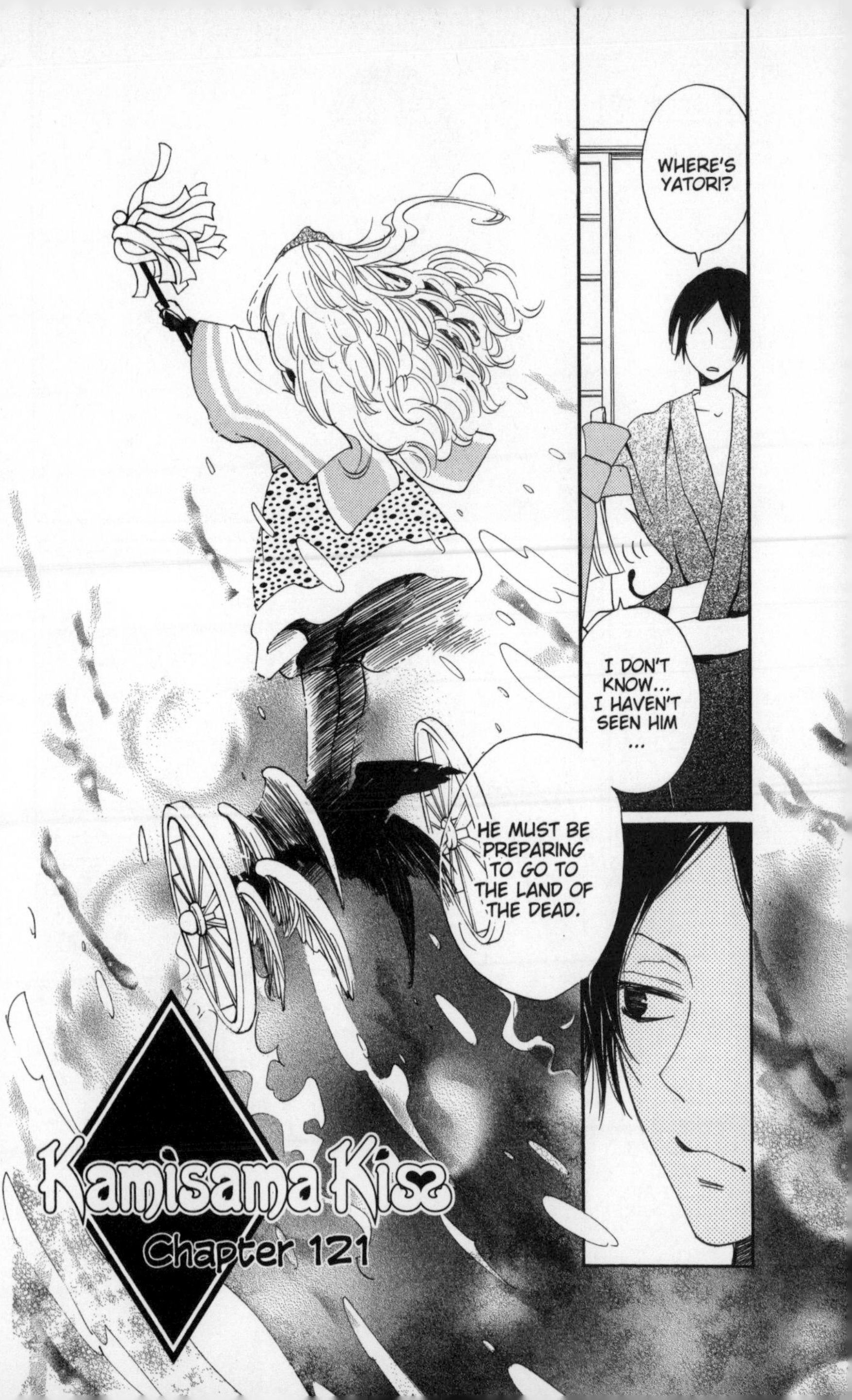
WHERE'S YATORI?
I DON'T KNOW... I HAVEN'T SEEN HIM ...
HE MUST BE PREPARING TO GO TO THE LAND OF THE DEAD.
Kamisama Kiss
Chapter 121

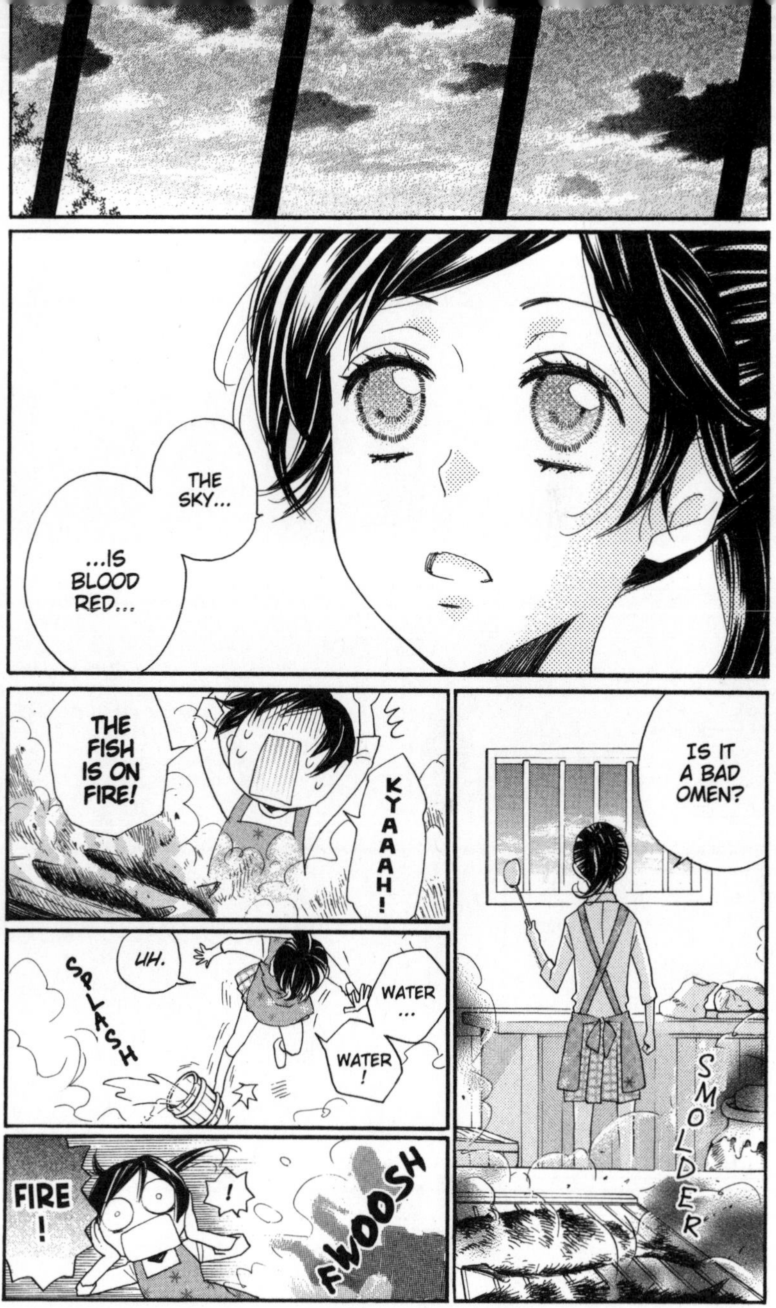
THE SKY...
...IS BLOOD RED...
IS IT A BAD OMEN?
SMOLDER
KYAAAH!
THE FISH IS ON FIRE!
WATER...
WATER!
UH.
SPLASH
FWOOSH
!
FIRE!

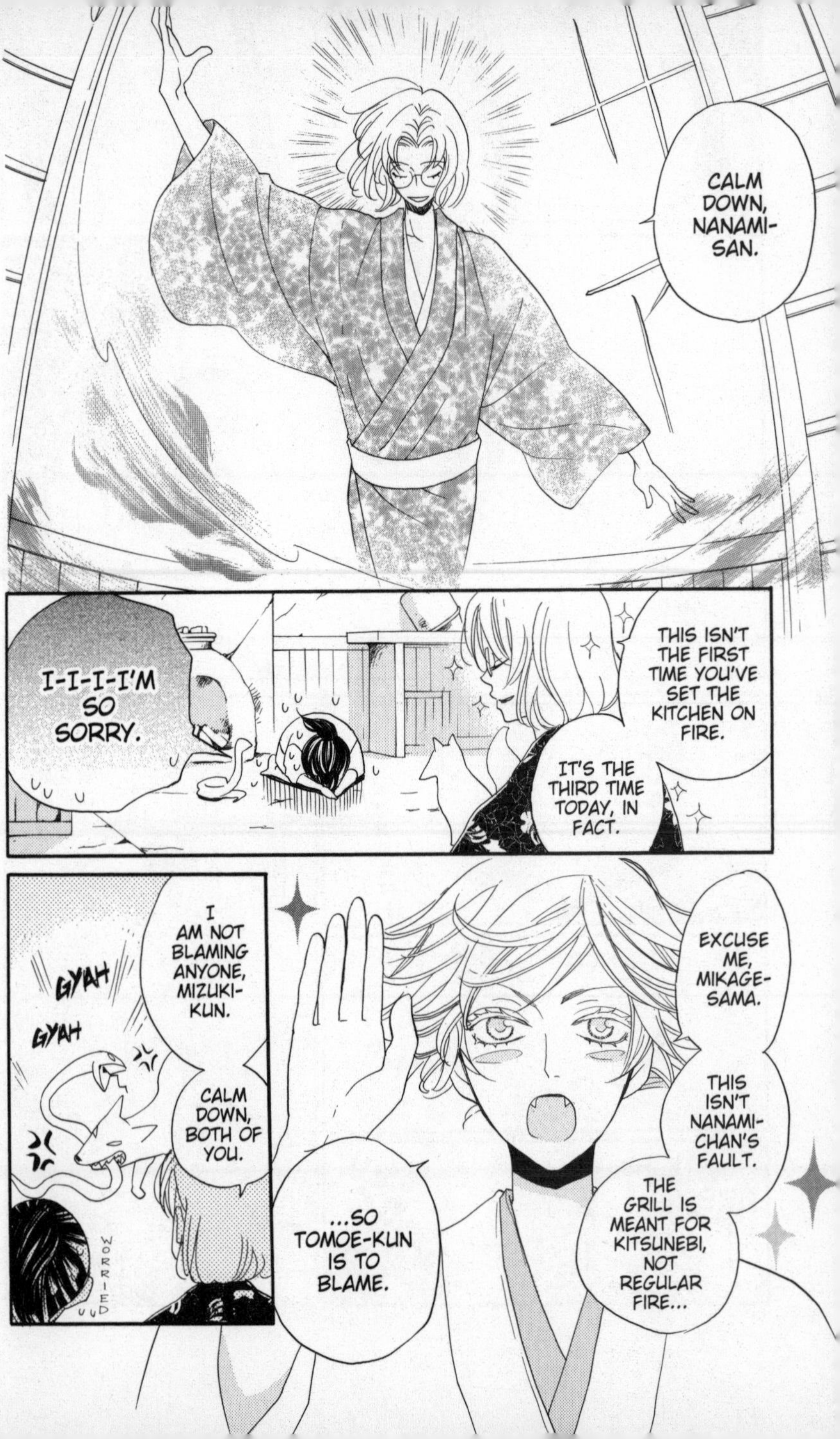
CALM DOWN, NANAMI-SAN.
THIS ISN'T THE FIRST TIME YOU'VE SET THE KITCHEN ON FIRE.
IT'S THE THIRD TIME TODAY, IN FACT.
I-I-I-I'M SO SORRY.
EXCUSE ME, MIKAGE-SAMA.
THIS ISN'T NANAMI-CHAN'S FAULT.
THE GRILL IS MEANT FOR KITSUNEBI, NOT REGULAR FIRE...
...SO TOMOE-KUN IS TO BLAME.
I AM NOT BLAMING ANYONE, MIZUKI-KUN.
CALM DOWN, BOTH OF YOU.
GYAH
GYAH
WORRIED

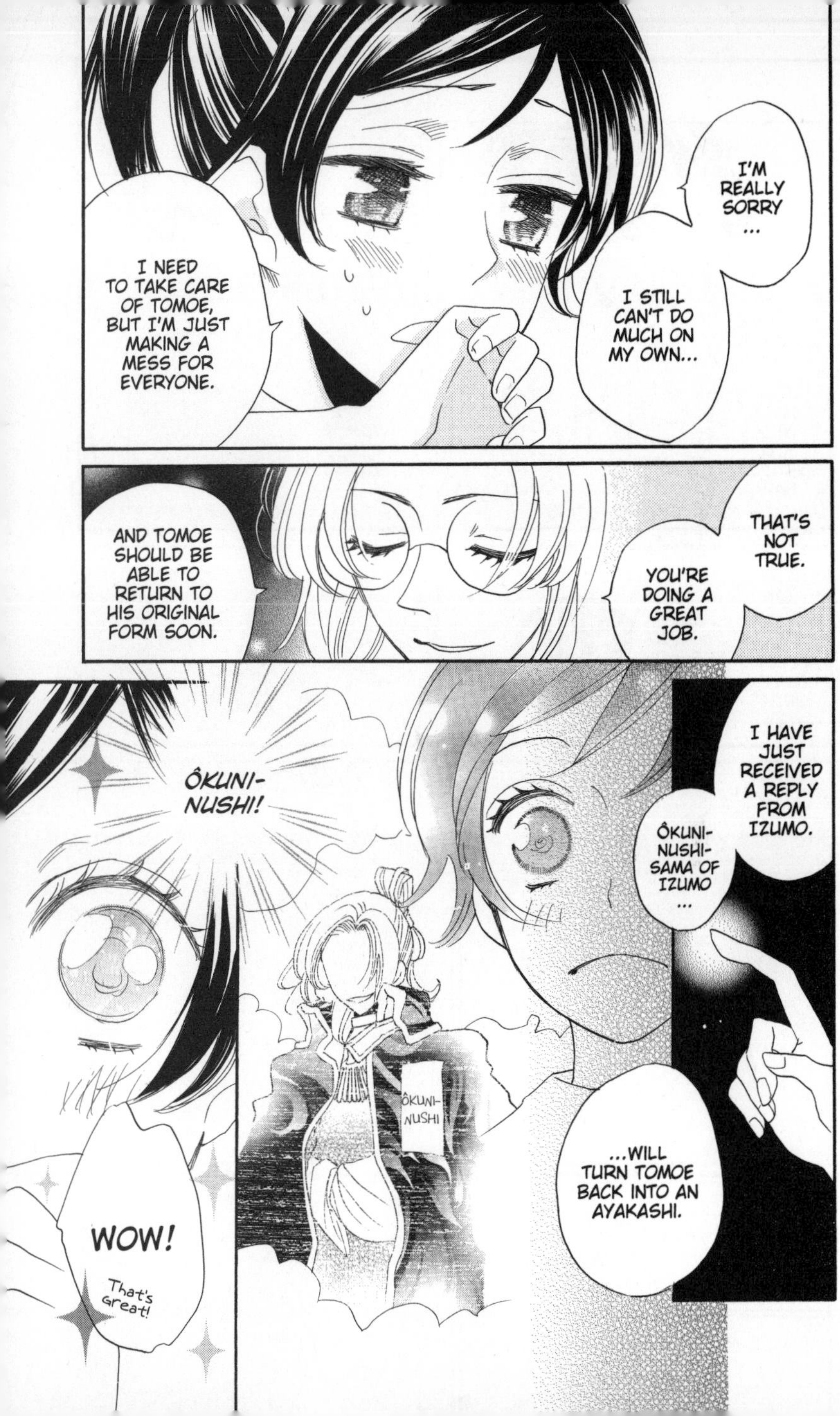
I'M REALLY SORRY...
I STILL CAN'T DO MUCH ON MY OWN...
I NEED TO TAKE CARE OF TOMOE, BUT I'M JUST MAKING A MESS FOR EVERYONE.
THAT'S NOT TRUE.
YOU'RE DOING A GREAT JOB.
AND TOMOE SHOULD BE ABLE TO RETURN TO HIS ORIGINAL FORM SOON.
I HAVE JUST RECEIVED A REPLY FROM IZUMO.
ÔKUNI-NUSHI-SAMA OF IZUMO...
...WILL TURN TOMOE BACK INTO AN AYAKASHI.
ÔKUNI-NUSHI
ÔKUNI-NUSHI!
WOW!
That's Great!

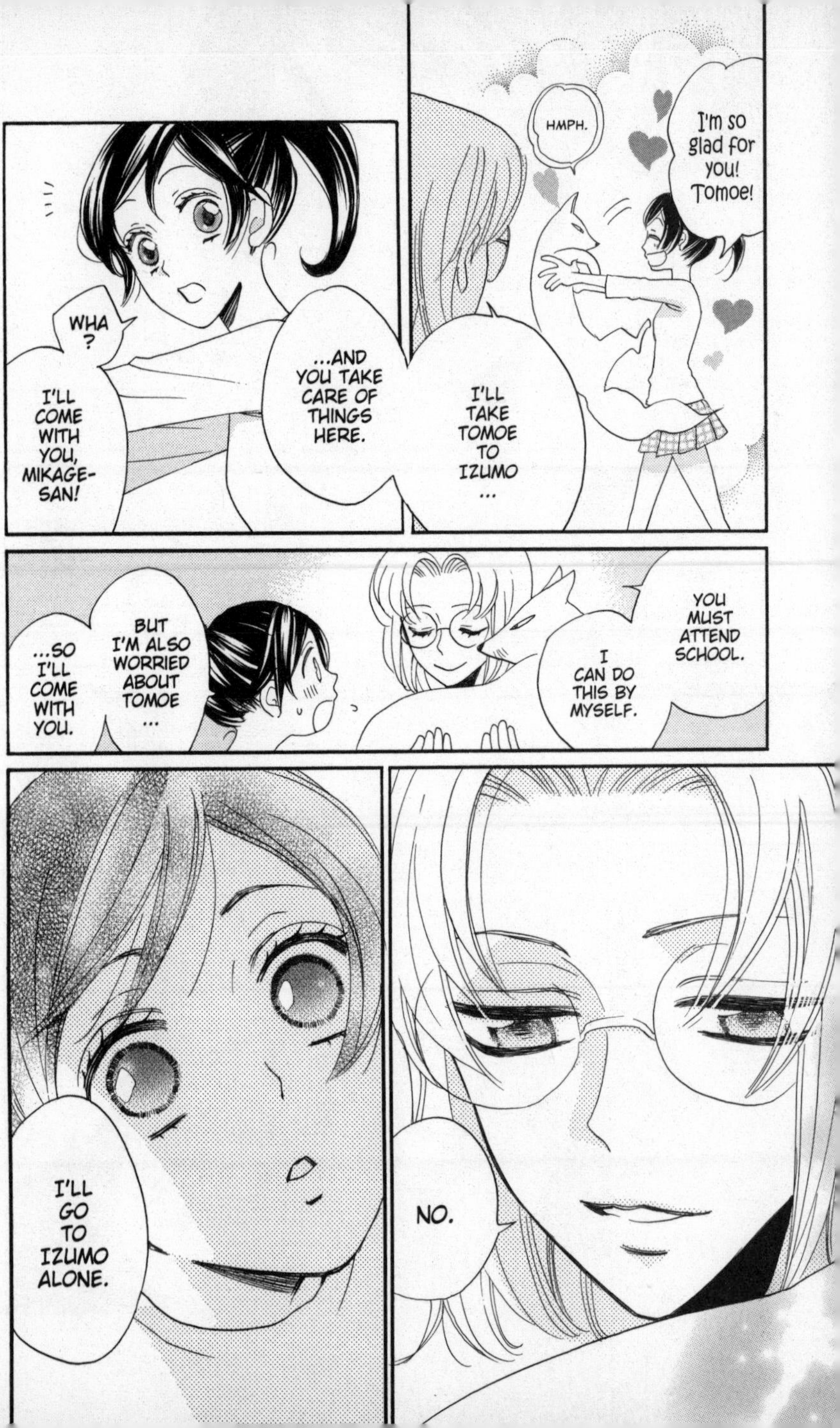
I'm so glad for you! Tomoe!
HMPH.
I'LL TAKE TOMOE TO IZUMO ...
...AND YOU TAKE CARE OF THINGS HERE.
WHA ?
I'LL COME WITH YOU, MIKAGE-SAN!
YOU MUST ATTEND SCHOOL.
I CAN DO THIS BY MYSELF.
BUT I'M ALSO WORRIED ABOUT TOMOE ...
...SO I'LL COME WITH YOU.
NO.
I'LL GO TO IZUMO ALONE.

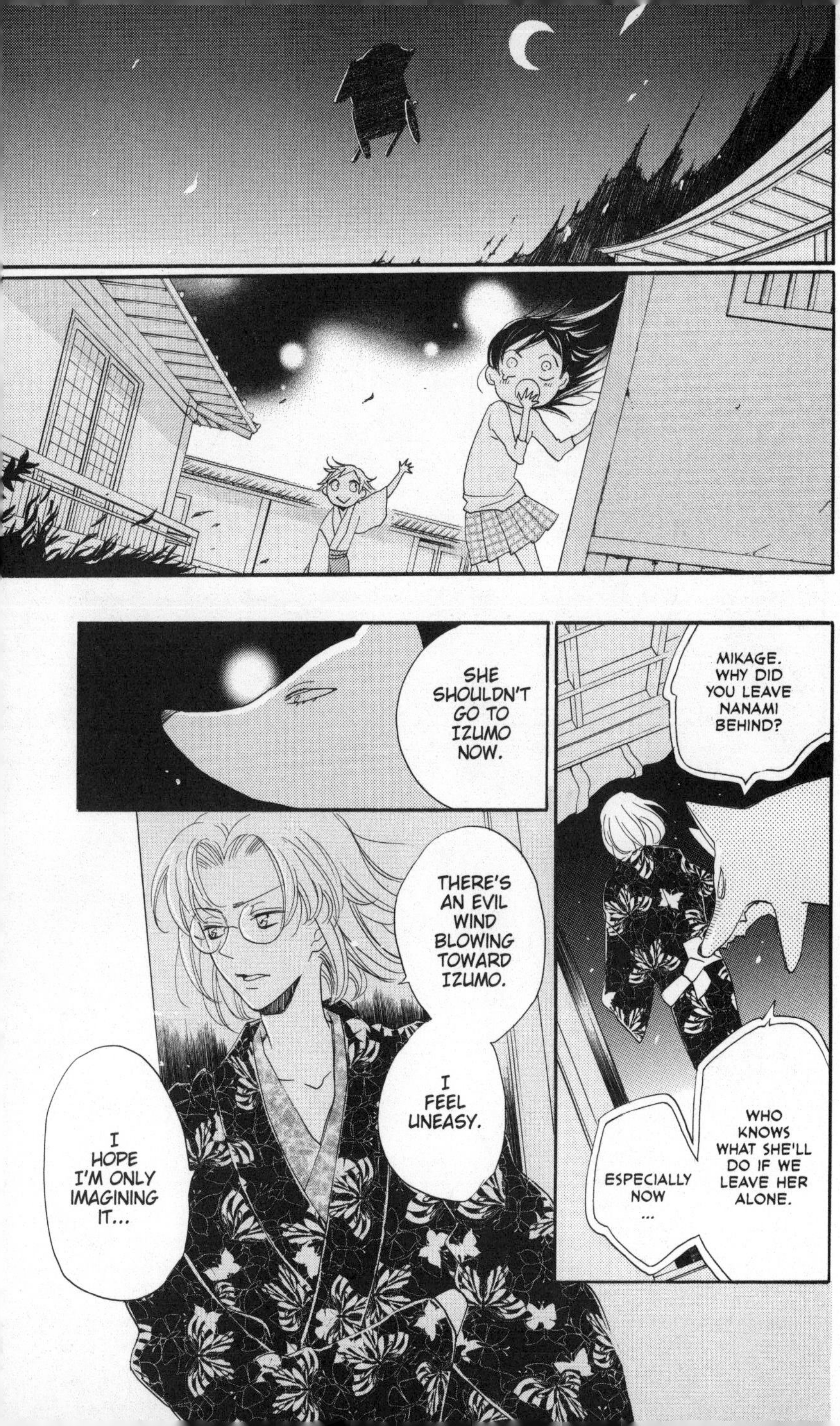
MIKAGE. WHY DID YOU LEAVE NANAMI BEHIND?
WHO KNOWS WHAT SHE'LL DO IF WE LEAVE HER ALONE.
ESPECIALLY NOW ...
SHE SHOULDN'T GO TO IZUMO NOW.
THERE'S AN EVIL WIND BLOWING TOWARD IZUMO.
I FEEL UNEASY.
I HOPE I'M ONLY IMAGINING IT...

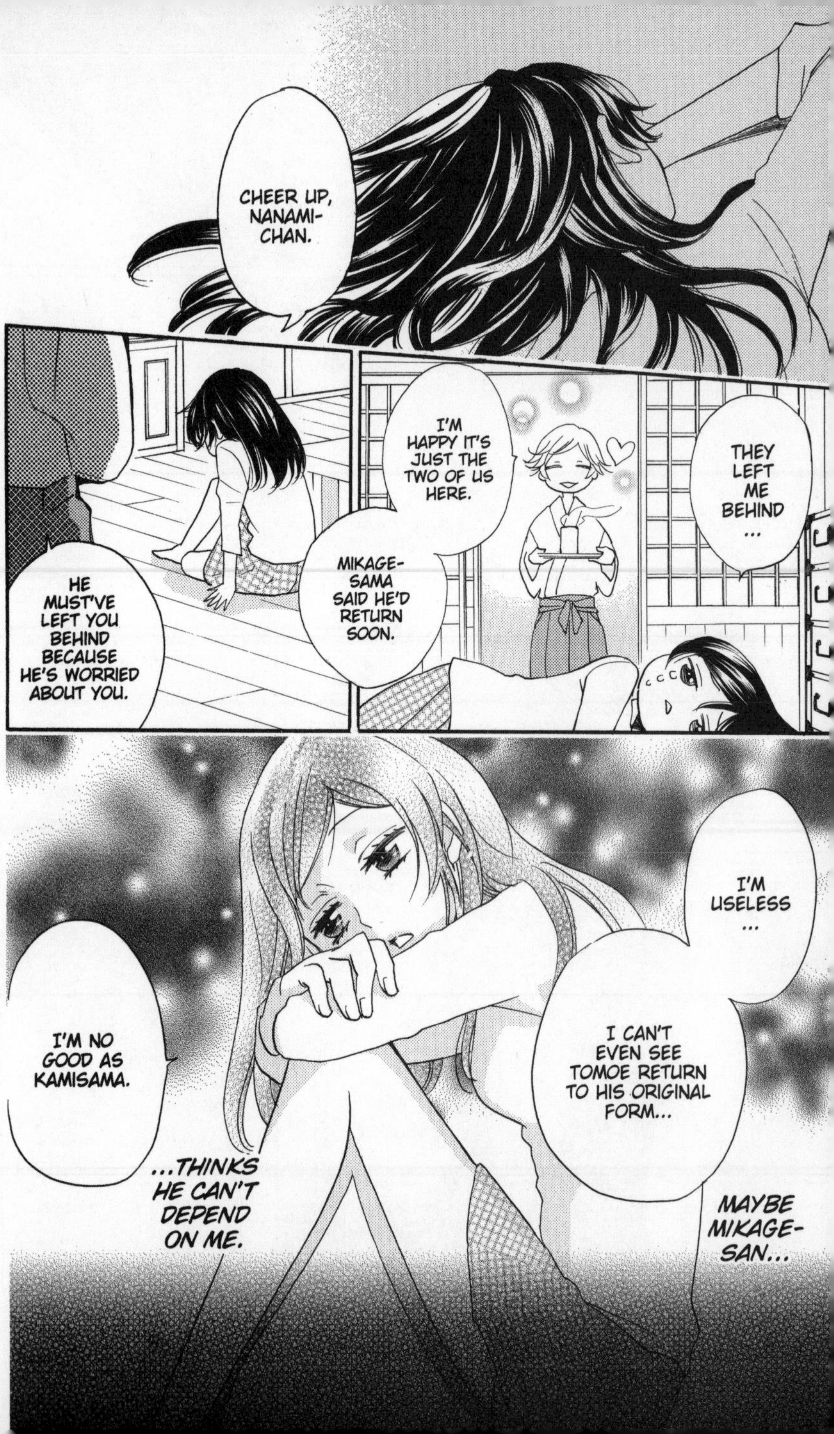
CHEER UP, NANAMI-CHAN.
THEY LEFT ME BEHIND ...
I'M HAPPY IT'S JUST THE TWO OF US HERE.
MIKAGE-SAMA SAID HE'D RETURN SOON.
HE MUST'VE LEFT YOU BEHIND BECAUSE HE'S WORRIED ABOUT YOU.
I'M USELESS ...
I CAN'T EVEN SEE TOMOE RETURN TO HIS ORIGINAL FORM...
I'M NO GOOD AS KAMISAMA.
MAYBE MIKAGE-SAN...
...THINKS HE CAN'T DEPEND ON ME.

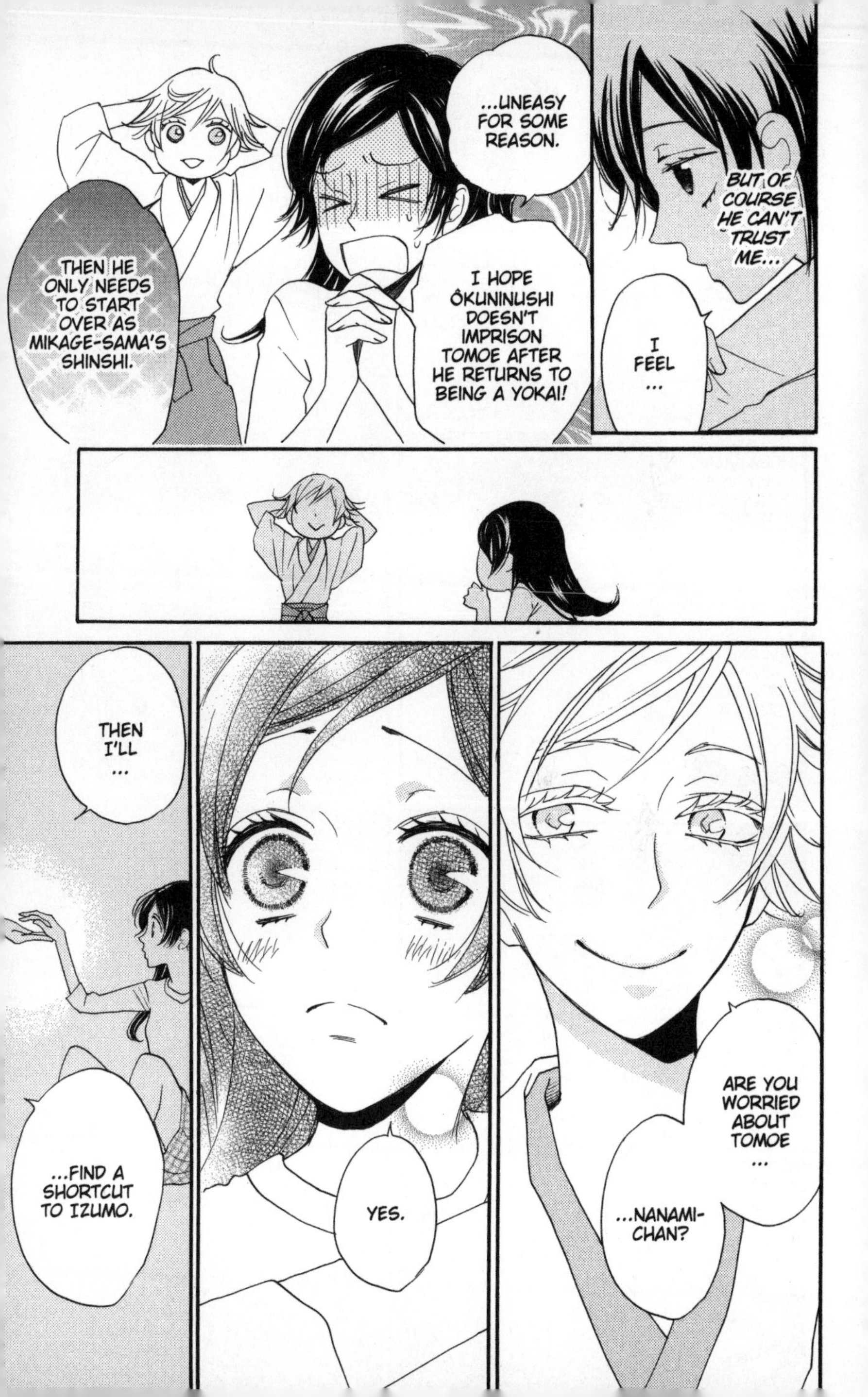
BUT OF COURSE HE CAN'T TRUST ME...
I FEEL ...
...UNEASY FOR SOME REASON.
I HOPE ÔKUNINUSHI DOESN'T IMPRISON TOMOE AFTER HE RETURNS TO BEING A YOKAI!
THEN HE ONLY NEEDS TO START OVER AS MIKAGE-SAMA'S SHINSHI.
ARE YOU WORRIED ABOUT TOMOE ...
...NANAMI-CHAN?
YES.
THEN I'LL ...
...FIND A SHORTCUT TO IZUMO.

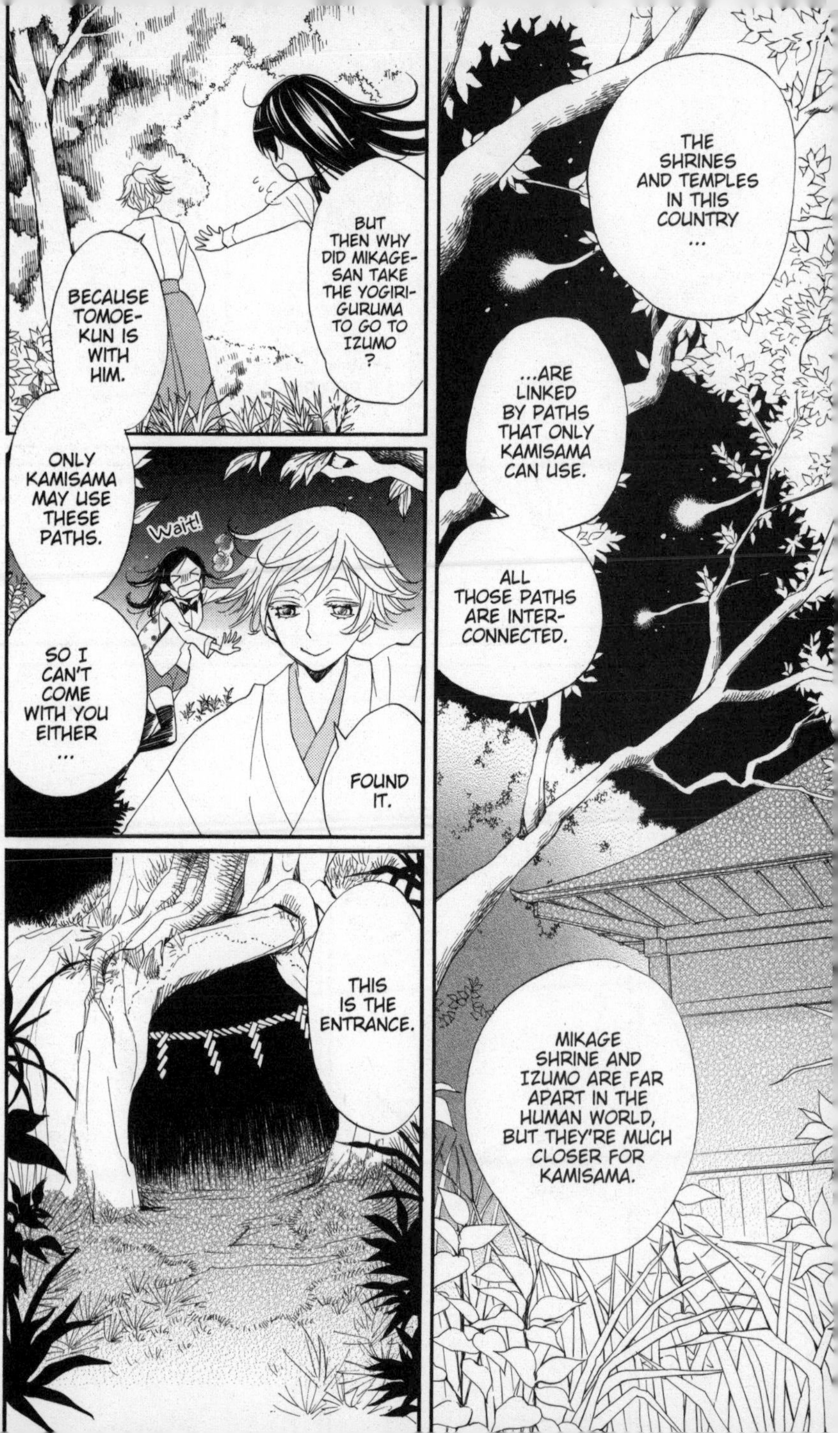
THE SHRINES AND TEMPLES IN THIS COUNTRY...
...ARE LINKED BY PATHS THAT ONLY KAMISAMA CAN USE.
ALL THOSE PATHS ARE INTER-CONNECTED.
MIKAGE SHRINE AND IZUMO ARE FAR APART IN THE HUMAN WORLD, BUT THEY'RE MUCH CLOSER FOR KAMISAMA.
BUT THEN WHY DID MIKAGE-SAN TAKE THE YOGIRI-GURUMA TO GO TO IZUMO?
BECAUSE TOMOE-KUN IS WITH HIM.
ONLY KAMISAMA MAY USE THESE PATHS.
Wait!
SO I CAN'T COME WITH YOU EITHER...
FOUND IT.
THIS IS THE ENTRANCE.

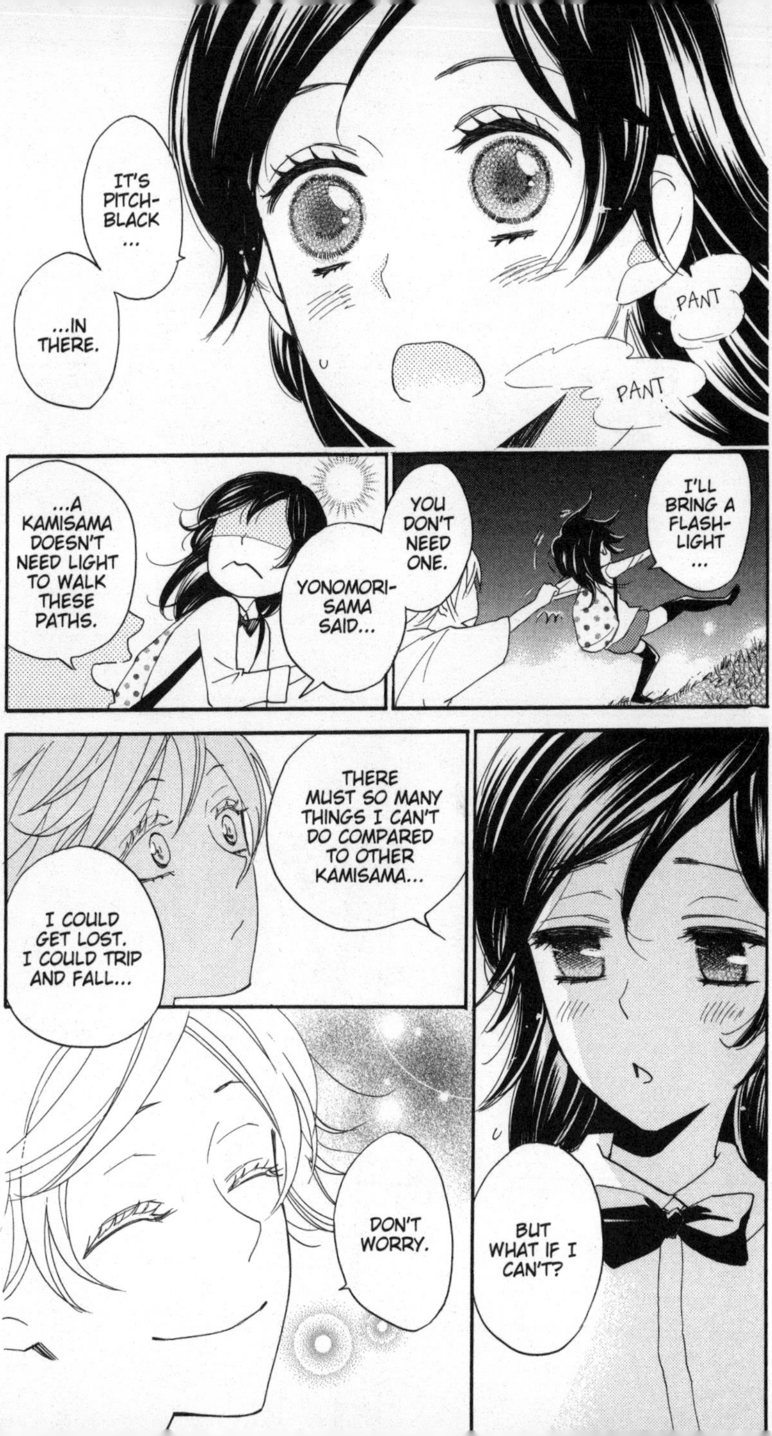
PANT
PANT
IT'S PITCH-BLACK...
...IN THERE.
I'LL BRING A FLASH-LIGHT...
YOU DON'T NEED ONE.
YONOMORI-SAMA SAID...
...A KAMISAMA DOESN'T NEED LIGHT TO WALK THESE PATHS.
BUT WHAT IF I CAN'T?
THERE MUST SO MANY THINGS I CAN'T DO COMPARED TO OTHER KAMISAMA...
I COULD GET LOST. I COULD TRIP AND FALL...
DON'T WORRY.

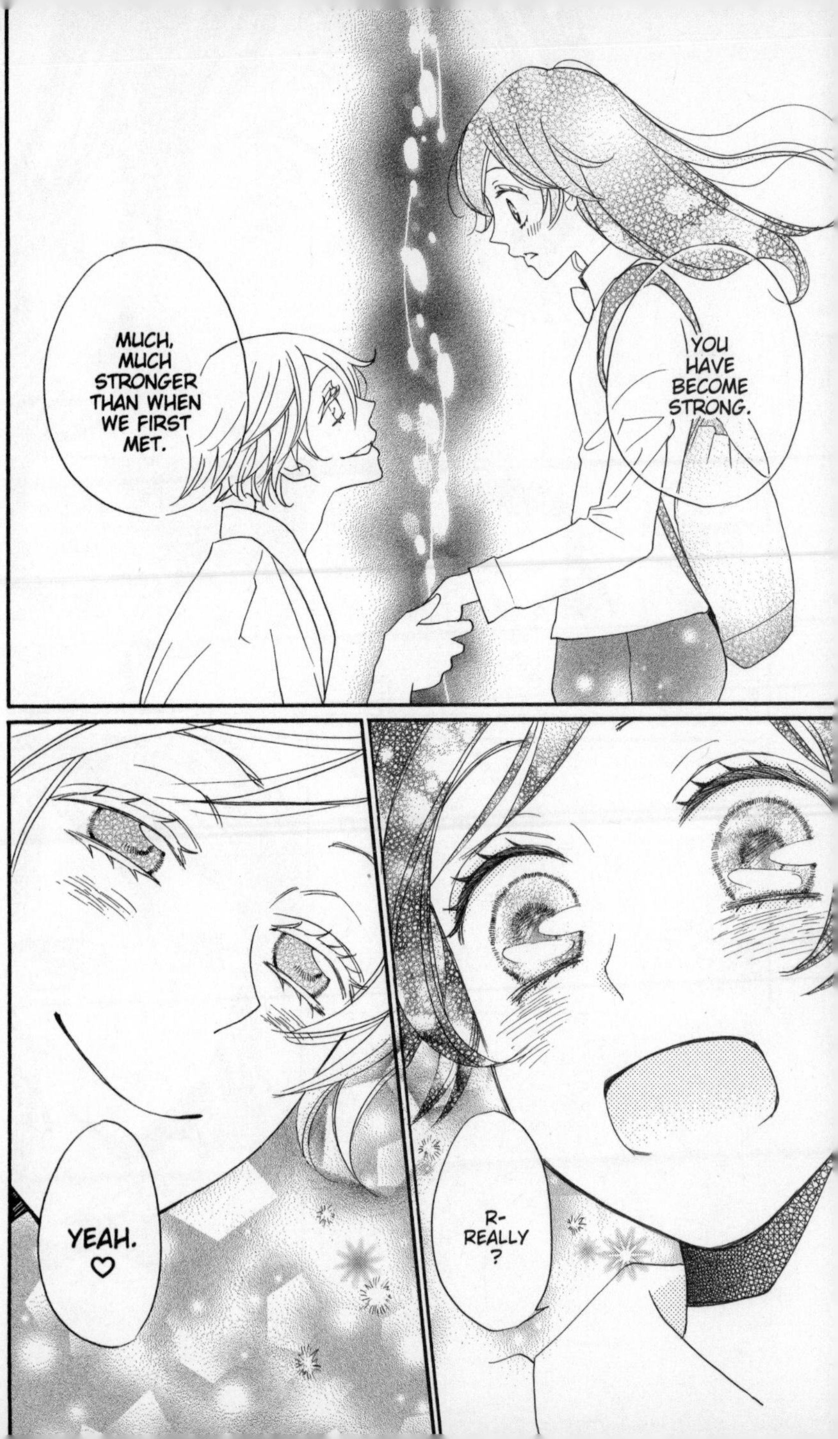
YOU HAVE BECOME STRONG.
MUCH, MUCH STRONGER THAN WHEN WE FIRST MET.
R-REALLY?
YEAH. ♡

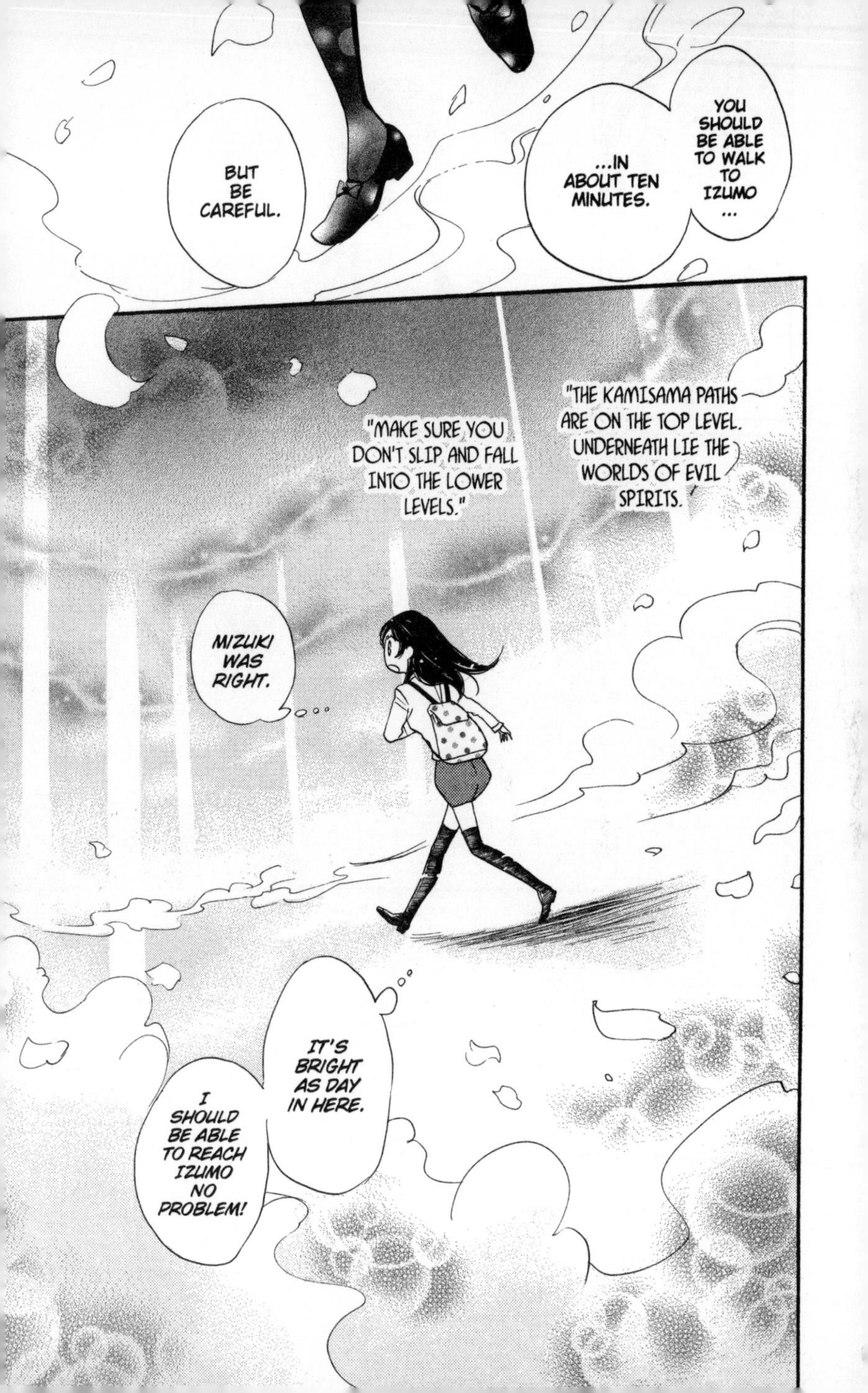
YOU SHOULD BE ABLE TO WALK TO IZUMO...
...IN ABOUT TEN MINUTES.
BUT BE CAREFUL.
"THE KAMISAMA PATHS ARE ON THE TOP LEVEL. UNDERNEATH LIE THE WORLDS OF EVIL SPIRITS.
"MAKE SURE YOU DON'T SLIP AND FALL INTO THE LOWER LEVELS."
MIZUKI WAS RIGHT.
IT'S BRIGHT AS DAY IN HERE.
I SHOULD BE ABLE TO REACH IZUMO NO PROBLEM!

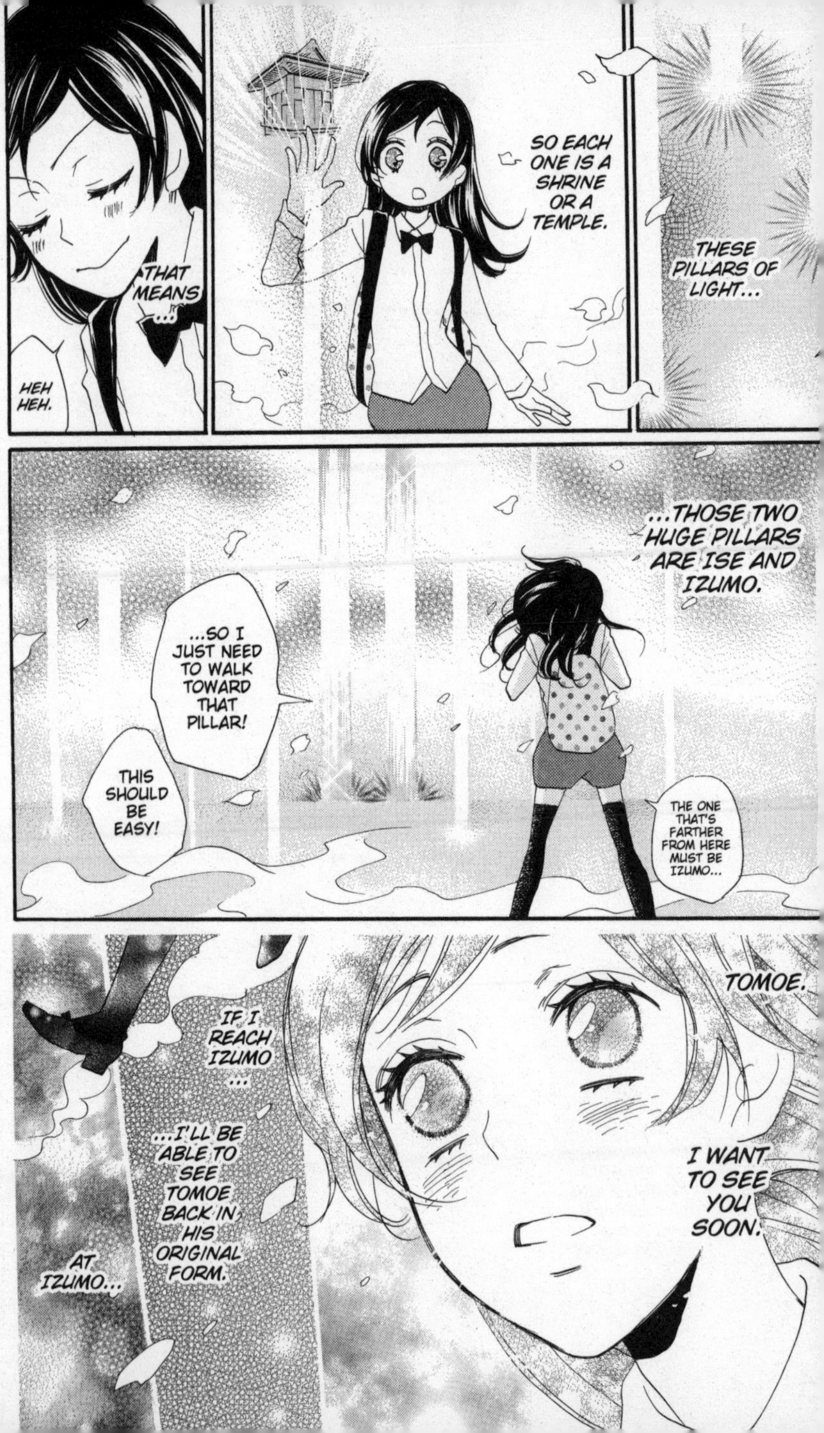
THESE PILLARS OF LIGHT...
SO EACH ONE IS A SHRINE OR A TEMPLE.
THAT MEANS...
HEH HEH.
...THOSE TWO HUGE PILLARS ARE ISE AND IZUMO.
THE ONE THAT'S FARTHER FROM HERE MUST BE IZUMO...
...SO I JUST NEED TO WALK TOWARD THAT PILLAR!
THIS SHOULD BE EASY!
TOMOE.
I WANT TO SEE YOU SOON.
IF I REACH IZUMO...
...I'LL BE ABLE TO SEE TOMOE BACK IN HIS ORIGINAL FORM.
AT IZUMO...

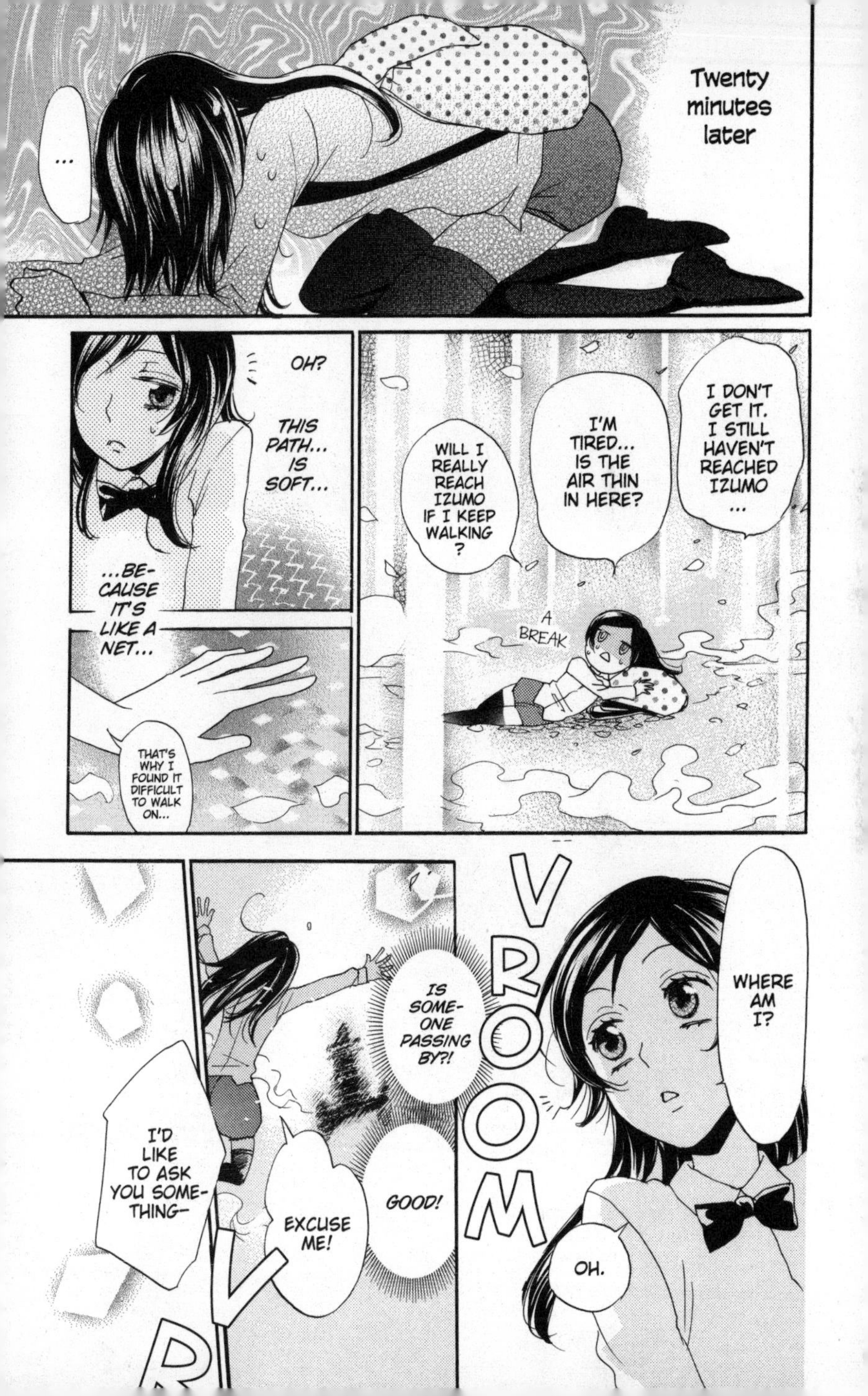
Twenty minutes later
...
I DON'T GET IT. I STILL HAVEN'T REACHED IZUMO ...
I'M TIRED... IS THE AIR THIN IN HERE?
WILL I REALLY REACH IZUMO IF I KEEP WALKING?
A BREAK
OH?
THIS PATH... IS SOFT...
...BECAUSE IT'S LIKE A NET...
THAT'S WHY I FOUND IT DIFFICULT TO WALK ON...
WHERE AM I?
OH.
VROOM
IS SOMEONE PASSING BY?!
GOOD!
EXCUSE ME!
I'D LIKE TO ASK YOU SOMETHING-

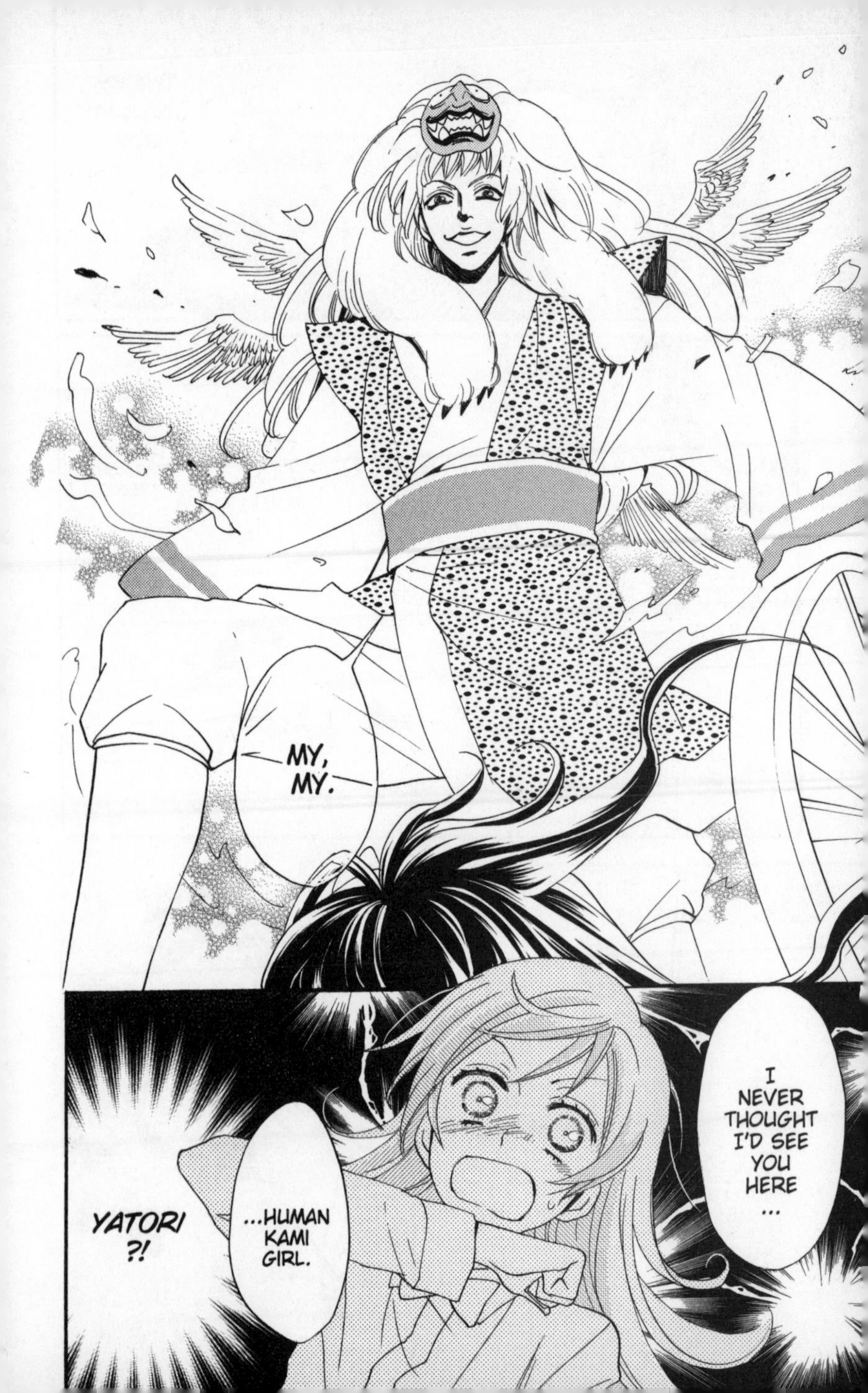
MY, MY.
I NEVER THOUGHT I'D SEE YOU HERE...
...HUMAN KAMI GIRL.
YATORI ?!

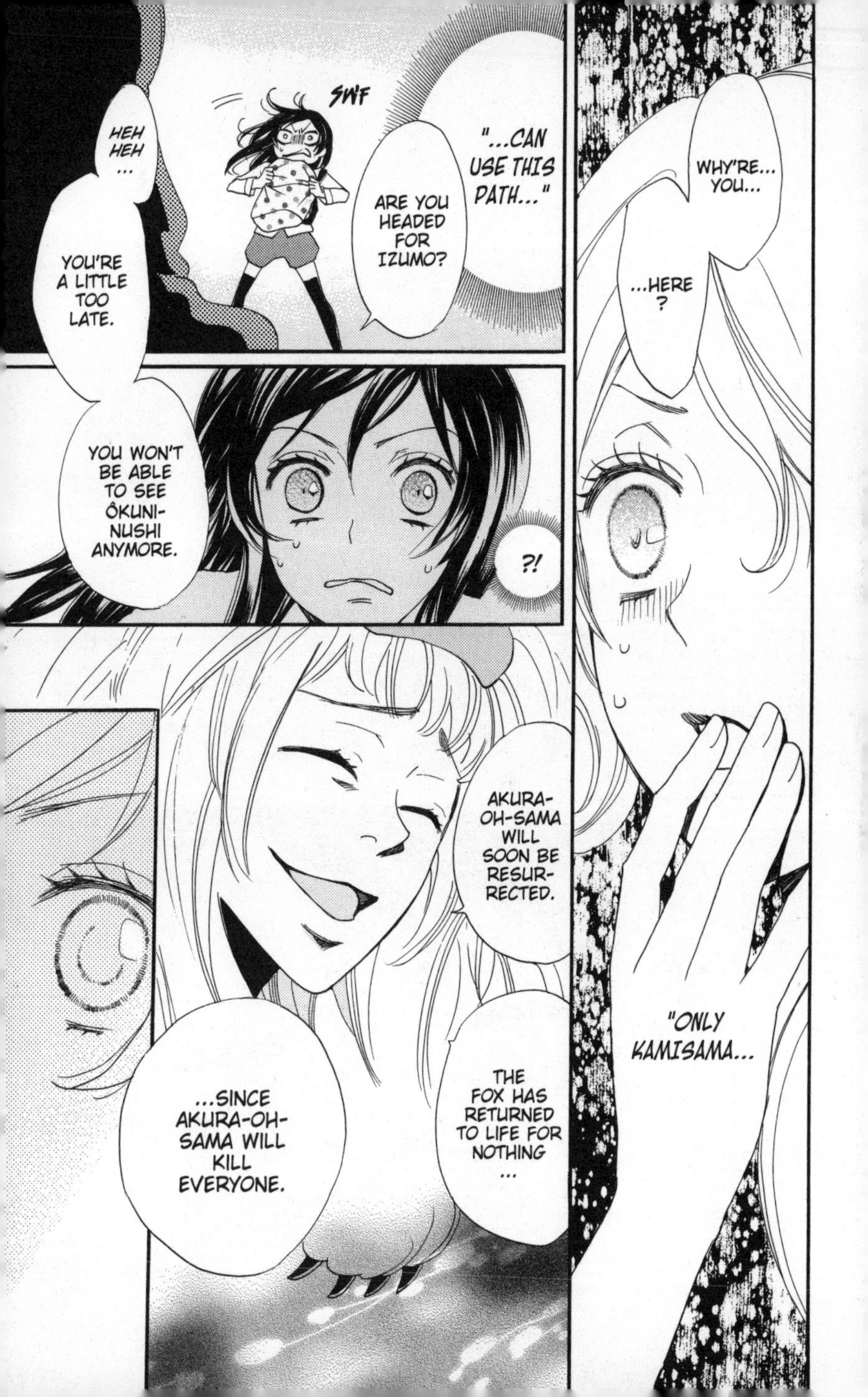
WHY'RE... YOU...
...HERE?
"ONLY KAMISAMA...
SW'F
"...CAN USE THIS PATH..."
ARE YOU HEADED FOR IZUMO?
HEH HEH ...
YOU'RE A LITTLE TOO LATE.
YOU WON'T BE ABLE TO SEE ÔKUNI-NUSHI ANYMORE.
?!
AKURA-OH-SAMA WILL SOON BE RESUR-RECTED.
THE FOX HAS RETURNED TO LIFE FOR NOTHING ...
...SINCE AKURA-OH-SAMA WILL KILL EVERYONE.

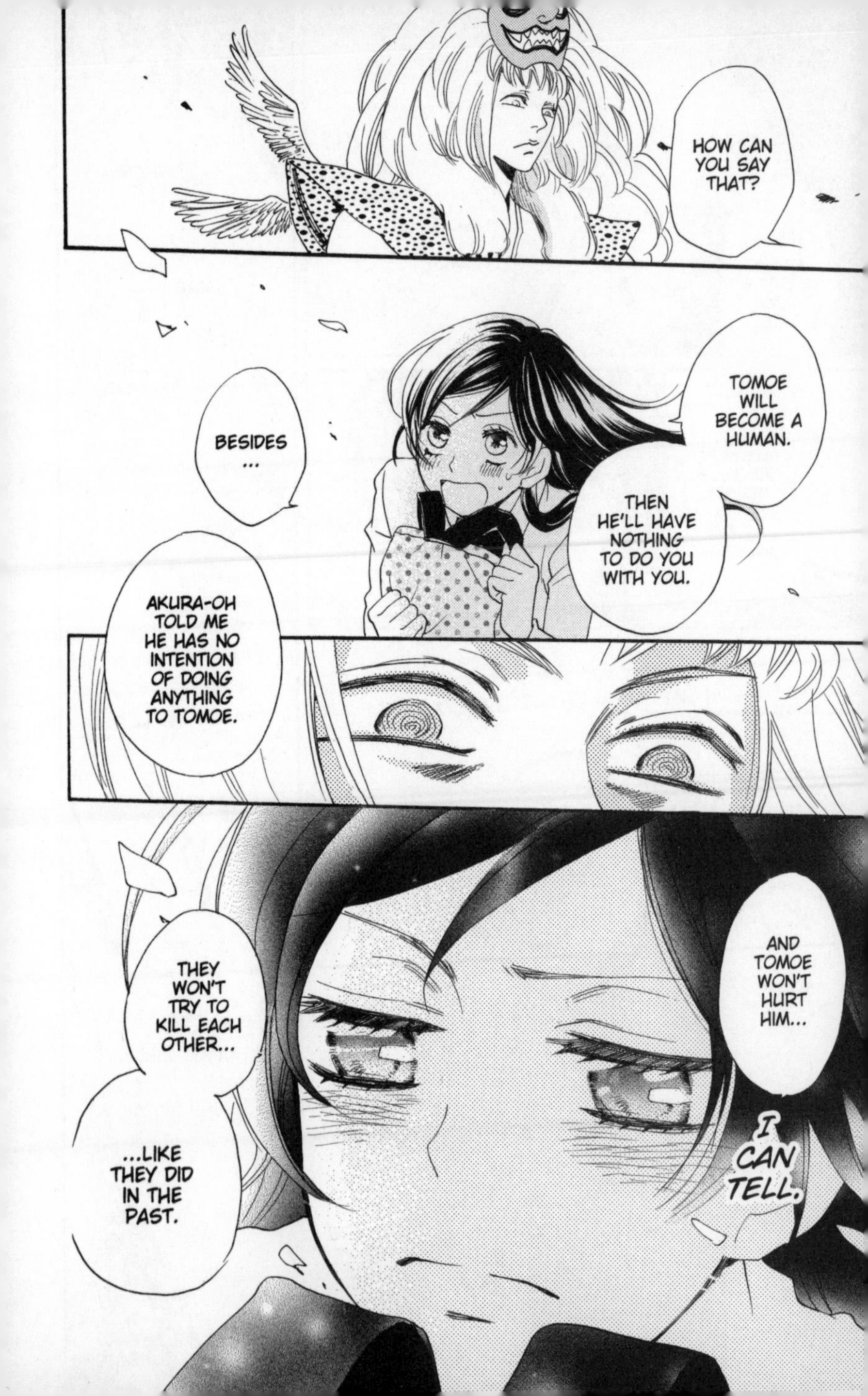
HOW CAN YOU SAY THAT?
TOMOE WILL BECOME A HUMAN.
THEN HE'LL HAVE NOTHING TO DO YOU WITH YOU.
BESIDES ...
AKURA-OH TOLD ME HE HAS NO INTENTION OF DOING ANYTHING TO TOMOE.
AND TOMOE WON'T HURT HIM...
THEY WON'T TRY TO KILL EACH OTHER...
...LIKE THEY DID IN THE PAST.
I CAN TELL.

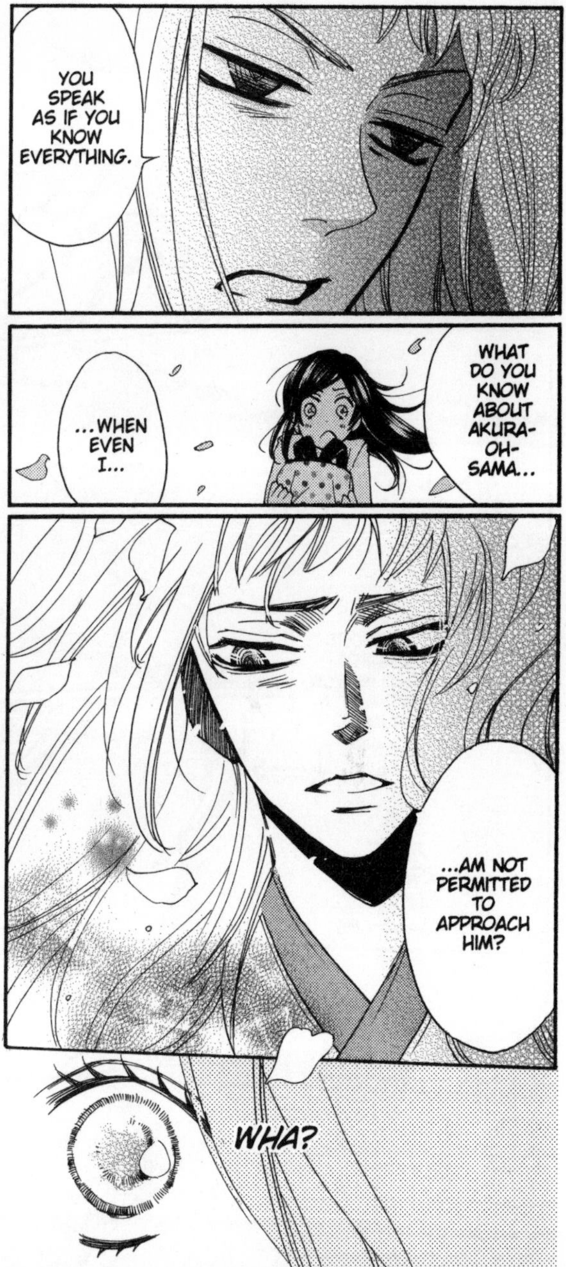
YOU SPEAK AS IF YOU KNOW EVERYTHING.
WHAT DO YOU KNOW ABOUT AKURA-OH-SAMA...
...WHEN EVEN I...
...AM NOT PERMITTED TO APPROACH HIM?
WHA?

One of my favorite sweets is Panda Pocky.

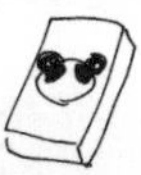

Once I start eating them, I just can't stop!

These chocolates were delicious.

Jean Michel Mortreau

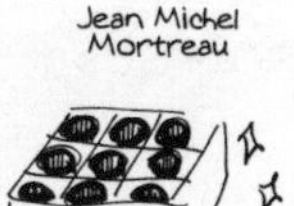

They were a gift. Thank you.

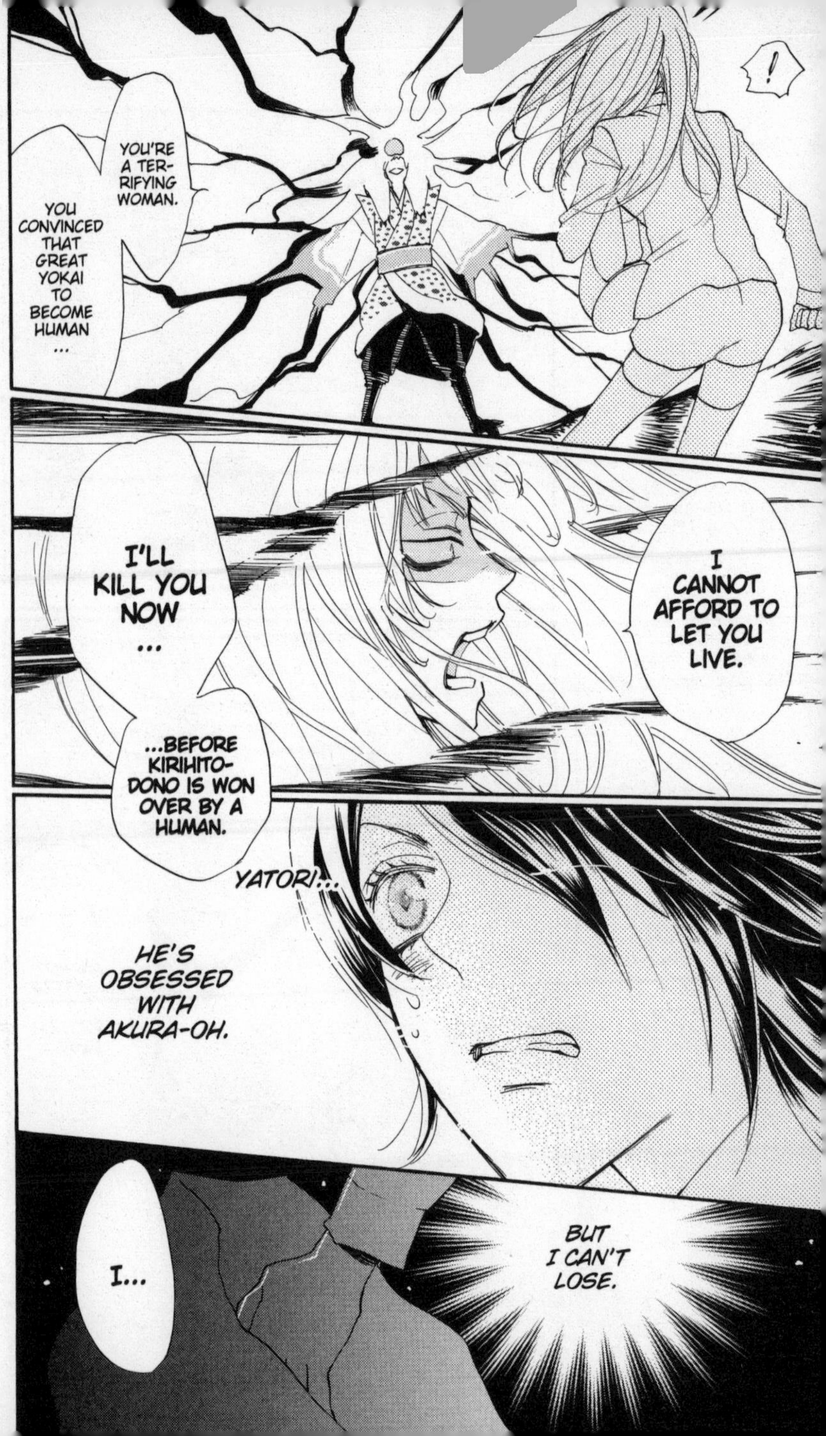
!
YOU'RE A TERRIFYING WOMAN.
YOU CONVINCED THAT GREAT YOKAI TO BECOME HUMAN...
I CANNOT AFFORD TO LET YOU LIVE.
I'LL KILL YOU NOW...
...BEFORE KIRIHITO-DONO IS WON OVER BY A HUMAN.
YATORI...
HE'S OBSESSED WITH AKURA-OH.
BUT I CAN'T LOSE.
I...

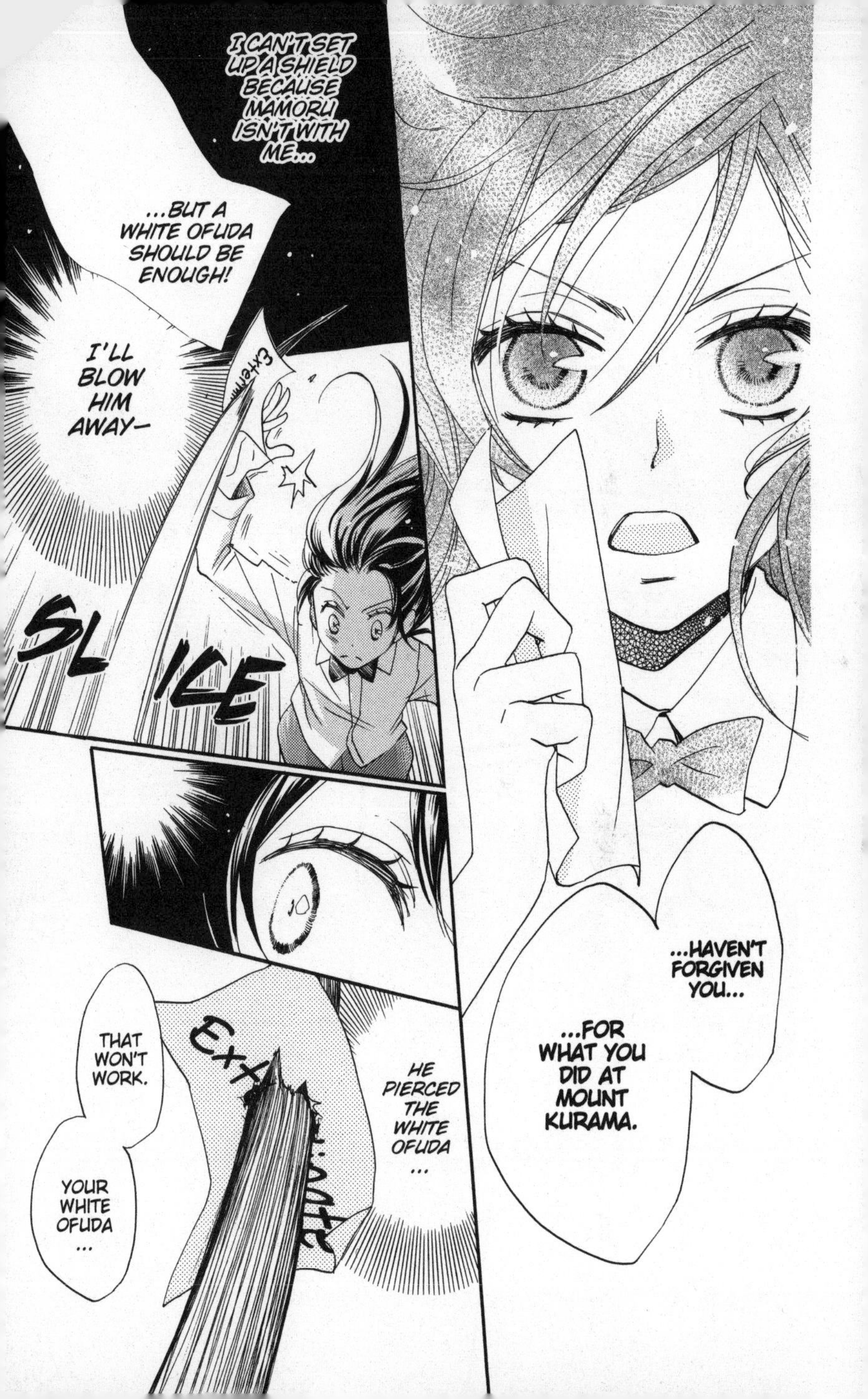
...HAVEN'T FORGIVEN YOU...
...FOR WHAT YOU DID AT MOUNT KURAMA.
I CAN'T SET UP A SHIELD BECAUSE MAMORU ISN'T WITH ME...
...BUT A WHITE OFUDA SHOULD BE ENOUGH!
Extermi
I'LL BLOW HIM AWAY—
SLICE
HE PIERCED THE WHITE OFUDA...
THAT WON'T WORK.
YOUR WHITE OFUDA...

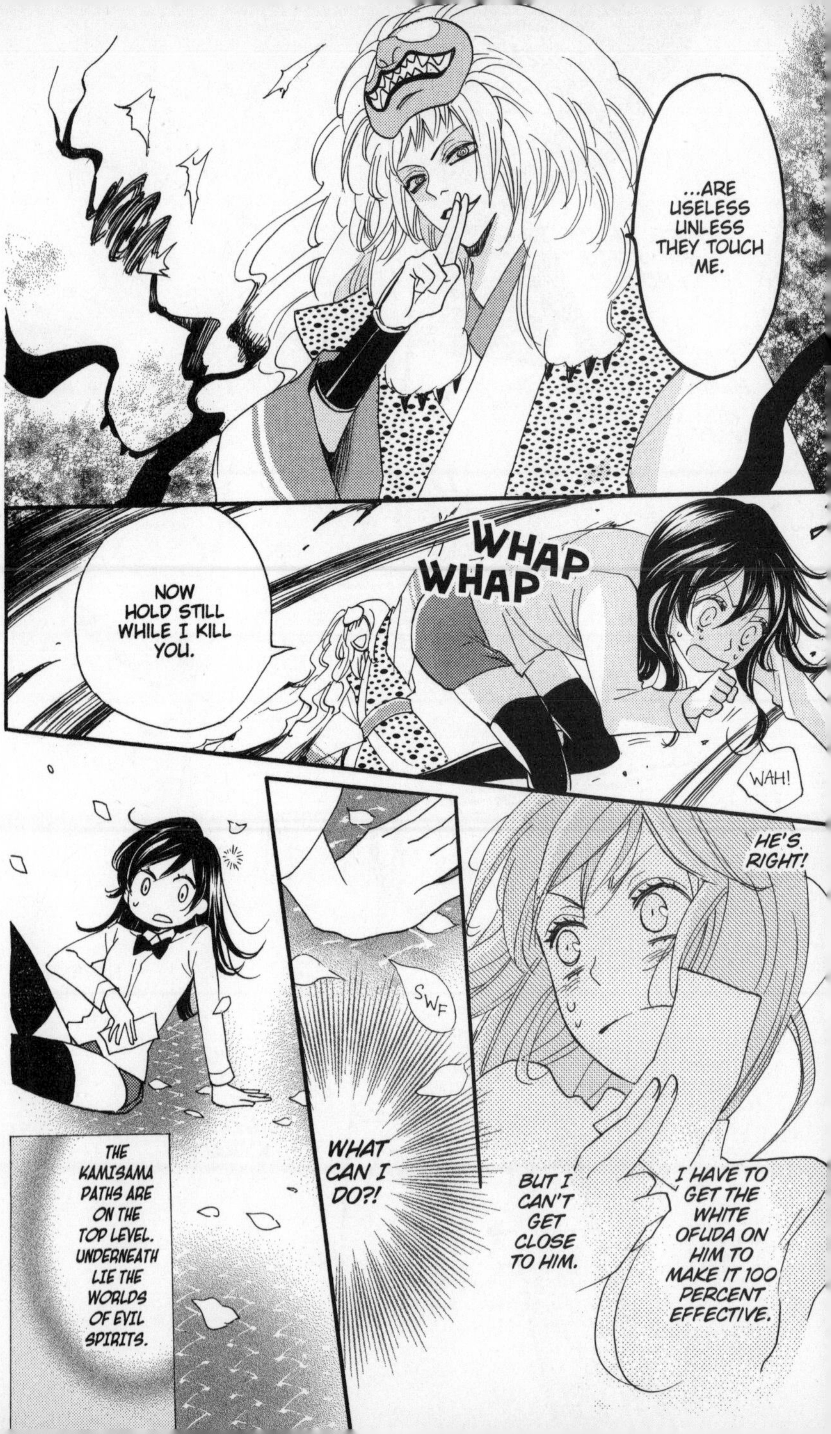
...ARE USELESS UNLESS THEY TOUCH ME.
WHAP WHAP
NOW HOLD STILL WHILE I KILL YOU.
WAH!
HE'S RIGHT!
I HAVE TO GET THE WHITE OFUDA ON HIM TO MAKE IT 100 PERCENT EFFECTIVE.
BUT I CAN'T GET CLOSE TO HIM.
SWF
WHAT CAN I DO?!
THE KAMISAMA PATHS ARE ON THE TOP LEVEL. UNDERNEATH LIE THE WORLDS OF EVIL SPIRITS.

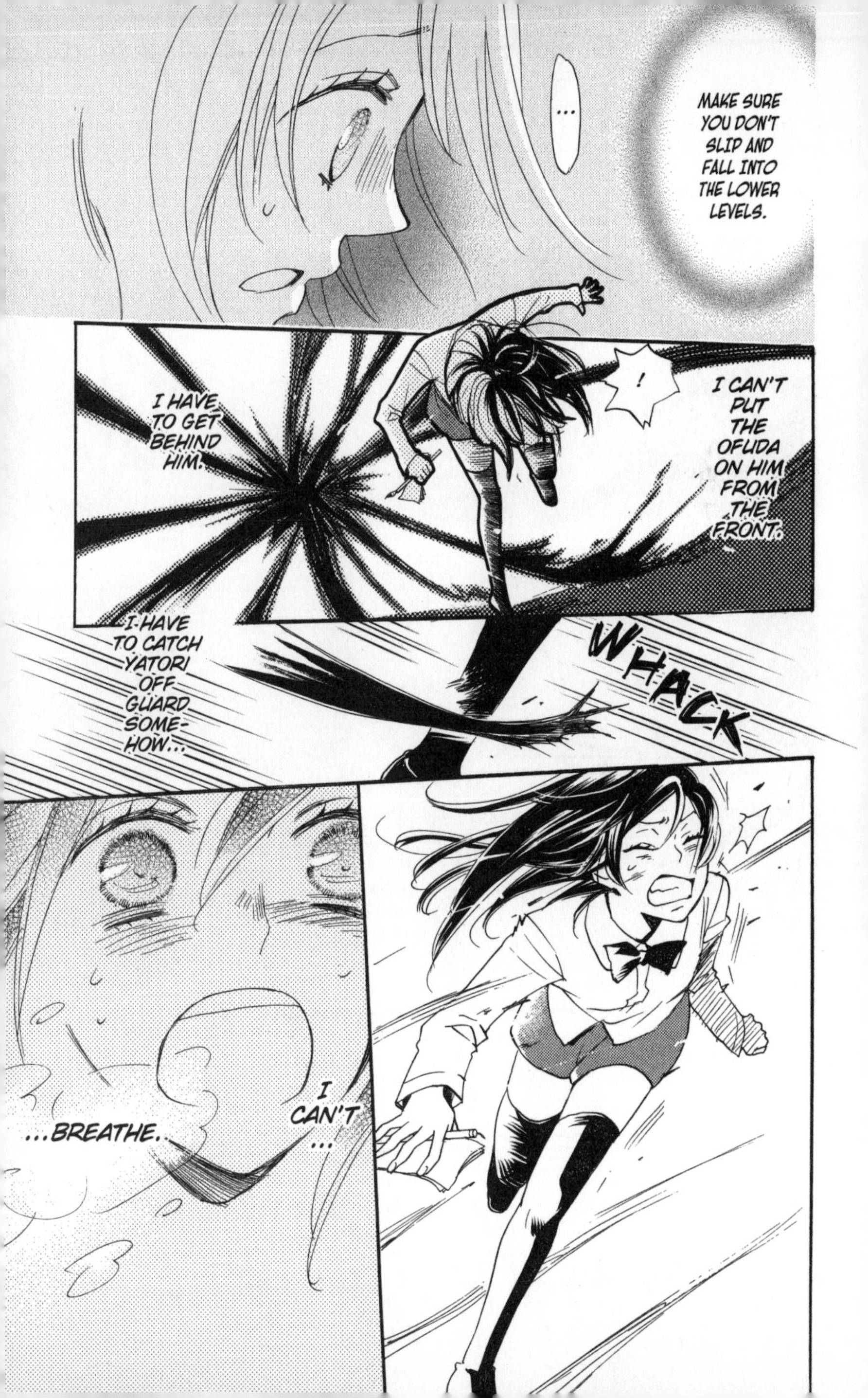
MAKE SURE YOU DON'T SLIP AND FALL INTO THE LOWER LEVELS.
...
!
I CAN'T PUT THE OFUDA ON HIM FROM THE FRONT.
I HAVE TO GET BEHIND HIM.
WHACK
I HAVE TO CATCH YATORI OFF GUARD SOME-HOW...
I CAN'T ...
...BREATHE...

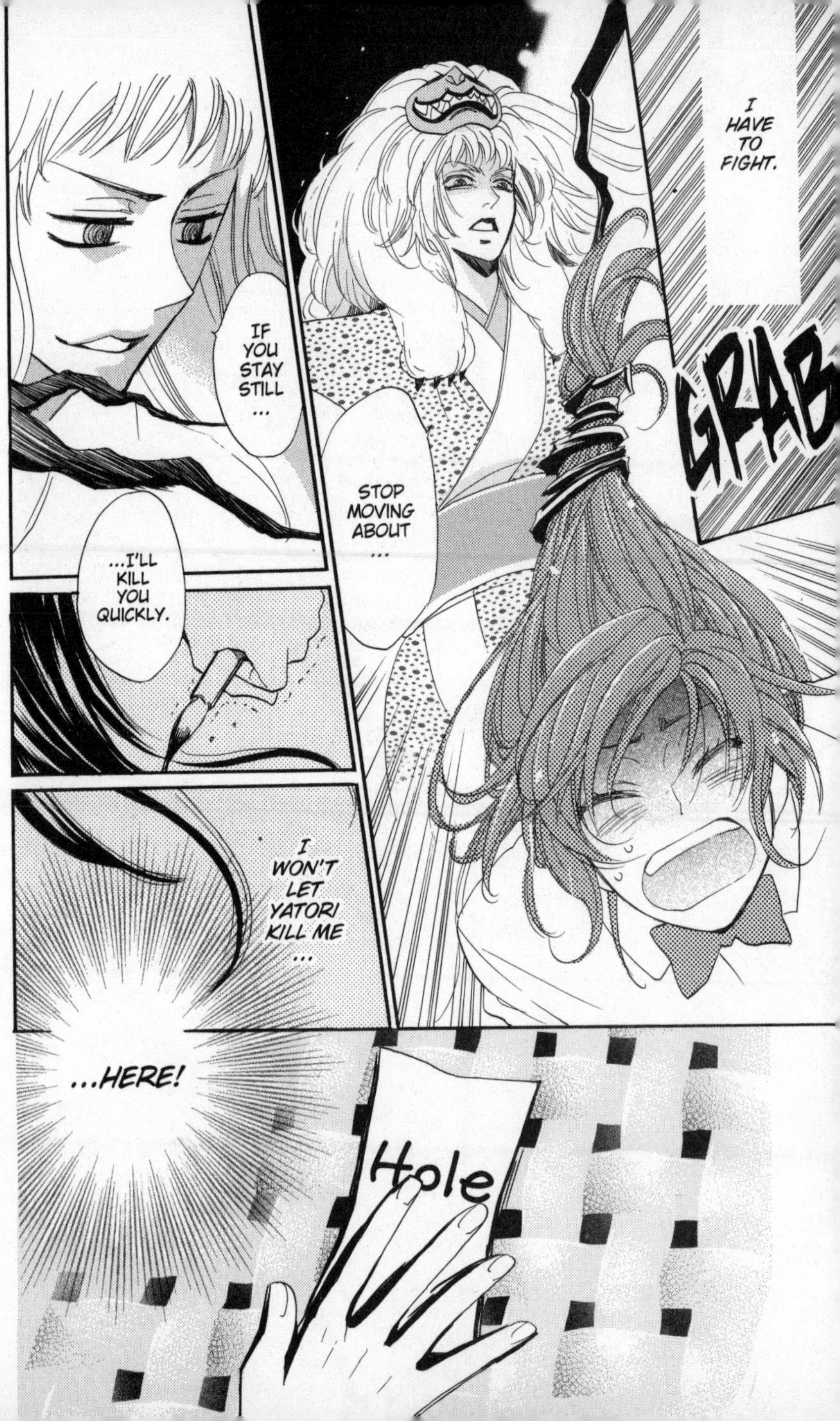

I HAVE TO FIGHT.
GRAB
STOP MOVING ABOUT...
IF YOU STAY STILL...
...I'LL KILL YOU QUICKLY.
I WON'T LET YATORI KILL ME...
...HERE!
Hole

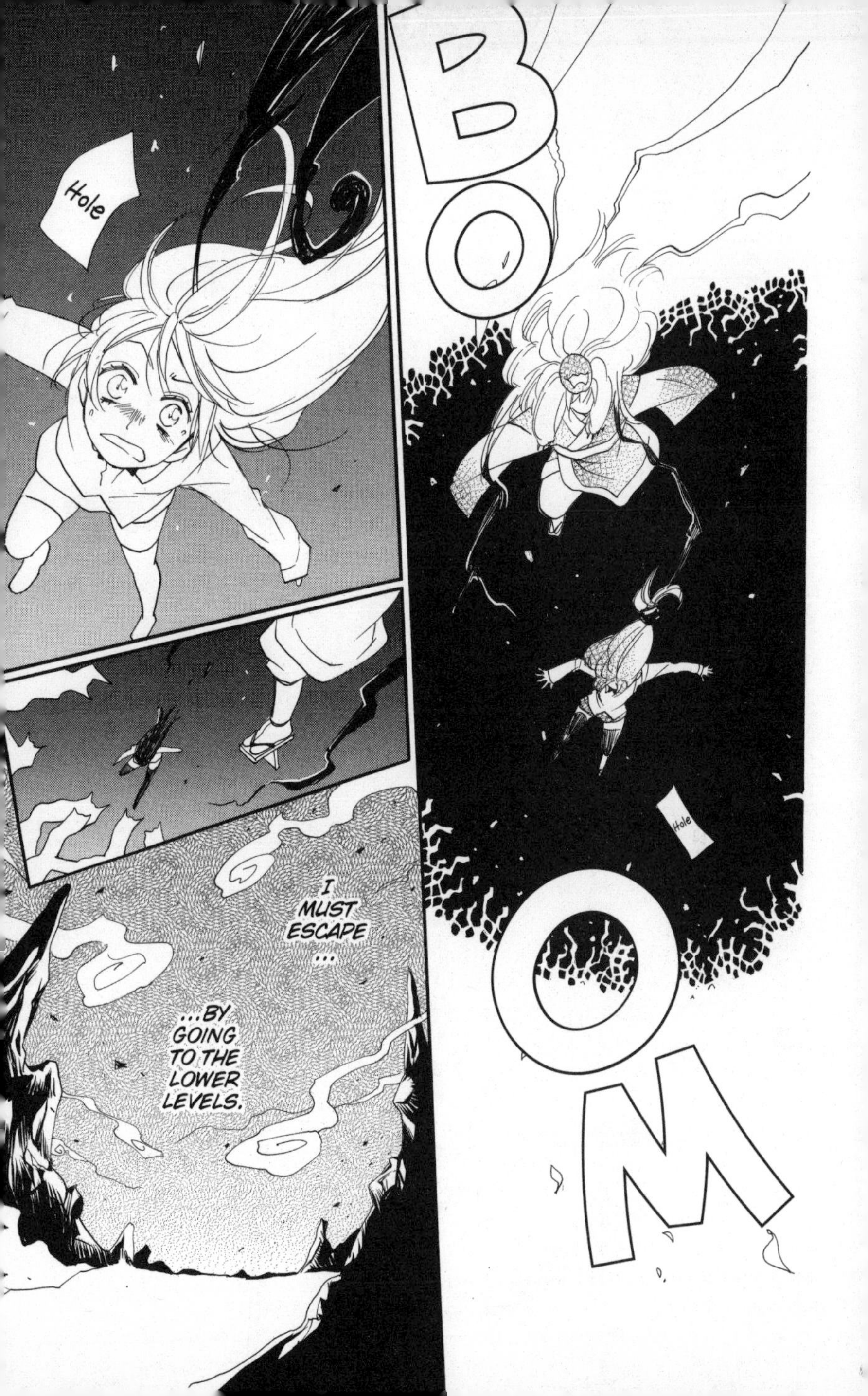
BOOM
Hole
Hole
I MUST ESCAPE...
...BY GOING TO THE LOWER LEVELS.

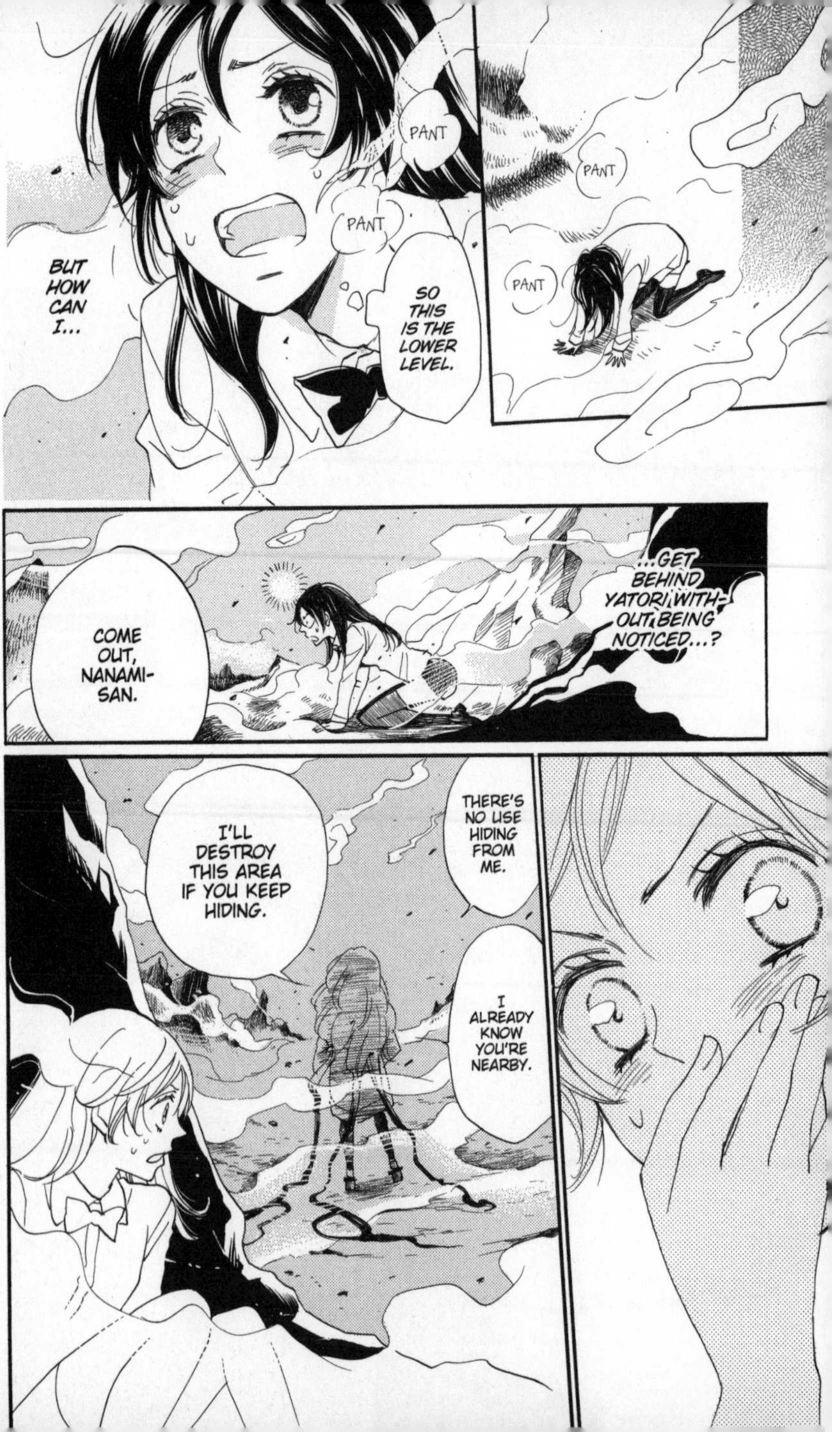
PANT
PANT
PANT
PANT
SO THIS IS THE LOWER LEVEL.
BUT HOW CAN I...
...GET BEHIND YATORI WITH-OUT BEING NOTICED...?
COME OUT, NANAMI-SAN.
THERE'S NO USE HIDING FROM ME.
I ALREADY KNOW YOU'RE NEARBY.
I'LL DESTROY THIS AREA IF YOU KEEP HIDING.

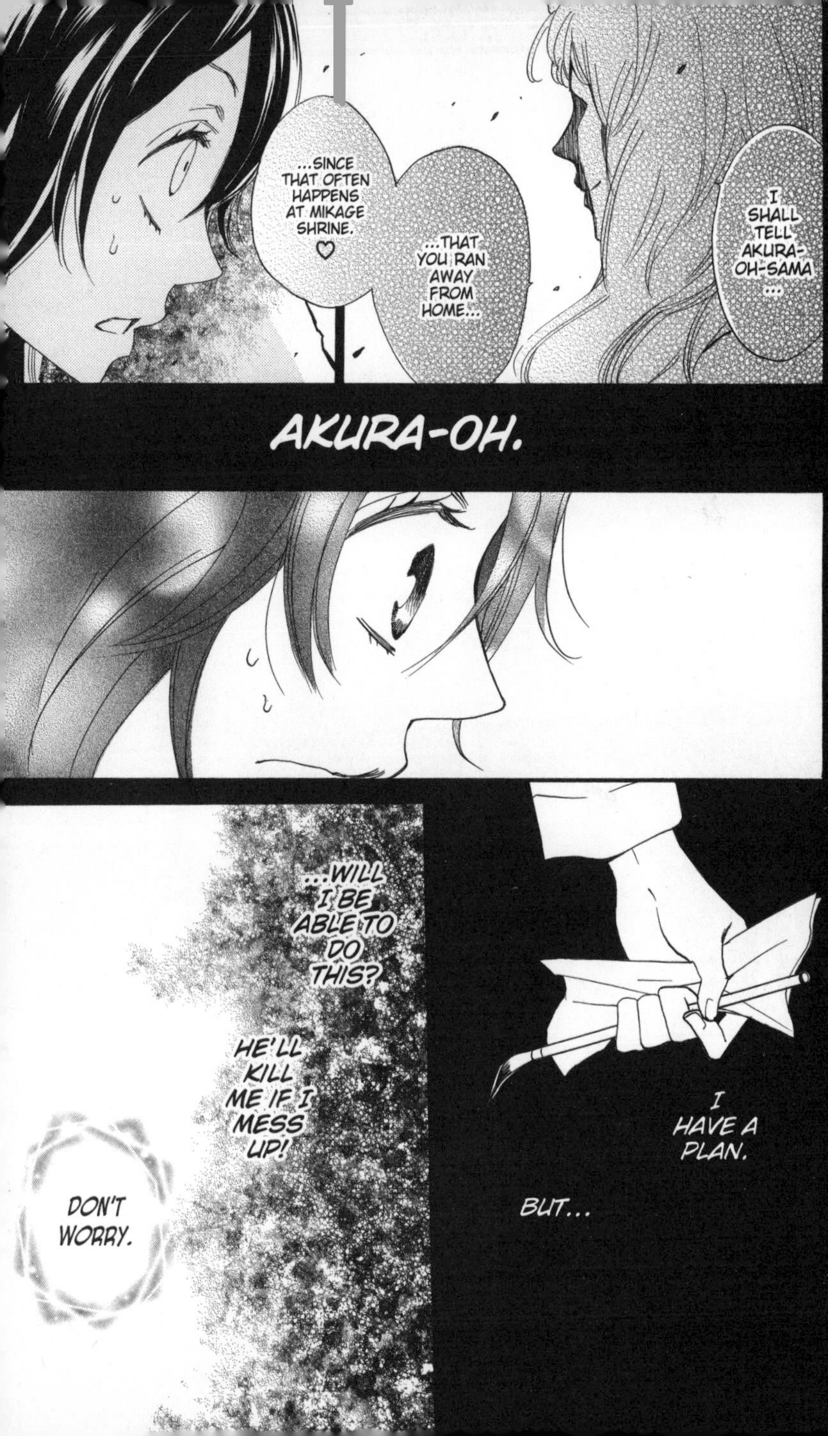
I SHALL TELL AKURA-OH-SAMA...
...THAT YOU RAN AWAY FROM HOME...
...SINCE THAT OFTEN HAPPENS AT MIKAGE SHRINE. ♡
AKURA-OH.
I HAVE A PLAN.
BUT...
...WILL I BE ABLE TO DO THIS?
HE'LL KILL ME IF I MESS UP!
DON'T WORRY.

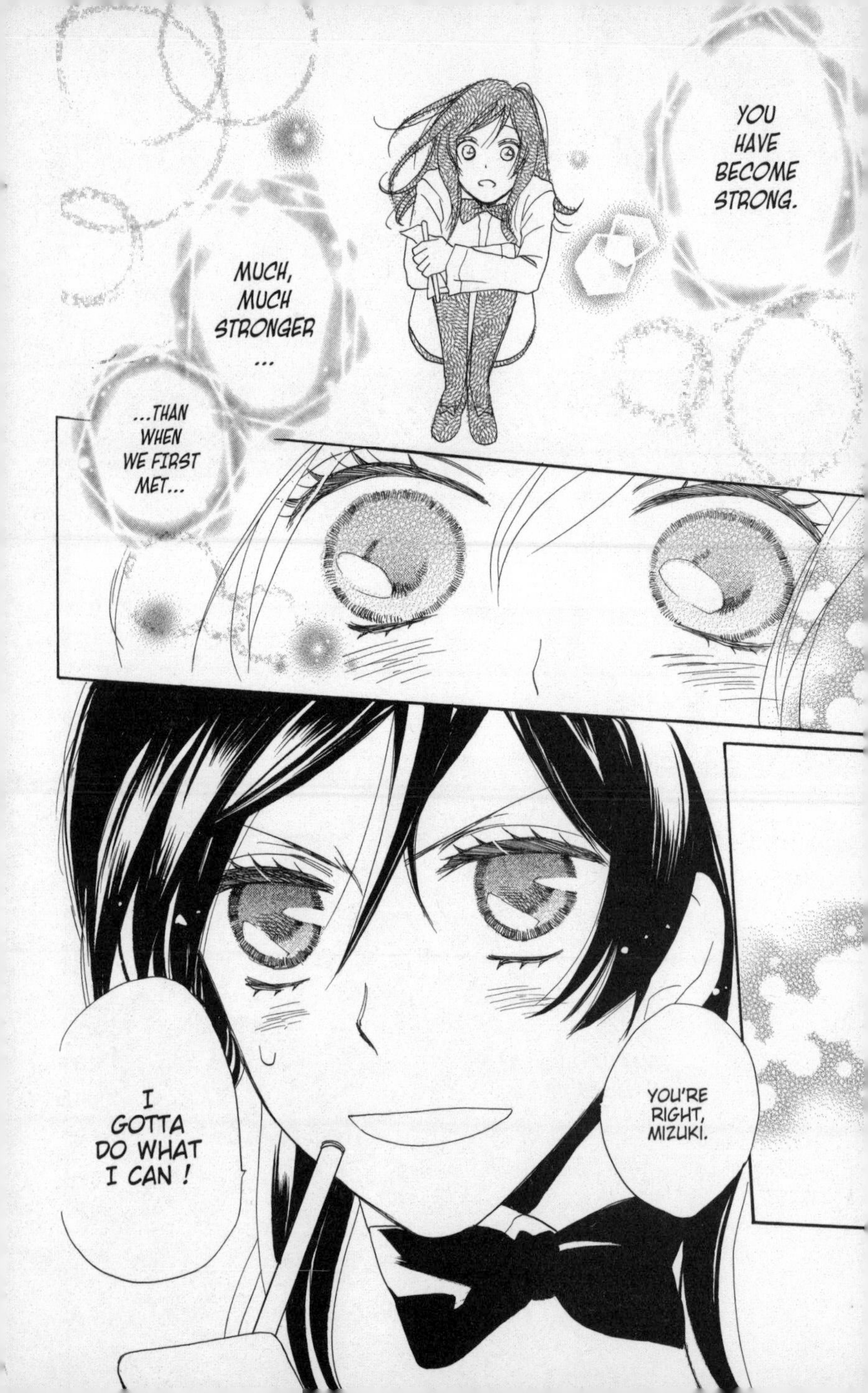
YOU HAVE BECOME STRONG.
MUCH, MUCH STRONGER ...
...THAN WHEN WE FIRST MET...
YOU'RE RIGHT, MIZUKI.
I GOTTA DO WHAT I CAN !

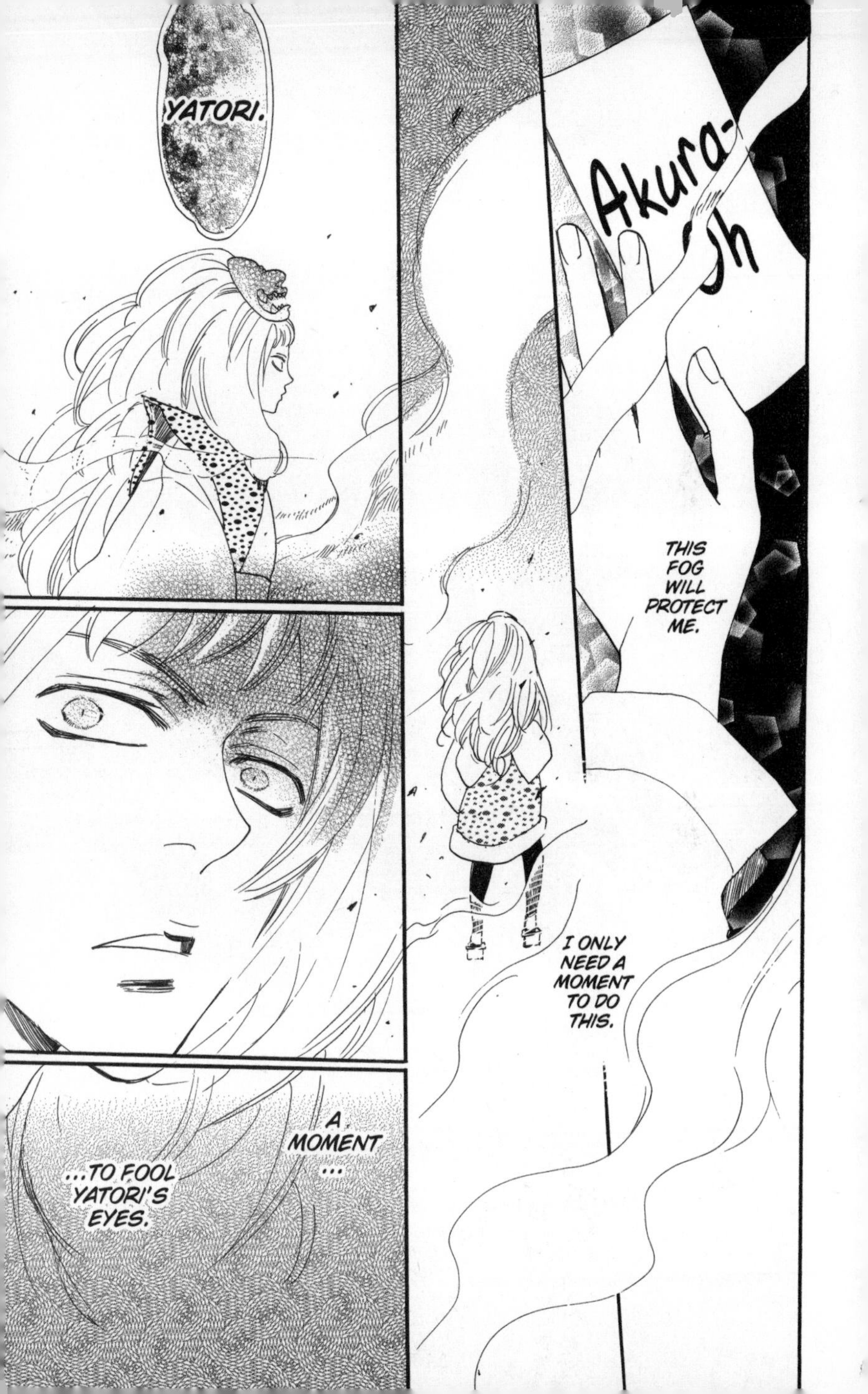
Akura-Oh
THIS FOG WILL PROTECT ME.
I ONLY NEED A MOMENT TO DO THIS.
YATORI.
A MOMENT ...
...TO FOOL YATORI'S EYES.

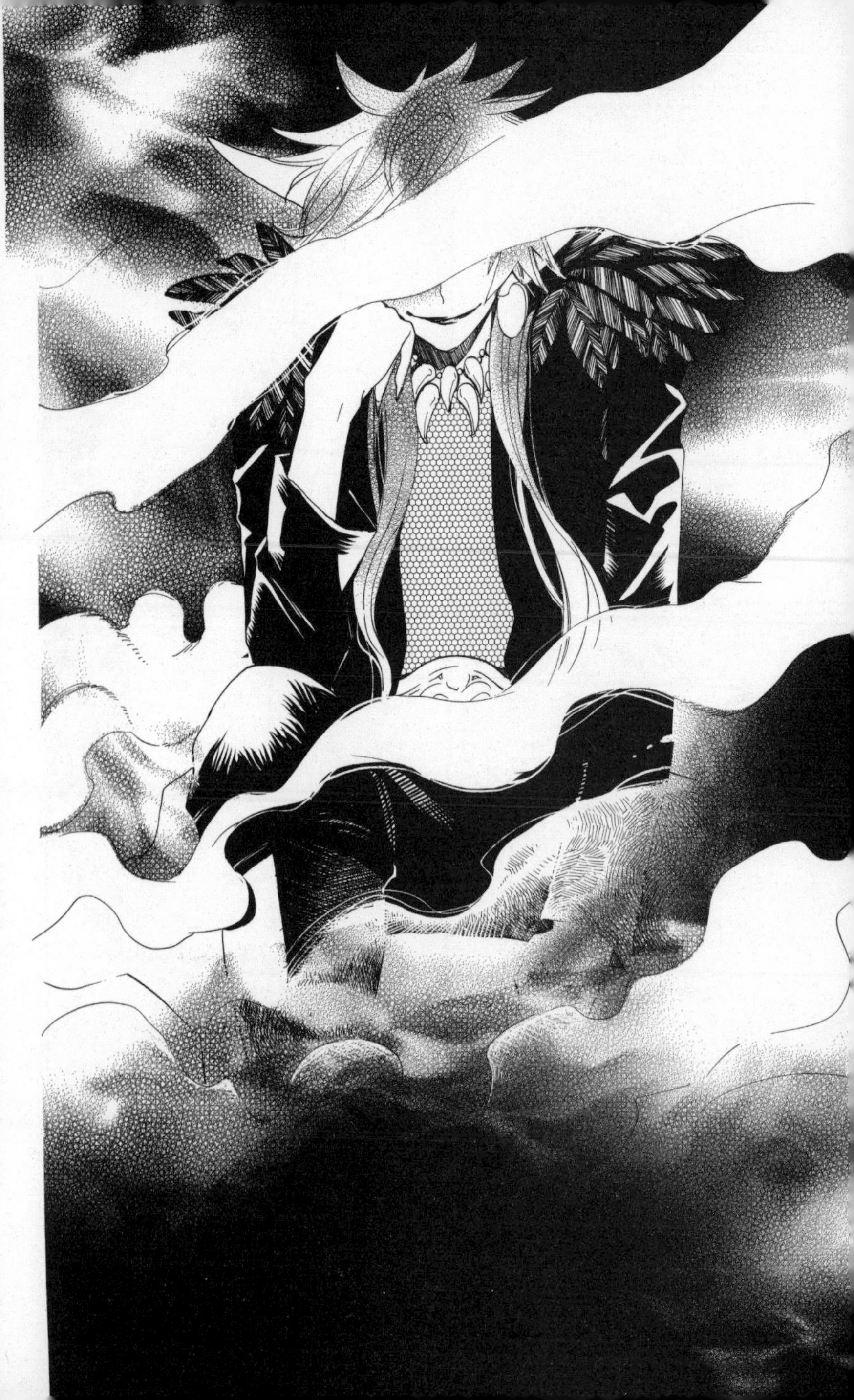

Chapter 122

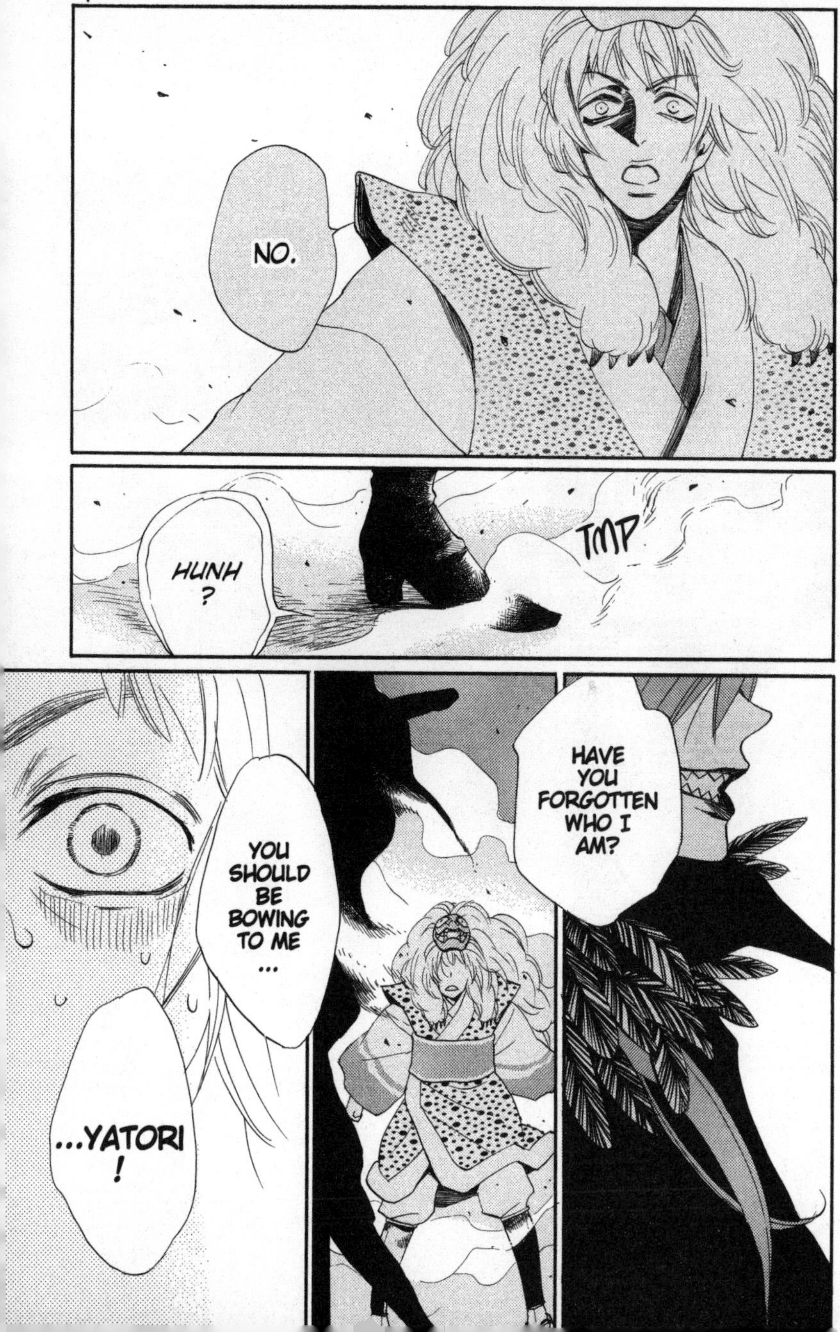
NO.
TMP
HUNH?
HAVE YOU FORGOTTEN WHO I AM?
YOU SHOULD BE BOWING TO ME ...
...YATORI!

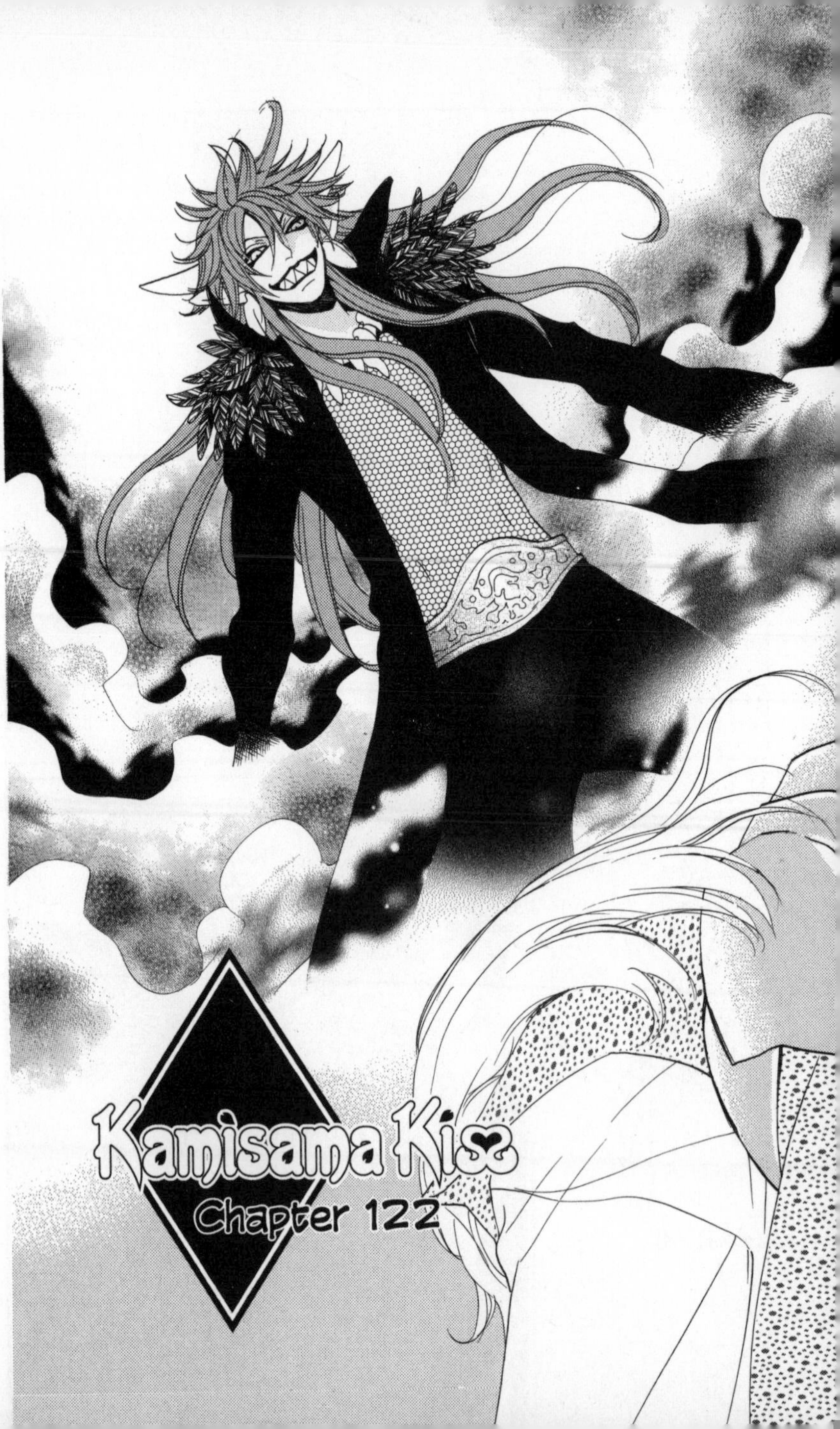
Kamisama Kiss
Chapter 122

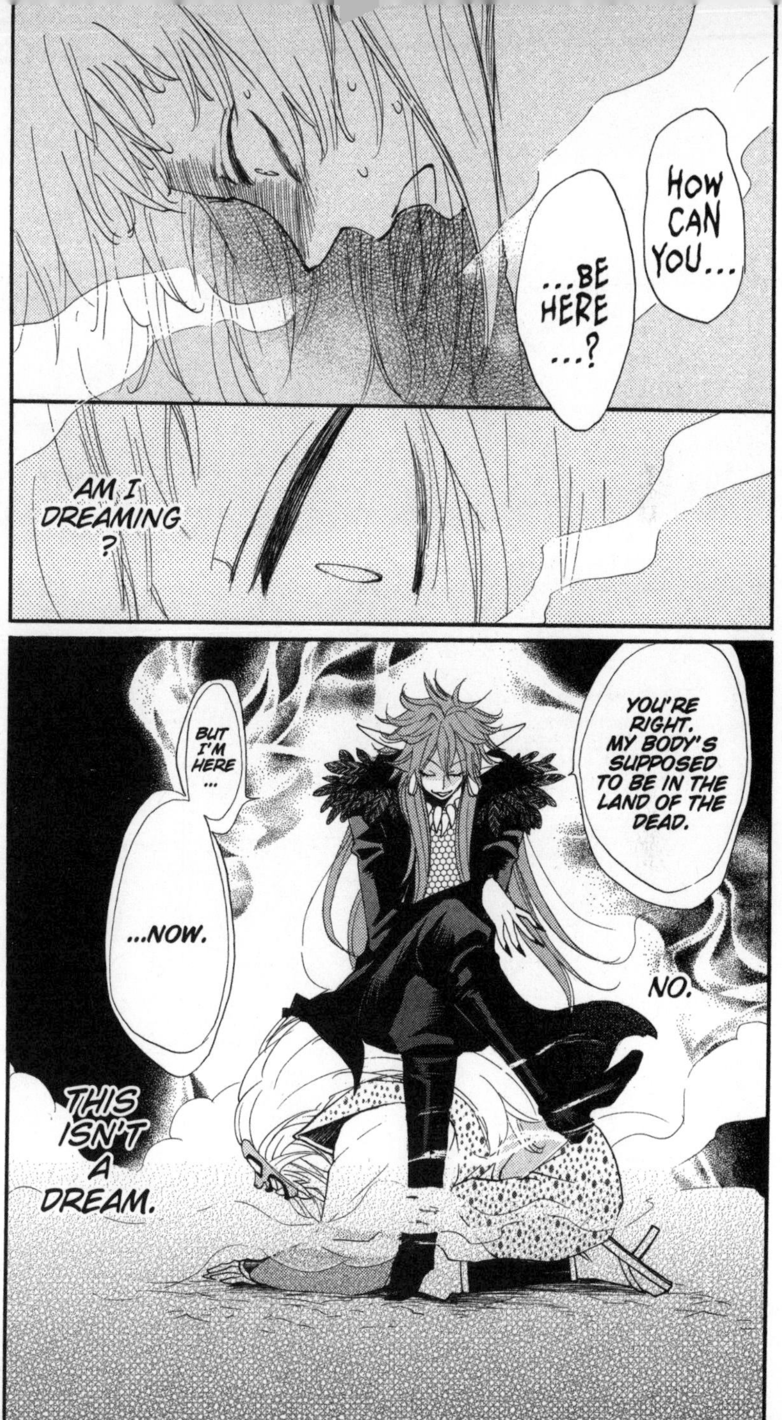
HOW CAN YOU...
...BE HERE...?
AM I DREAMING?
YOU'RE RIGHT. MY BODY'S SUPPOSED TO BE IN THE LAND OF THE DEAD.
BUT I'M HERE...
...NOW.
NO.
THIS ISN'T A DREAM.

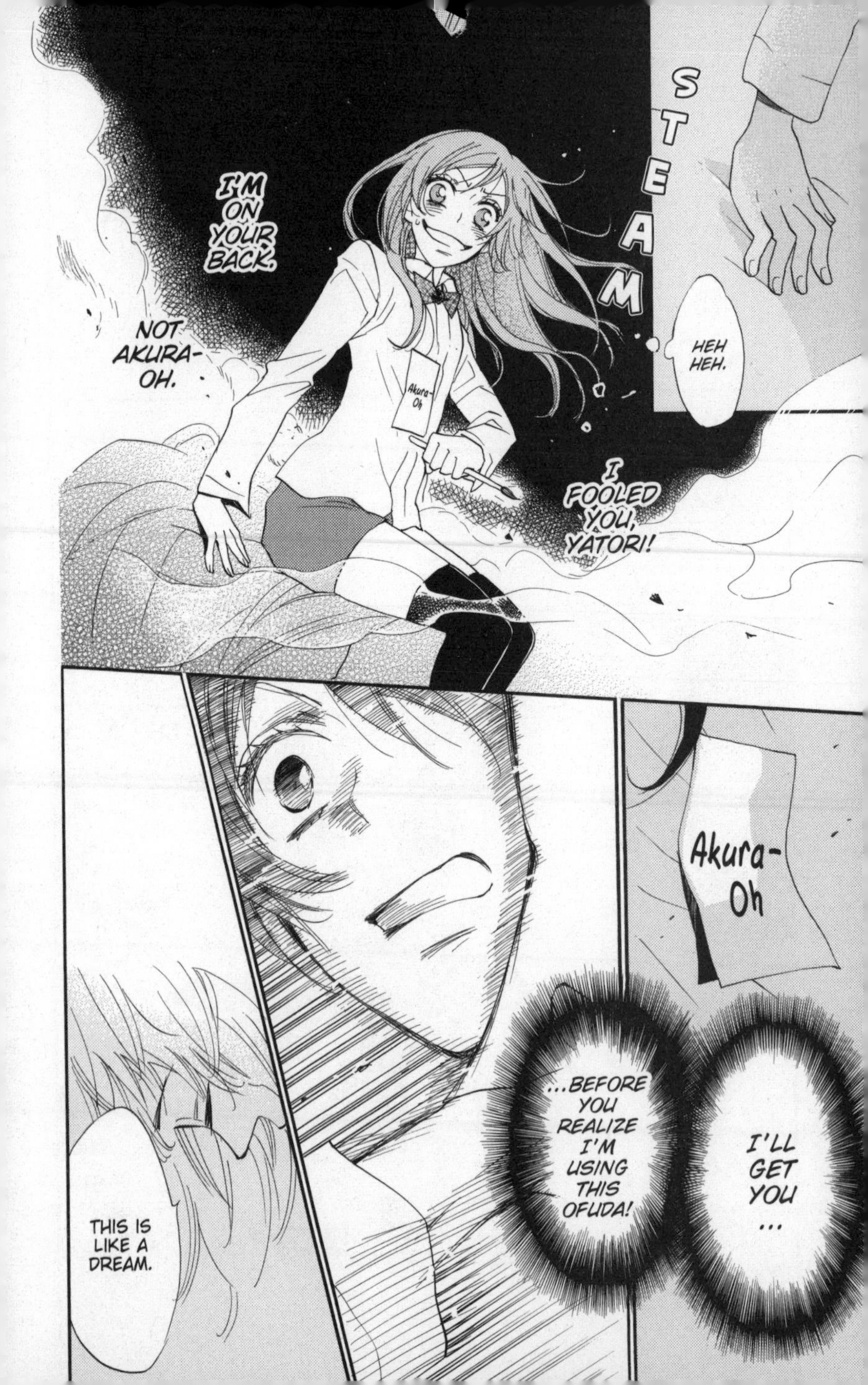
STEAM
HEH HEH.
I'M ON YOUR BACK.
NOT AKURA-OH.
Akura-Oh
I FOOLED YOU, YATORI!
Akura-Oh
I'LL GET YOU ...
...BEFORE YOU REALIZE I'M USING THIS OFUDA!
THIS IS LIKE A DREAM.

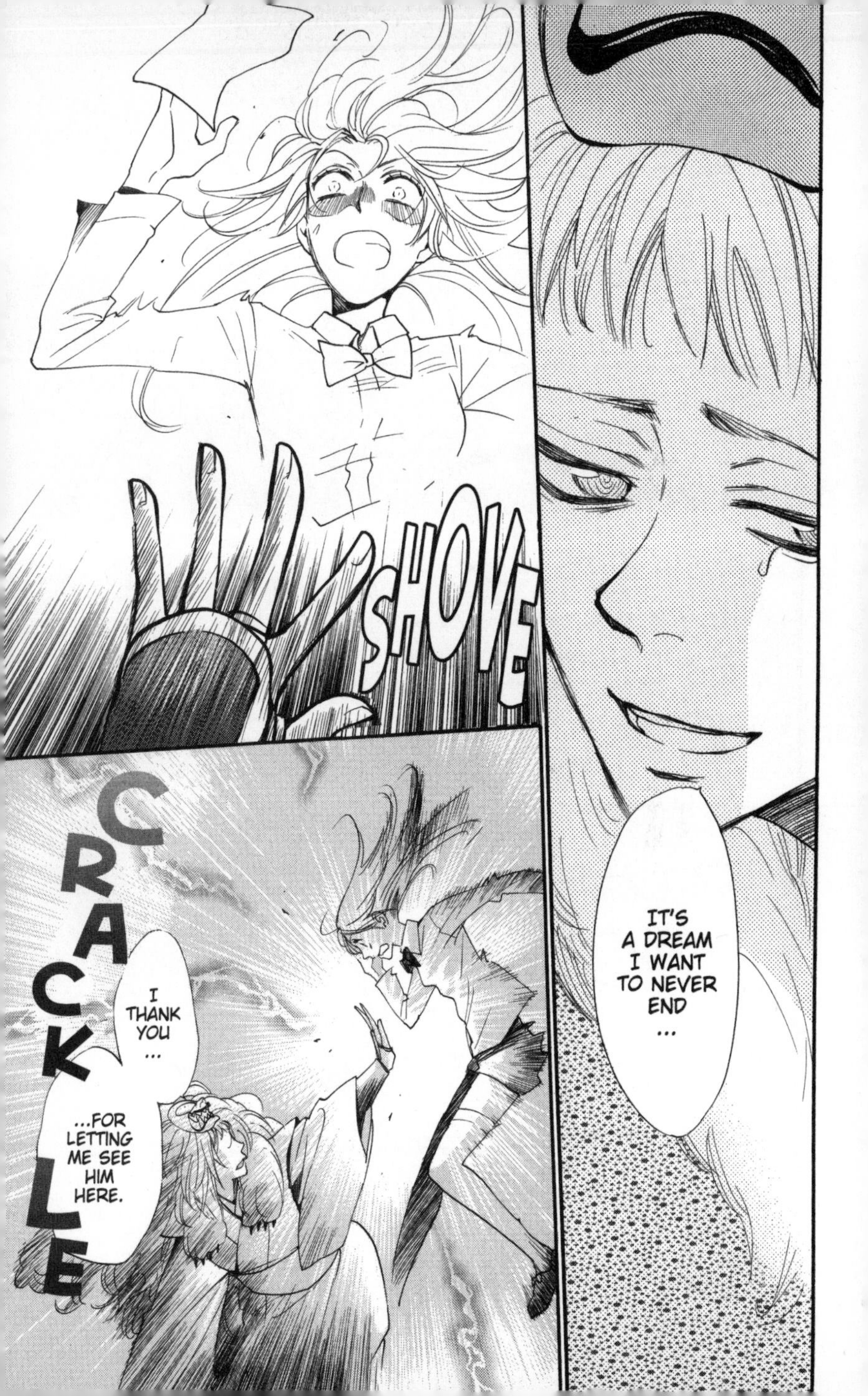
IT'S A DREAM I WANT TO NEVER END ...
SHOVE
CRACKLE
I THANK YOU ...
...FOR LETTING ME SEE HIM HERE.

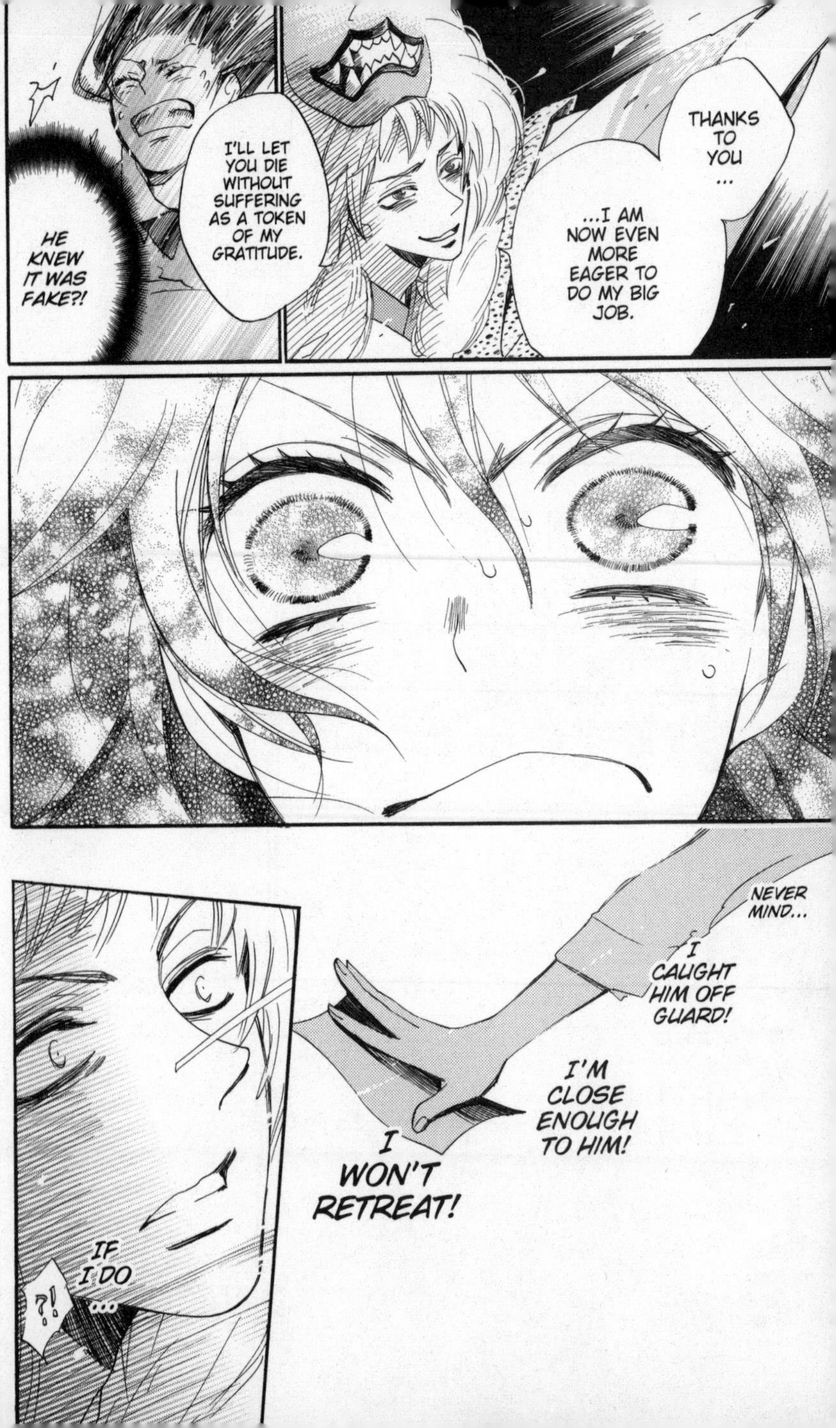
THANKS TO YOU...
...I AM NOW EVEN MORE EAGER TO DO MY BIG JOB.
I'LL LET YOU DIE WITHOUT SUFFERING AS A TOKEN OF MY GRATITUDE.
HE KNEW IT WAS FAKE?!
NEVER MIND...
I CAUGHT HIM OFF GUARD!
I'M CLOSE ENOUGH TO HIM!
I WON'T RETREAT!
IF I DO...
?!

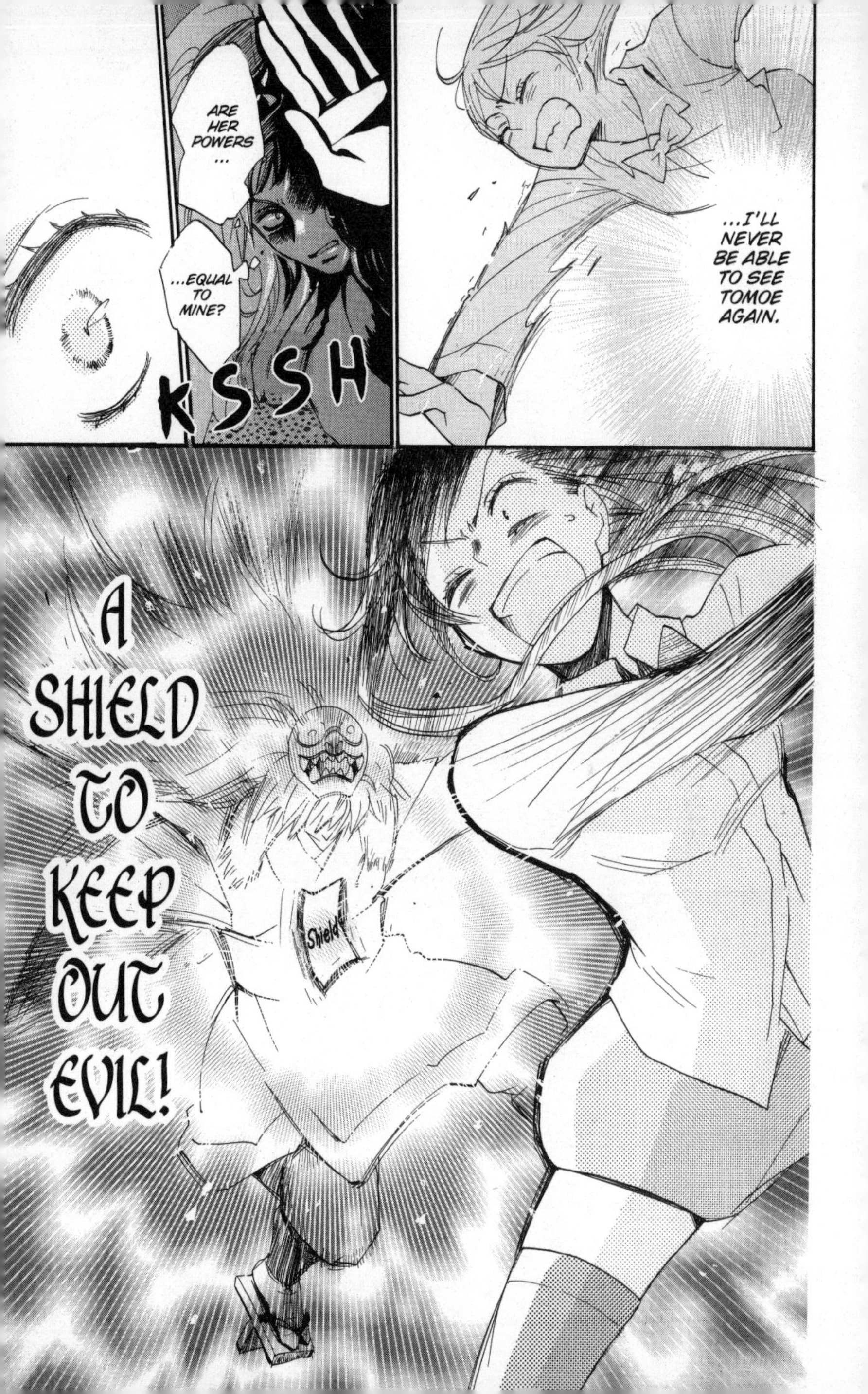
...I'LL NEVER BE ABLE TO SEE TOMOE AGAIN.
ARE HER POWERS ...
...EQUAL TO MINE?
KSSH
A SHIELD TO KEEP OUT EVIL!
Shield

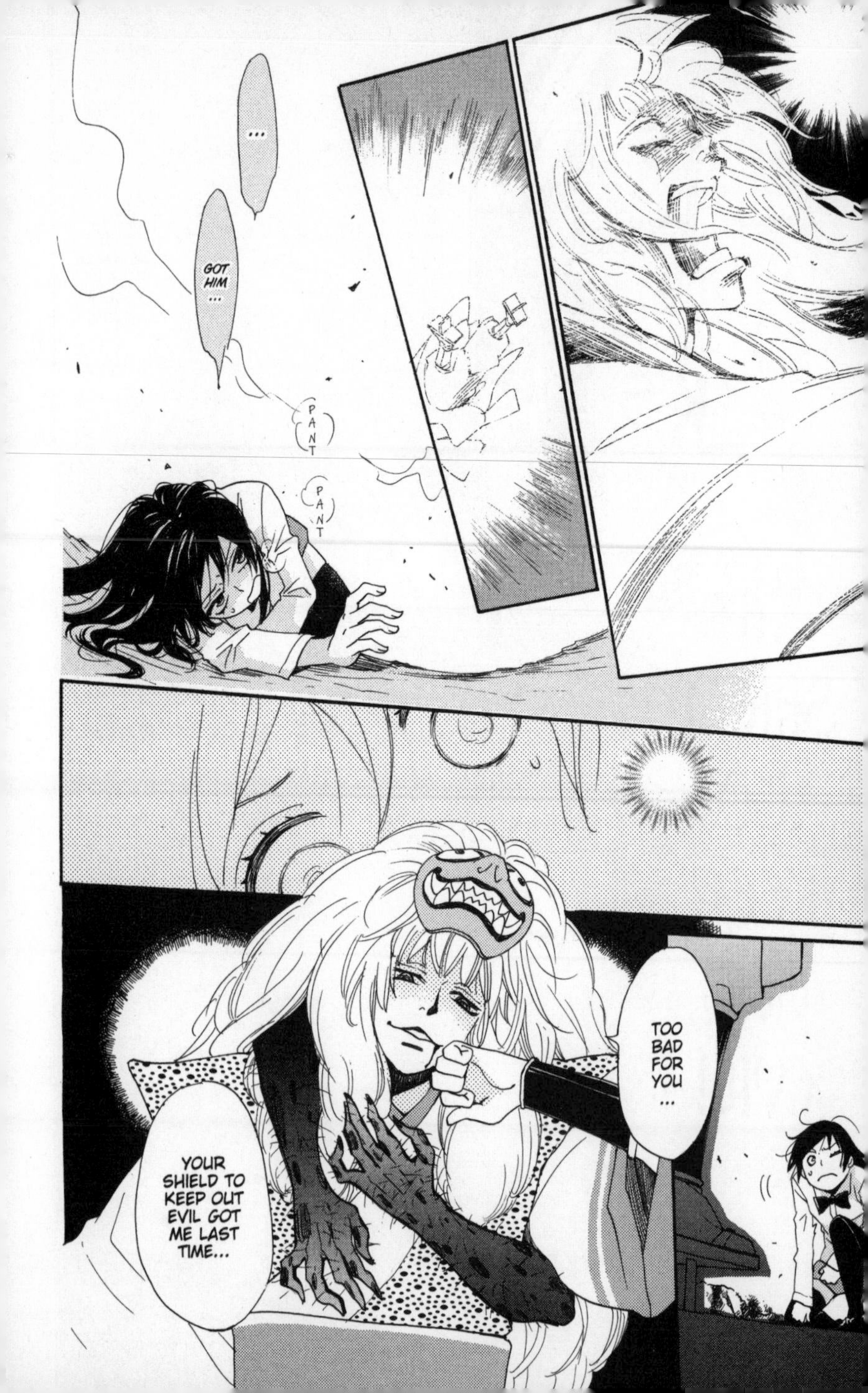
...
GOT HIM ...
PANT PANT
TOO BAD FOR YOU ...
YOUR SHIELD TO KEEP OUT EVIL GOT ME LAST TIME...

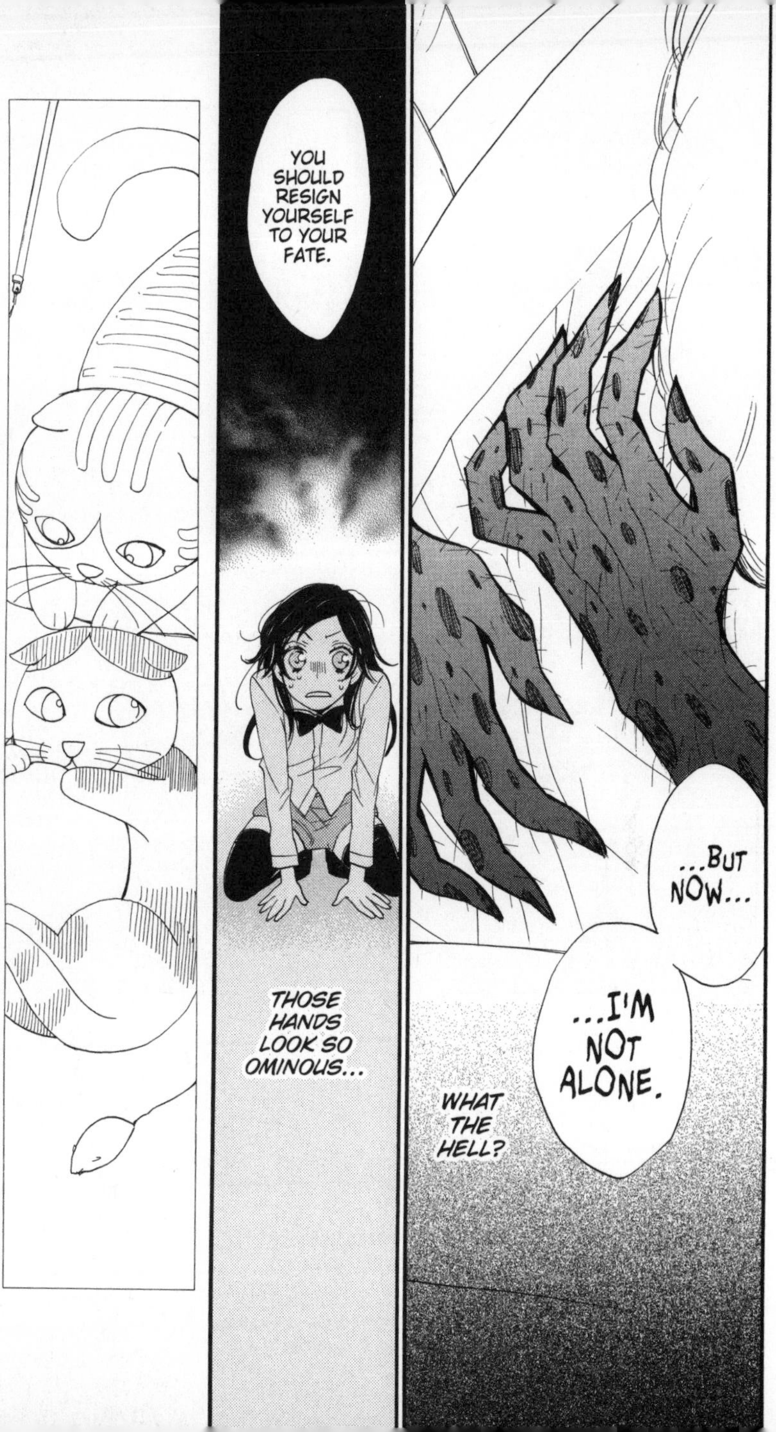
...BUT NOW...
...I'M NOT ALONE.
WHAT THE HELL?
YOU SHOULD RESIGN YOURSELF TO YOUR FATE.
THOSE HANDS LOOK SO OMINOUS...

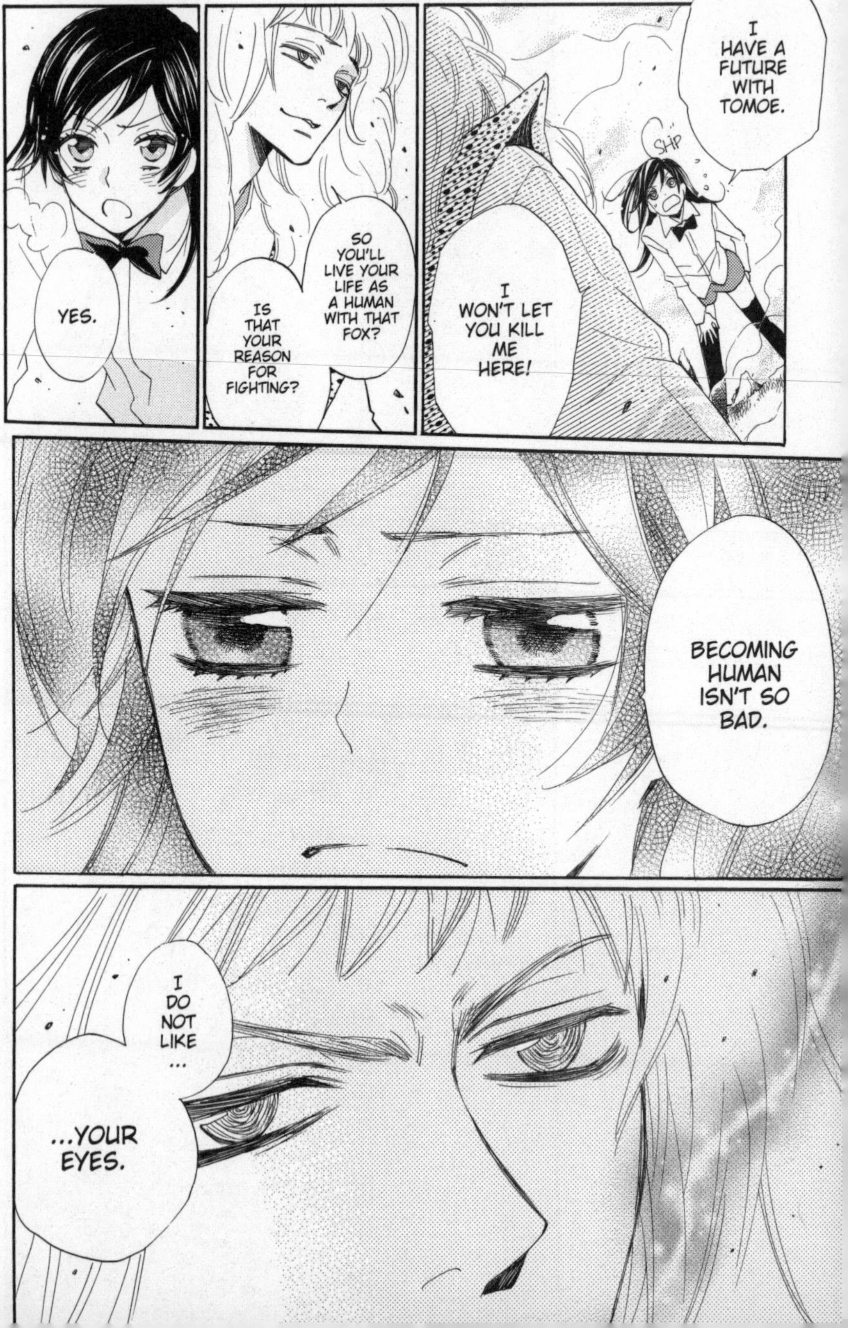
I HAVE A FUTURE WITH TOMOE.
SHP
I WON'T LET YOU KILL ME HERE!
SO YOU'LL LIVE YOUR LIFE AS A HUMAN WITH THAT FOX?
IS THAT YOUR REASON FOR FIGHTING?
YES.
BECOMING HUMAN ISN'T SO BAD.
I DO NOT LIKE ...
...YOUR EYES.

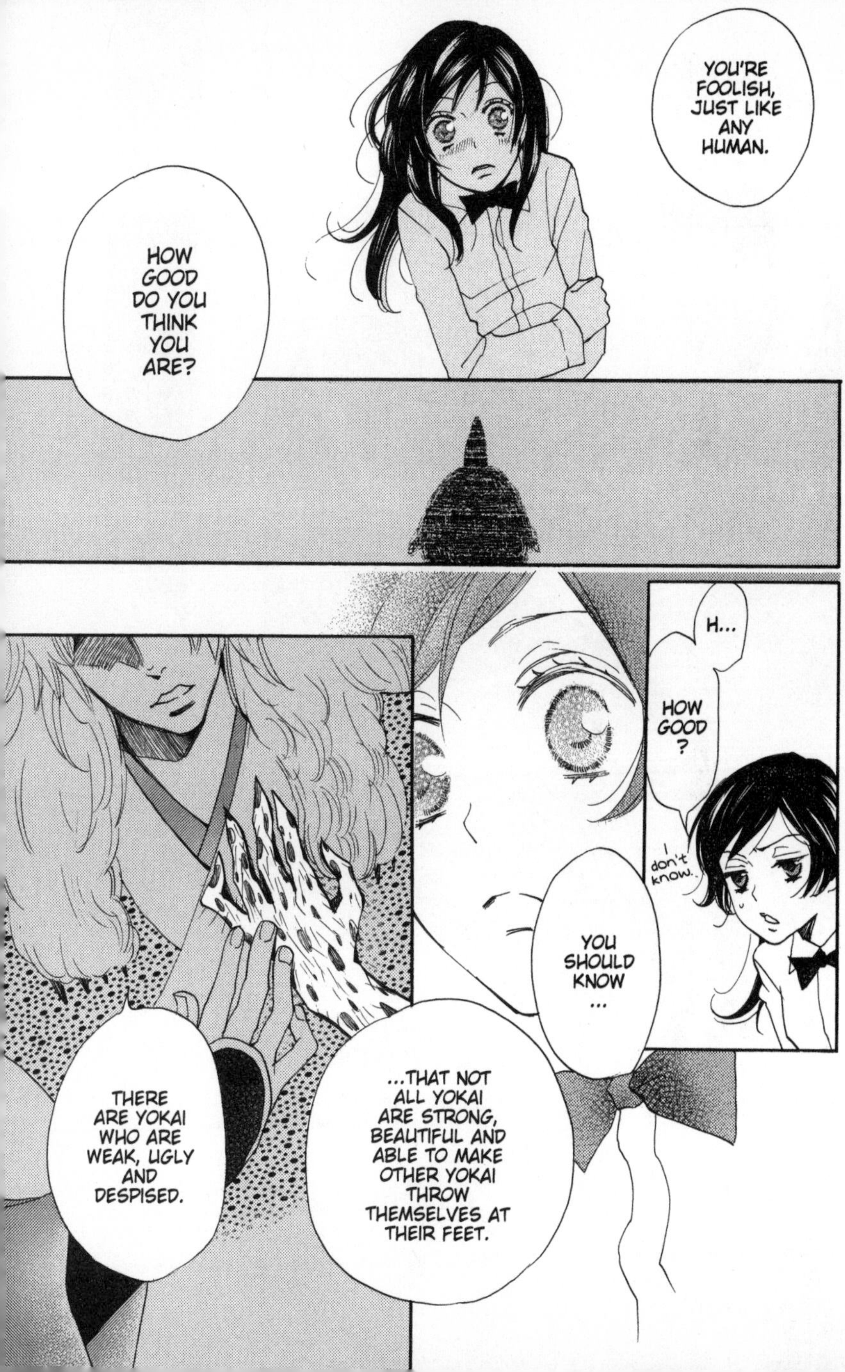
YOU'RE FOOLISH, JUST LIKE ANY HUMAN.
HOW GOOD DO YOU THINK YOU ARE?
H...
HOW GOOD ?
I don't know..
YOU SHOULD KNOW ...
...THAT NOT ALL YOKAI ARE STRONG, BEAUTIFUL AND ABLE TO MAKE OTHER YOKAI THROW THEMSELVES AT THEIR FEET.
THERE ARE YOKAI WHO ARE WEAK, UGLY AND DESPISED.

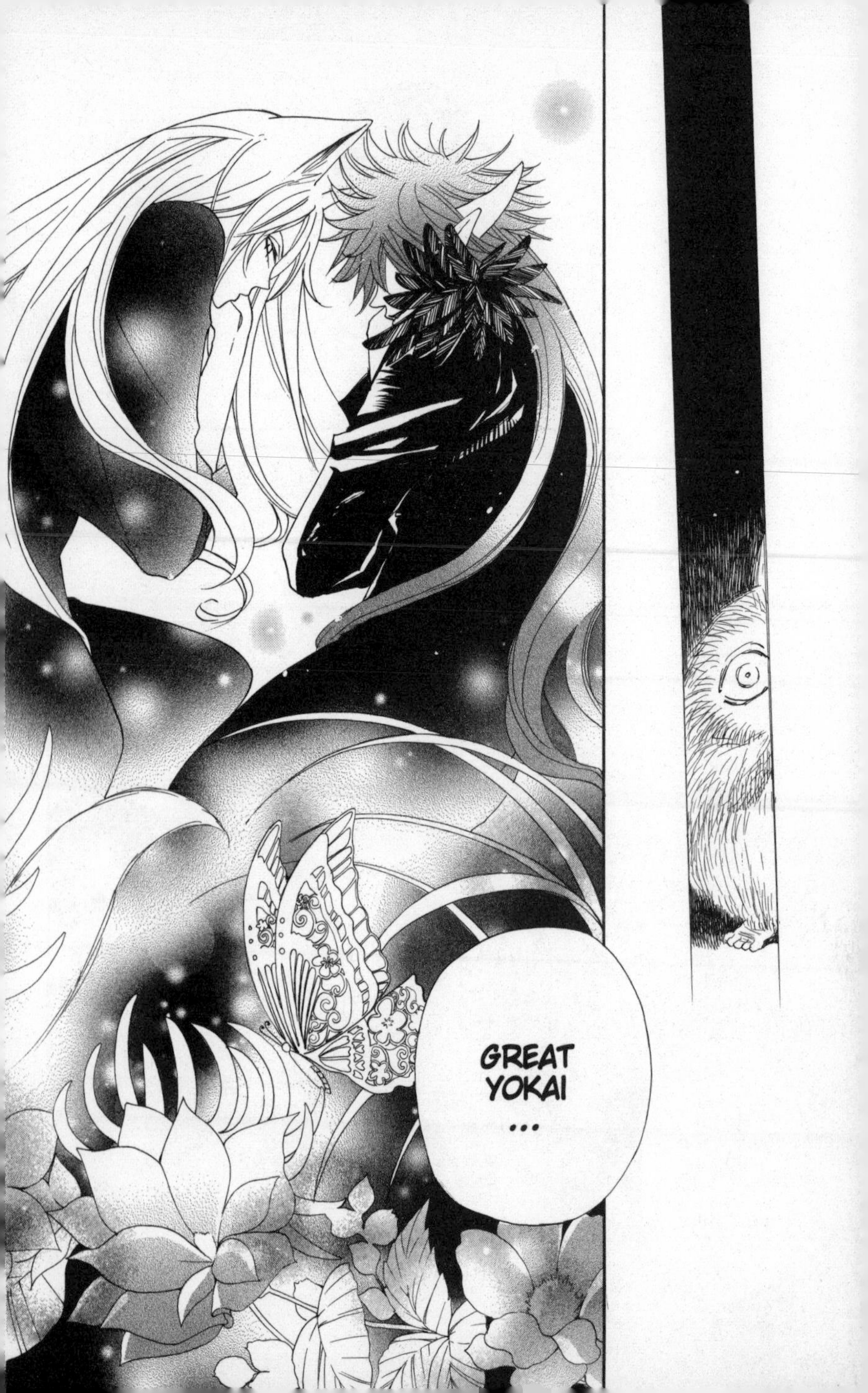
GREAT YOKAI ...

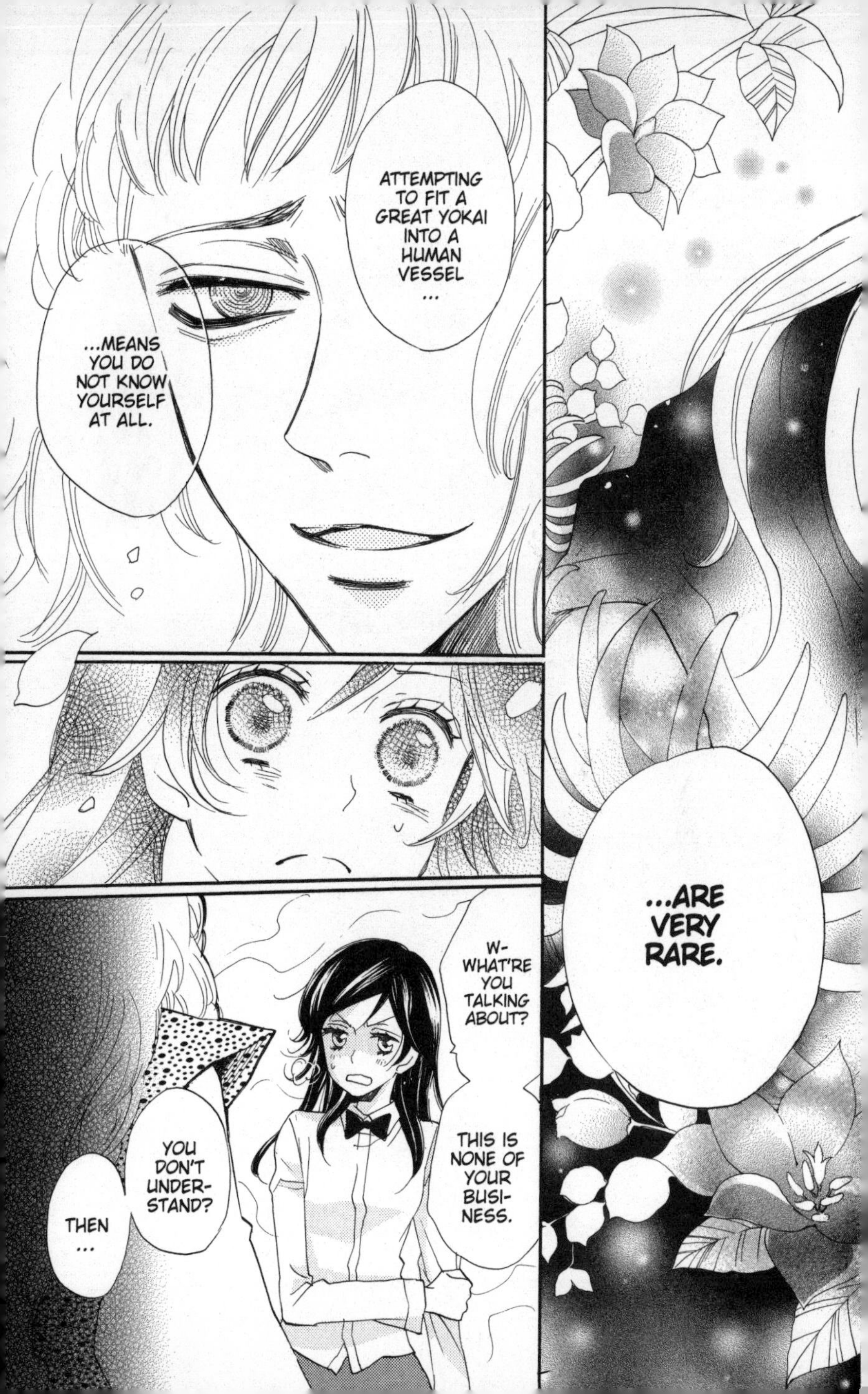
...ARE VERY RARE.
ATTEMPTING TO FIT A GREAT YOKAI INTO A HUMAN VESSEL ...
...MEANS YOU DO NOT KNOW YOURSELF AT ALL.
W-WHAT'RE YOU TALKING ABOUT?
THIS IS NONE OF YOUR BUSI-NESS.
YOU DON'T UNDER-STAND?
THEN ...

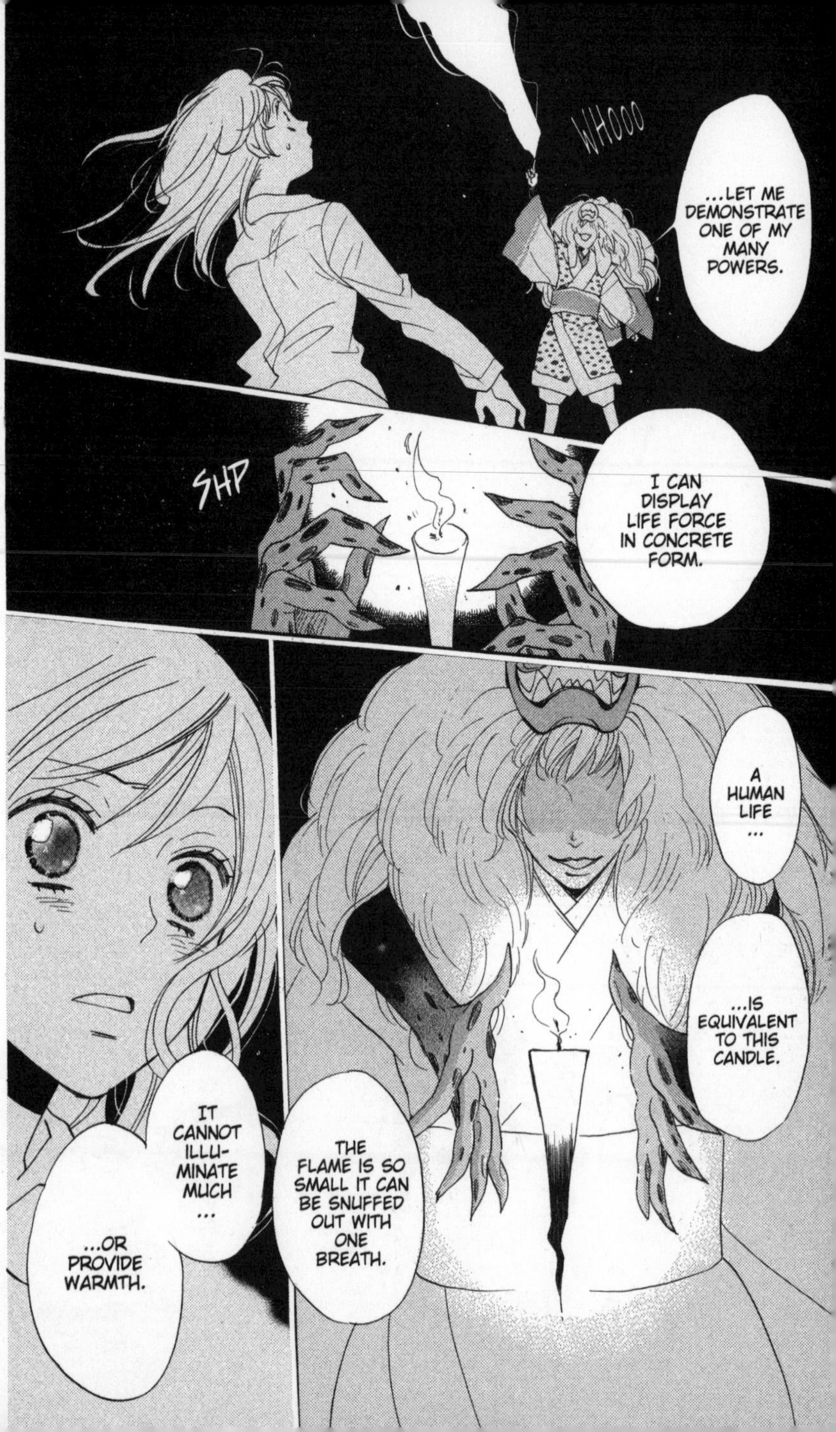
...LET ME DEMONSTRATE ONE OF MY MANY POWERS.
WHOOO
I CAN DISPLAY LIFE FORCE IN CONCRETE FORM.
SHP
A HUMAN LIFE ...
...IS EQUIVALENT TO THIS CANDLE.
THE FLAME IS SO SMALL IT CAN BE SNUFFED OUT WITH ONE BREATH.
IT CANNOT ILLU-MINATE MUCH ...
...OR PROVIDE WARMTH.

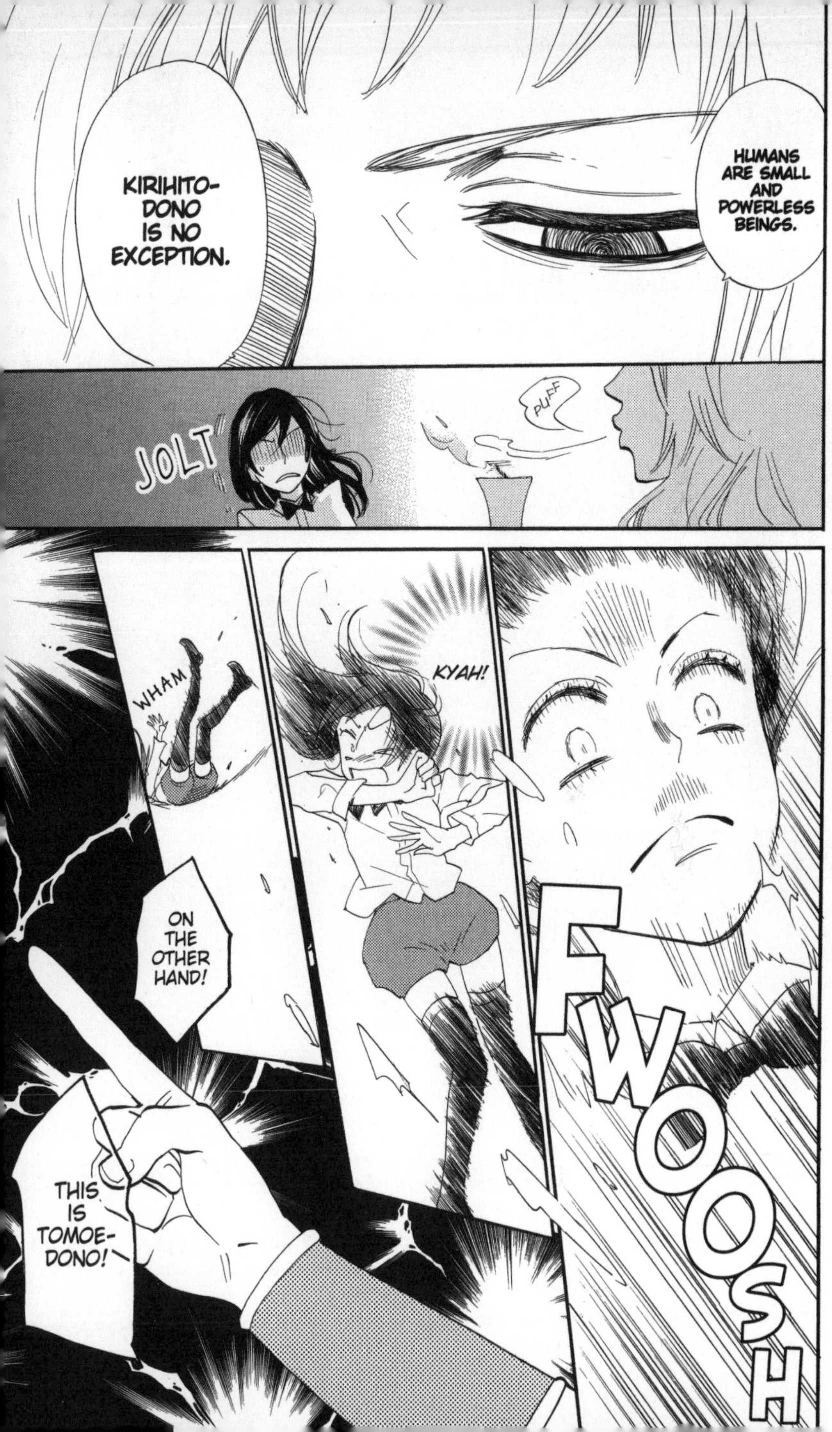
HUMANS ARE SMALL AND POWERLESS BEINGS.
KIRIHITO-DONO IS NO EXCEPTION.
PUFF
JOLT
FWOOSH
KYAH!
WHAM
ON THE OTHER HAND!
THIS IS TOMOE-DONO!

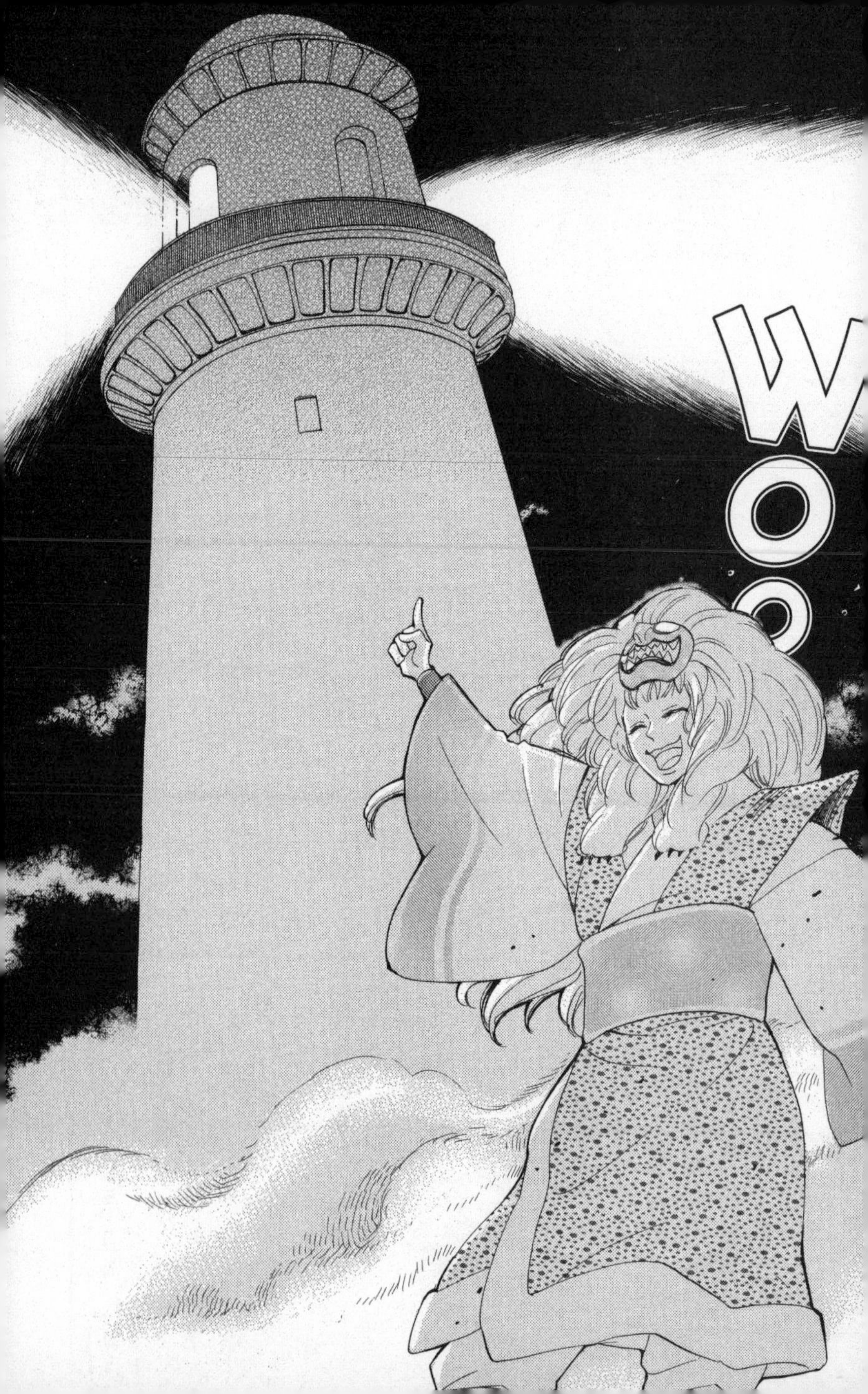
WOO

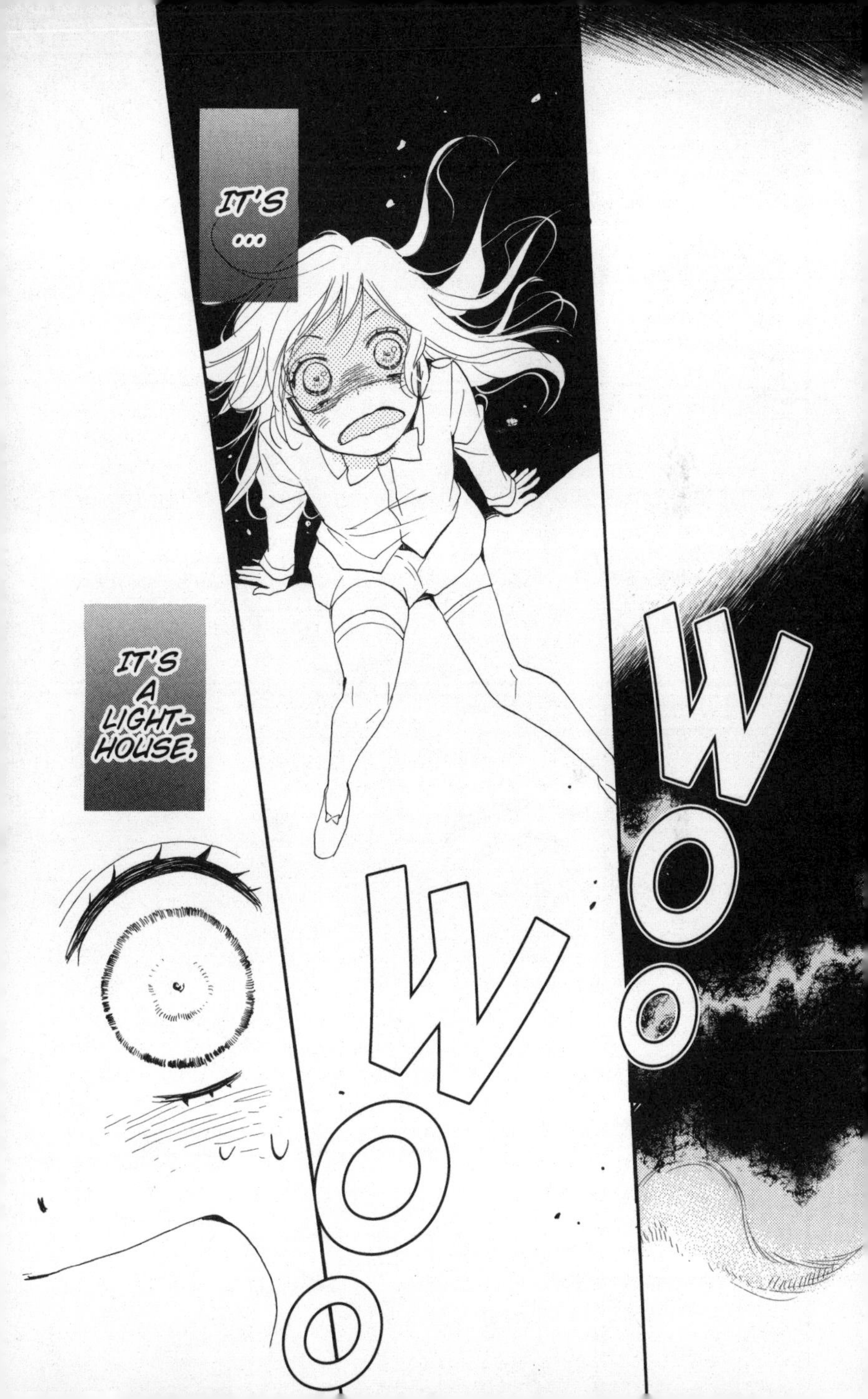
WOO
IT'S...
IT'S A LIGHT-HOUSE.
WOO

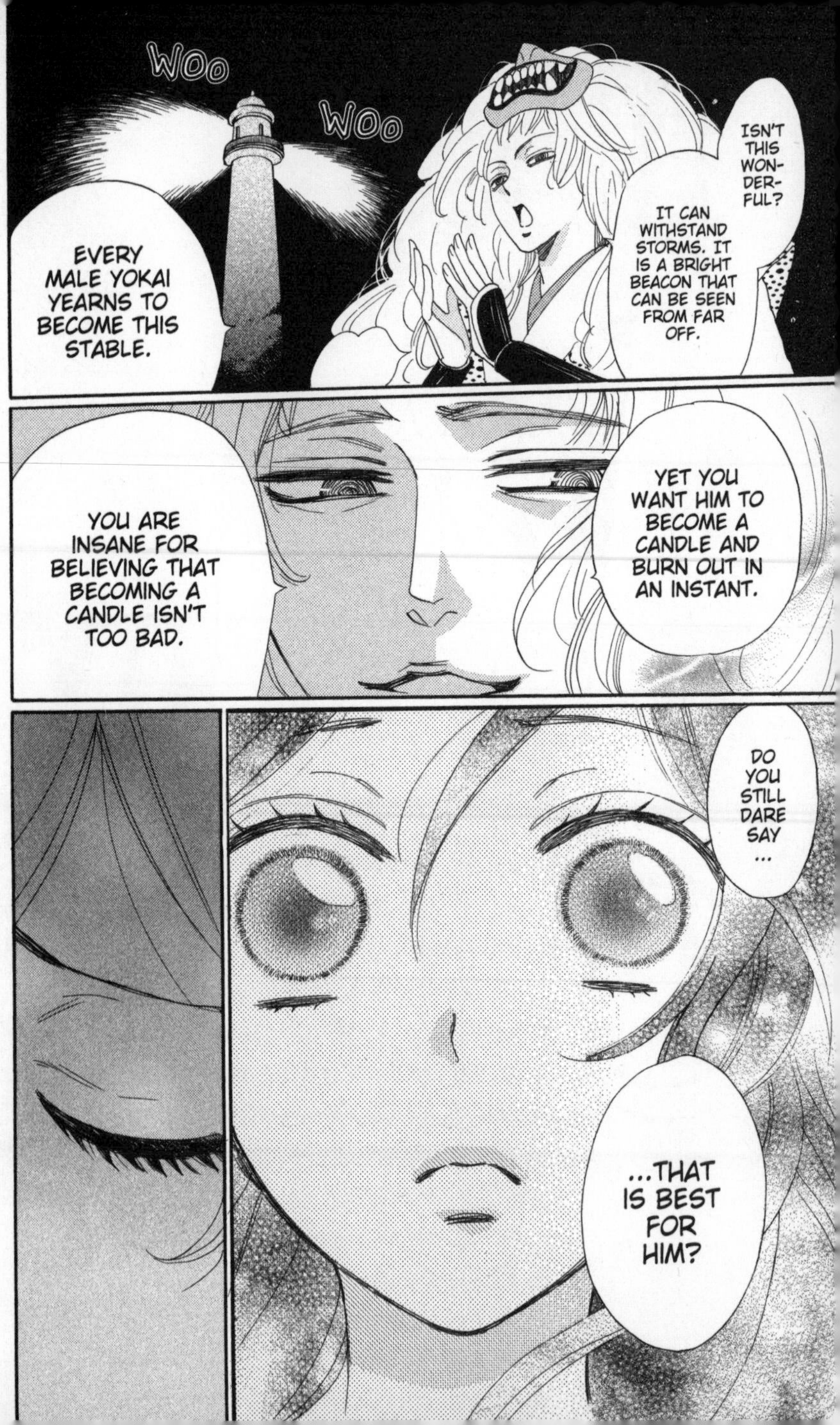
WOO
WOO
ISN'T THIS WONDERFUL?
IT CAN WITHSTAND STORMS. IT IS A BRIGHT BEACON THAT CAN BE SEEN FROM FAR OFF.
EVERY MALE YOKAI YEARNS TO BECOME THIS STABLE.
YET YOU WANT HIM TO BECOME A CANDLE AND BURN OUT IN AN INSTANT.
YOU ARE INSANE FOR BELIEVING THAT BECOMING A CANDLE ISN'T TOO BAD.
DO YOU STILL DARE SAY ...
...THAT IS BEST FOR HIM?

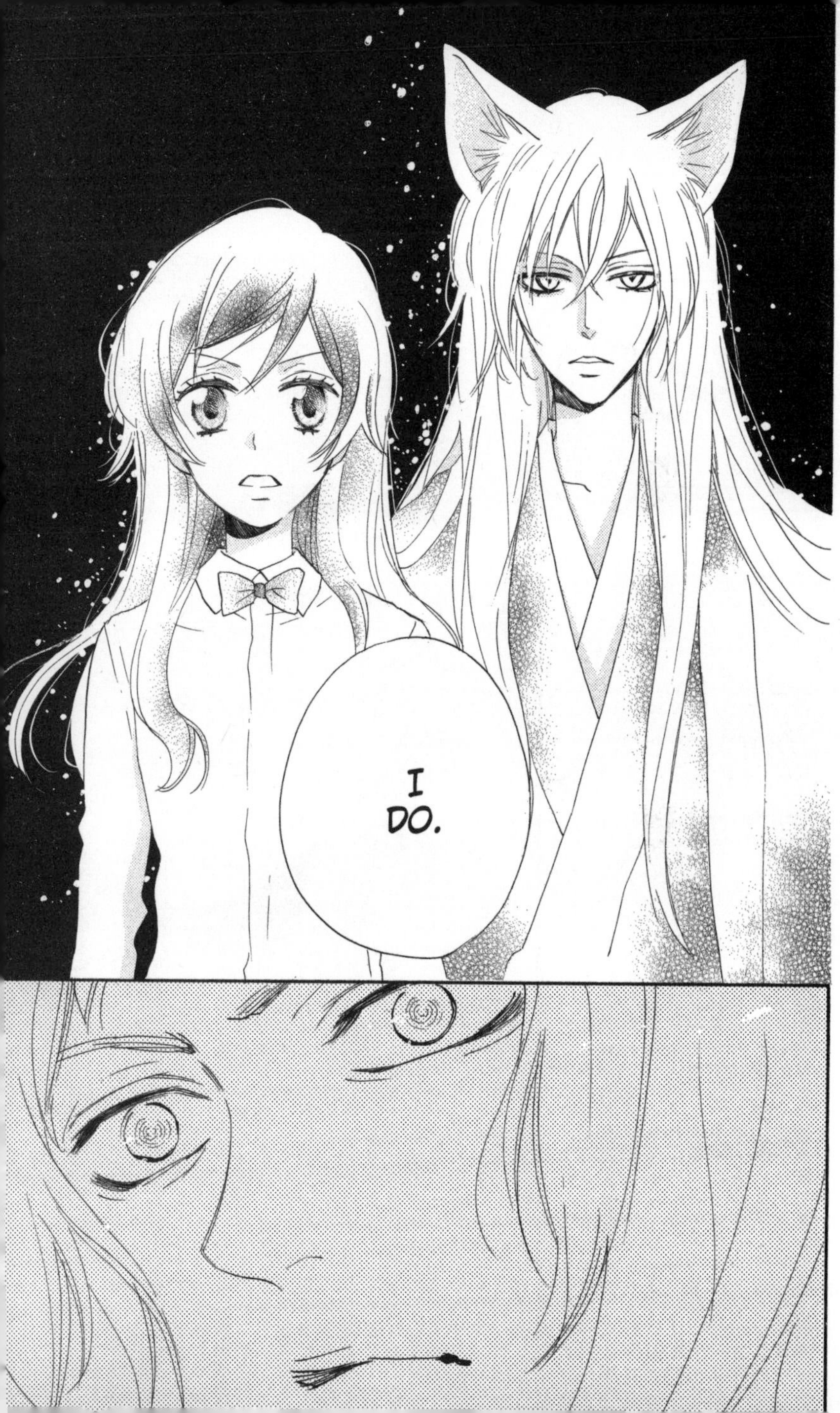
I DO.

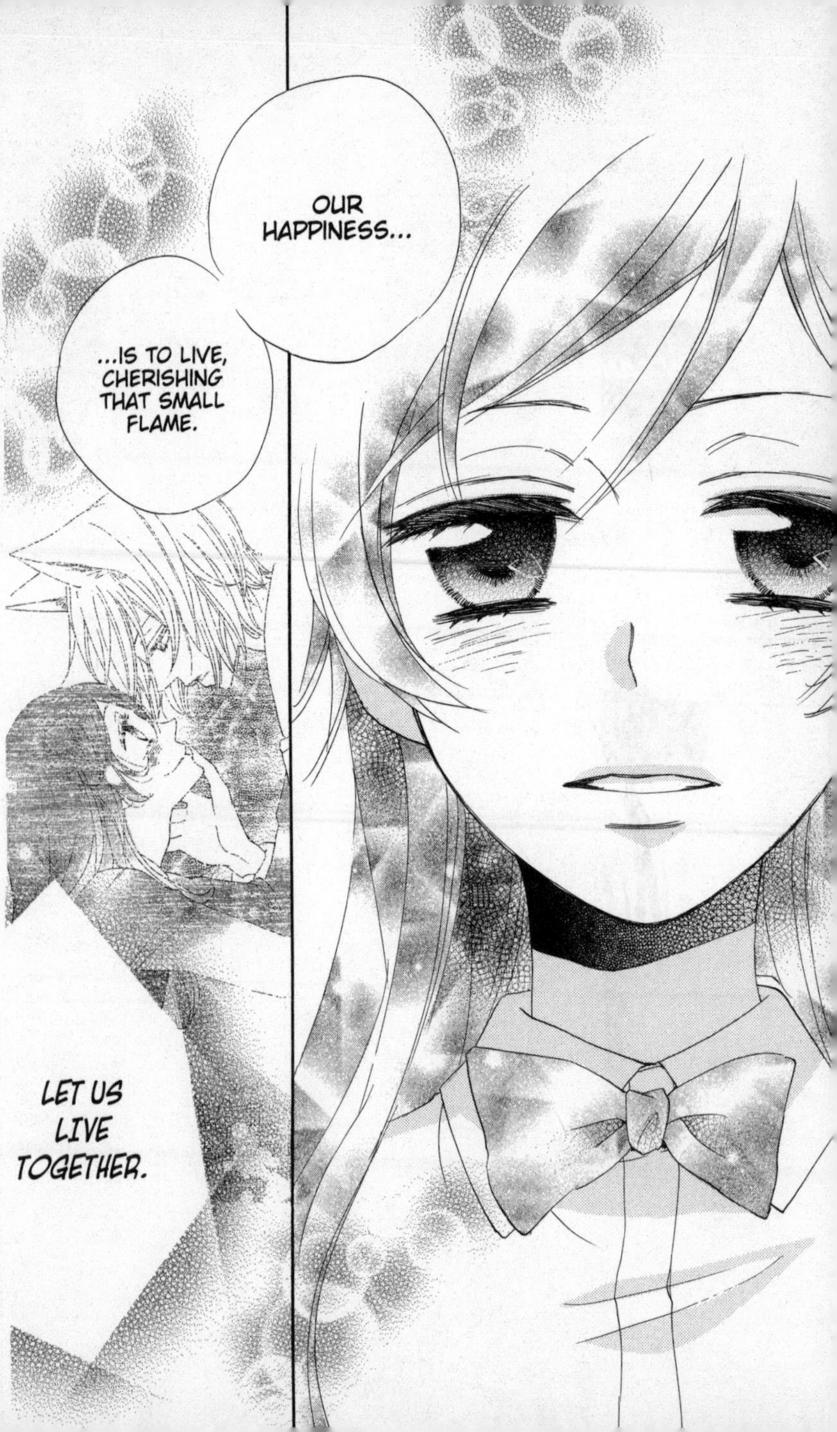
OUR HAPPINESS...
...IS TO LIVE, CHERISHING THAT SMALL FLAME.
LET US LIVE TOGETHER.

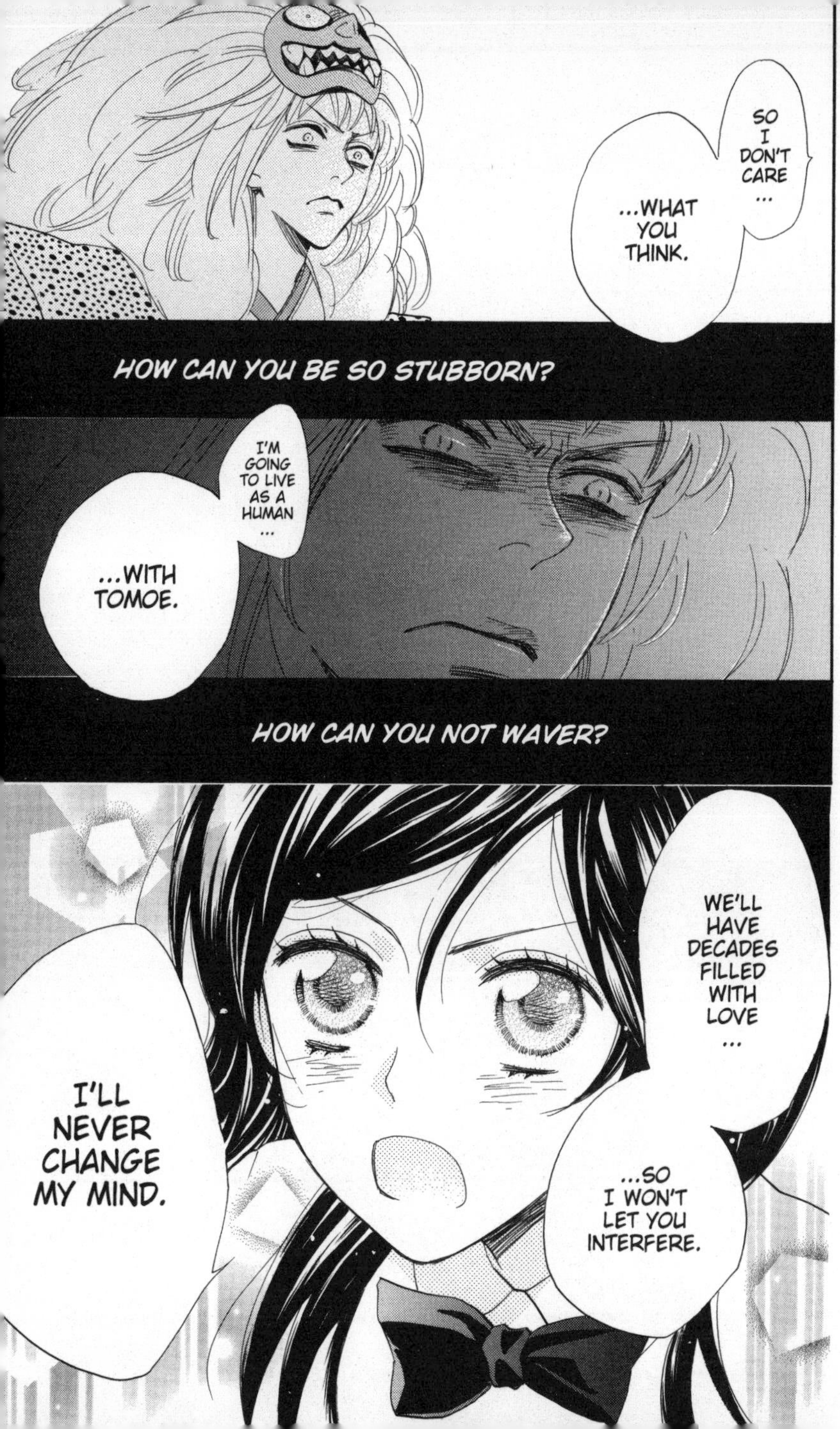
SO I DON'T CARE...
...WHAT YOU THINK.
HOW CAN YOU BE SO STUBBORN?
I'M GOING TO LIVE AS A HUMAN...
...WITH TOMOE.
HOW CAN YOU NOT WAVER?
WE'LL HAVE DECADES FILLED WITH LOVE...
...SO I WON'T LET YOU INTERFERE.
I'LL NEVER CHANGE MY MIND.

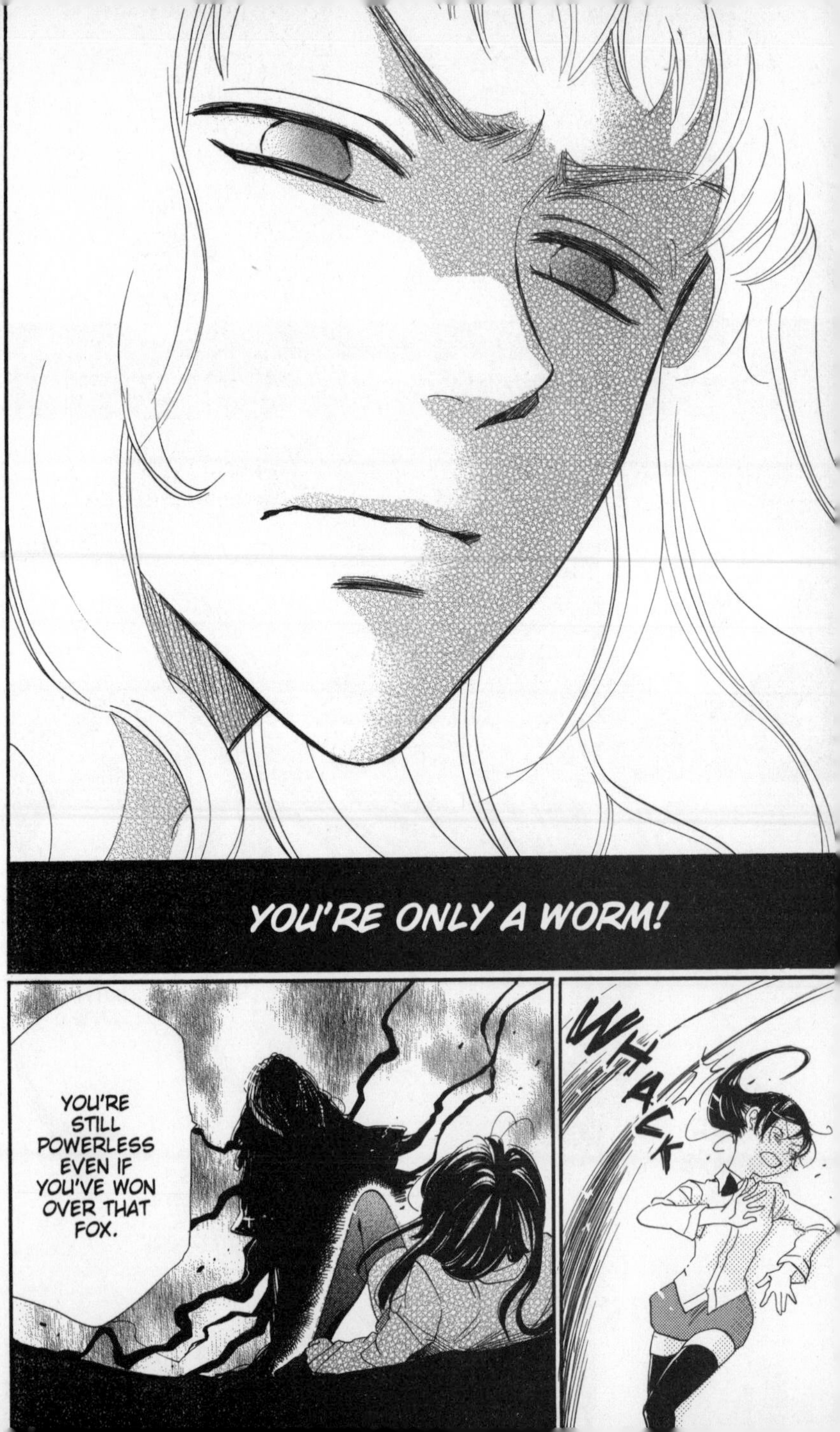
YOU'RE ONLY A WORM!
WHACK
YOU'RE STILL POWERLESS EVEN IF YOU'VE WON OVER THAT FOX.

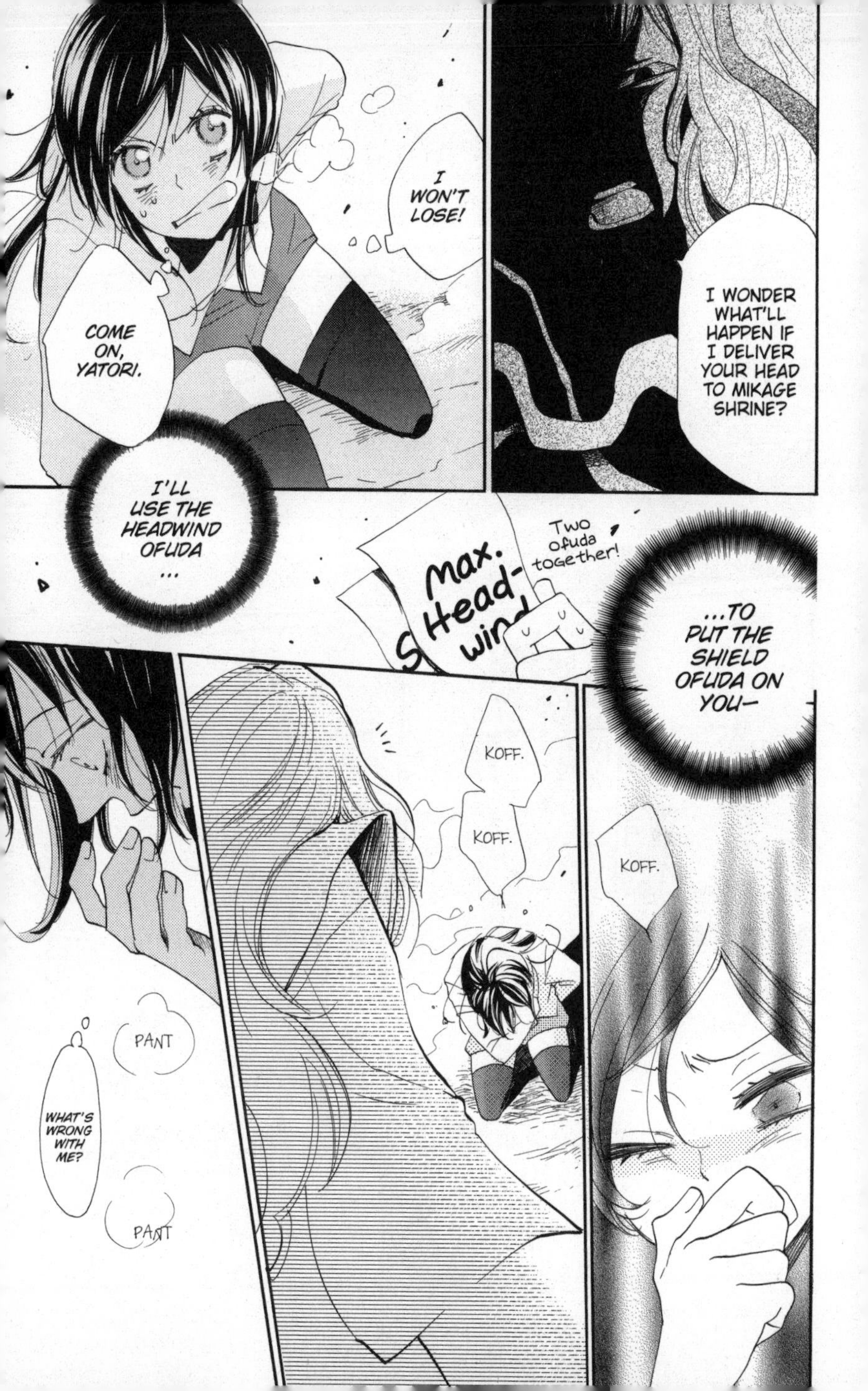
I WONDER WHAT'LL HAPPEN IF I DELIVER YOUR HEAD TO MIKAGE SHRINE?
I WON'T LOSE!
COME ON, YATORI.
I'LL USE THE HEADWIND OFUDA ...
Two ofuda together!
Max. Head-wind
...TO PUT THE SHIELD OFUDA ON YOU—
KOFF.
KOFF.
KOFF.
PANT
WHAT'S WRONG WITH ME?
PANT

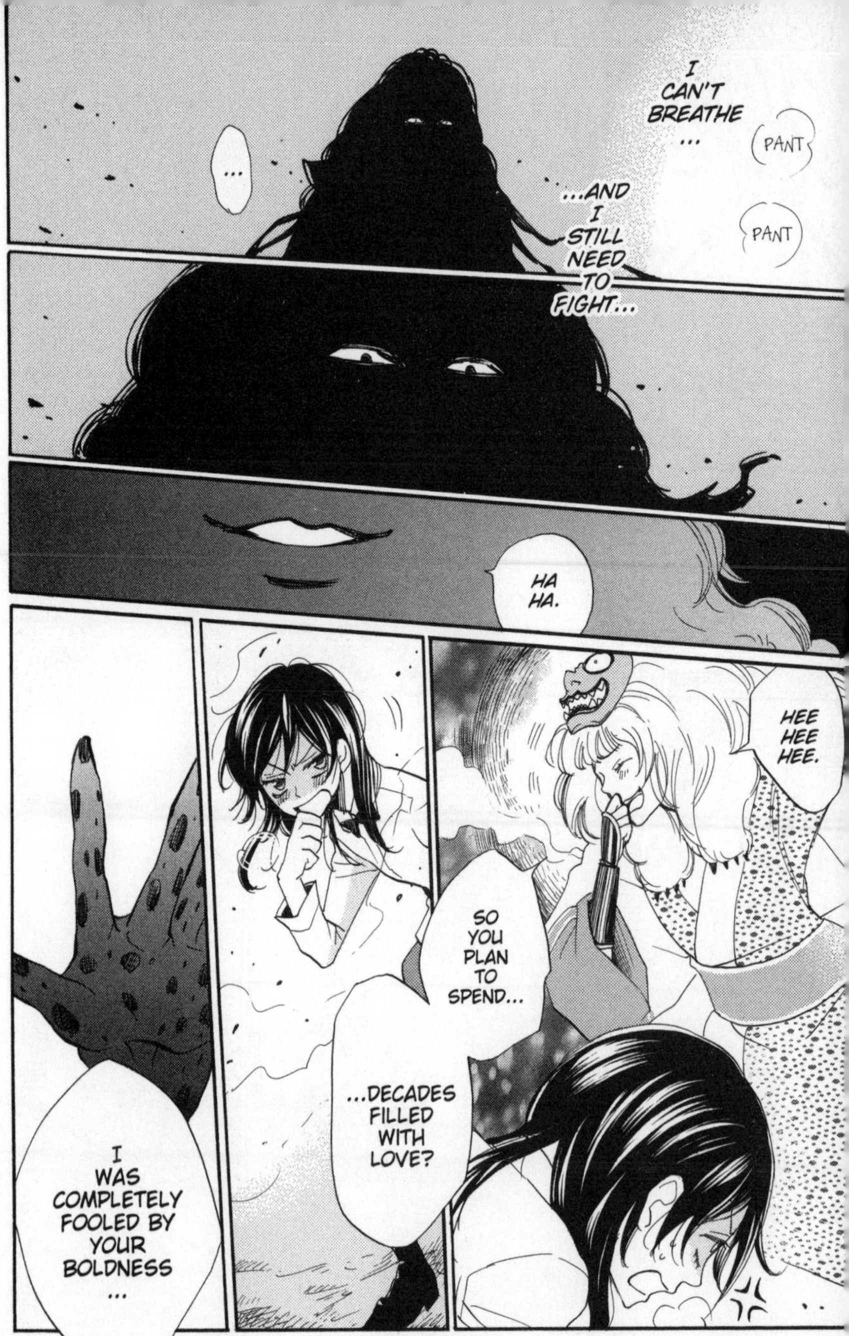
I CAN'T BREATHE ...
PANT
...AND I STILL NEED TO FIGHT...
PANT
...
HA HA.
HEE HEE HEE.
SO YOU PLAN TO SPEND...
...DECADES FILLED WITH LOVE?
I WAS COMPLETELY FOOLED BY YOUR BOLDNESS ...

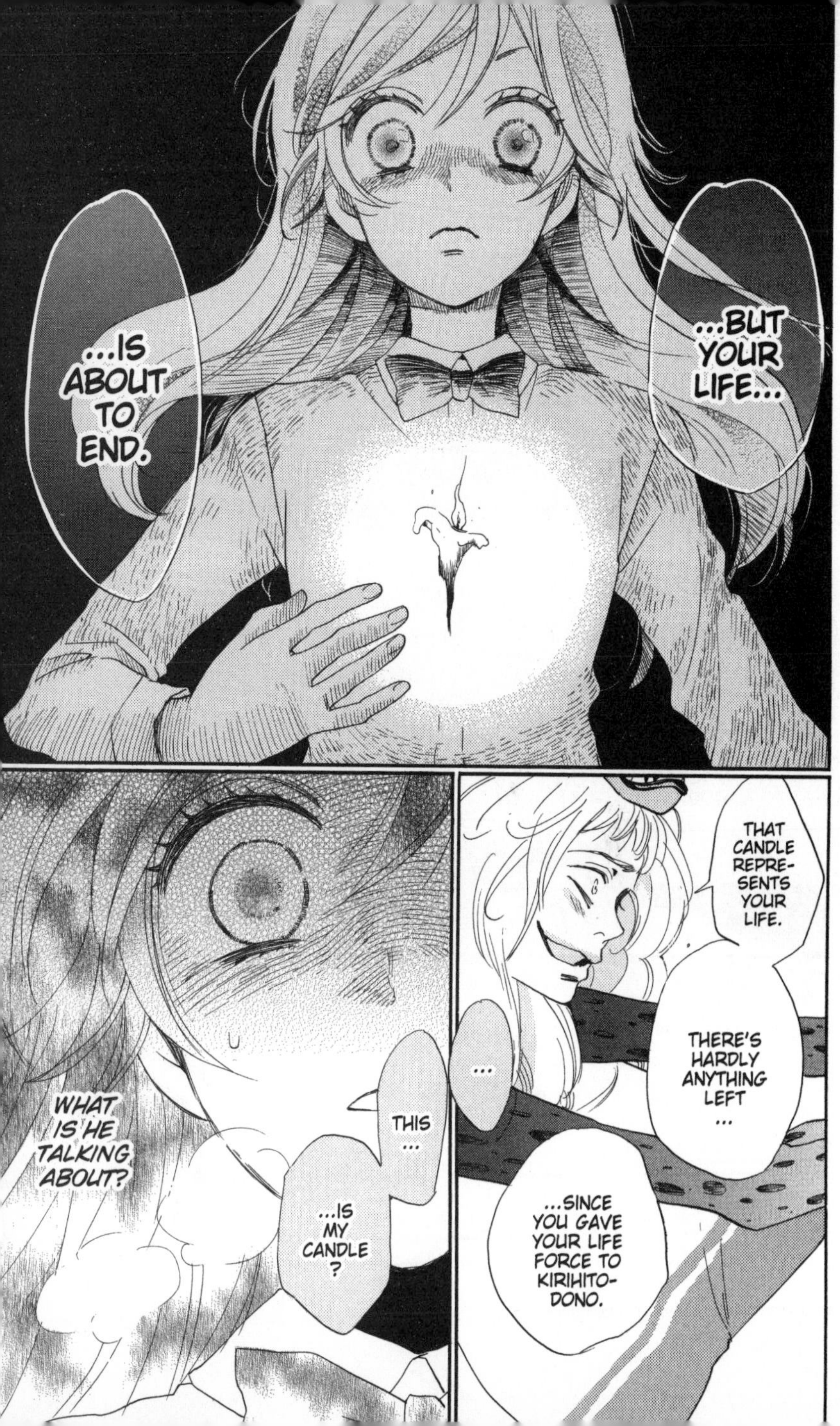
...BUT YOUR LIFE...
...IS ABOUT TO END.
THAT CANDLE REPRESENTS YOUR LIFE.
THERE'S HARDLY ANYTHING LEFT ...
...
...SINCE YOU GAVE YOUR LIFE FORCE TO KIRIHITO-DONO.
THIS ...
...IS MY CANDLE ?
WHAT IS HE TALKING ABOUT?

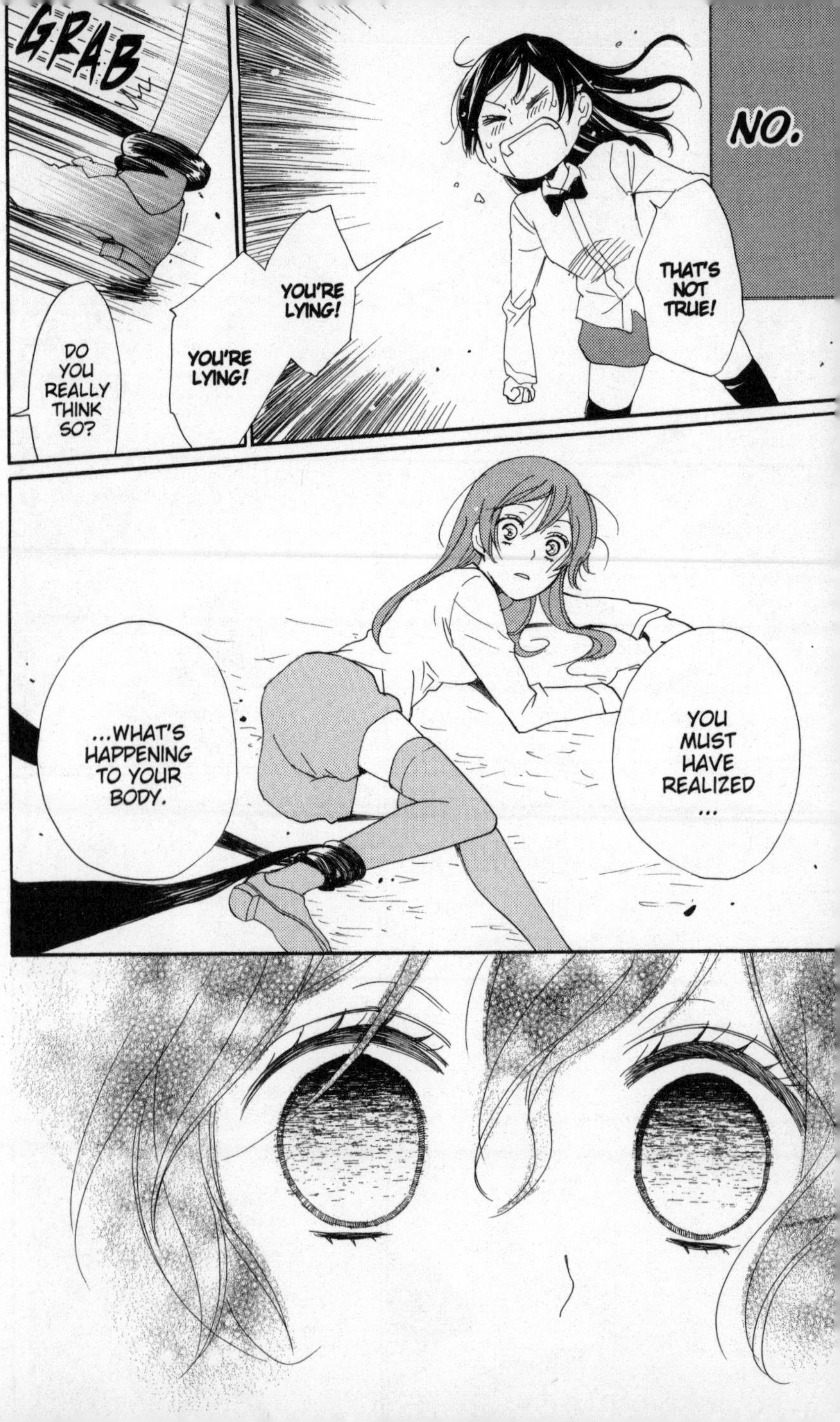
NO.
THAT'S NOT TRUE!
YOU'RE LYING!
YOU'RE LYING!
GRAB
DO YOU REALLY THINK SO?
YOU MUST HAVE REALIZED ...
...WHAT'S HAPPENING TO YOUR BODY.

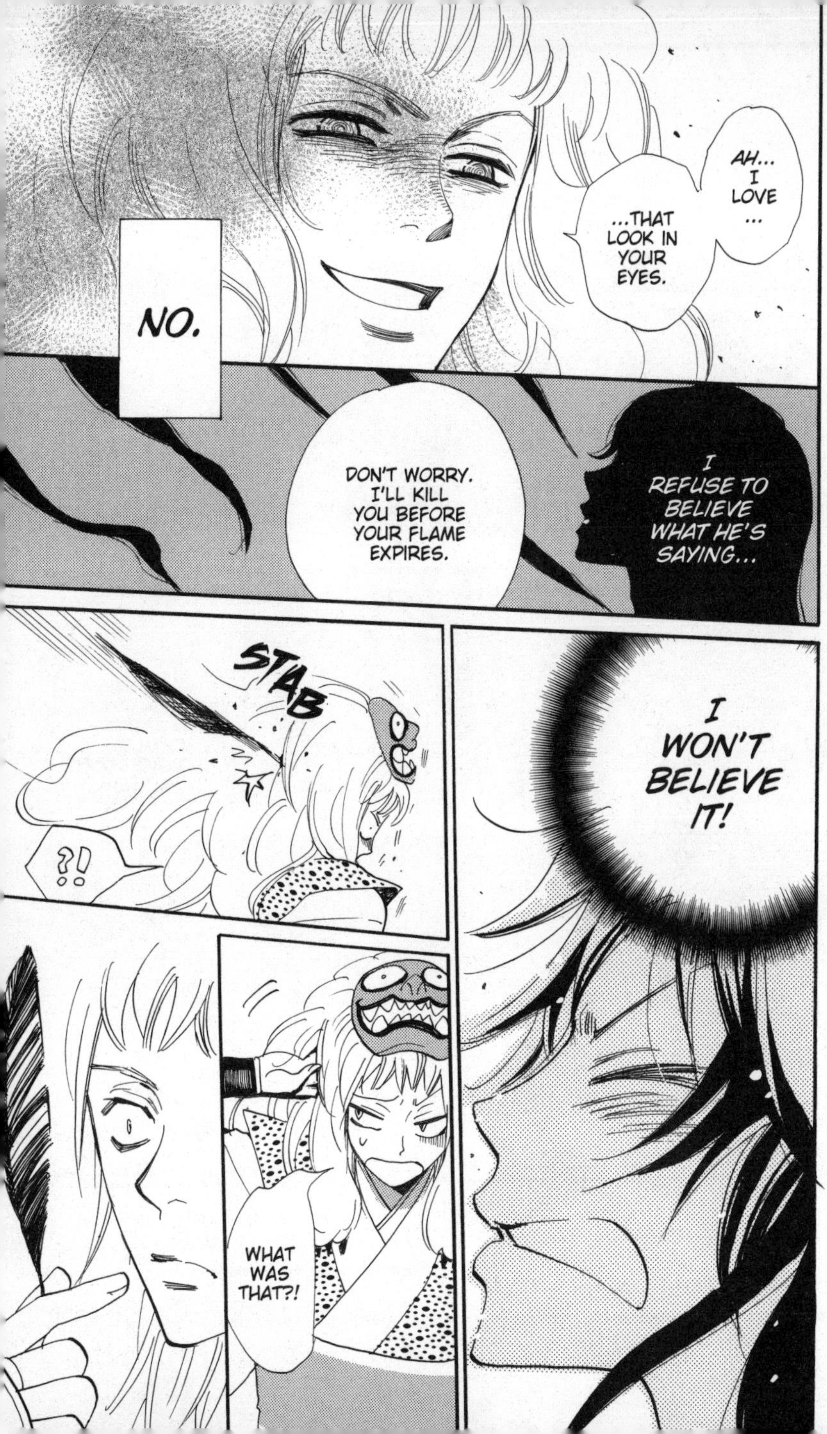
AH... I LOVE ...
...THAT LOOK IN YOUR EYES.
NO.
I REFUSE TO BELIEVE WHAT HE'S SAYING...
DON'T WORRY. I'LL KILL YOU BEFORE YOUR FLAME EXPIRES.
I WON'T BELIEVE IT!
STAB
?!
WHAT WAS THAT?!

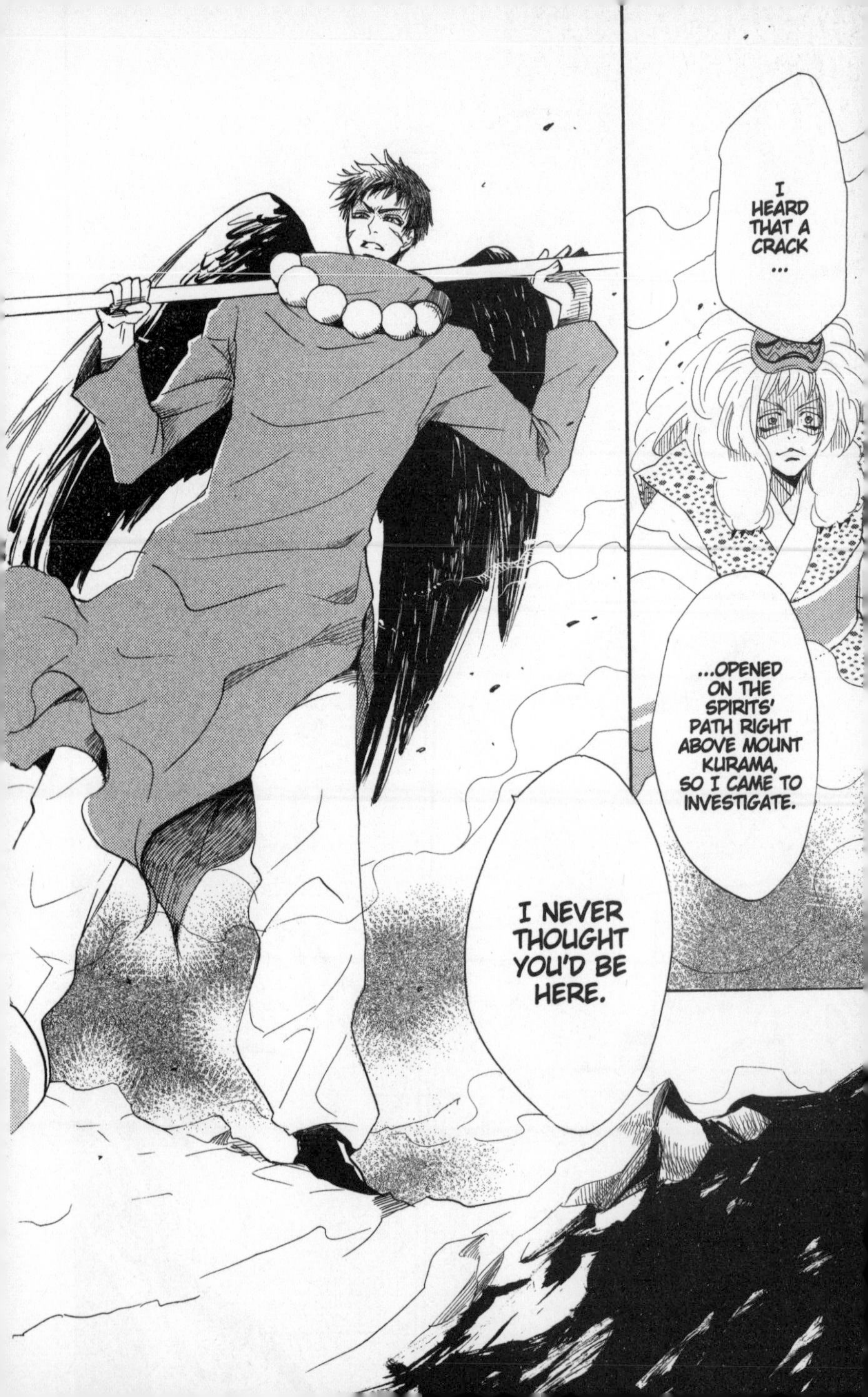
I HEARD THAT A CRACK ...
...OPENED ON THE SPIRITS' PATH RIGHT ABOVE MOUNT KURAMA, SO I CAME TO INVESTIGATE.
I NEVER THOUGHT YOU'D BE HERE.

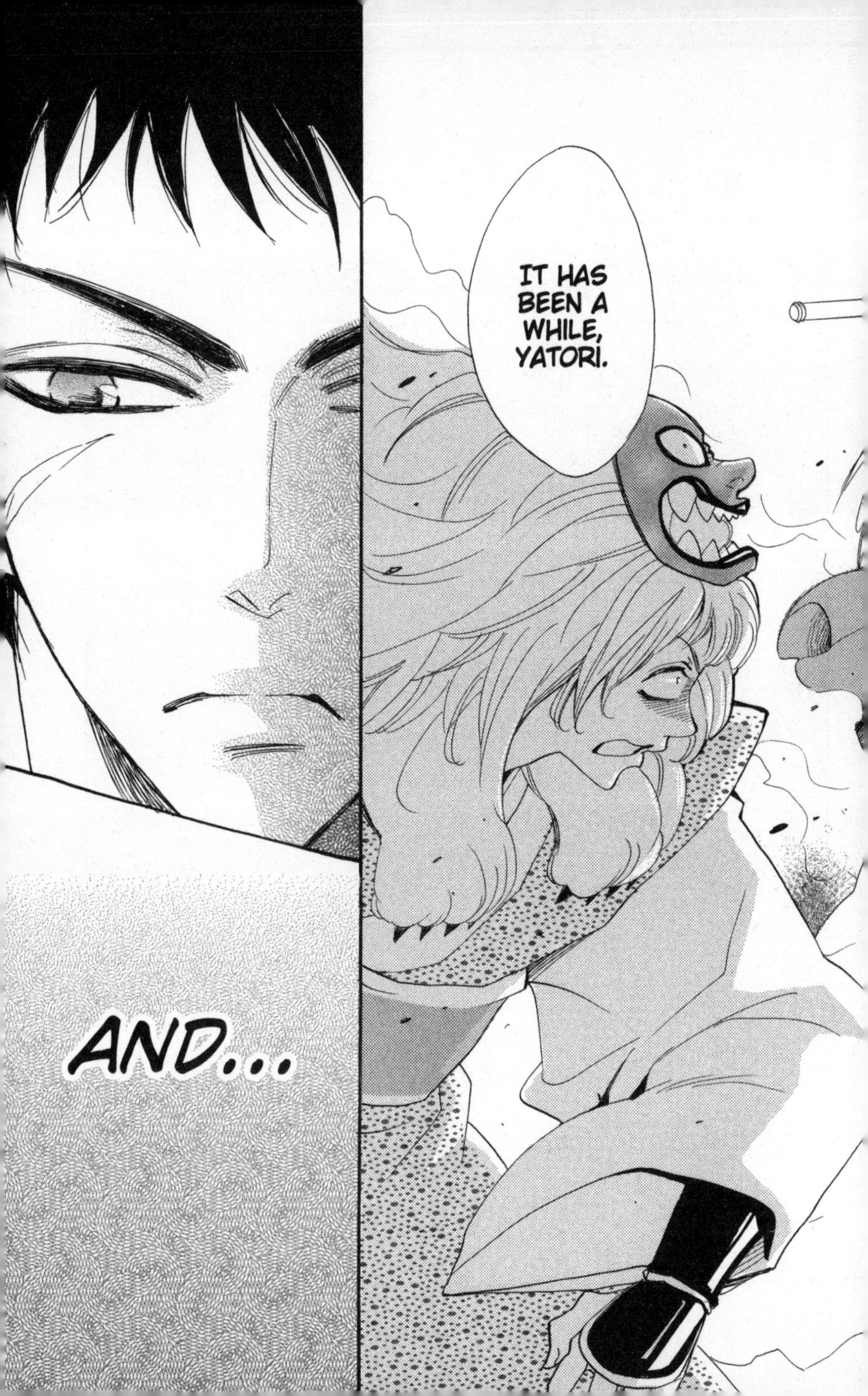
IT HAS BEEN A WHILE, YATORI.
AND...

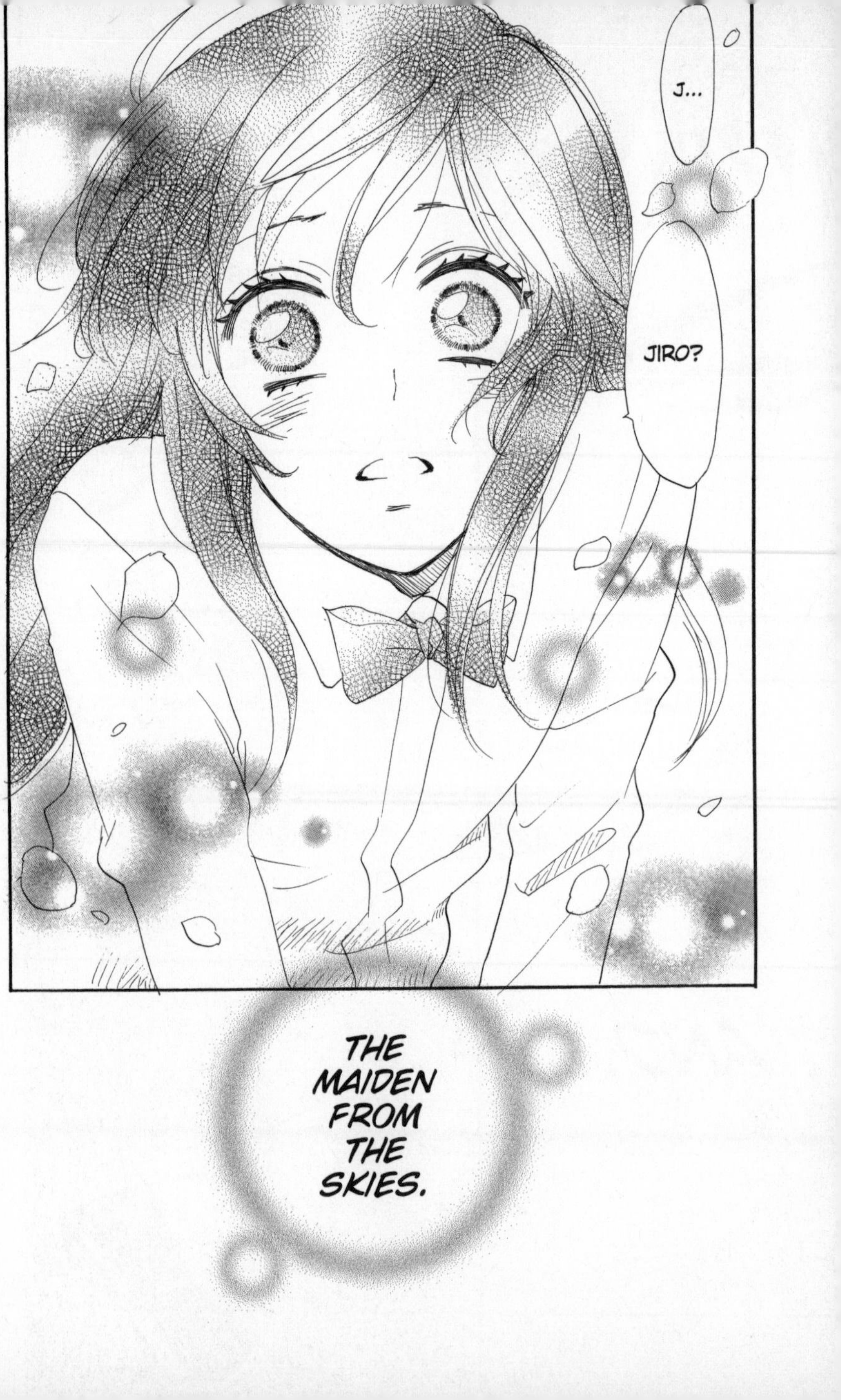
J...
JIRO?
THE MAIDEN FROM THE SKIES.

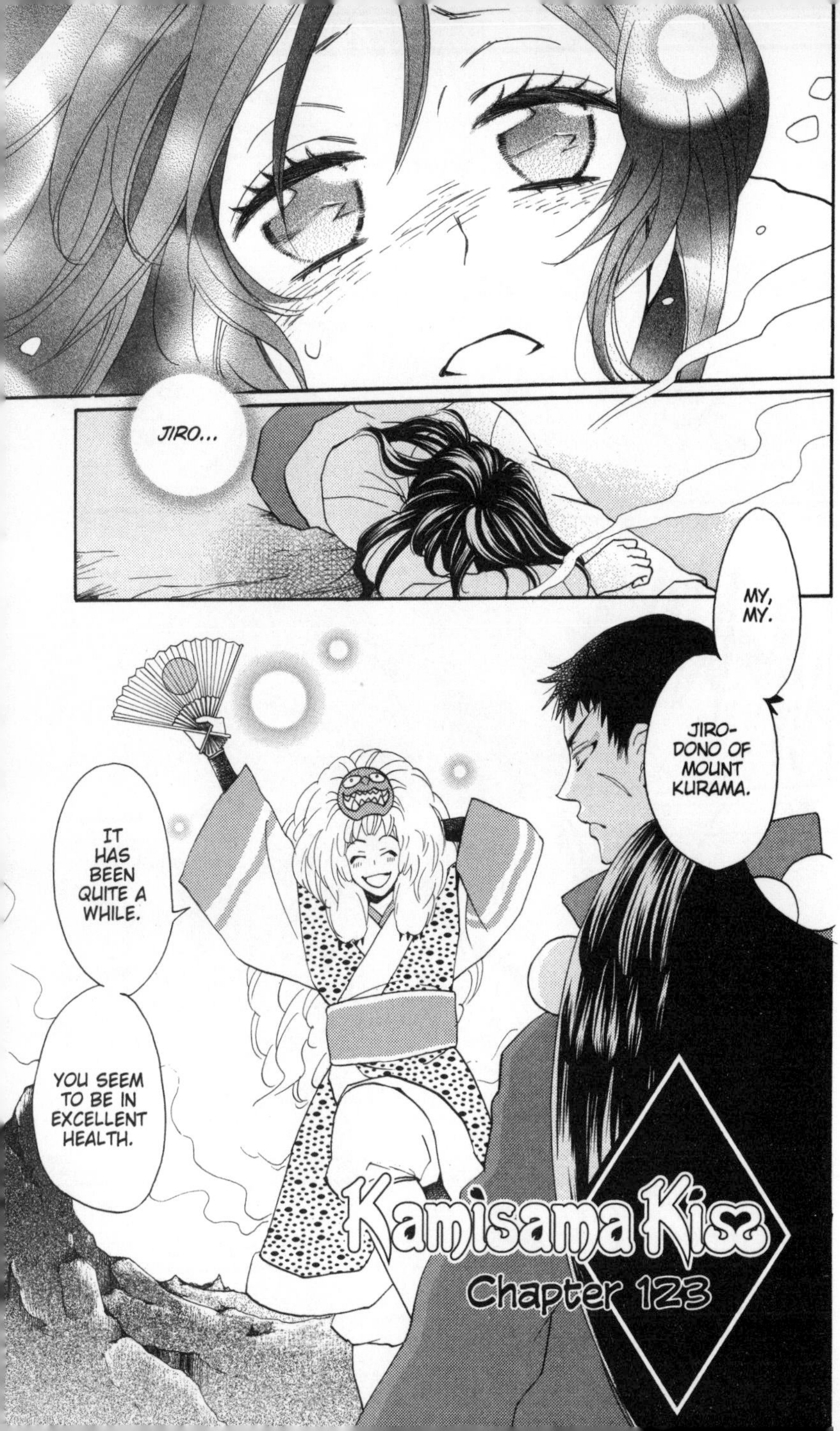
JIRO...
MY, MY.
JIRO-DONO OF MOUNT KURAMA.
IT HAS BEEN QUITE A WHILE.
YOU SEEM TO BE IN EXCELLENT HEALTH.
Kamisama Kiss
Chapter 123

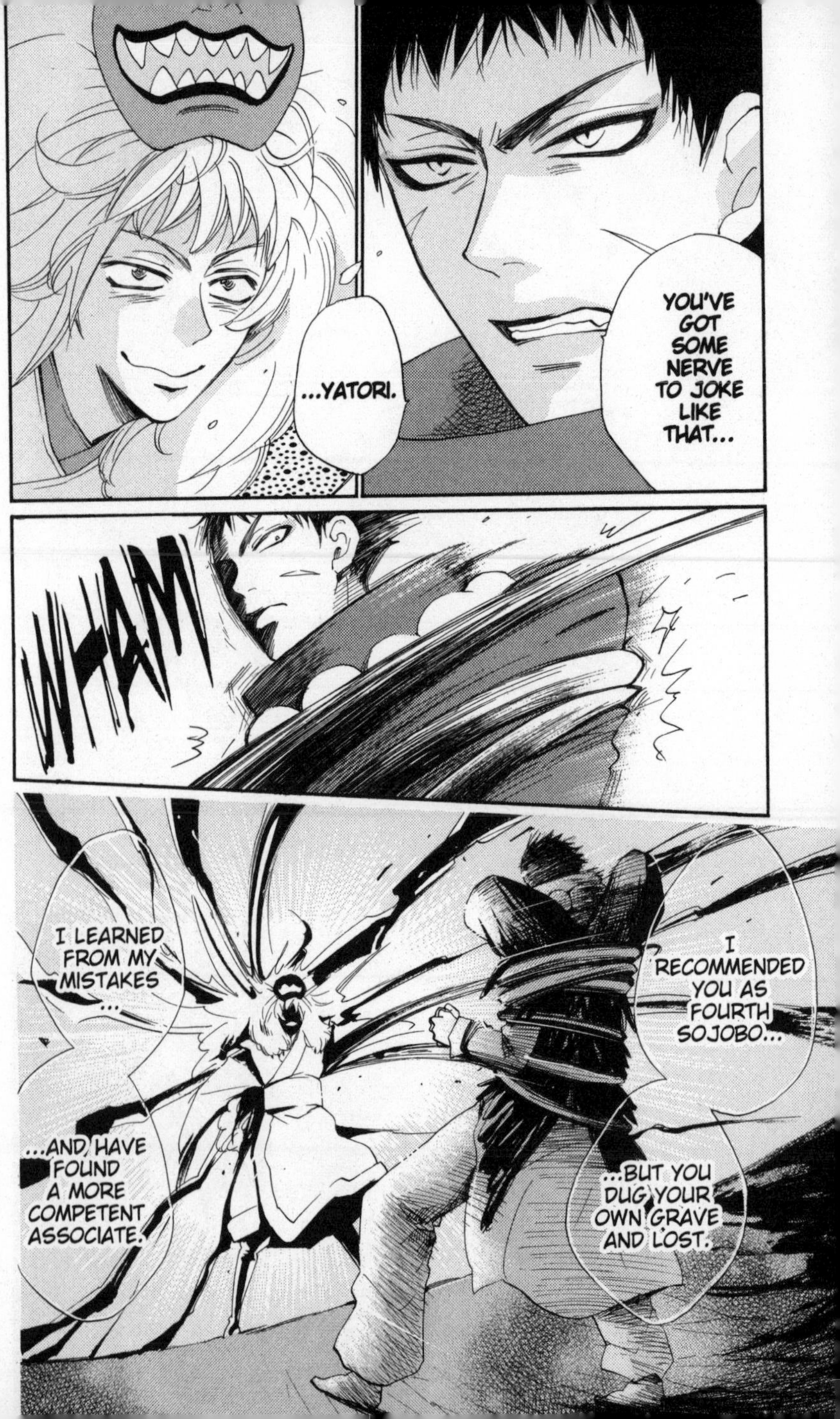
YOU'VE GOT SOME NERVE TO JOKE LIKE THAT...
...YATORI.
WHAM
I RECOMMENDED YOU AS FOURTH SOJOBO...
I LEARNED FROM MY MISTAKES...
...BUT YOU DUG YOUR OWN GRAVE AND LOST.
...AND HAVE FOUND A MORE COMPETENT ASSOCIATE.

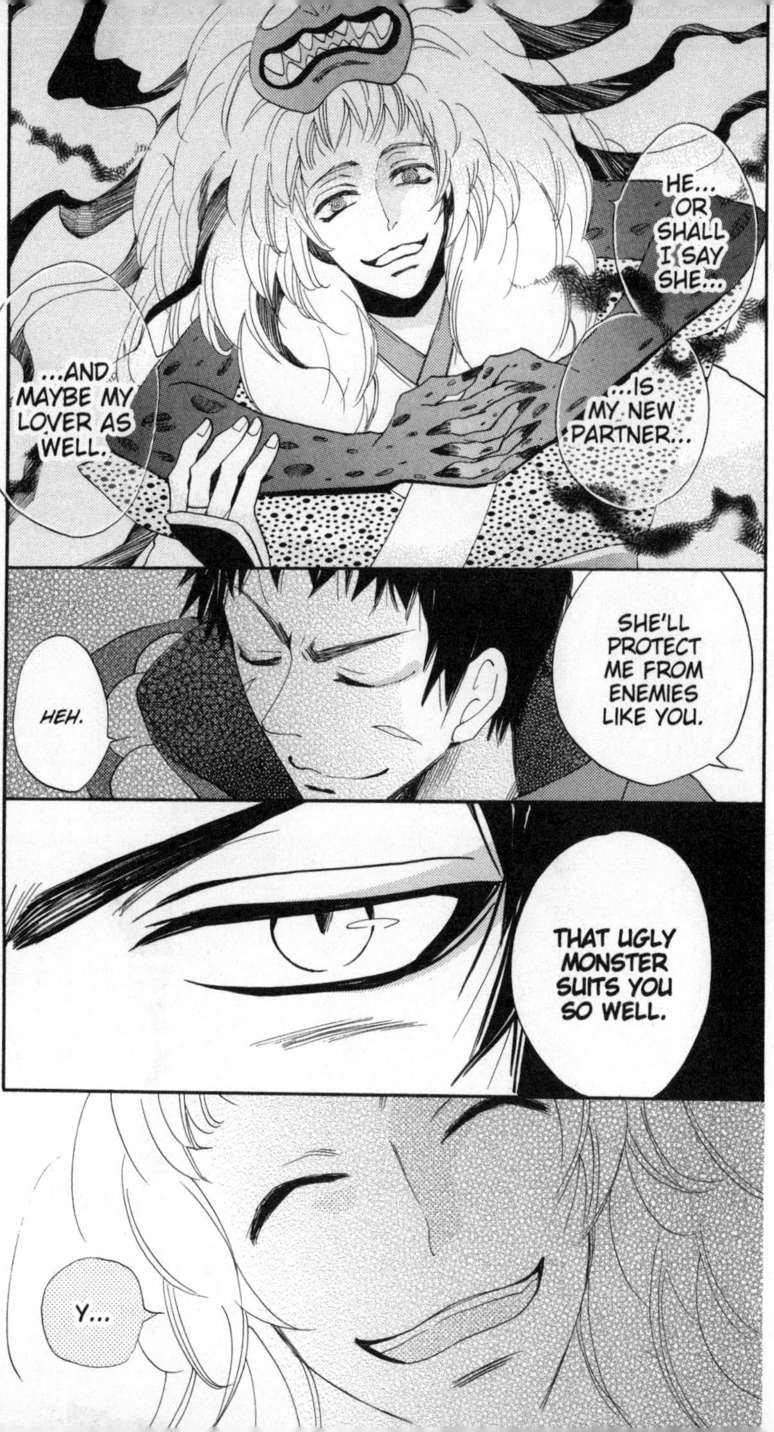
HE... OR SHALL I SAY SHE...
...IS MY NEW PARTNER...
...AND MAYBE MY LOVER AS WELL.
SHE'LL PROTECT ME FROM ENEMIES LIKE YOU.
HEH.
THAT UGLY MONSTER SUITS YOU SO WELL.
Y...

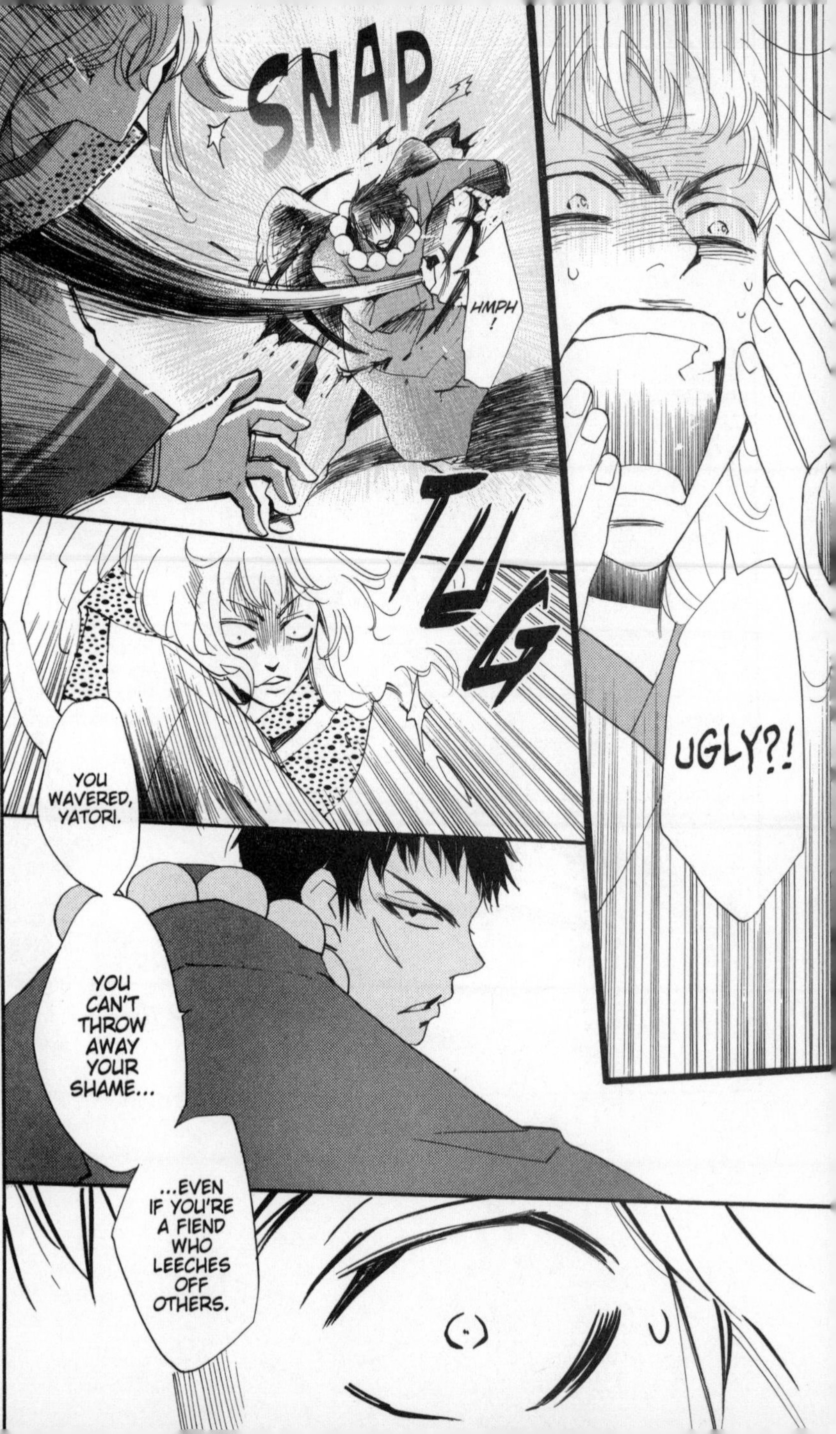
UGLY?!
SNAP
HMPH!
TUG
YOU WAVERED, YATORI.
YOU CAN'T THROW AWAY YOUR SHAME...
...EVEN IF YOU'RE A FIEND WHO LEECHES OFF OTHERS.

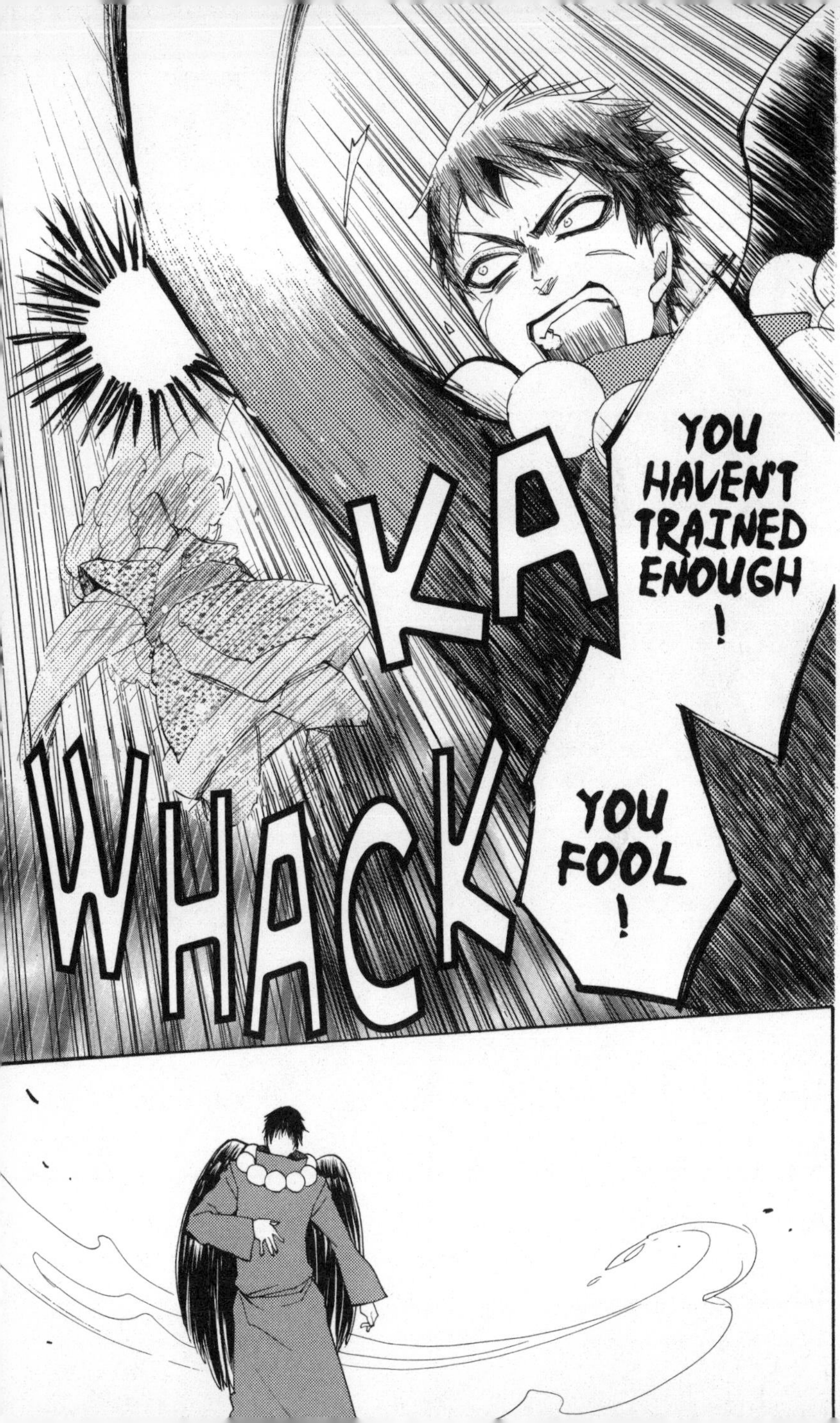
YOU HAVEN'T TRAINED ENOUGH!
YOU FOOL!
KA WHACK

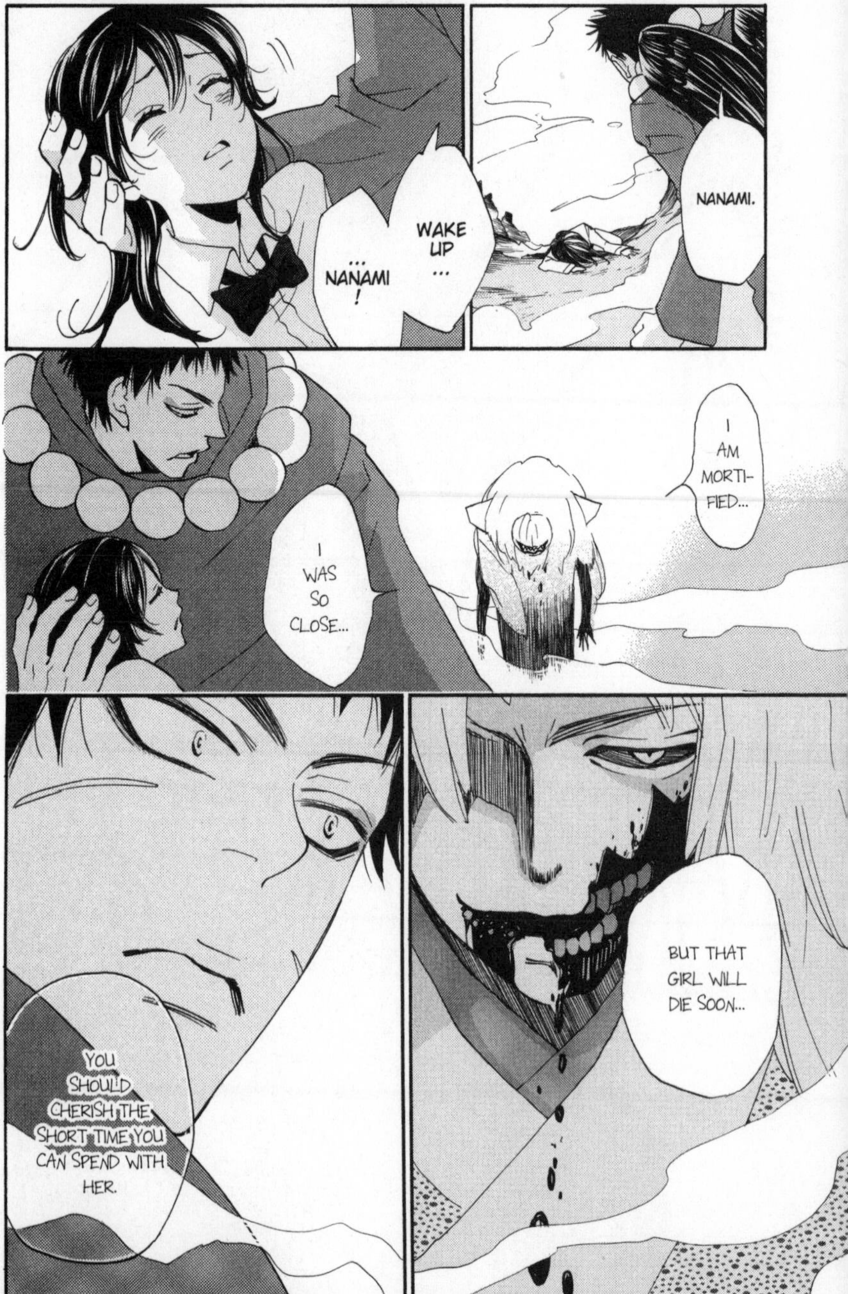
NANAMI.
WAKE UP ...
... NANAMI!
I AM MORTIFIED...
I WAS SO CLOSE...
BUT THAT GIRL WILL DIE SOON...
YOU SHOULD CHERISH THE SHORT TIME YOU CAN SPEND WITH HER.

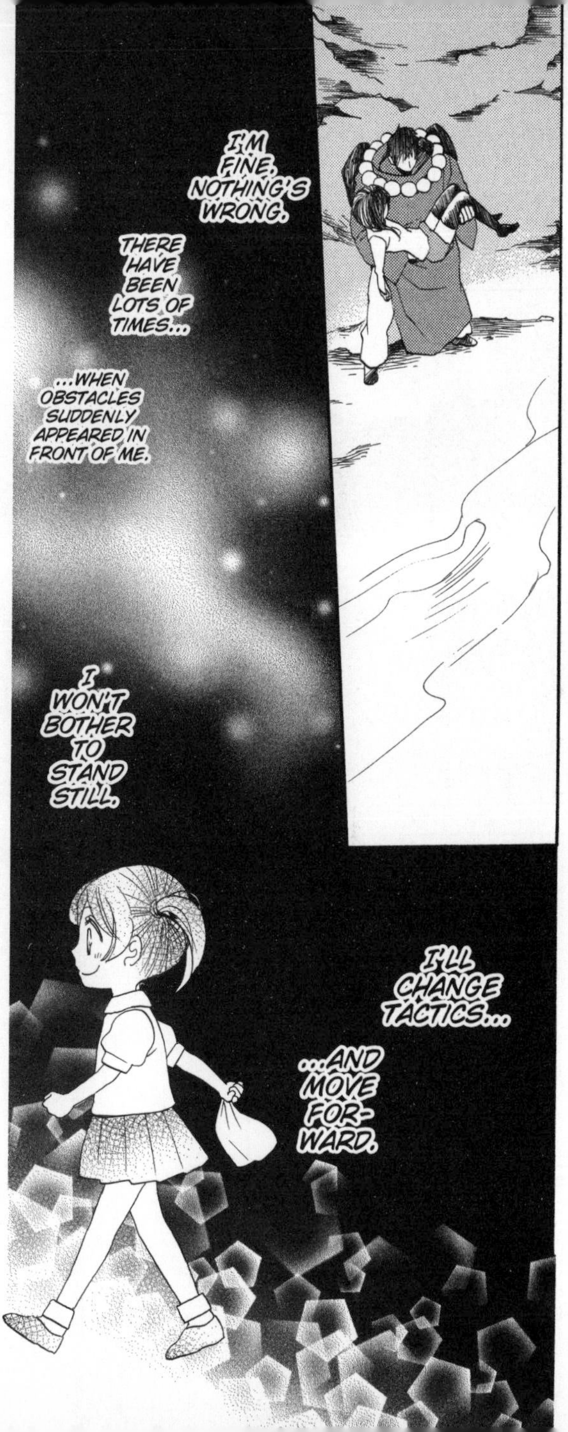
I'M FINE. NOTHING'S WRONG.
THERE HAVE BEEN LOTS OF TIMES...
...WHEN OBSTACLES SUDDENLY APPEARED IN FRONT OF ME.
I WON'T BOTHER TO STAND STILL.
I'LL CHANGE TACTICS...
...AND MOVE FOR-WARD.

Nowadays, I'm into

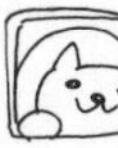

the Neko Atsume Game app.

I rarely play Games, But the cats are so so cute...

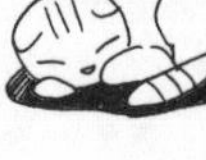

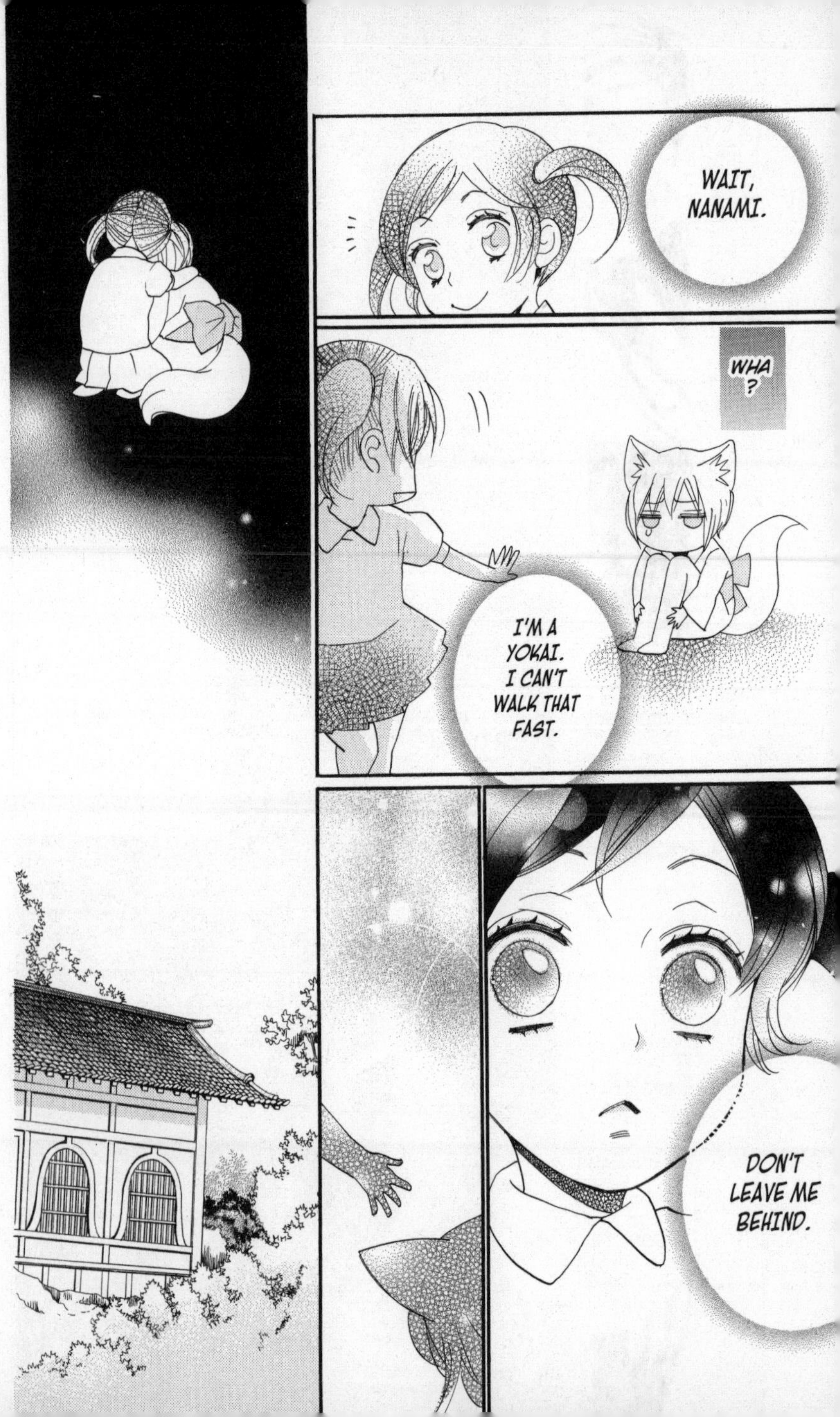
WAIT, NANAMI.
WHA ?
I'M A YOKAI. I CAN'T WALK THAT FAST.
DON'T LEAVE ME BEHIND.

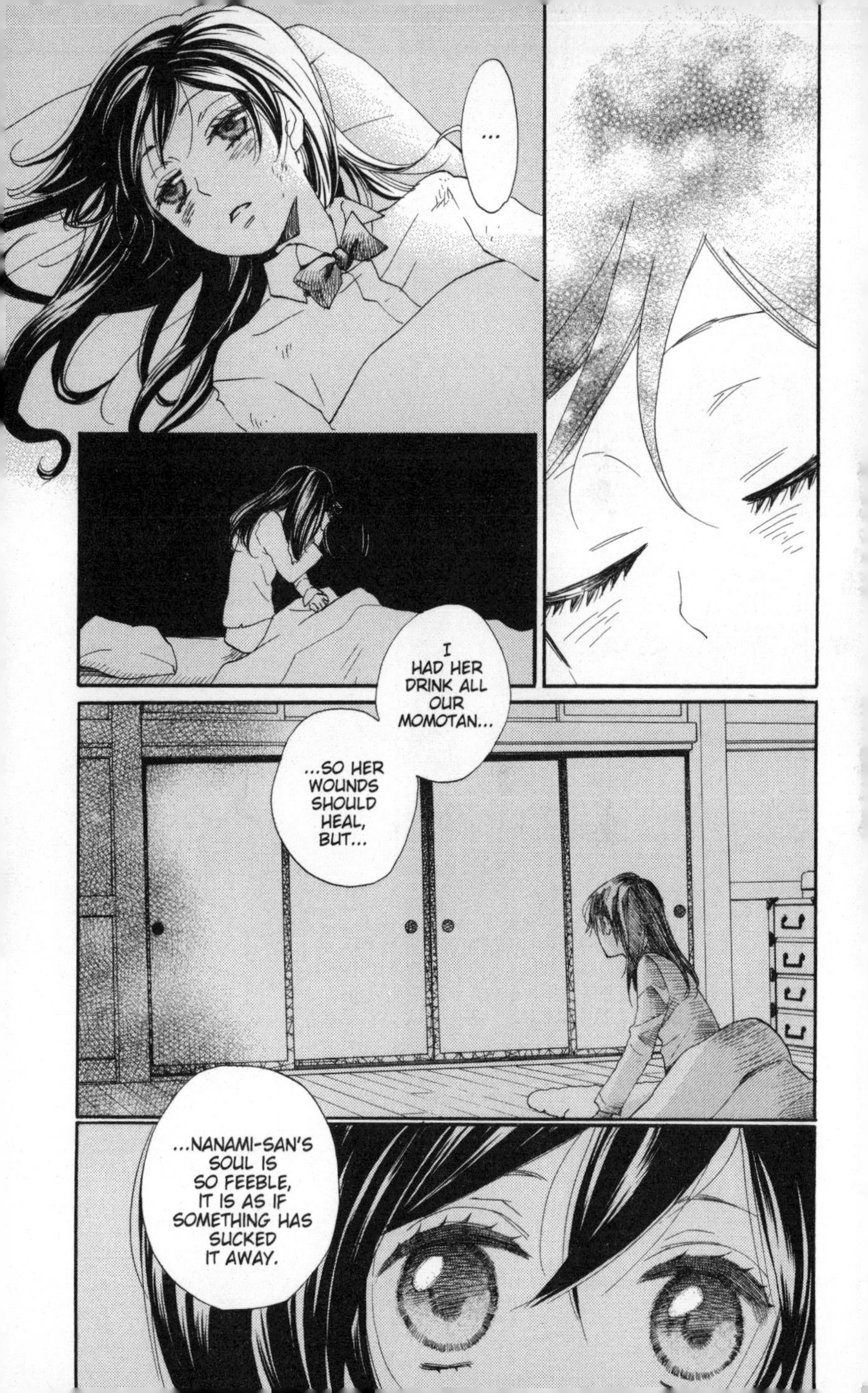
...
I HAD HER DRINK ALL OUR MOMOTAN...
...SO HER WOUNDS SHOULD HEAL, BUT...
...NANAMI-SAN'S SOUL IS SO FEEBLE, IT IS AS IF SOMETHING HAS SUCKED IT AWAY.

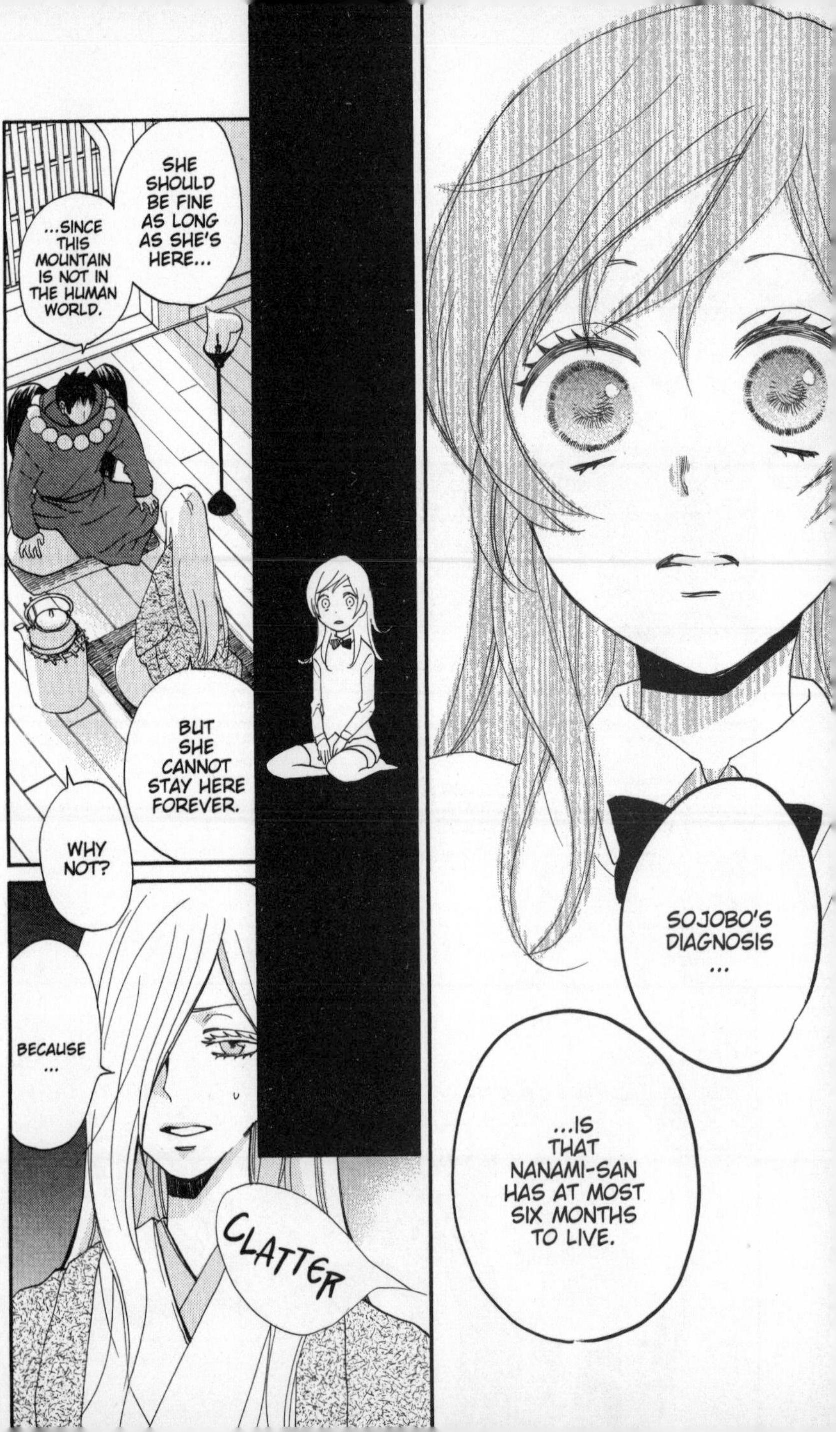
SOJOBO'S DIAGNOSIS...
...IS THAT NANAMI-SAN HAS AT MOST SIX MONTHS TO LIVE.
SHE SHOULD BE FINE AS LONG AS SHE'S HERE...
...SINCE THIS MOUNTAIN IS NOT IN THE HUMAN WORLD.
BUT SHE CANNOT STAY HERE FOREVER.
WHY NOT?
BECAUSE...
CLATTER

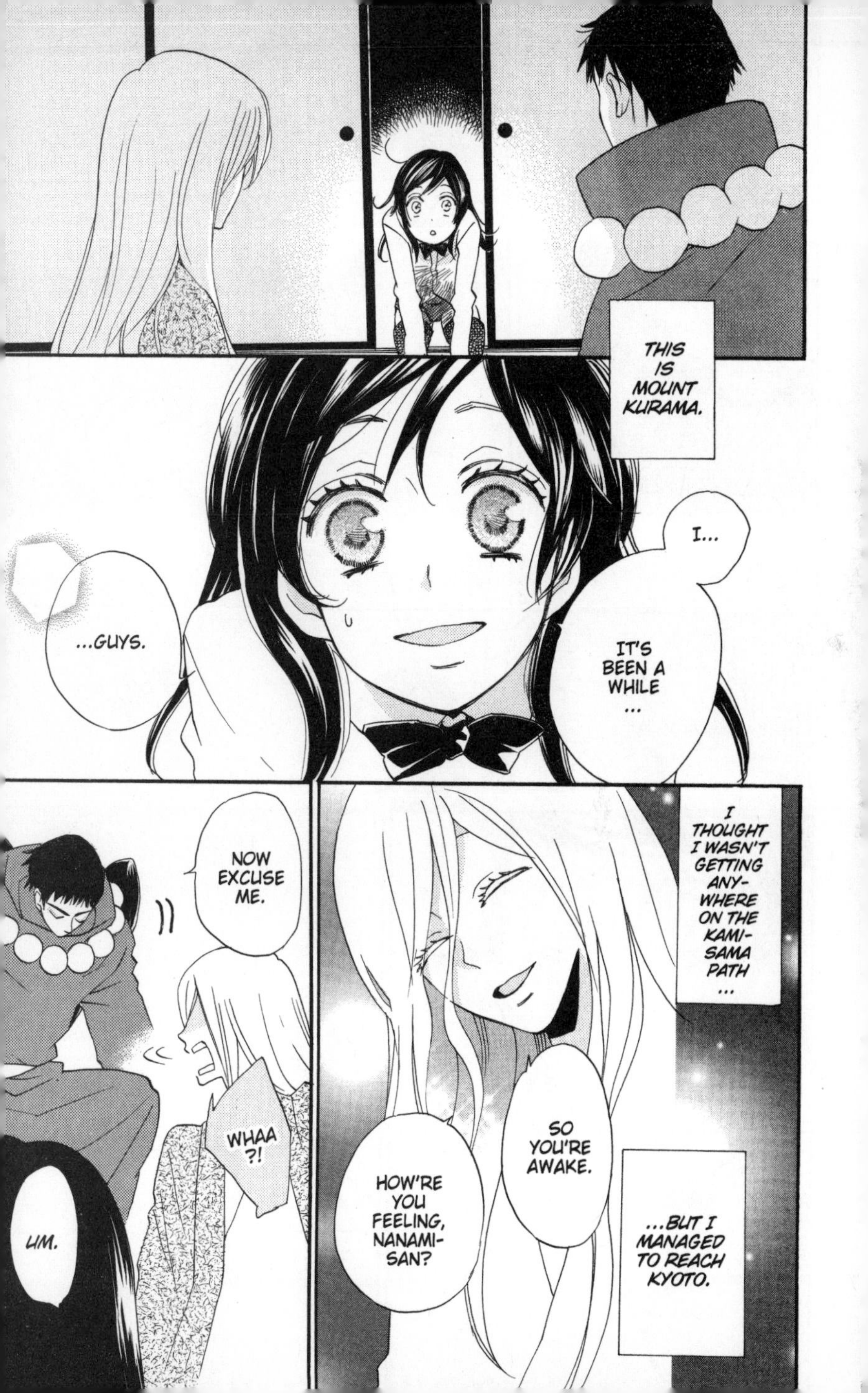
THIS IS MOUNT KURAMA.
I...
IT'S BEEN A WHILE...
...GUYS.
I THOUGHT I WASN'T GETTING ANY-WHERE ON THE KAMI-SAMA PATH...
SO YOU'RE AWAKE.
...BUT I MANAGED TO REACH KYOTO.
HOW'RE YOU FEELING, NANAMI-SAN?
NOW EXCUSE ME.
WHAA?!
UM.

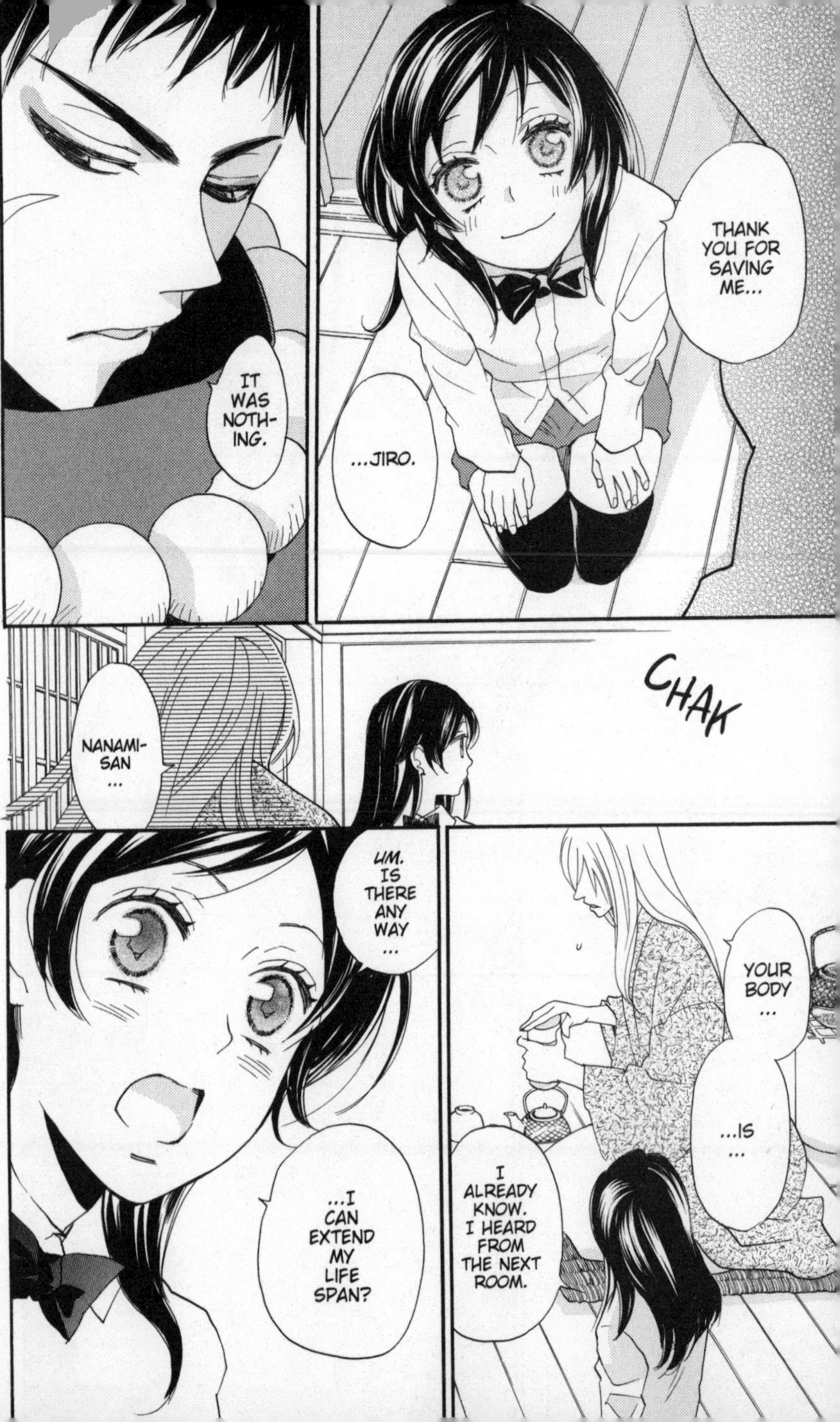
THANK YOU FOR SAVING ME...
...JIRO.
IT WAS NOTHING.
CHAK
NANAMI-SAN...
YOUR BODY...
...IS...
I ALREADY KNOW. I HEARD FROM THE NEXT ROOM.
UM. IS THERE ANY WAY...
...I CAN EXTEND MY LIFE SPAN?

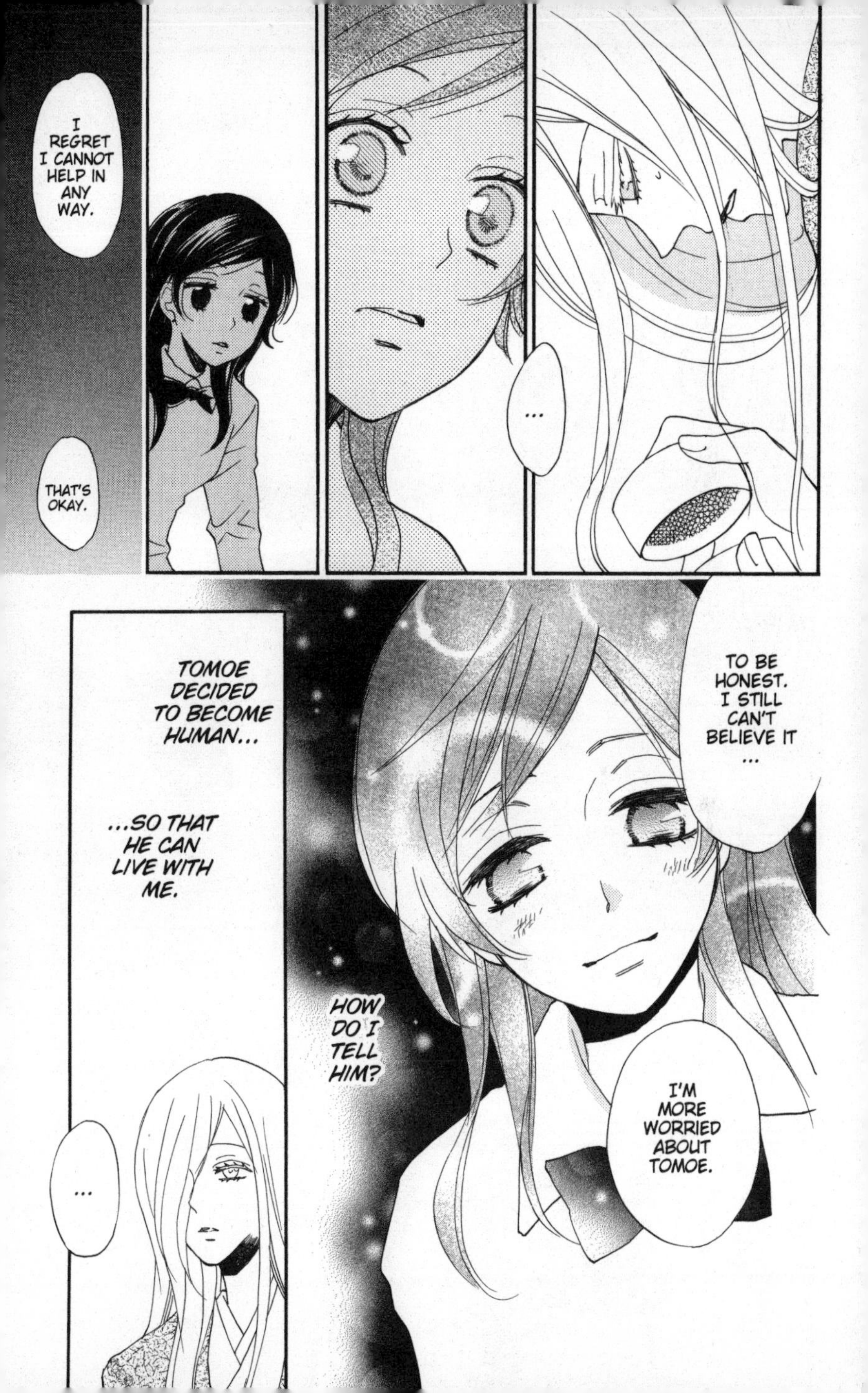
...
I REGRET I CANNOT HELP IN ANY WAY.
THAT'S OKAY.
TO BE HONEST. I STILL CAN'T BELIEVE IT ...
I'M MORE WORRIED ABOUT TOMOE.
HOW DO I TELL HIM?
TOMOE DECIDED TO BECOME HUMAN...
...SO THAT HE CAN LIVE WITH ME.
...

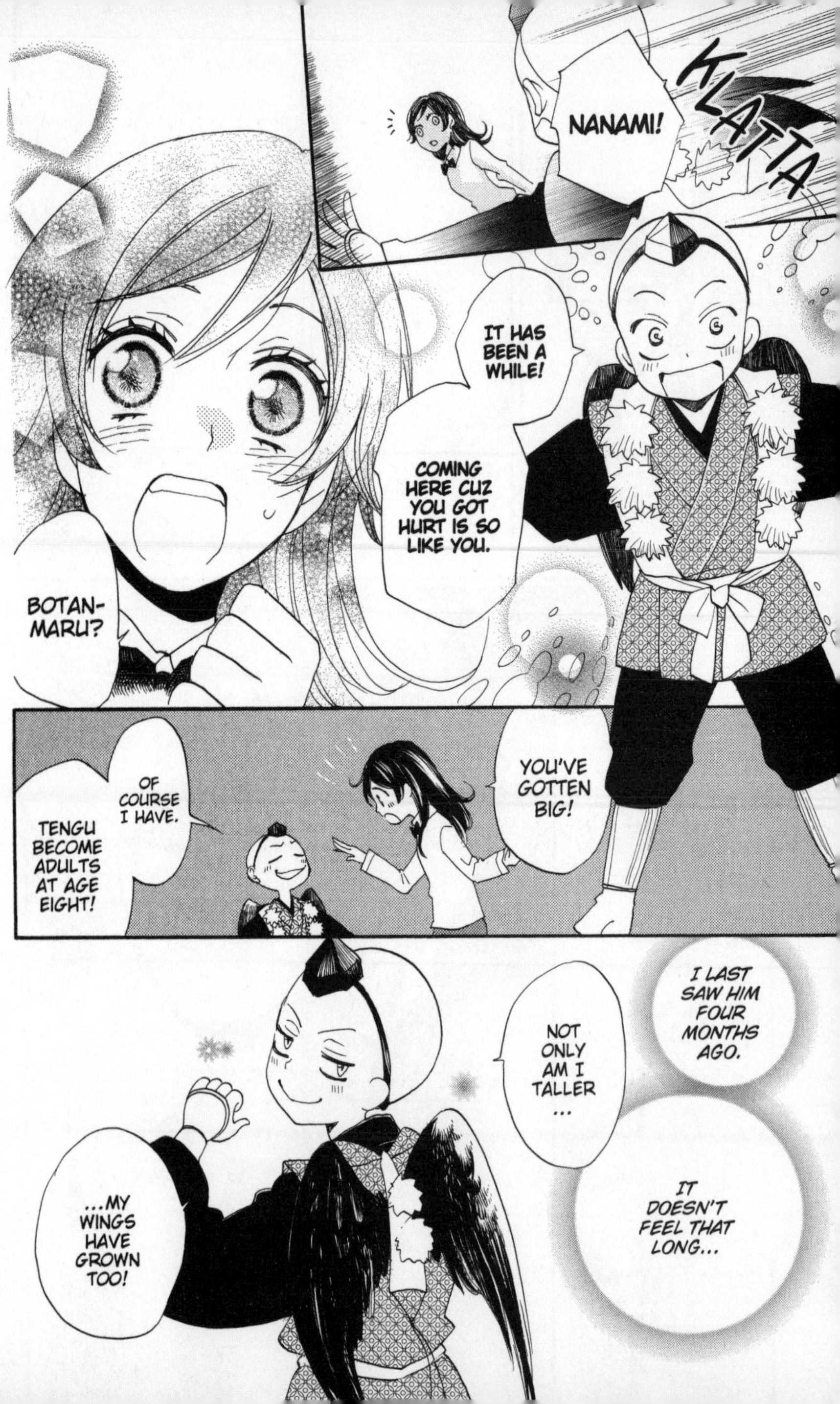
KLATTA
NANAMI!
IT HAS BEEN A WHILE!
COMING HERE CUZ YOU GOT HURT IS SO LIKE YOU.
BOTAN-MARU?
YOU'VE GOTTEN BIG!
OF COURSE I HAVE.
TENGU BECOME ADULTS AT AGE EIGHT!
I LAST SAW HIM FOUR MONTHS AGO.
IT DOESN'T FEEL THAT LONG...
NOT ONLY AM I TALLER...
...MY WINGS HAVE GROWN TOO!

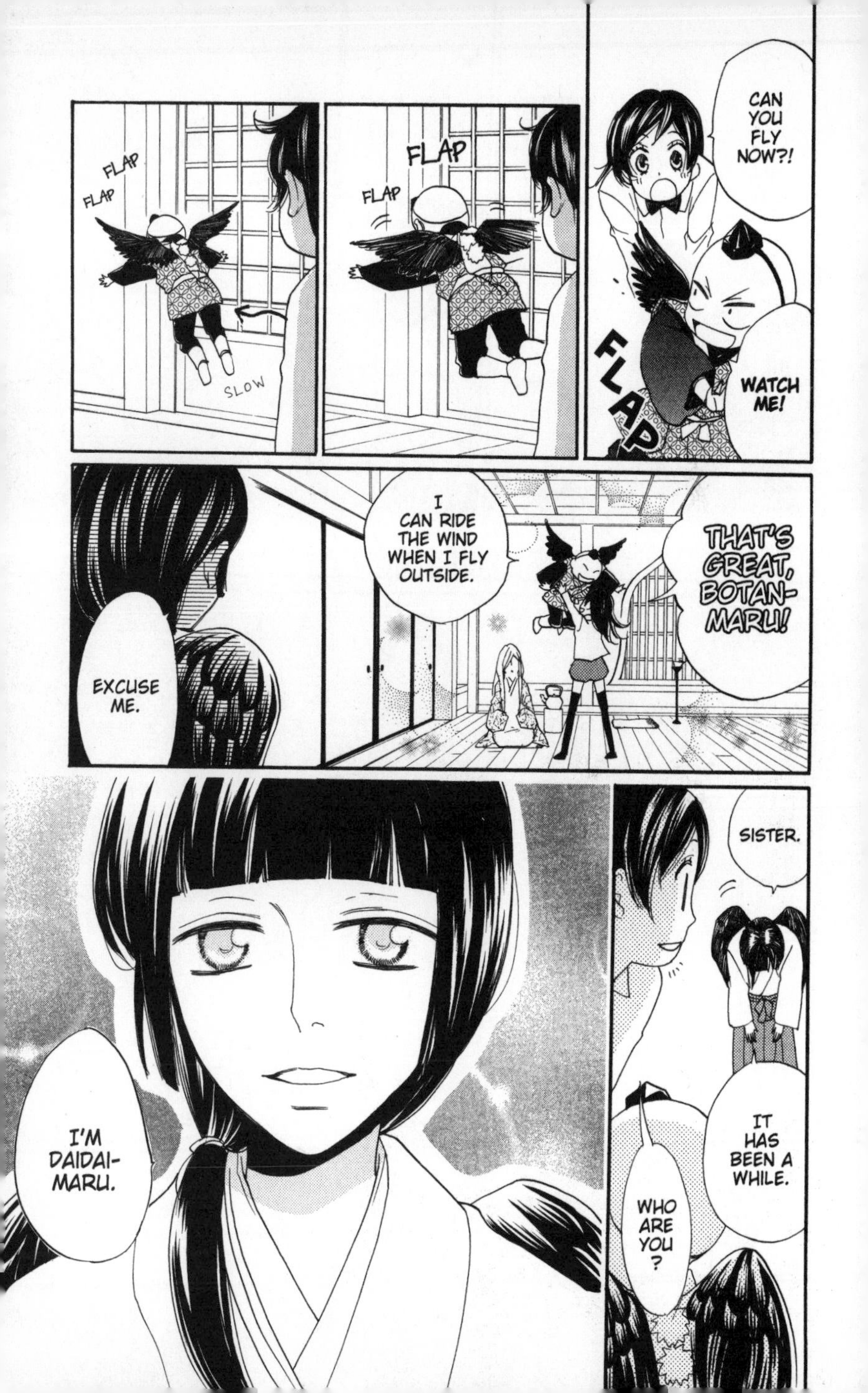
CAN YOU FLY NOW?!
WATCH ME!
FLAP
FLAP
FLAP
FLAP
FLAP
SLOW
THAT'S GREAT, BOTAN-MARU!
I CAN RIDE THE WIND WHEN I FLY OUTSIDE.
EXCUSE ME.
SISTER.
IT HAS BEEN A WHILE.
WHO ARE YOU?
I'M DAIDAI-MARU.

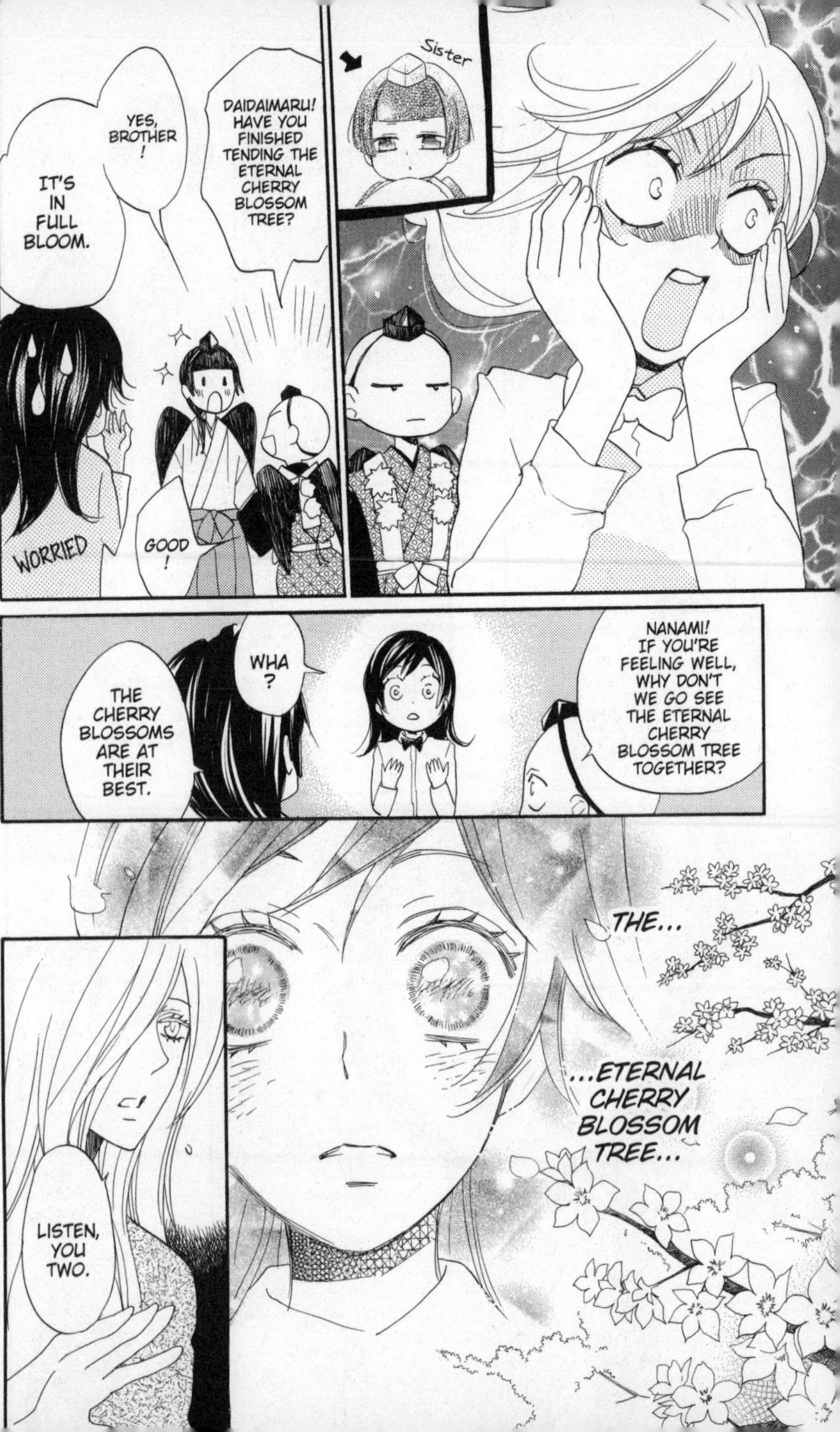
Sister
DAIDAIMARU! HAVE YOU FINISHED TENDING THE ETERNAL CHERRY BLOSSOM TREE?
YES, BROTHER!
IT'S IN FULL BLOOM.
GOOD!
WORRIED
NANAMI! IF YOU'RE FEELING WELL, WHY DON'T WE GO SEE THE ETERNAL CHERRY BLOSSOM TREE TOGETHER?
WHA?
THE CHERRY BLOSSOMS ARE AT THEIR BEST.
THE...
...ETERNAL CHERRY BLOSSOM TREE...
LISTEN, YOU TWO.

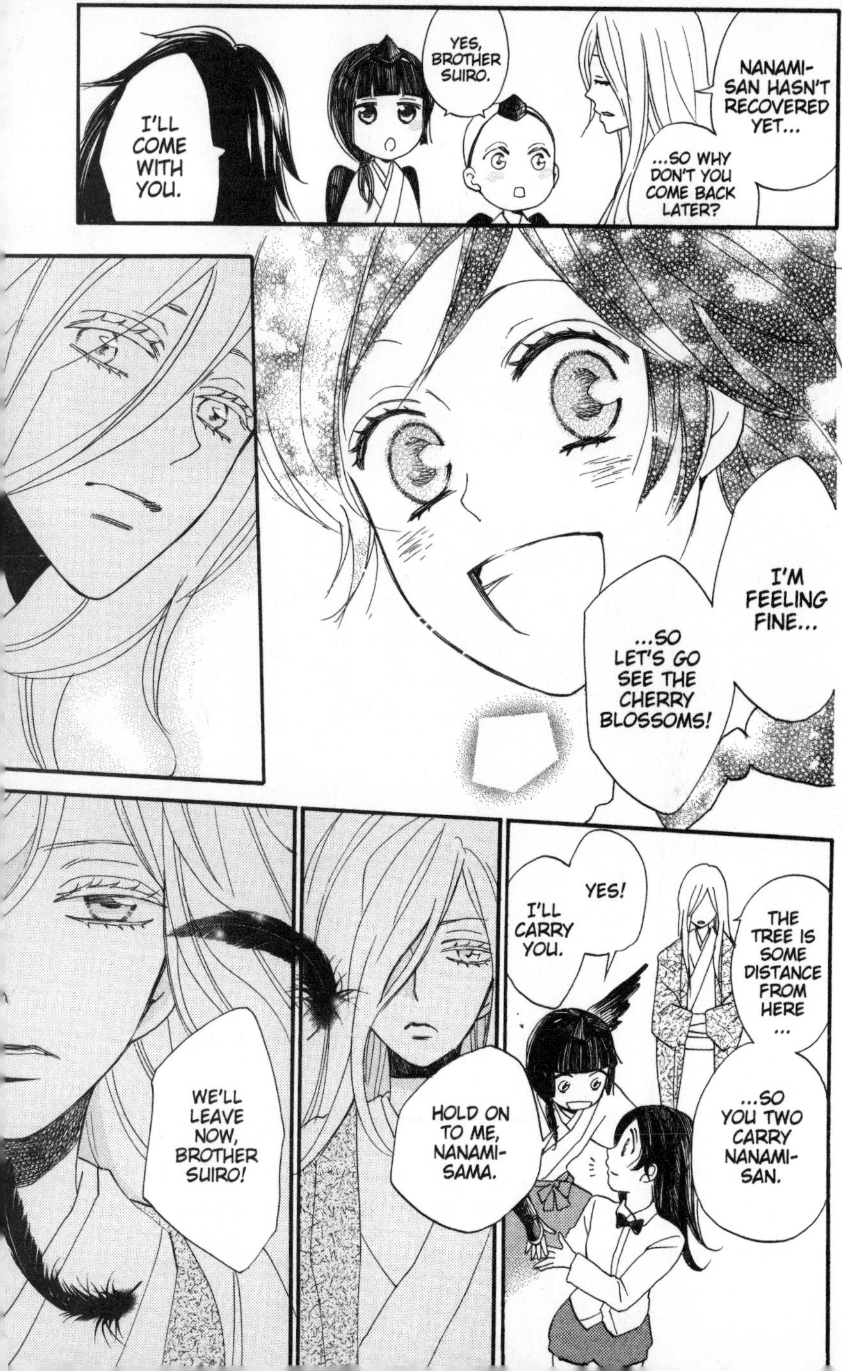
NANAMI-SAN HASN'T RECOVERED YET...
...SO WHY DON'T YOU COME BACK LATER?
YES, BROTHER SUIRO.
I'LL COME WITH YOU.
I'M FEELING FINE...
...SO LET'S GO SEE THE CHERRY BLOSSOMS!
THE TREE IS SOME DISTANCE FROM HERE ...
...SO YOU TWO CARRY NANAMI-SAN.
YES!
I'LL CARRY YOU.
HOLD ON TO ME, NANAMI-SAMA.
WE'LL LEAVE NOW, BROTHER SUIRO!

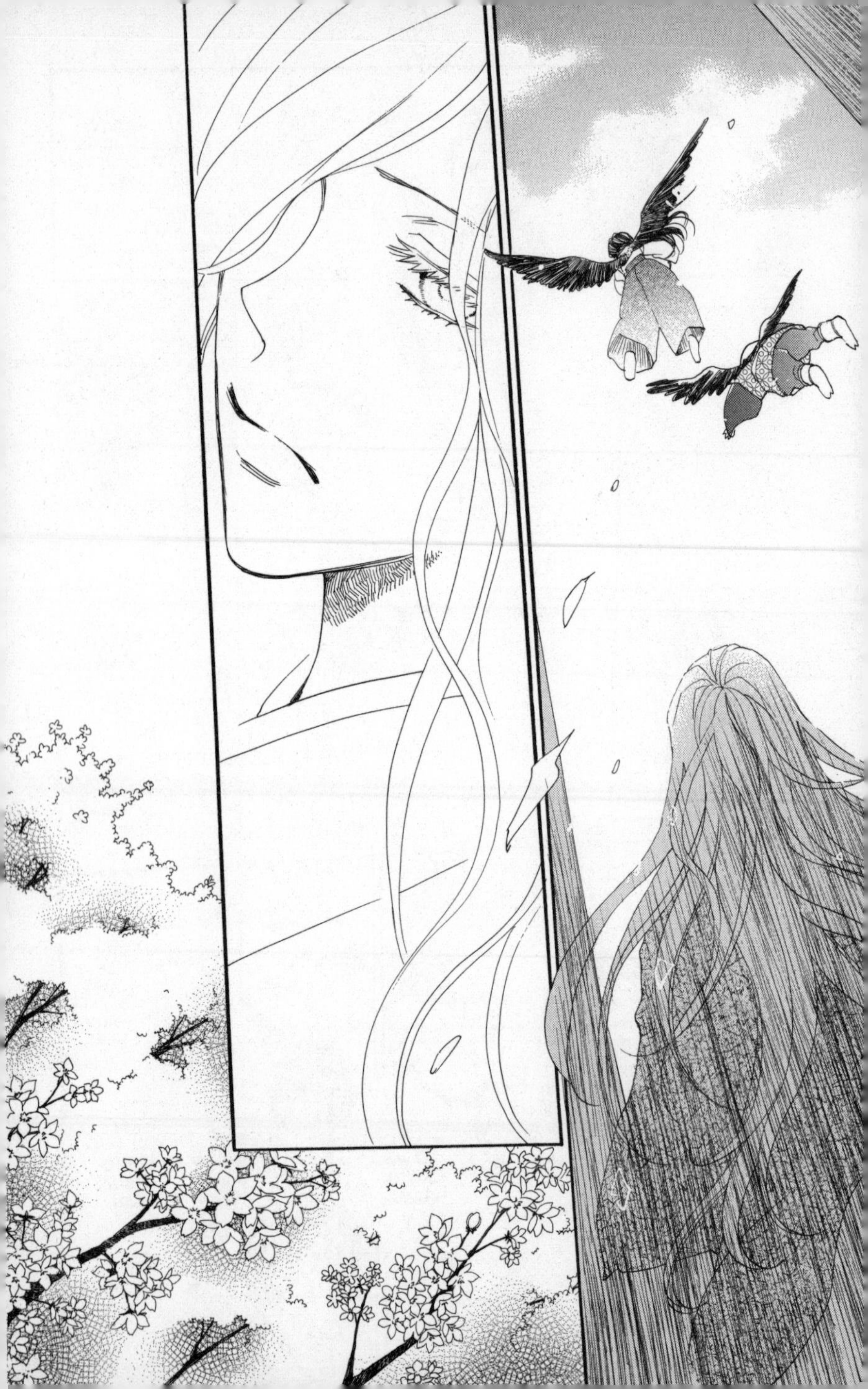

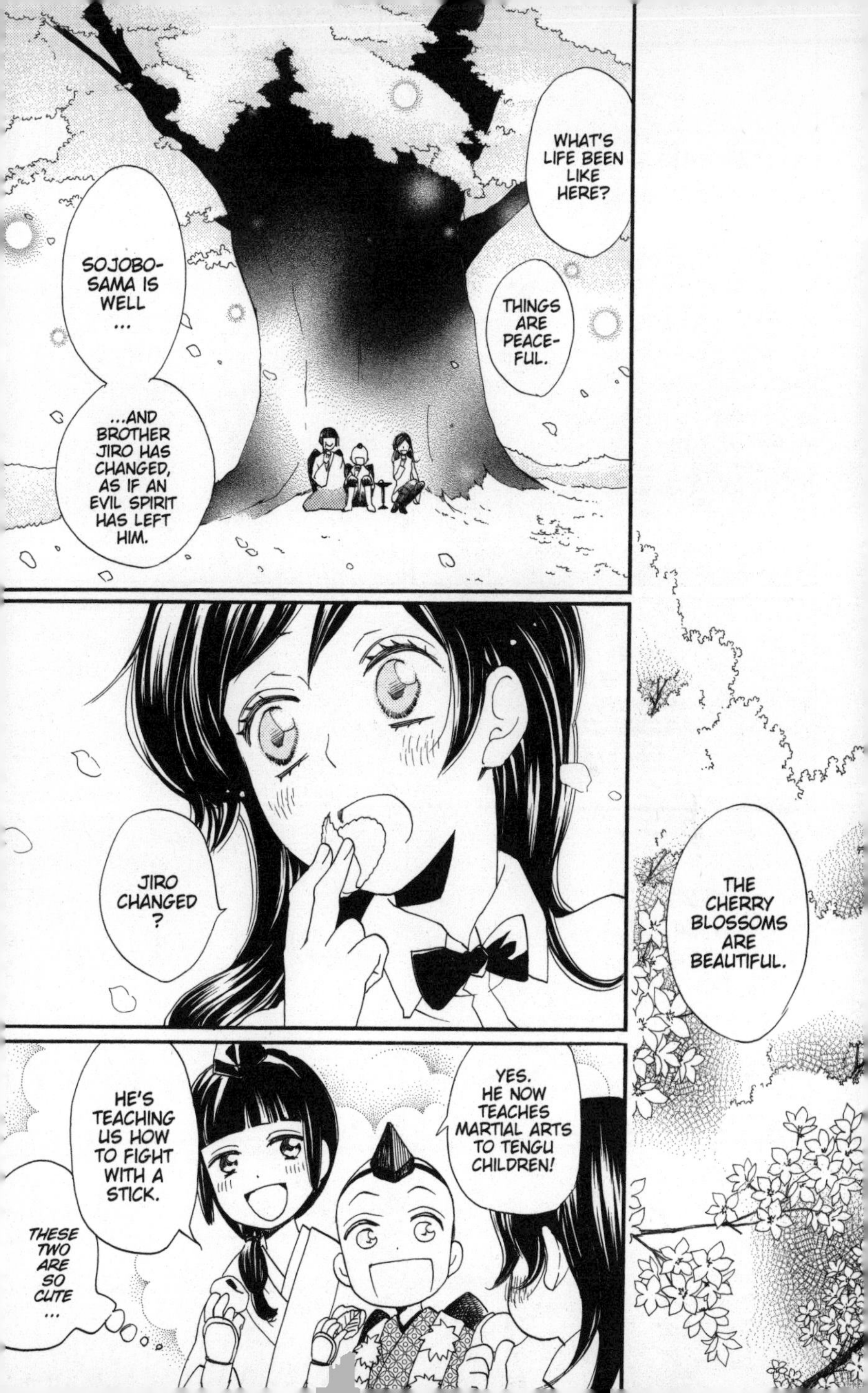
THE CHERRY BLOSSOMS ARE BEAUTIFUL.
WHAT'S LIFE BEEN LIKE HERE?
THINGS ARE PEACE-FUL.
SOJOBO-SAMA IS WELL...
...AND BROTHER JIRO HAS CHANGED, AS IF AN EVIL SPIRIT HAS LEFT HIM.
JIRO CHANGED?
YES. HE NOW TEACHES MARTIAL ARTS TO TENGU CHILDREN!
HE'S TEACHING US HOW TO FIGHT WITH A STICK.
THESE TWO ARE SO CUTE...

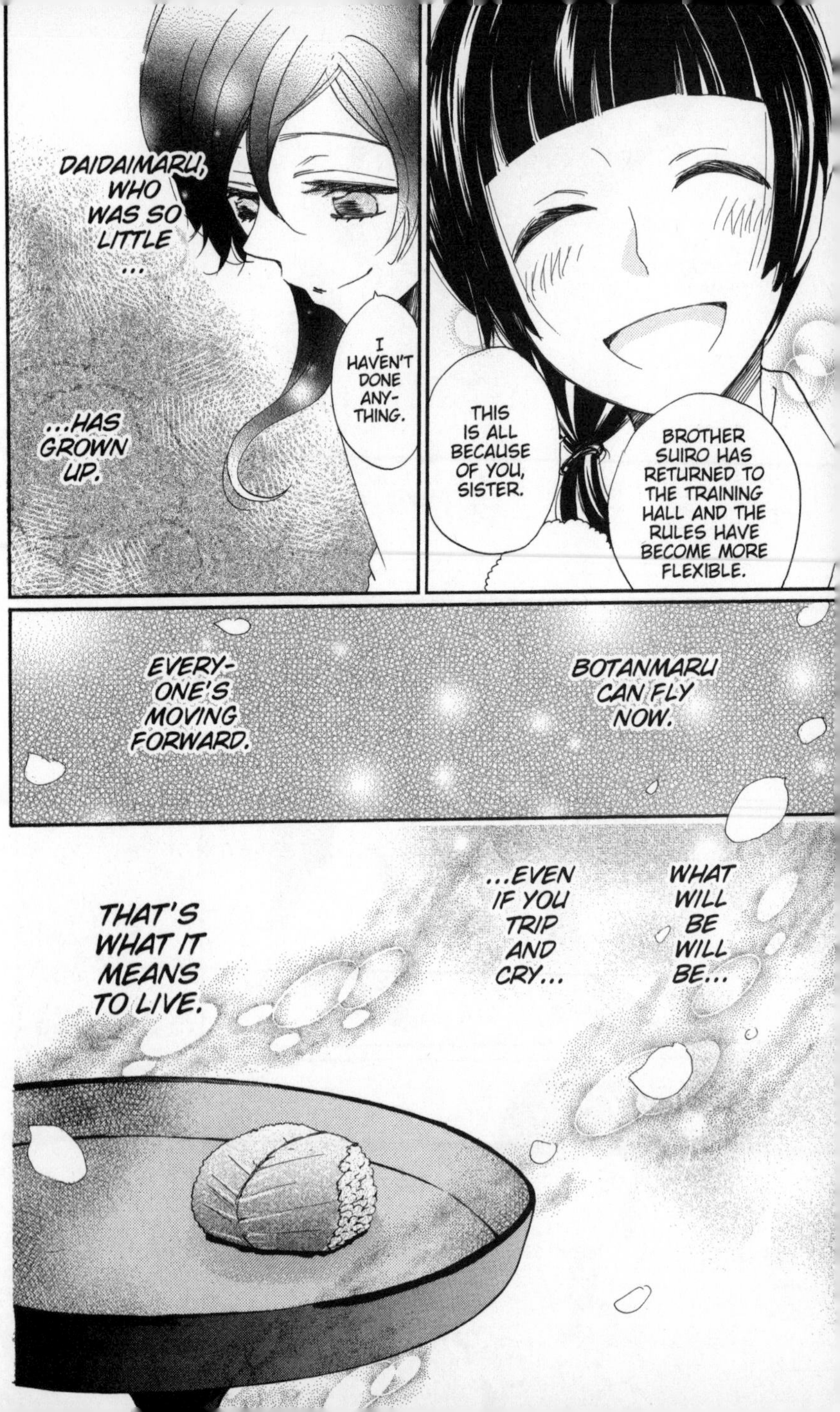
BROTHER SUIRO HAS RETURNED TO THE TRAINING HALL AND THE RULES HAVE BECOME MORE FLEXIBLE.
THIS IS ALL BECAUSE OF YOU, SISTER.
DAIDAIMARU, WHO WAS SO LITTLE ...
I HAVEN'T DONE ANY-THING.
...HAS GROWN UP.
BOTANMARU CAN FLY NOW.
EVERY-ONE'S MOVING FORWARD.
WHAT WILL BE WILL BE...
...EVEN IF YOU TRIP AND CRY...
THAT'S WHAT IT MEANS TO LIVE.

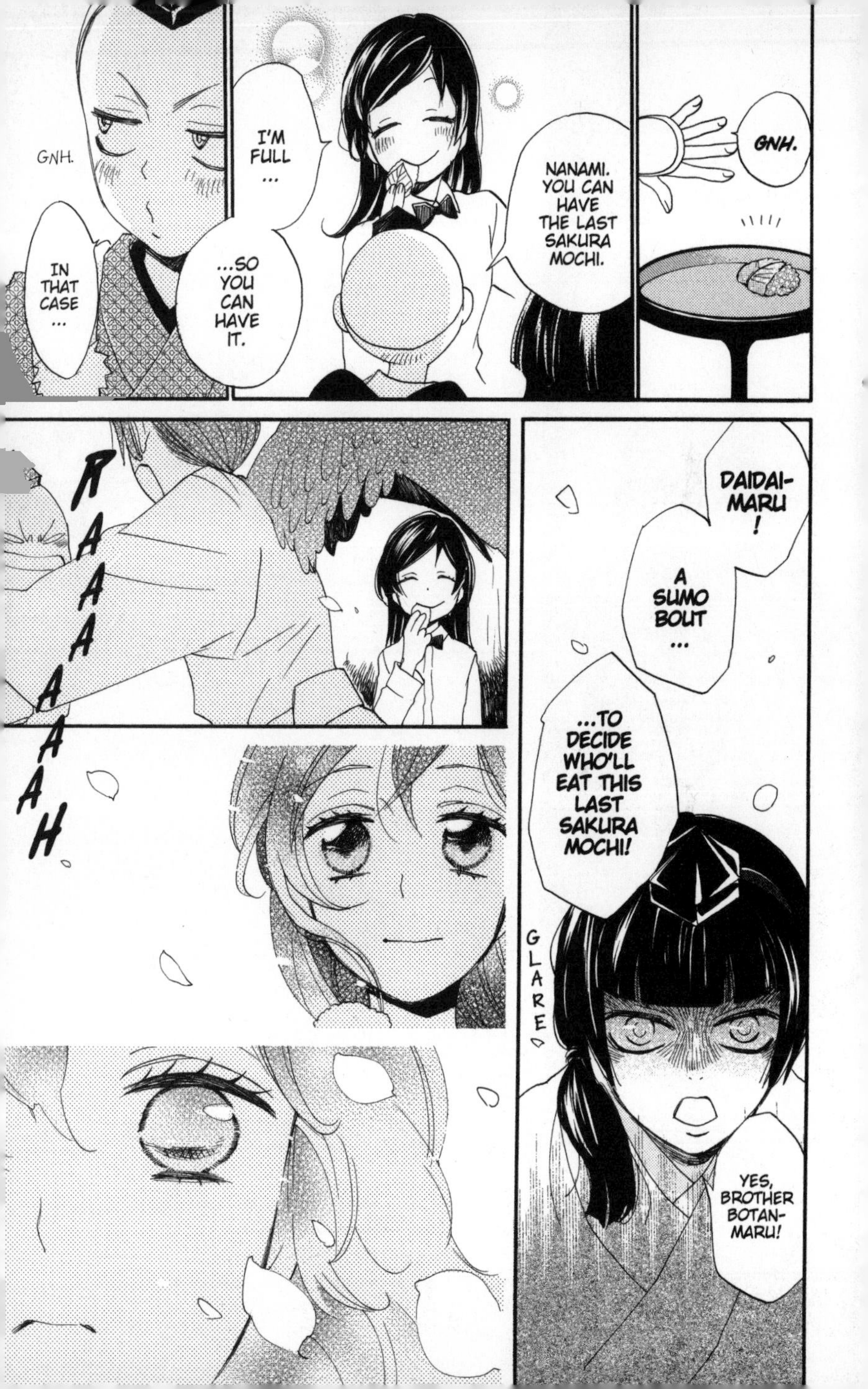

GNH.
NANAMI. YOU CAN HAVE THE LAST SAKURA MOCHI.
I'M FULL...
...SO YOU CAN HAVE IT.
GNH.
IN THAT CASE...
DAIDAI-MARU!
A SUMO BOUT...
...TO DECIDE WHO'LL EAT THIS LAST SAKURA MOCHI!
GLARE
YES, BROTHER BOTAN-MARU!
RAAAAAAAH.

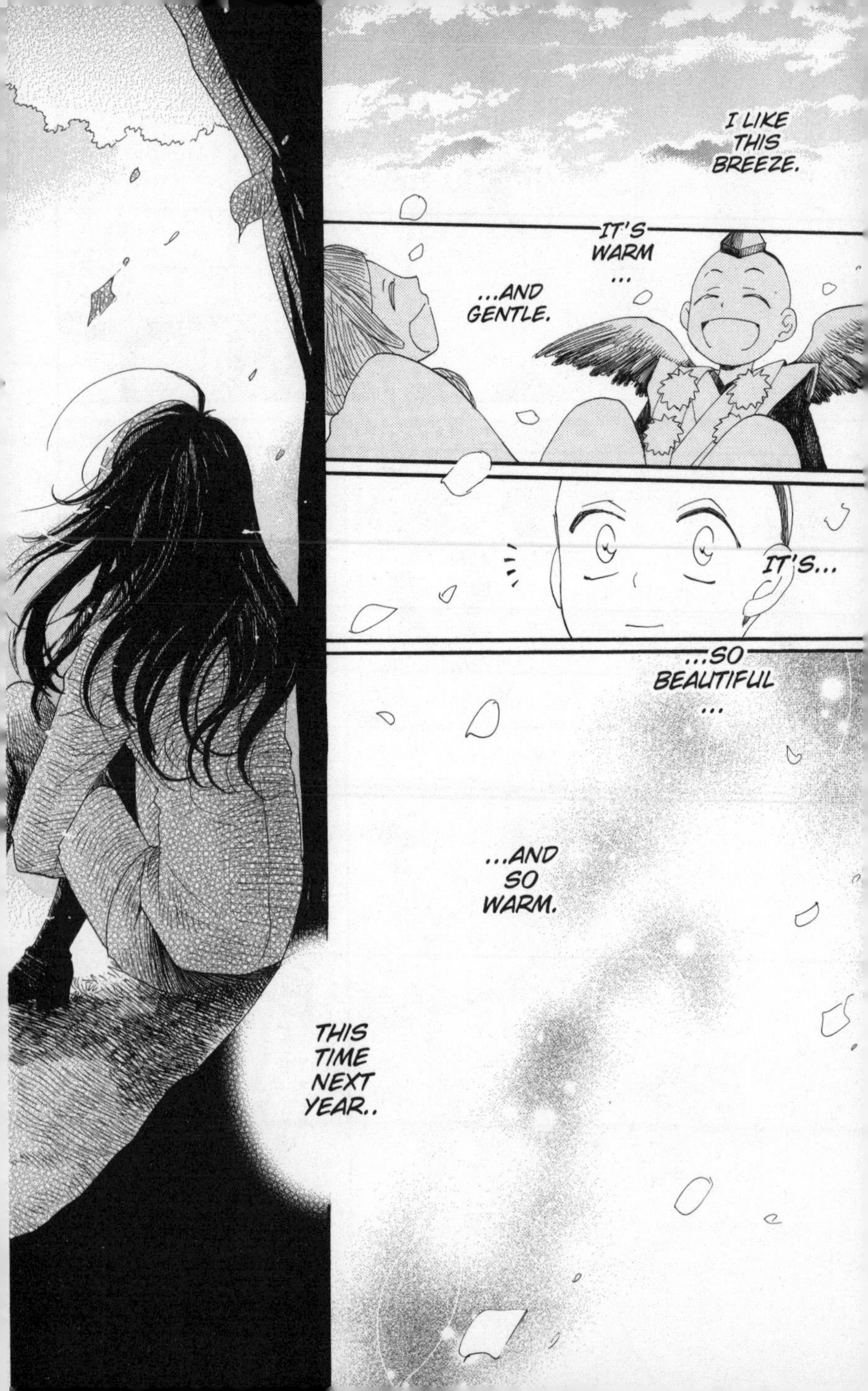
I LIKE THIS BREEZE.
IT'S WARM ...
...AND GENTLE.
IT'S...
...SO BEAUTIFUL ...
...AND SO WARM.
THIS TIME NEXT YEAR..

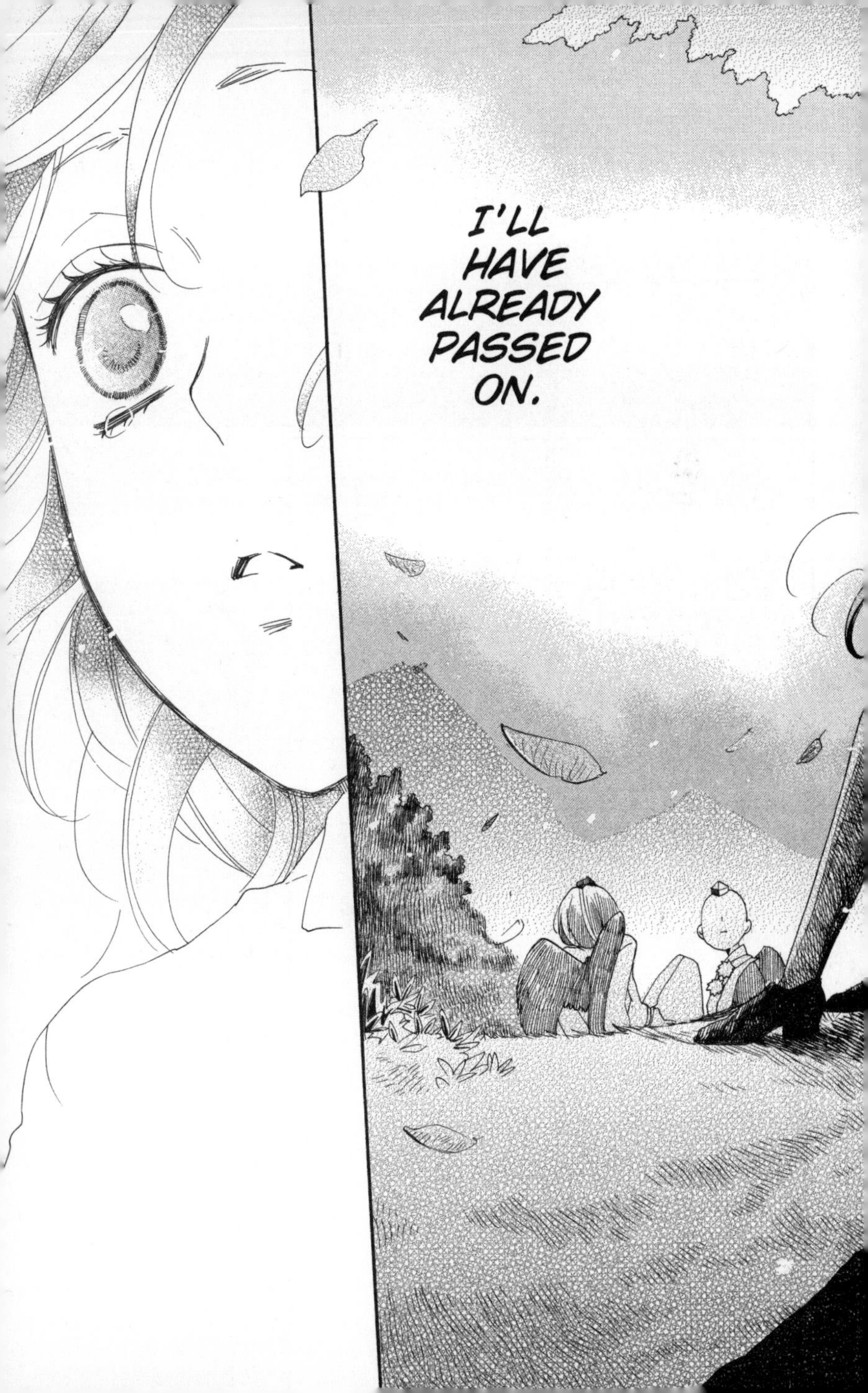
I'LL HAVE ALREADY PASSED ON.

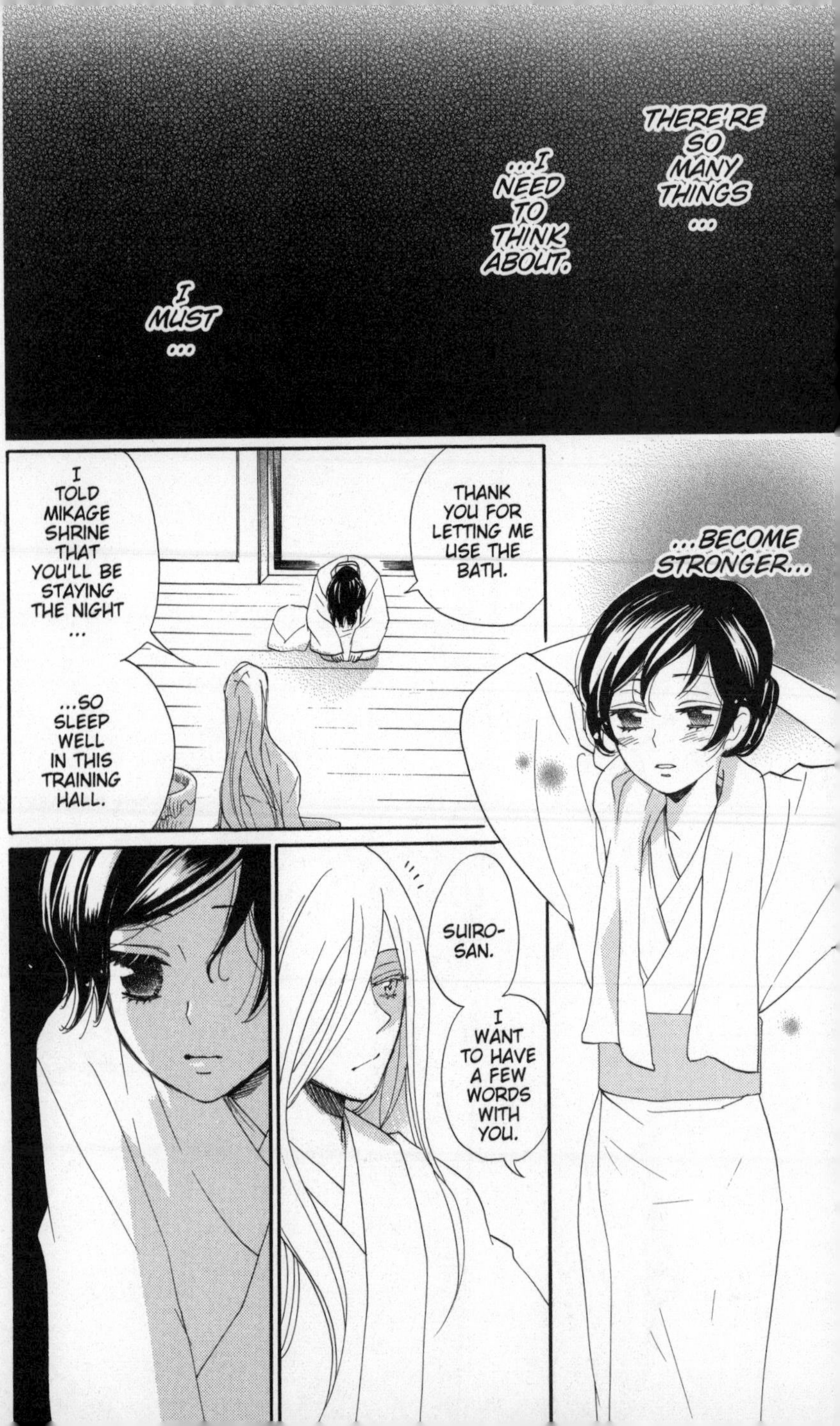
THERE'RE SO MANY THINGS...
...I NEED TO THINK ABOUT.
I MUST...
...BECOME STRONGER...
THANK YOU FOR LETTING ME USE THE BATH.
I TOLD MIKAGE SHRINE THAT YOU'LL BE STAYING THE NIGHT...
...SO SLEEP WELL IN THIS TRAINING HALL.
SUIRO-SAN.
I WANT TO HAVE A FEW WORDS WITH YOU.

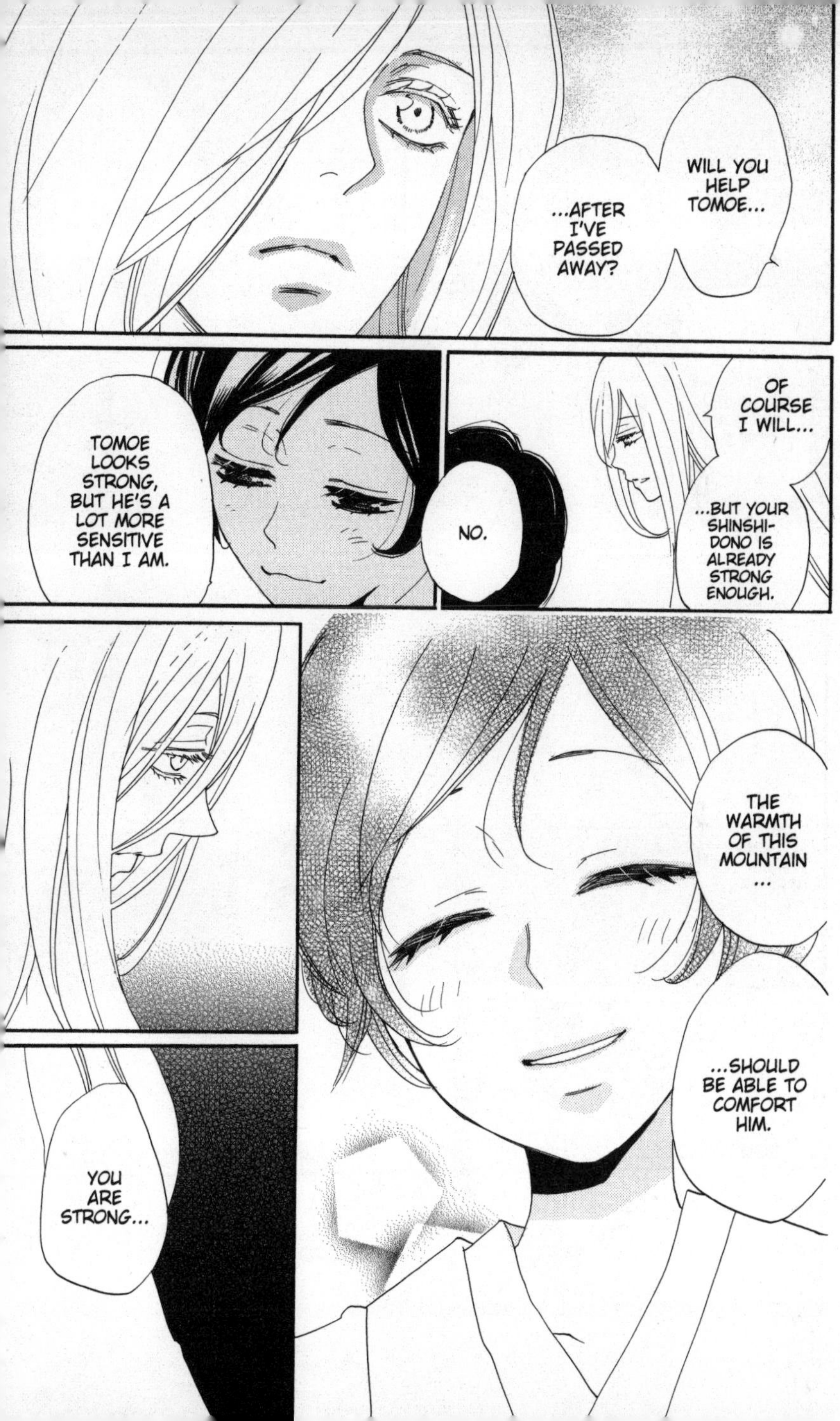
WILL YOU HELP TOMOE...
...AFTER I'VE PASSED AWAY?
OF COURSE I WILL...
...BUT YOUR SHINSHI-DONO IS ALREADY STRONG ENOUGH.
NO.
TOMOE LOOKS STRONG, BUT HE'S A LOT MORE SENSITIVE THAN I AM.
THE WARMTH OF THIS MOUNTAIN...
...SHOULD BE ABLE TO COMFORT HIM.
YOU ARE STRONG...

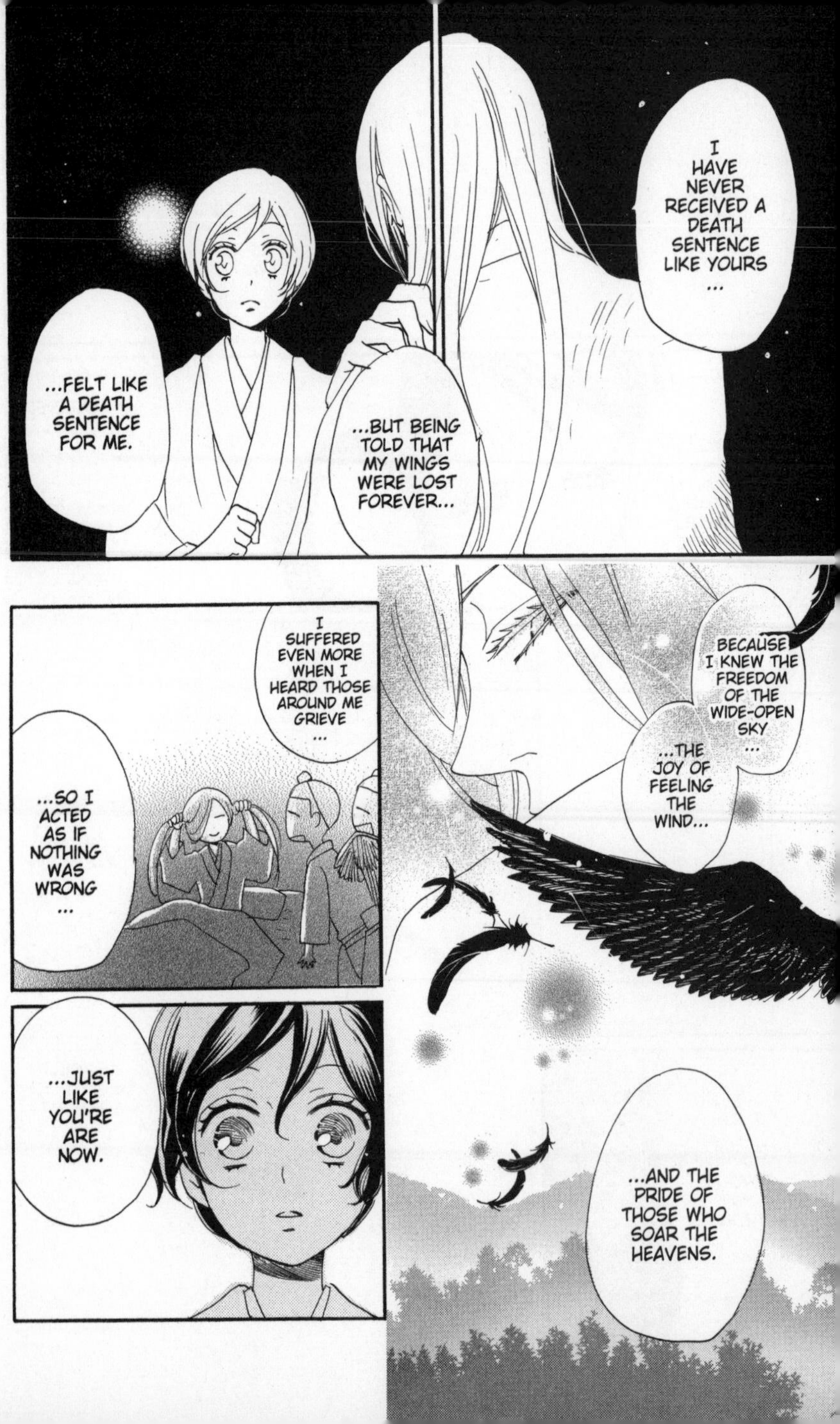
I HAVE NEVER RECEIVED A DEATH SENTENCE LIKE YOURS ...
...BUT BEING TOLD THAT MY WINGS WERE LOST FOREVER...
...FELT LIKE A DEATH SENTENCE FOR ME.
BECAUSE I KNEW THE FREEDOM OF THE WIDE-OPEN SKY ...
...THE JOY OF FEELING THE WIND...
...AND THE PRIDE OF THOSE WHO SOAR THE HEAVENS.
I SUFFERED EVEN MORE WHEN I HEARD THOSE AROUND ME GRIEVE ...
...SO I ACTED AS IF NOTHING WAS WRONG ...
...JUST LIKE YOU'RE ARE NOW.

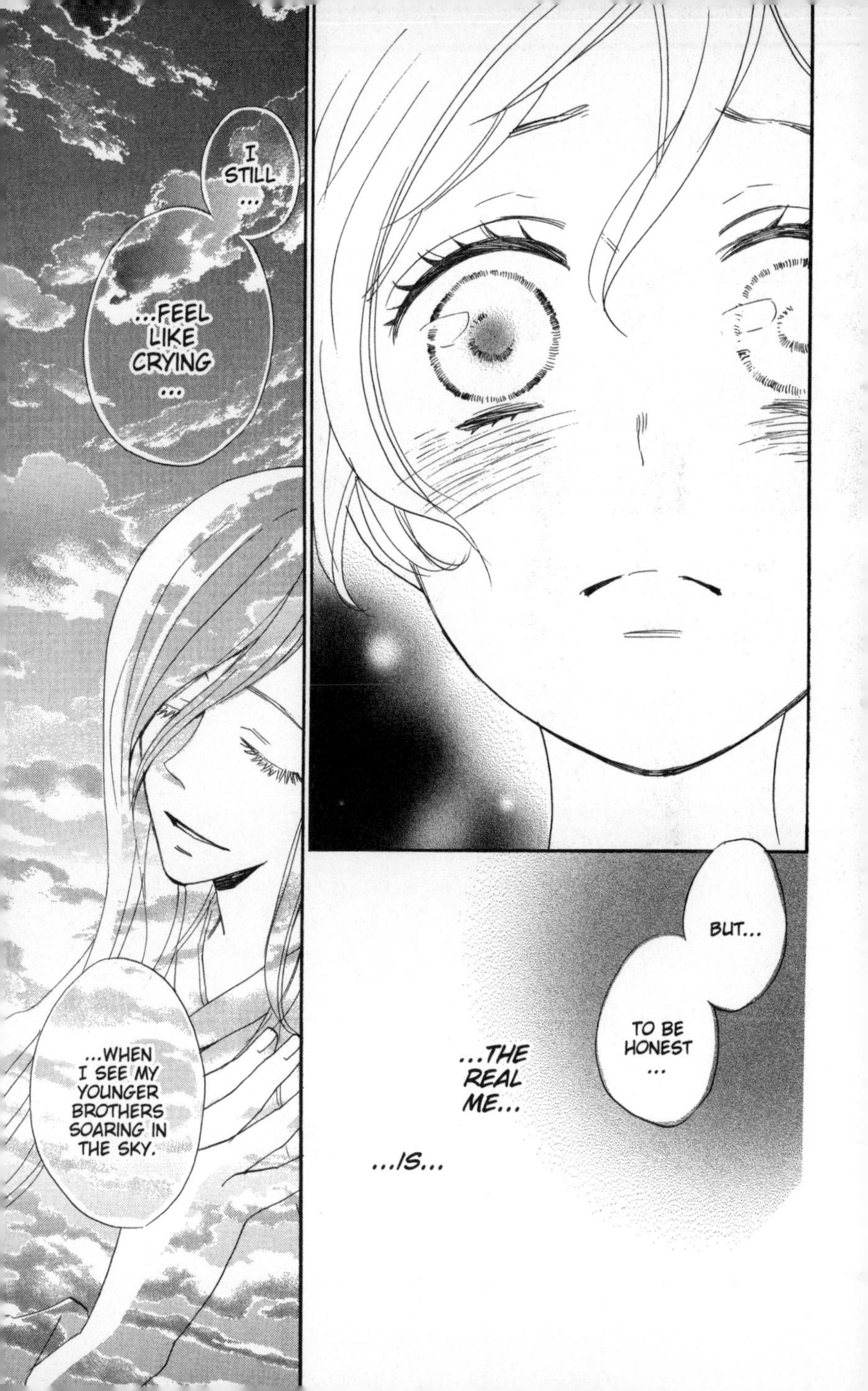
BUT...
TO BE HONEST ...
...THE REAL ME...
...IS...
I STILL ...
...FEEL LIKE CRYING ...
...WHEN I SEE MY YOUNGER BROTHERS SOARING IN THE SKY.

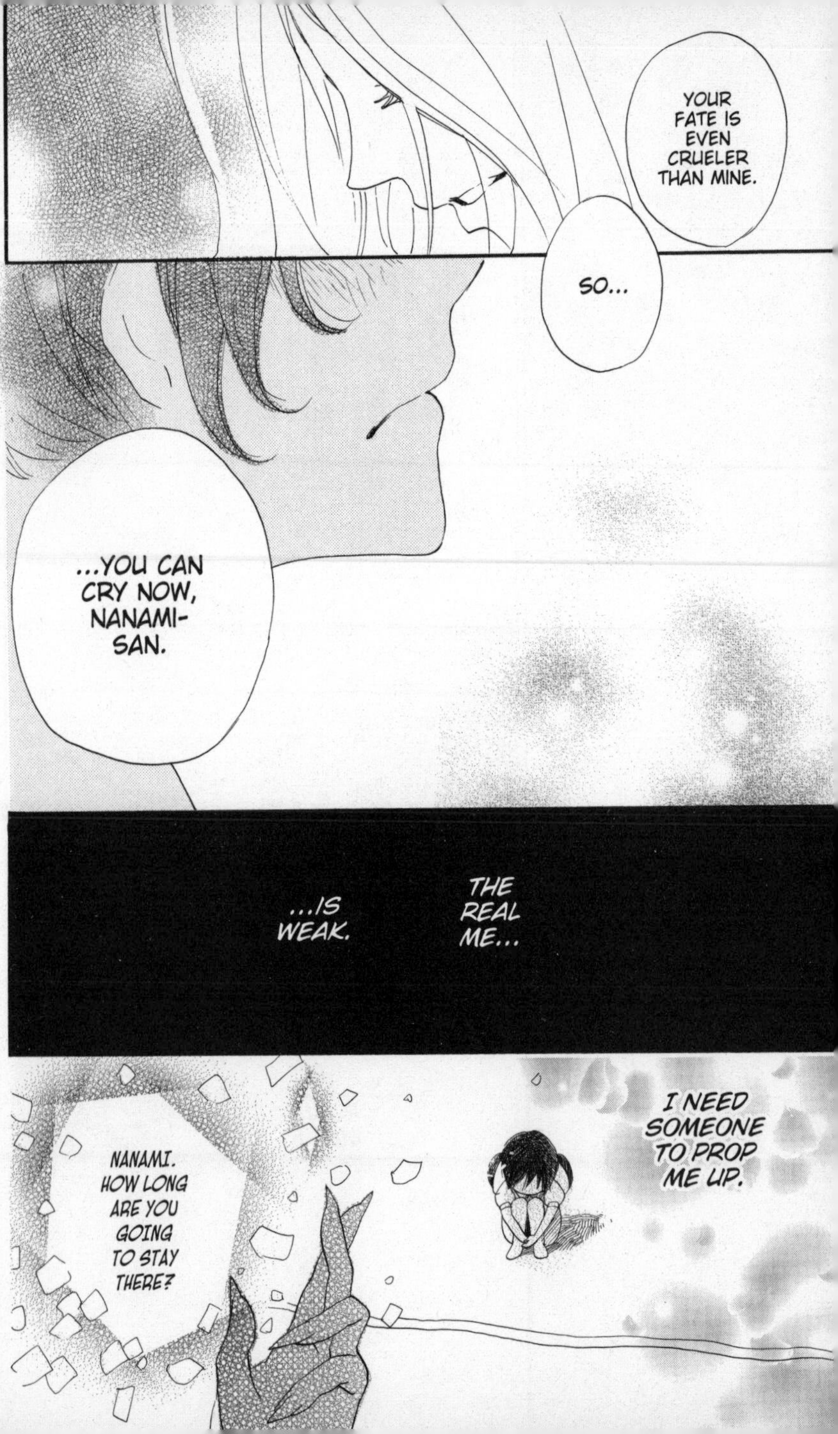
YOUR FATE IS EVEN CRUELER THAN MINE.
SO...
...YOU CAN CRY NOW, NANAMI-SAN.
THE REAL ME...
...IS WEAK.
I NEED SOMEONE TO PROP ME UP.
NANAMI. HOW LONG ARE YOU GOING TO STAY THERE?

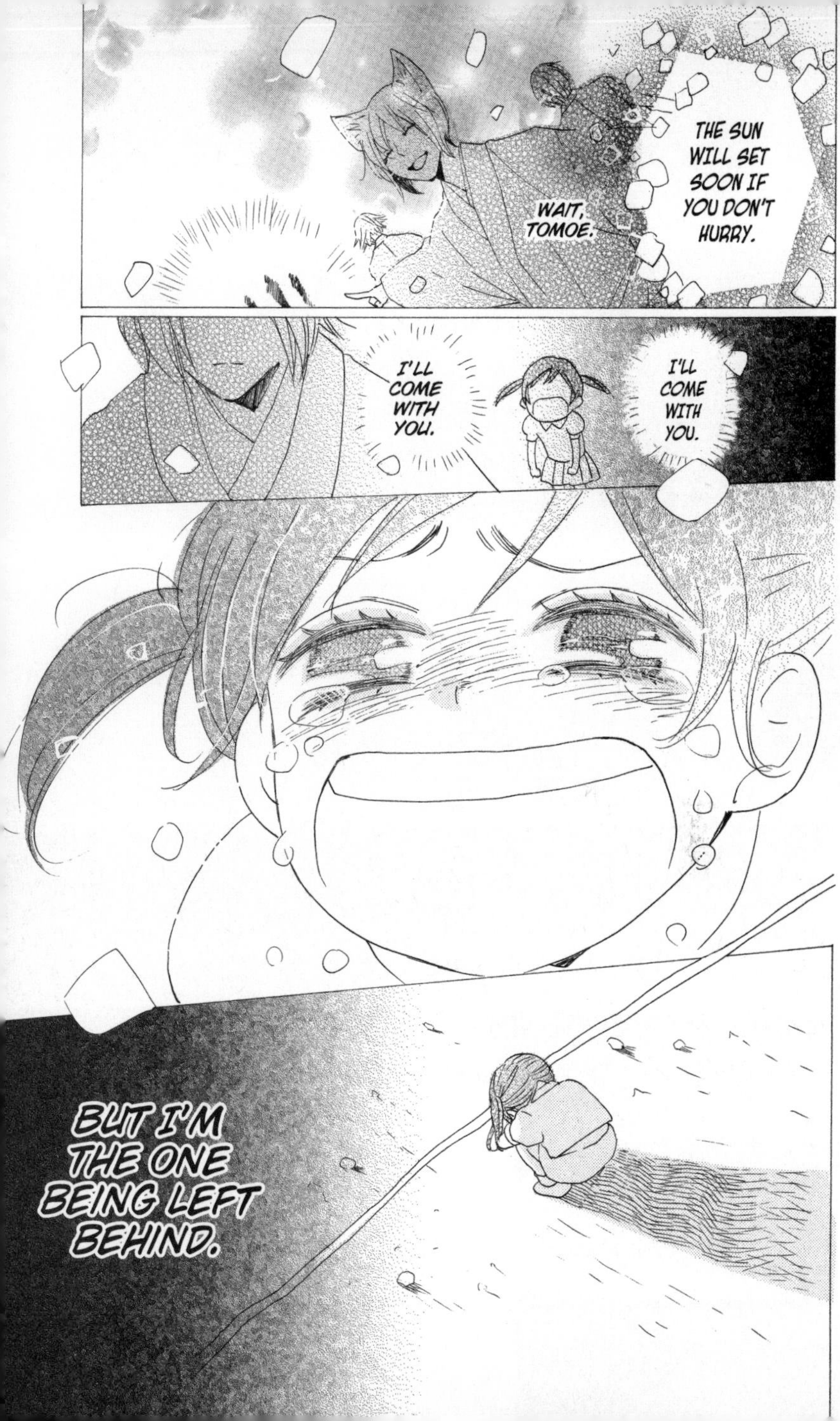
THE SUN WILL SET SOON IF YOU DON'T HURRY.
WAIT, TOMOE.
I'LL COME WITH YOU.
I'LL COME WITH YOU.
BUT I'M THE ONE BEING LEFT BEHIND.

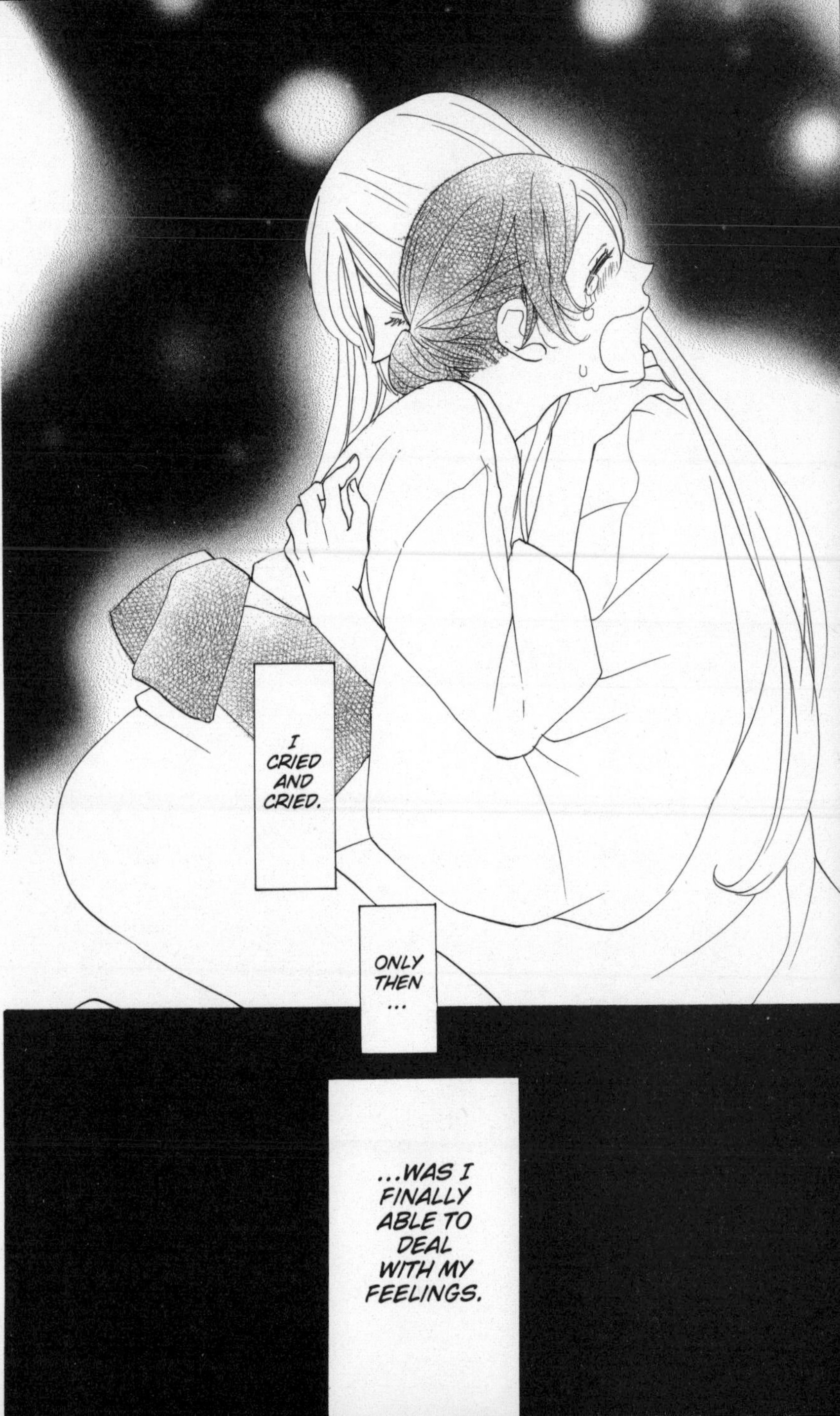
I CRIED AND CRIED.
ONLY THEN ...
...WAS I FINALLY ABLE TO DEAL WITH MY FEELINGS.

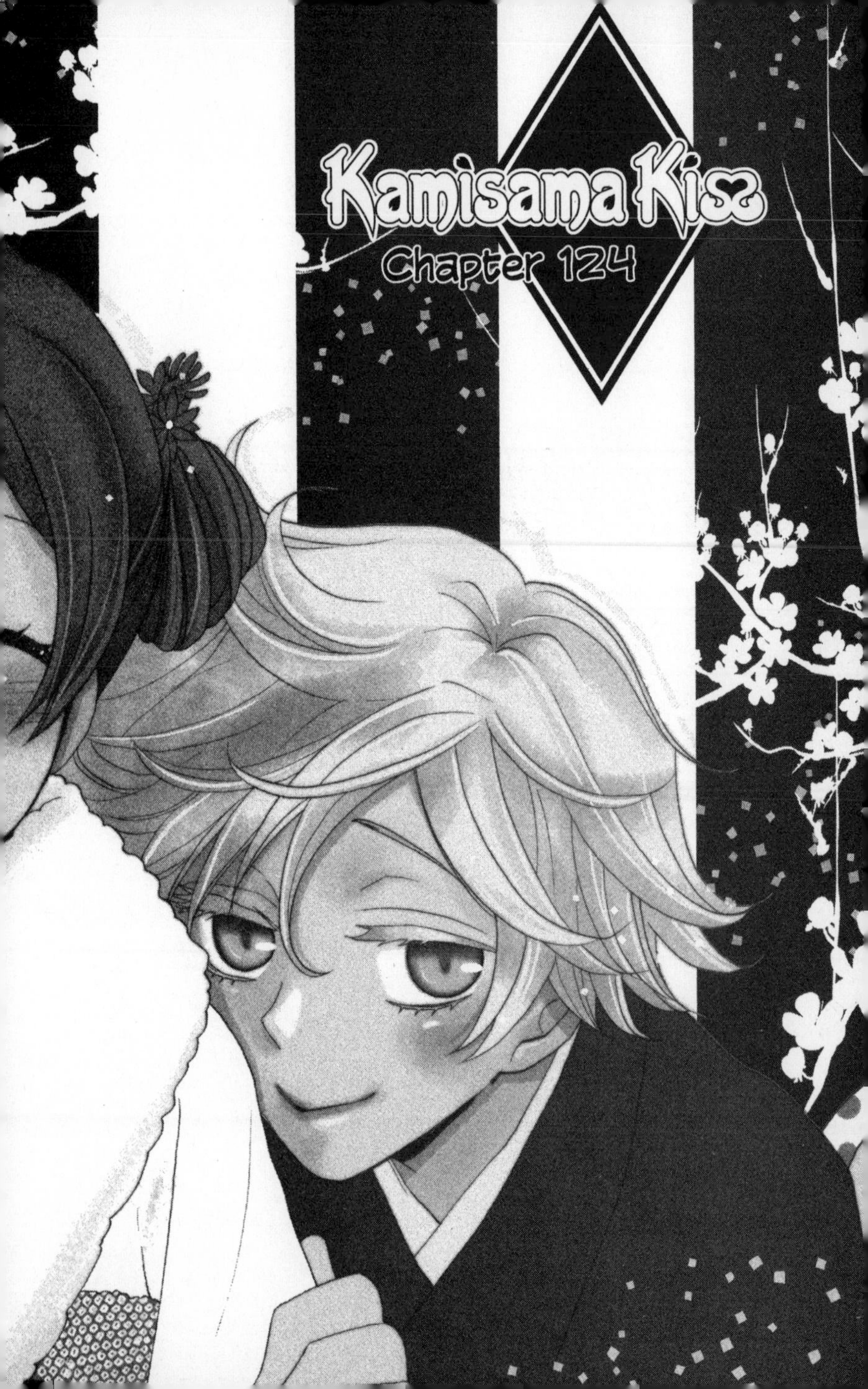
Kamisama Kiss
Chapter 124

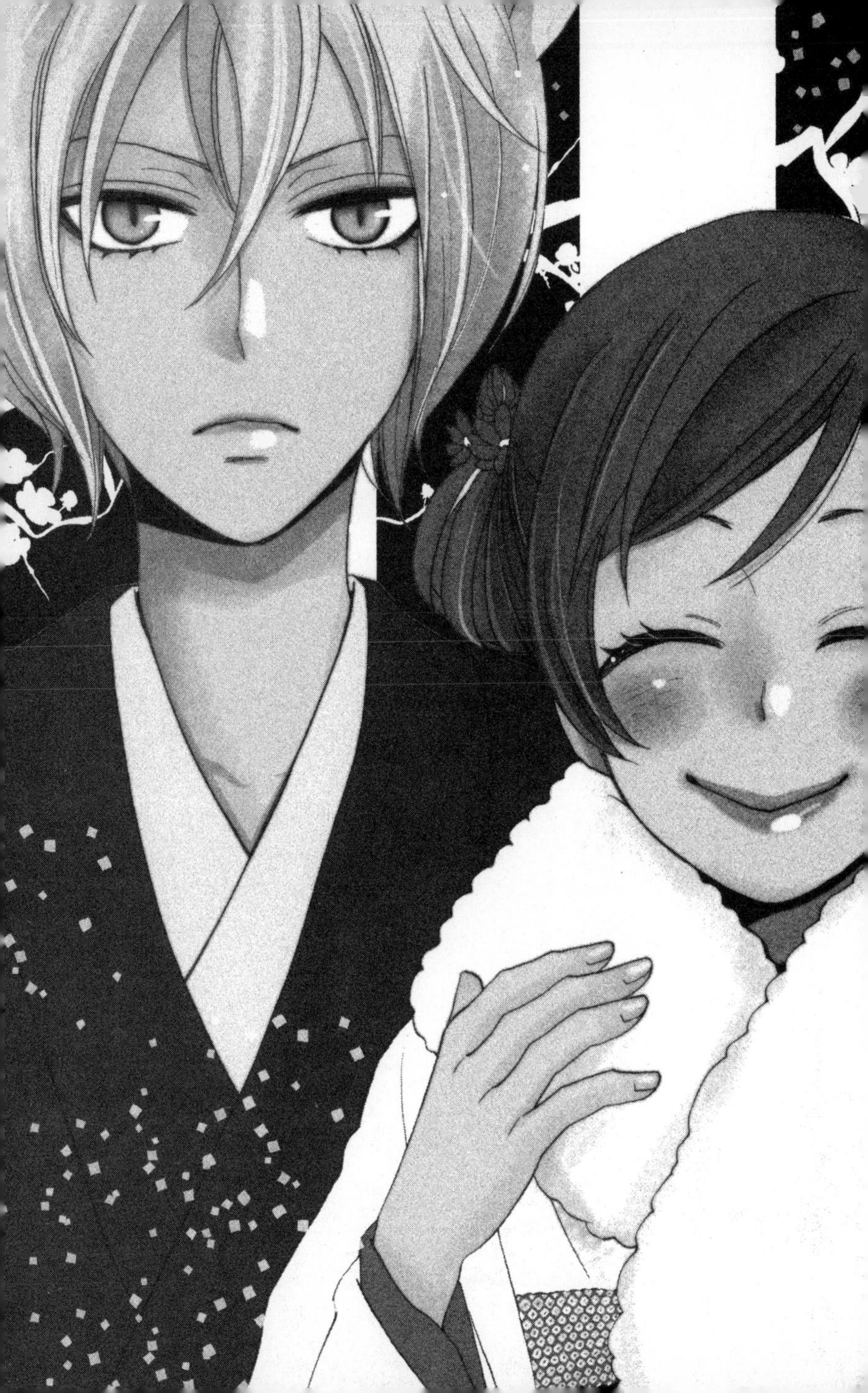

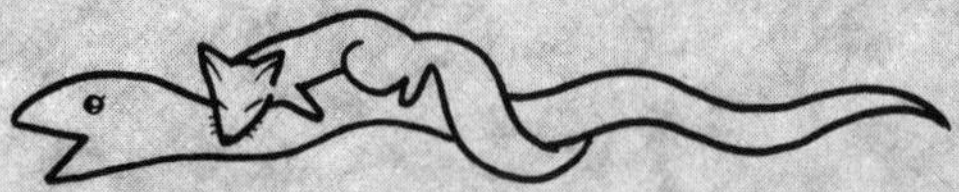

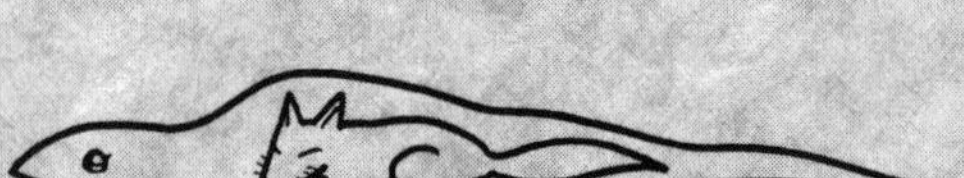

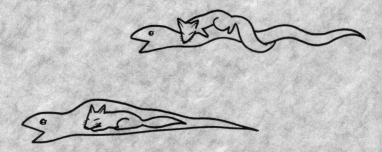

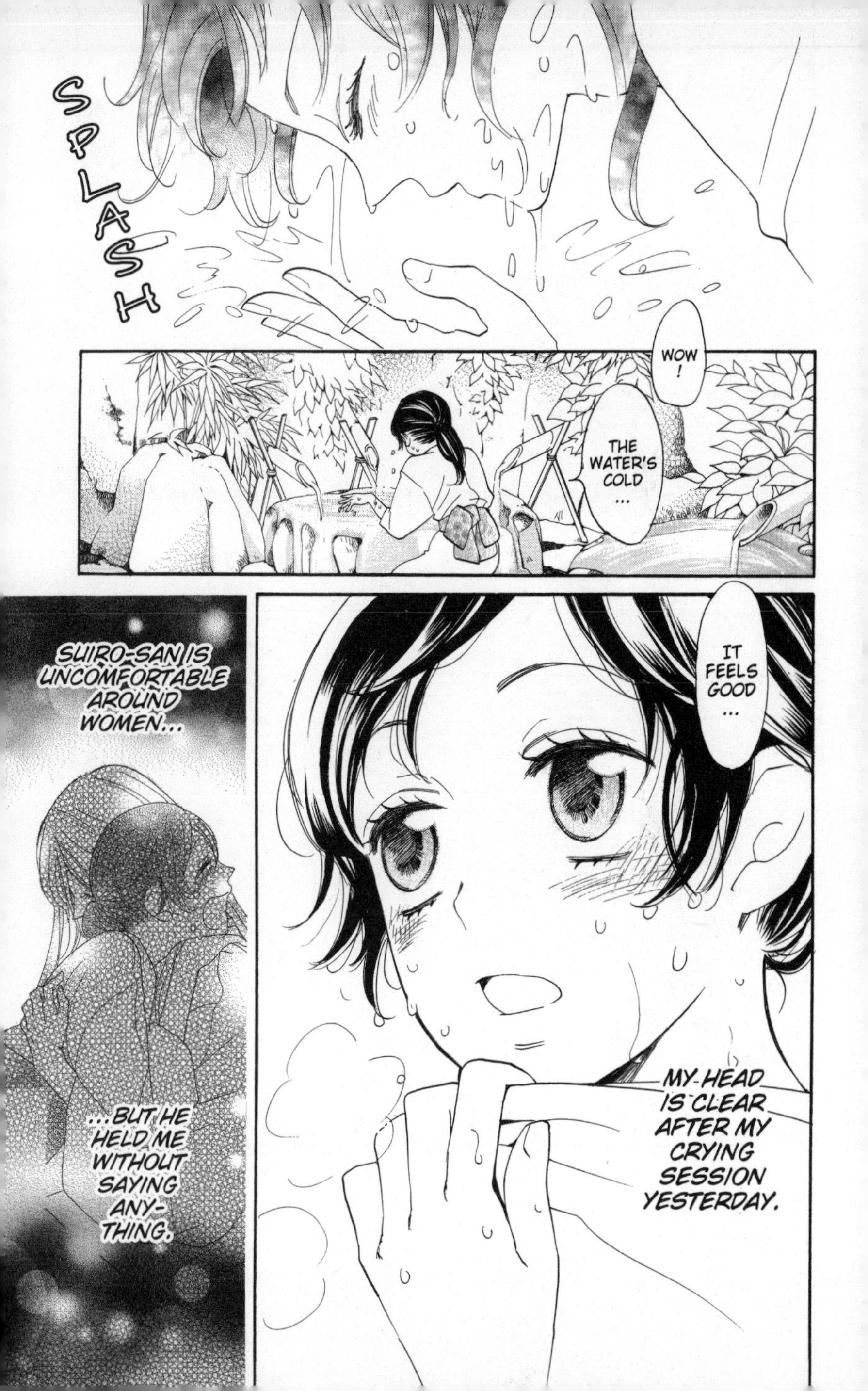
SPLASH
WOW!
THE WATER'S COLD...
IT FEELS GOOD...
MY HEAD IS CLEAR AFTER MY CRYING SESSION YESTERDAY.
SUIRO-SAN IS UNCOMFORTABLE AROUND WOMEN...
...BUT HE HELD ME WITHOUT SAYING ANY-THING.

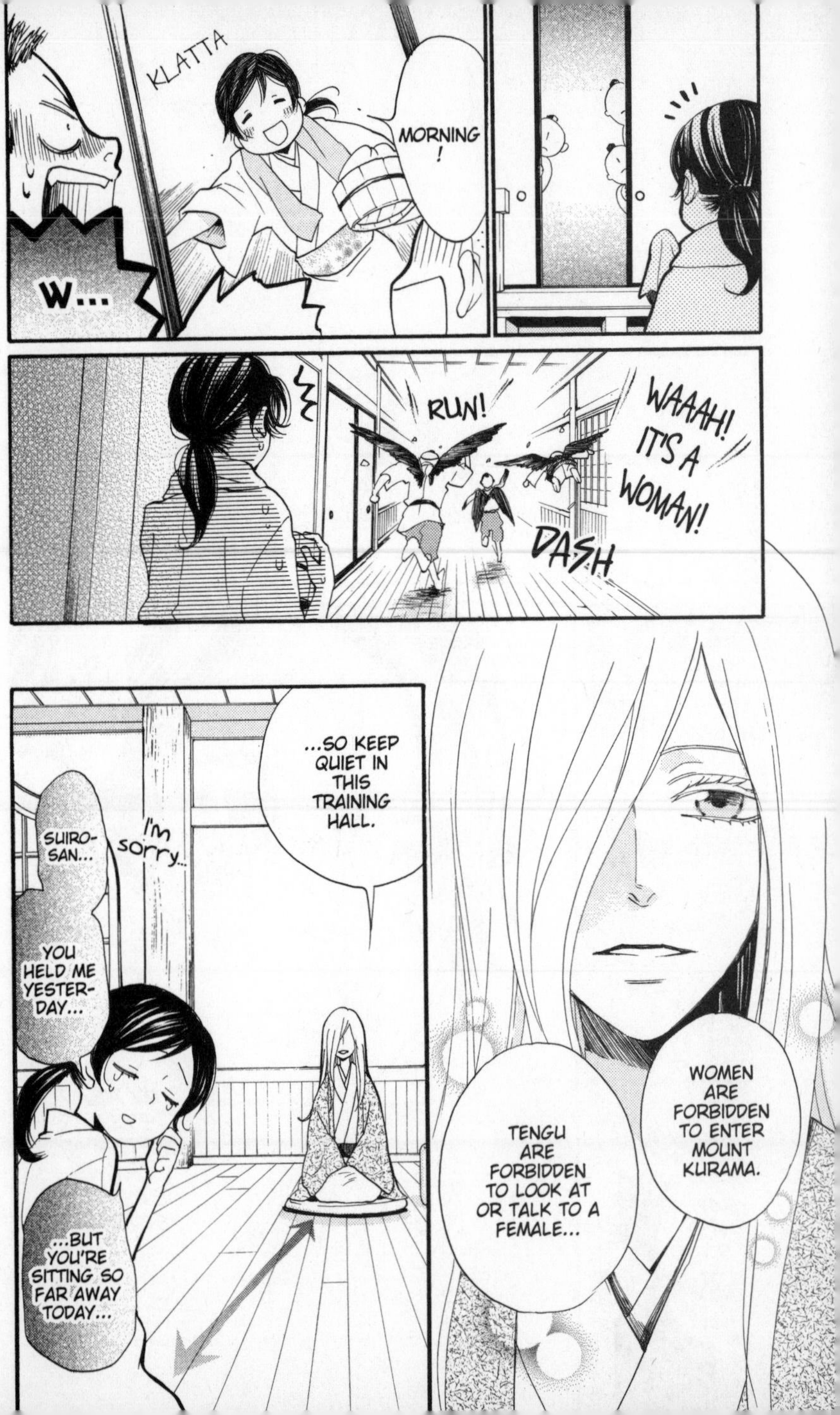
MORNING!
KLATTA
W...
WAAAH! IT'S A WOMAN!
RUN!
DASH
WOMEN ARE FORBIDDEN TO ENTER MOUNT KURAMA.
TENGU ARE FORBIDDEN TO LOOK AT OR TALK TO A FEMALE...
...SO KEEP QUIET IN THIS TRAINING HALL.
I'm sorry...
SUIRO-SAN...
YOU HELD ME YESTERDAY...
...BUT YOU'RE SITTING SO FAR AWAY TODAY...

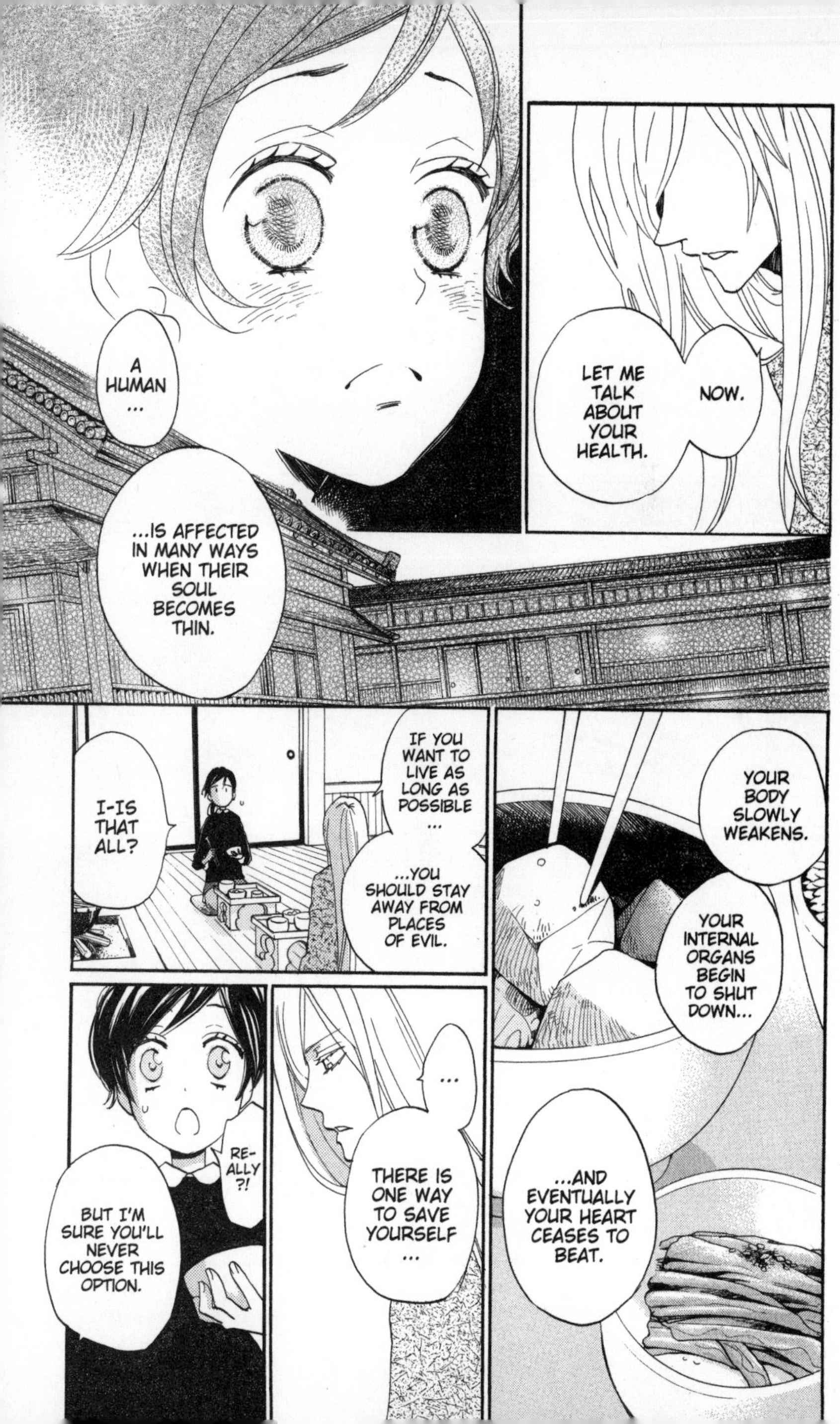
NOW.
LET ME TALK ABOUT YOUR HEALTH.
A HUMAN ...
...IS AFFECTED IN MANY WAYS WHEN THEIR SOUL BECOMES THIN.
YOUR BODY SLOWLY WEAKENS.
YOUR INTERNAL ORGANS BEGIN TO SHUT DOWN...
...AND EVENTUALLY YOUR HEART CEASES TO BEAT.
IF YOU WANT TO LIVE AS LONG AS POSSIBLE ...
...YOU SHOULD STAY AWAY FROM PLACES OF EVIL.
I-IS THAT ALL?
...
THERE IS ONE WAY TO SAVE YOURSELF ...
RE-ALLY?!
BUT I'M SURE YOU'LL NEVER CHOOSE THIS OPTION.

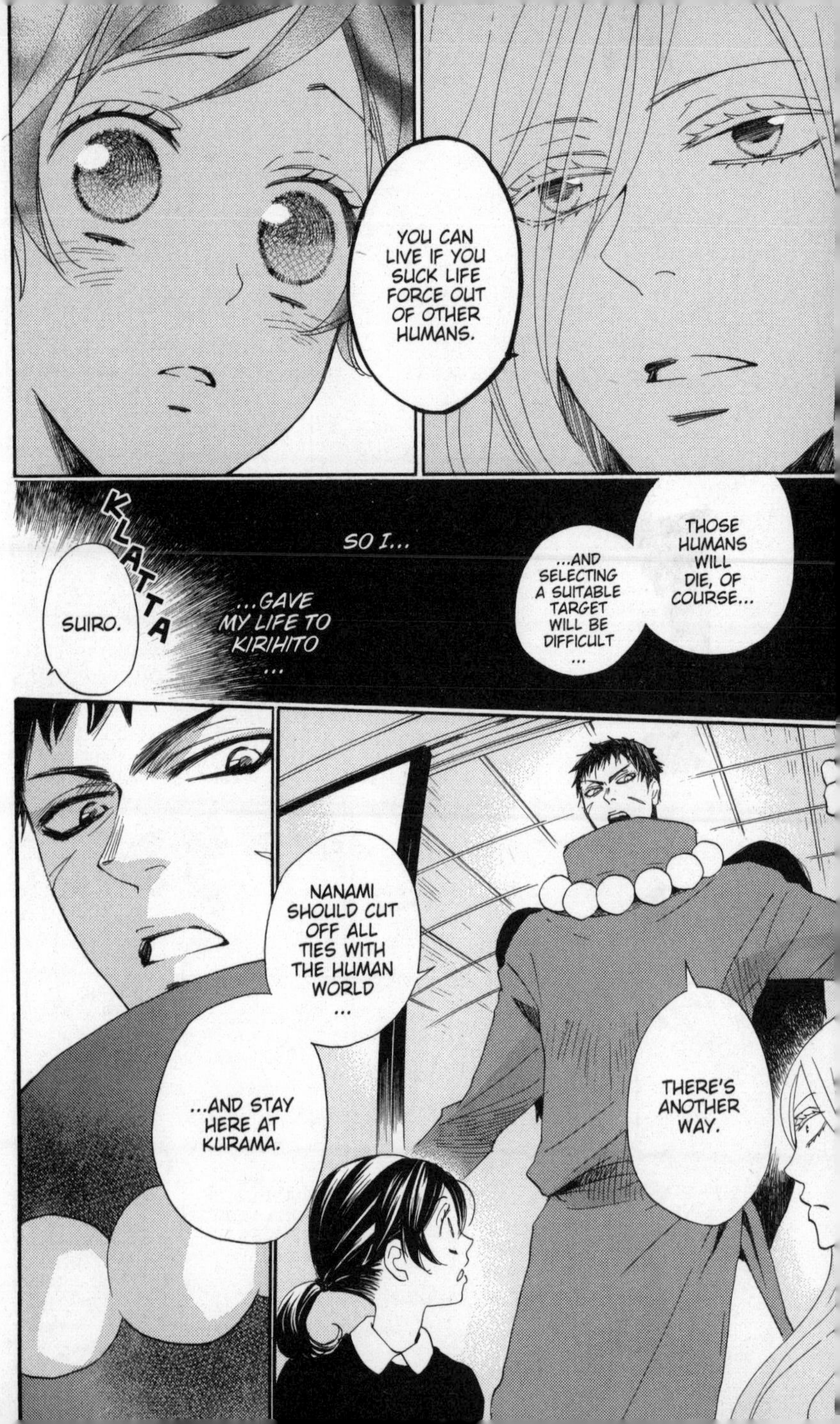
YOU CAN LIVE IF YOU SUCK LIFE FORCE OUT OF OTHER HUMANS.
THOSE HUMANS WILL DIE, OF COURSE...
...AND SELECTING A SUITABLE TARGET WILL BE DIFFICULT ...
SO I...
...GAVE MY LIFE TO KIRIHITO ...
KLATTA
SUIRO.
NANAMI SHOULD CUT OFF ALL TIES WITH THE HUMAN WORLD ...
...AND STAY HERE AT KURAMA.
THERE'S ANOTHER WAY.

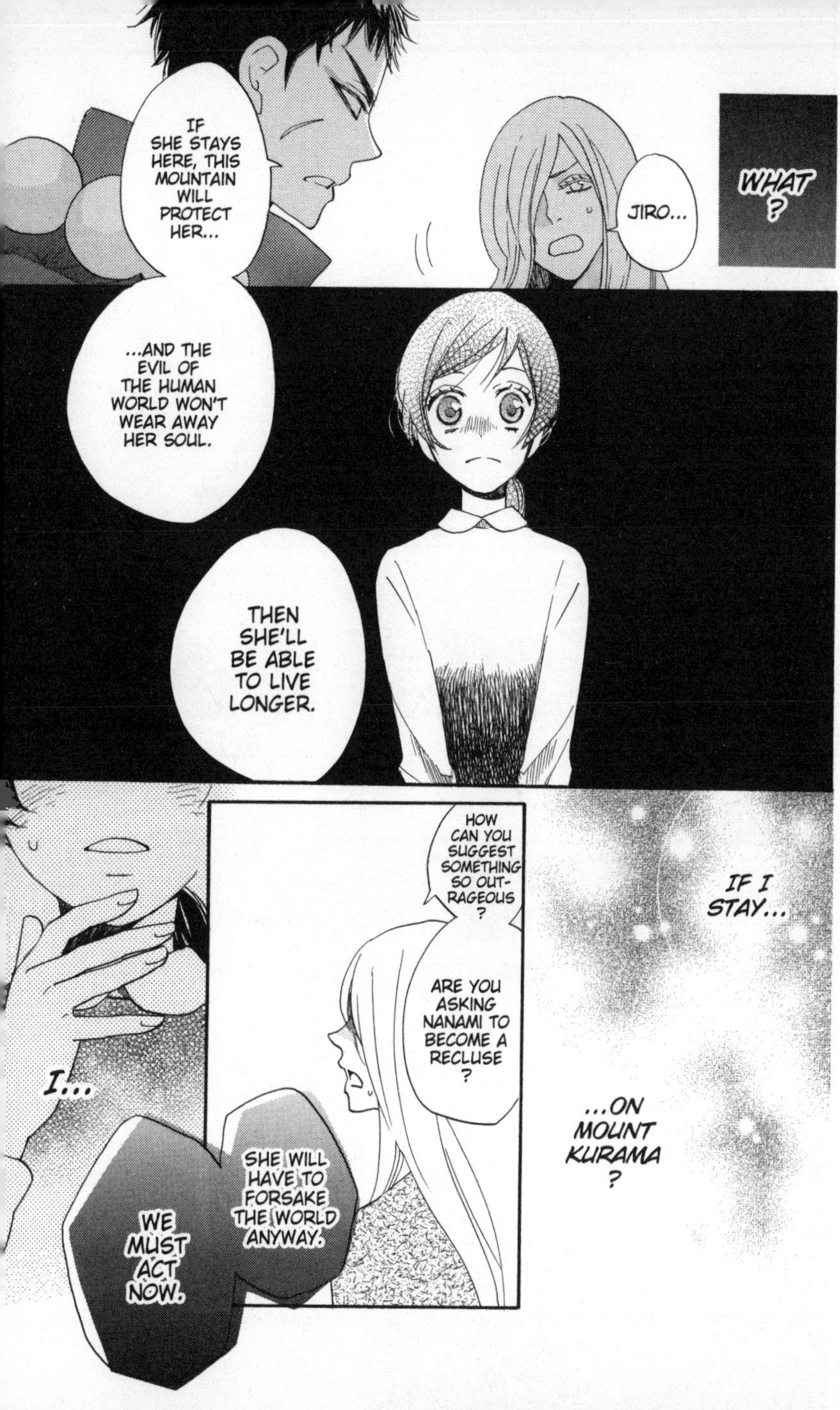
WHAT?
JIRO...
IF SHE STAYS HERE, THIS MOUNTAIN WILL PROTECT HER...
...AND THE EVIL OF THE HUMAN WORLD WON'T WEAR AWAY HER SOUL.
THEN SHE'LL BE ABLE TO LIVE LONGER.
IF I STAY...
...ON MOUNT KURAMA?
HOW CAN YOU SUGGEST SOMETHING SO OUTRAGEOUS?
ARE YOU ASKING NANAMI TO BECOME A RECLUSE?
SHE WILL HAVE TO FORSAKE THE WORLD ANYWAY.
WE MUST ACT NOW.
I...

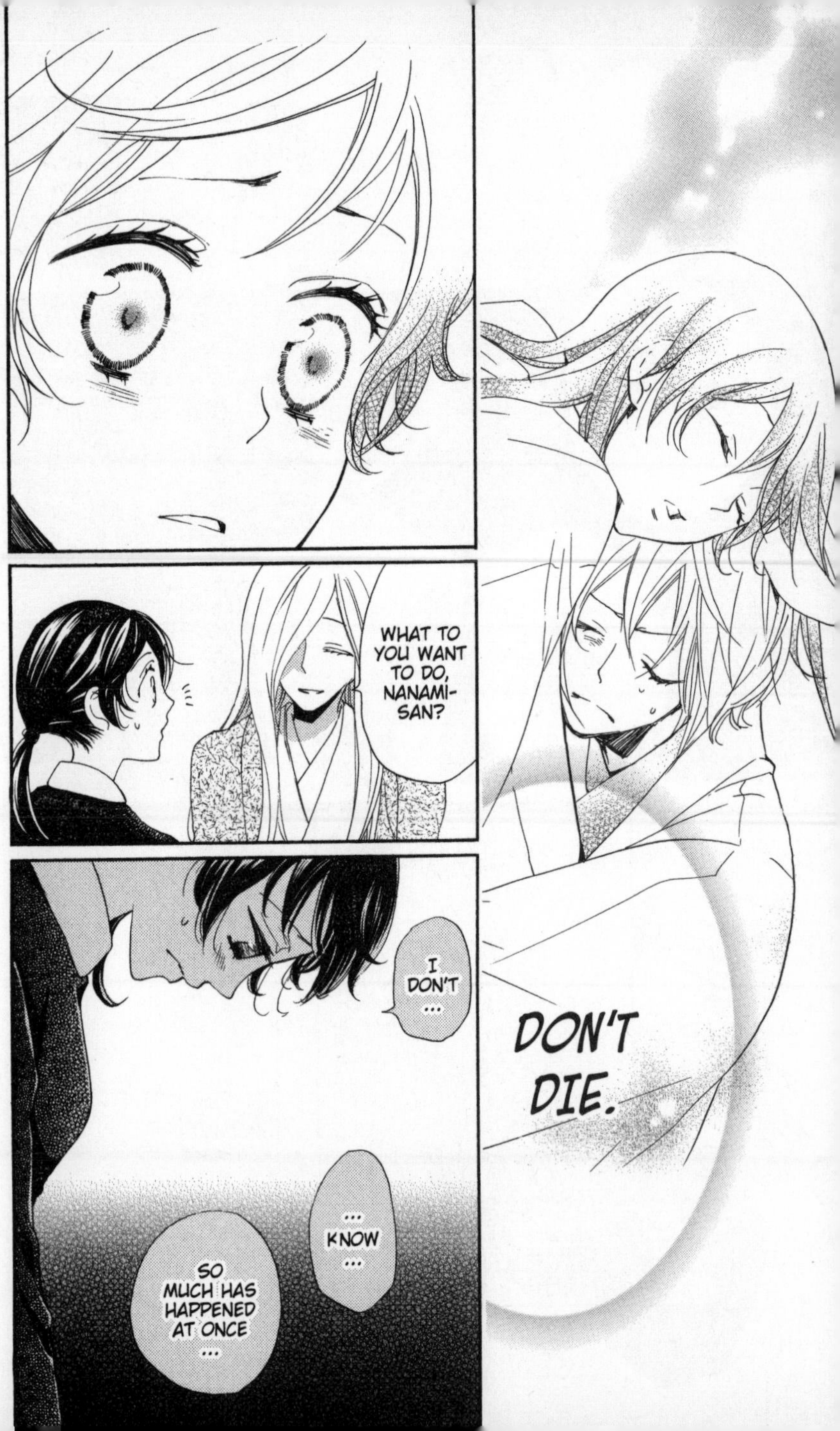
DON'T DIE.
WHAT TO YOU WANT TO DO, NANAMI-SAN?
I DON'T ...
... KNOW ...
SO MUCH HAS HAPPENED AT ONCE ...

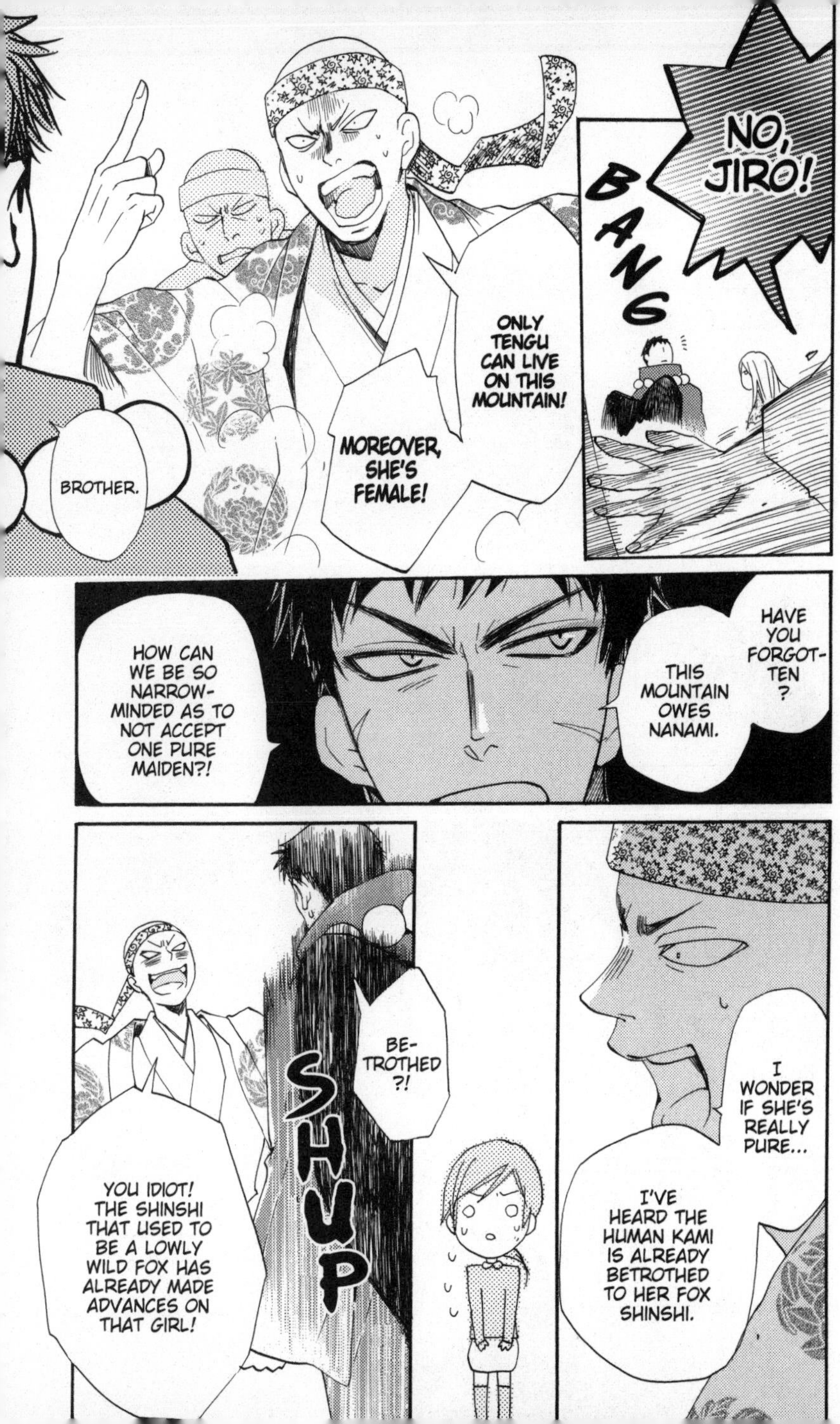
NO, JIRO!
BANG
ONLY TENGU CAN LIVE ON THIS MOUNTAIN!
MOREOVER, SHE'S FEMALE!
BROTHER.
HAVE YOU FORGOT-TEN?
THIS MOUNTAIN OWES NANAMI.
HOW CAN WE BE SO NARROW-MINDED AS TO NOT ACCEPT ONE PURE MAIDEN?!
I WONDER IF SHE'S REALLY PURE...
I'VE HEARD THE HUMAN KAMI IS ALREADY BETROTHED TO HER FOX SHINSHI.
BE-TROTHED?!
SHUP
YOU IDIOT! THE SHINSHI THAT USED TO BE A LOWLY WILD FOX HAS ALREADY MADE ADVANCES ON THAT GIRL!

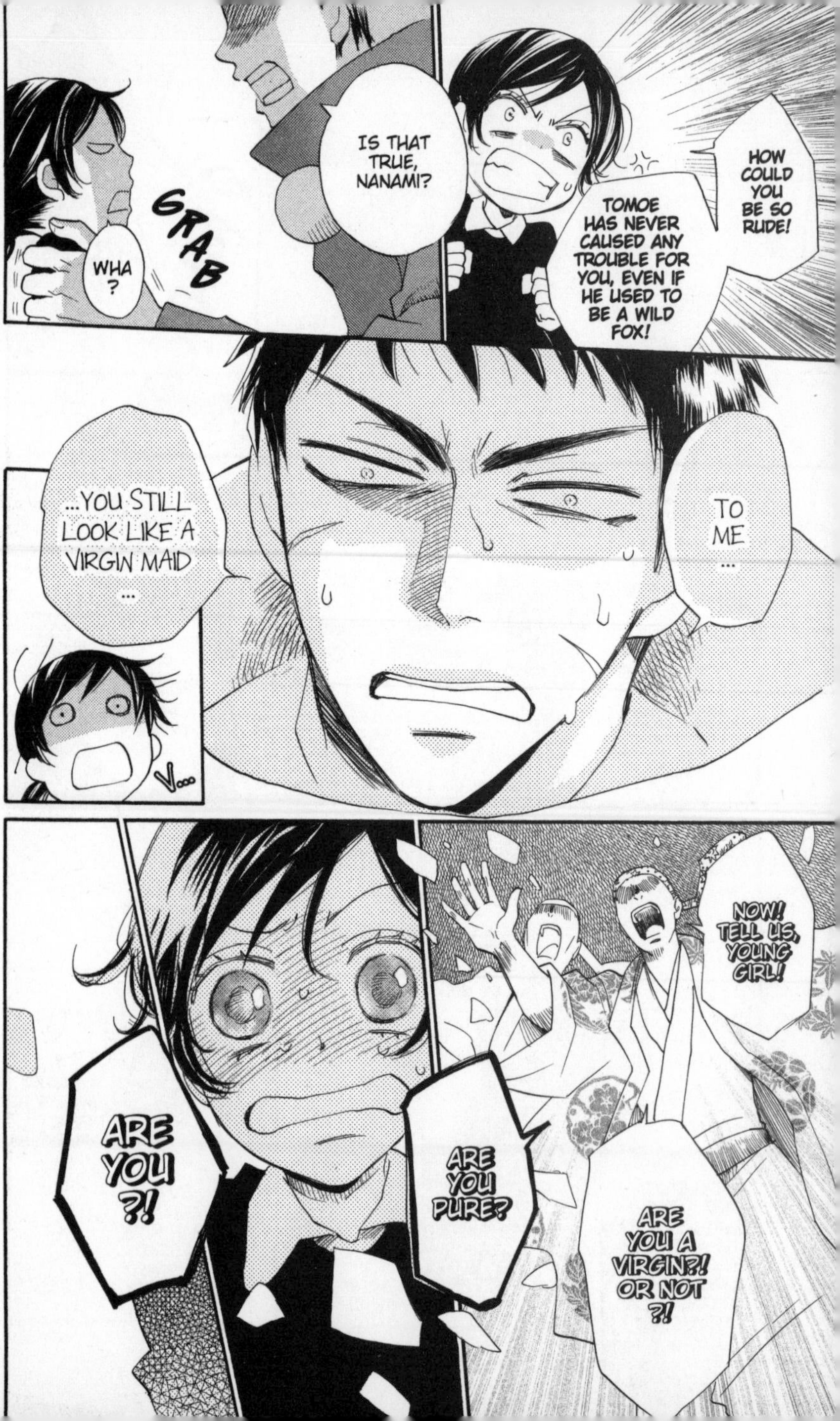
HOW COULD YOU BE SO RUDE!
TOMOE HAS NEVER CAUSED ANY TROUBLE FOR YOU, EVEN IF HE USED TO BE A WILD FOX!
IS THAT TRUE, NANAMI?
GRAB
WHA ?
TO ME ...
...YOU STILL LOOK LIKE A VIRGIN MAID ...
V...
NOW! TELL US, YOUNG GIRL!
ARE YOU A VIRGIN?! OR NOT ?!
ARE YOU PURE?
ARE YOU ?!

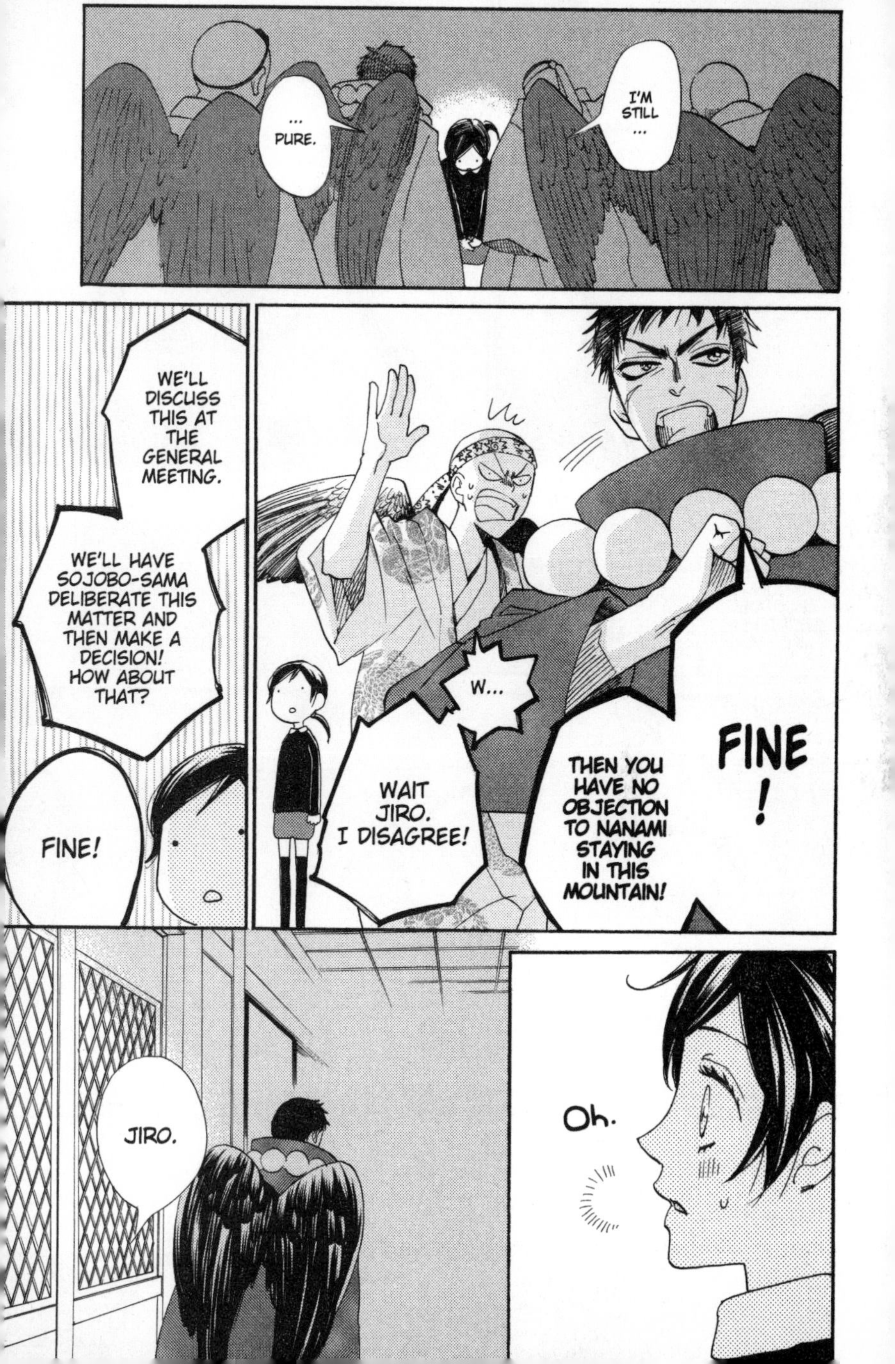
I'M STILL ...
... PURE.
FINE !
THEN YOU HAVE NO OBJECTION TO NANAMI STAYING IN THIS MOUNTAIN!
W...
WAIT JIRO. I DISAGREE!
WE'LL DISCUSS THIS AT THE GENERAL MEETING.
WE'LL HAVE SOJOBO-SAMA DELIBERATE THIS MATTER AND THEN MAKE A DECISION! HOW ABOUT THAT?
FINE!
Oh.
JIRO.

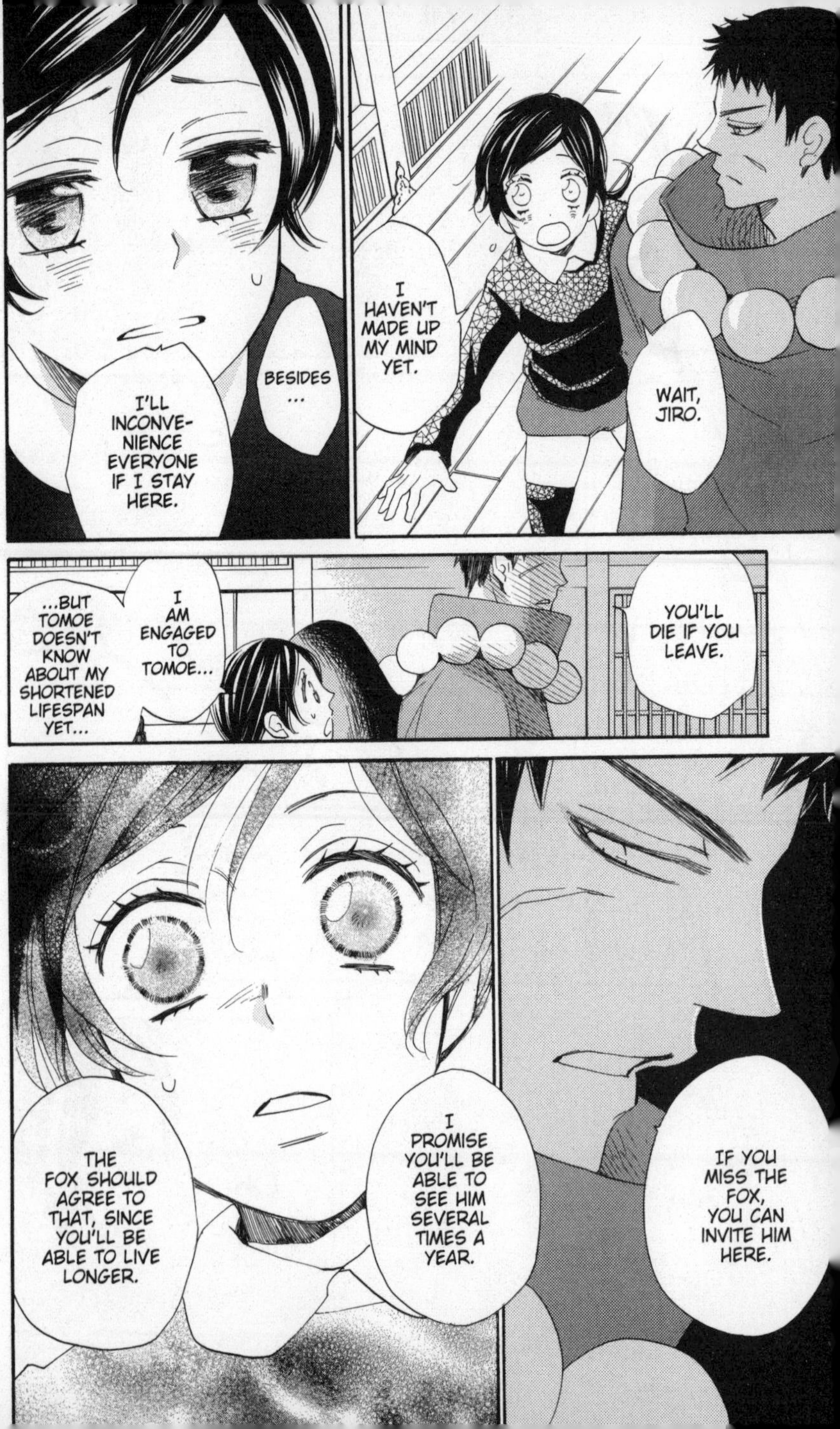
WAIT, JIRO.
I HAVEN'T MADE UP MY MIND YET.
BESIDES...
I'LL INCONVENIENCE EVERYONE IF I STAY HERE.
YOU'LL DIE IF YOU LEAVE.
I AM ENGAGED TO TOMOE...
...BUT TOMOE DOESN'T KNOW ABOUT MY SHORTENED LIFESPAN YET...
IF YOU MISS THE FOX, YOU CAN INVITE HIM HERE.
I PROMISE YOU'LL BE ABLE TO SEE HIM SEVERAL TIMES A YEAR.
THE FOX SHOULD AGREE TO THAT, SINCE YOU'LL BE ABLE TO LIVE LONGER.

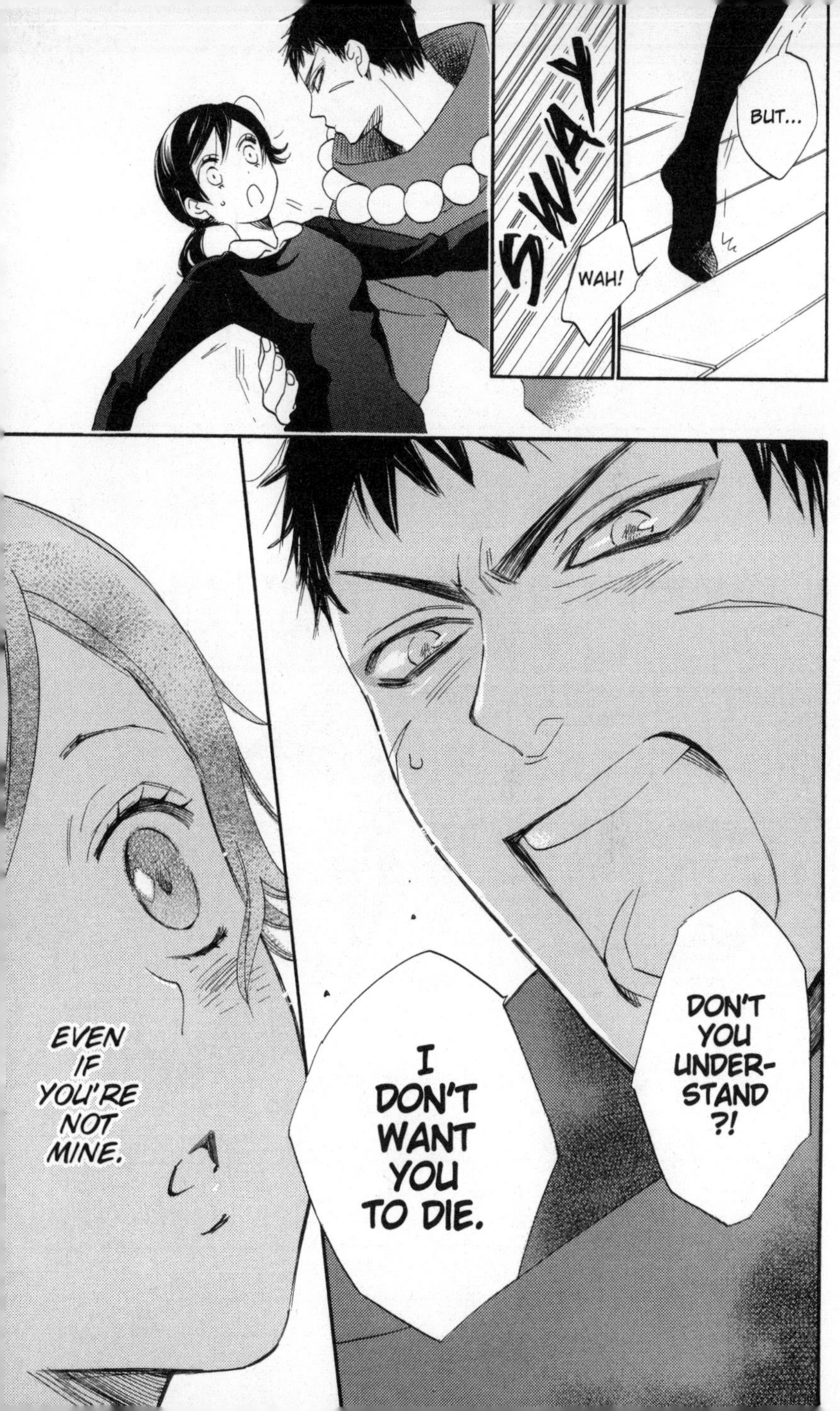
BUT...
SWAY
WAH!
DON'T YOU UNDER-STAND?!
I DON'T WANT YOU TO DIE.
EVEN IF YOU'RE NOT MINE.

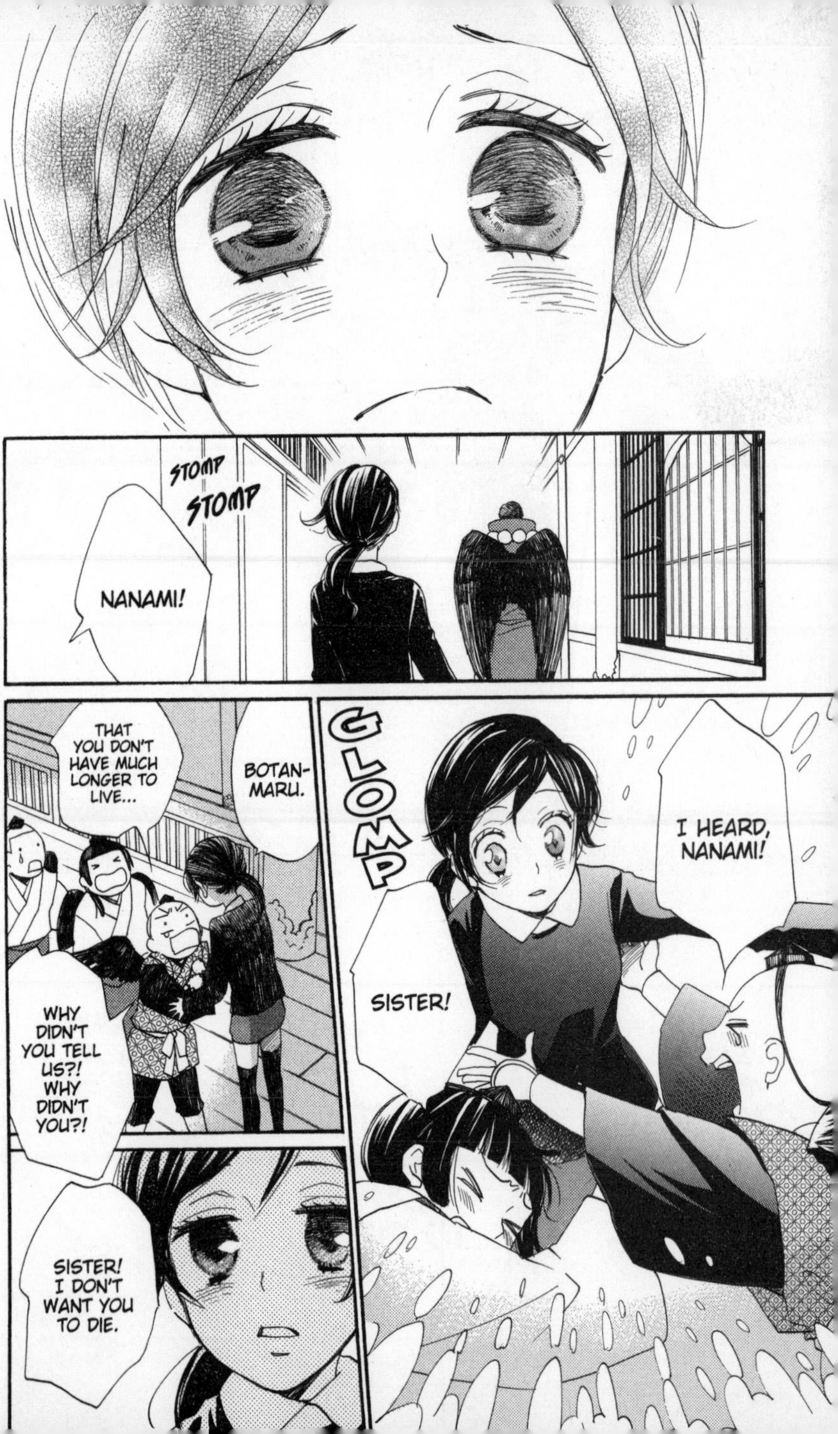
STOMP
STOMP
NANAMI!
GLOMP
I HEARD, NANAMI!
SISTER!
BOTAN-MARU.
THAT YOU DON'T HAVE MUCH LONGER TO LIVE...
WHY DIDN'T YOU TELL US?! WHY DIDN'T YOU?!
SISTER! I DON'T WANT YOU TO DIE.

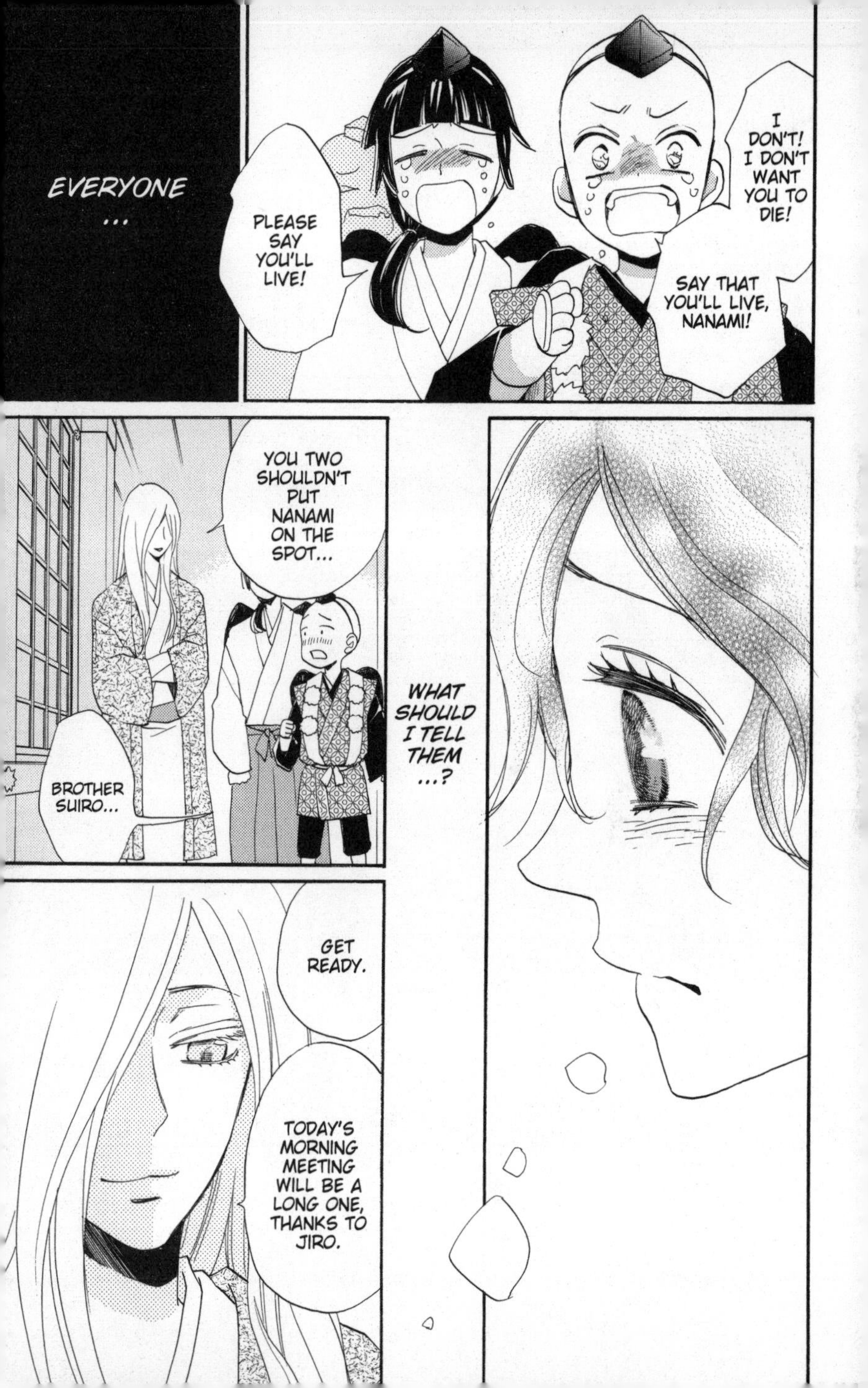
I DON'T! I DON'T WANT YOU TO DIE!
SAY THAT YOU'LL LIVE, NANAMI!
PLEASE SAY YOU'LL LIVE!
EVERYONE ...
WHAT SHOULD I TELL THEM ...?
YOU TWO SHOULDN'T PUT NANAMI ON THE SPOT...
BROTHER SUIRO...
GET READY.
TODAY'S MORNING MEETING WILL BE A LONG ONE, THANKS TO JIRO.

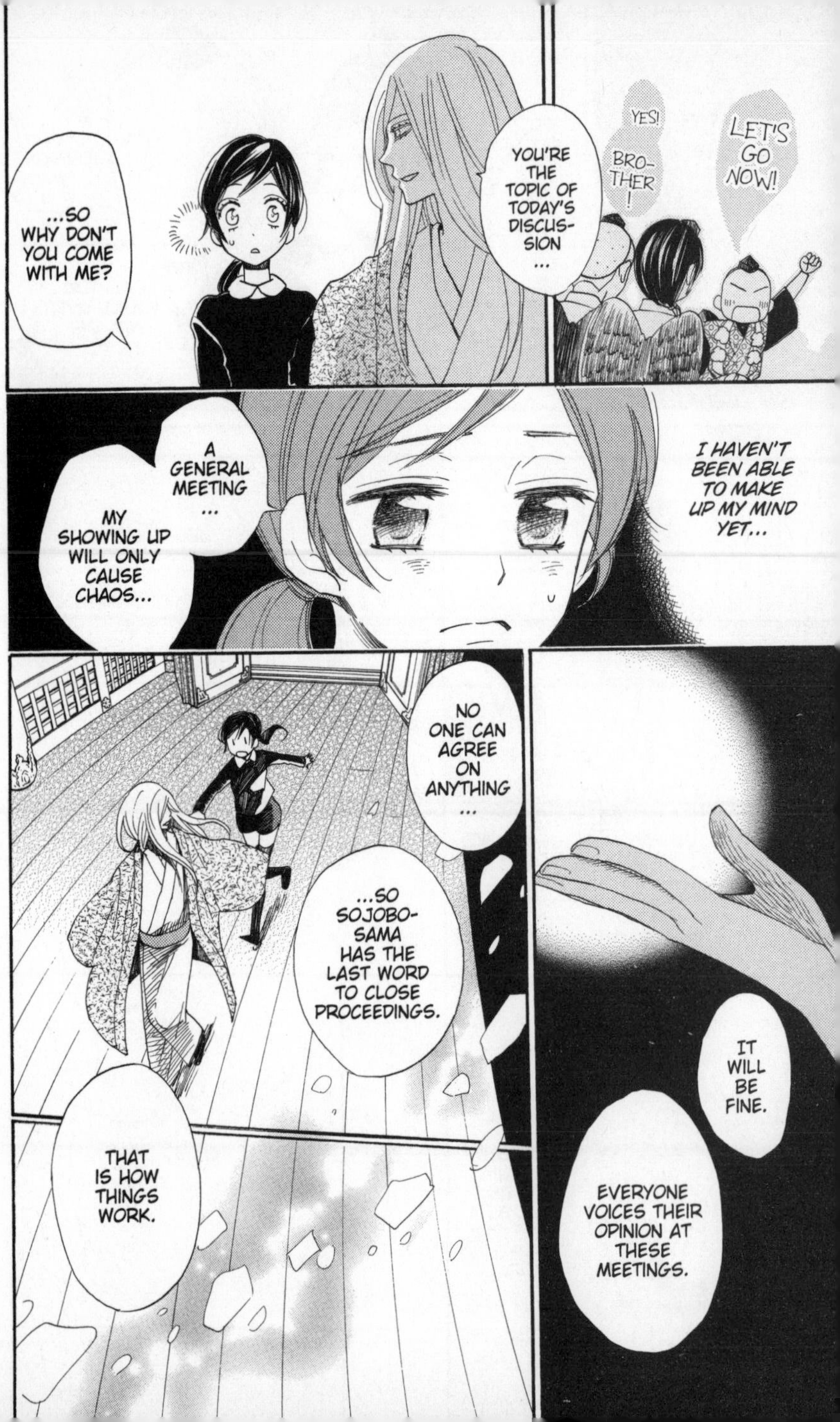
LET'S GO NOW!
YES!
BROTHER!
YOU'RE THE TOPIC OF TODAY'S DISCUSSION...
...SO WHY DON'T YOU COME WITH ME?
I HAVEN'T BEEN ABLE TO MAKE UP MY MIND YET...
A GENERAL MEETING...
MY SHOWING UP WILL ONLY CAUSE CHAOS...
IT WILL BE FINE.
EVERYONE VOICES THEIR OPINION AT THESE MEETINGS.
NO ONE CAN AGREE ON ANYTHING...
...SO SOJOBO-SAMA HAS THE LAST WORD TO CLOSE PROCEEDINGS.
THAT IS HOW THINGS WORK.

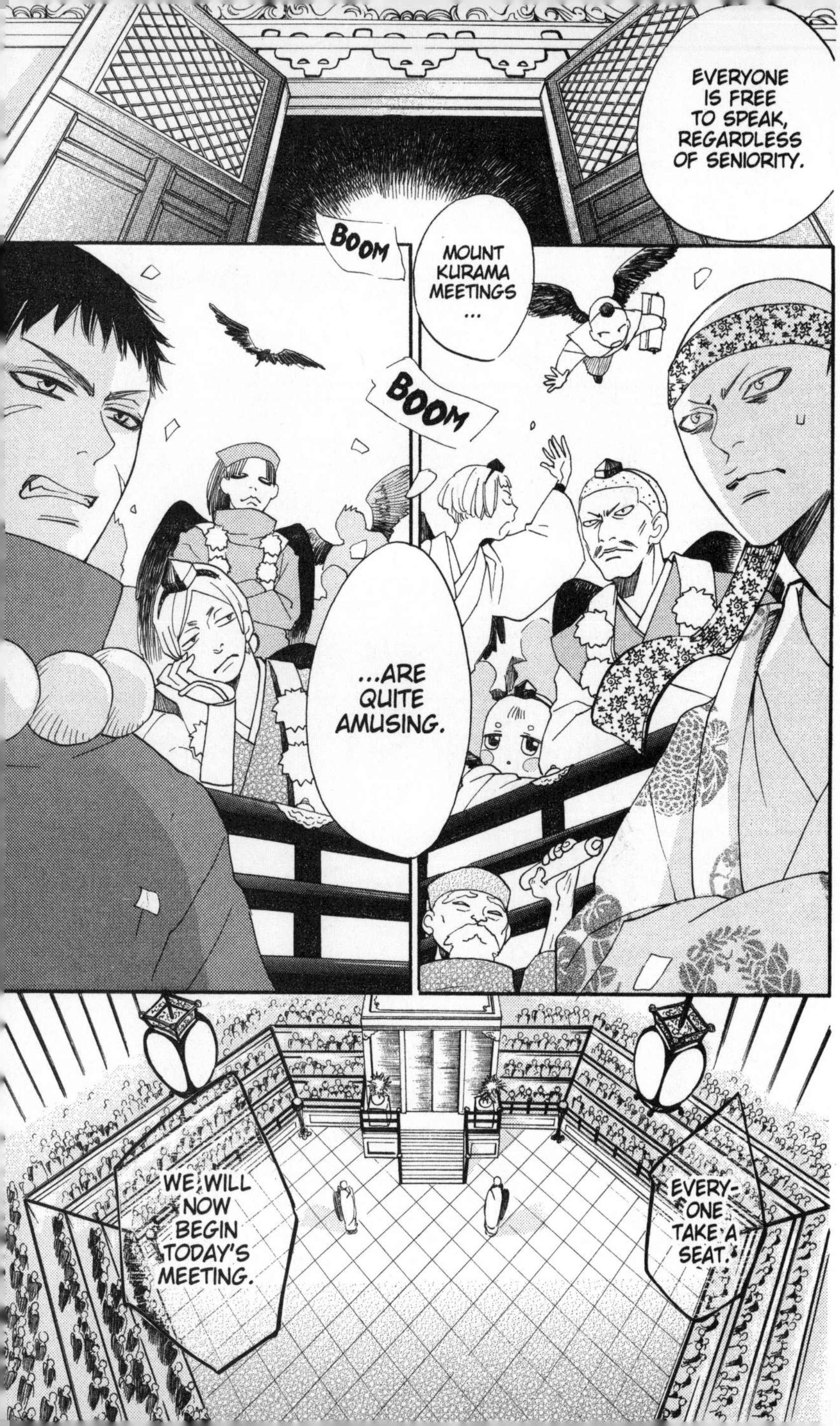
EVERYONE IS FREE TO SPEAK, REGARDLESS OF SENIORITY.
MOUNT KURAMA MEETINGS ...
...ARE QUITE AMUSING.
BOOM
BOOM
EVERY-ONE TAKE A SEAT.
WE WILL NOW BEGIN TODAY'S MEETING.

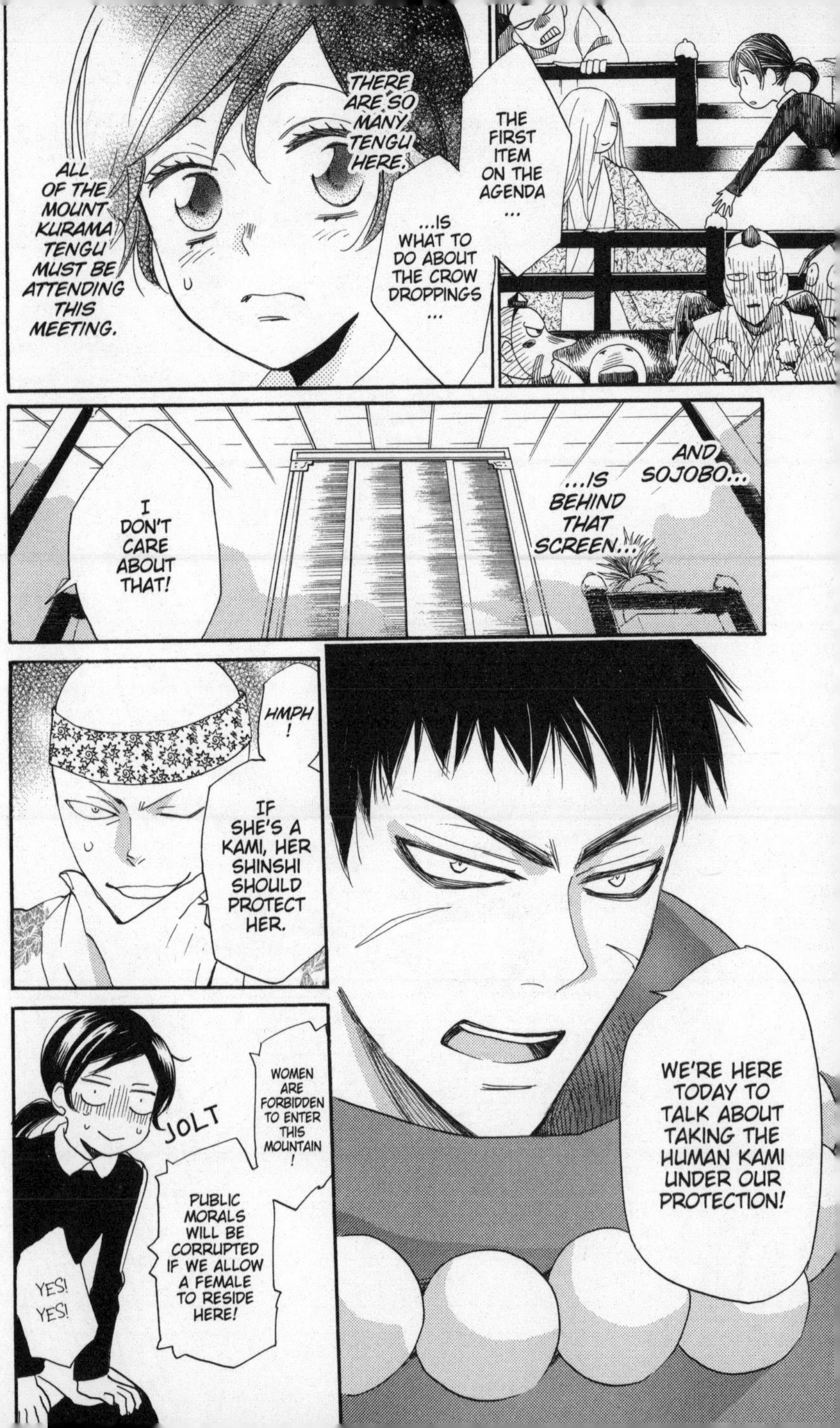
THE FIRST ITEM ON THE AGENDA ...
...IS WHAT TO DO ABOUT THE CROW DROPPINGS ...
THERE ARE SO MANY TENGU HERE.
ALL OF THE MOUNT KURAMA TENGU MUST BE ATTENDING THIS MEETING.
AND SOJOBO...
...IS BEHIND THAT SCREEN...
I DON'T CARE ABOUT THAT!
WE'RE HERE TODAY TO TALK ABOUT TAKING THE HUMAN KAMI UNDER OUR PROTECTION!
HMPH!
IF SHE'S A KAMI, HER SHINSHI SHOULD PROTECT HER.
WOMEN ARE FORBIDDEN TO ENTER THIS MOUNTAIN!
JOLT
PUBLIC MORALS WILL BE CORRUPTED IF WE ALLOW A FEMALE TO RESIDE HERE!
YES! YES!

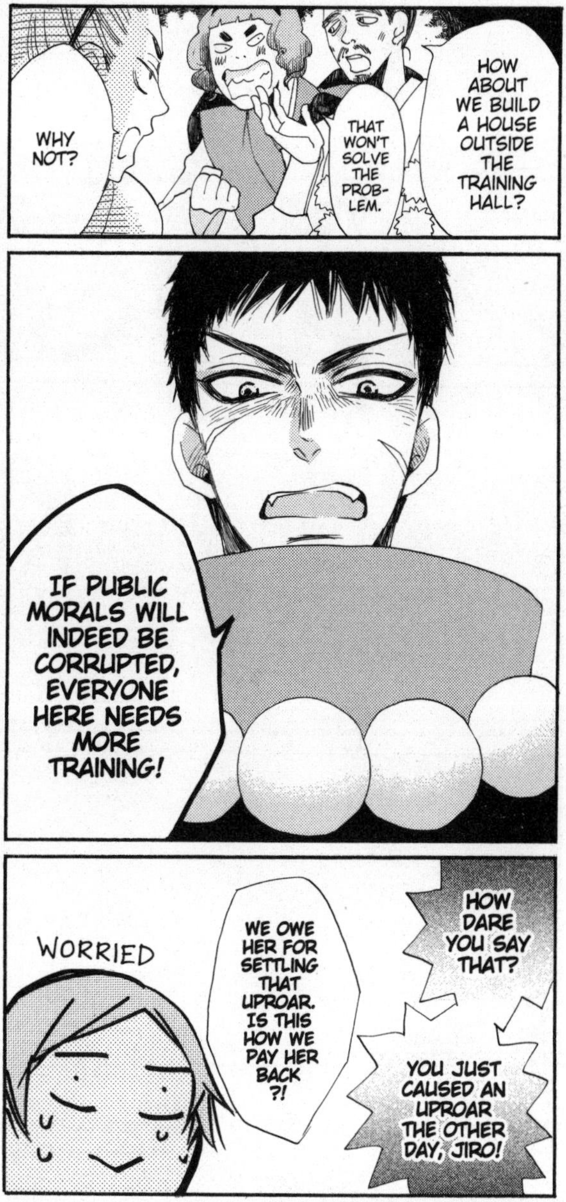
HOW ABOUT WE BUILD A HOUSE OUTSIDE THE TRAINING HALL?
THAT WON'T SOLVE THE PROB-LEM.
WHY NOT?
IF PUBLIC MORALS WILL INDEED BE CORRUPTED, EVERYONE HERE NEEDS MORE TRAINING!
HOW DARE YOU SAY THAT?
YOU JUST CAUSED AN UPROAR THE OTHER DAY, JIRO!
WE OWE HER FOR SETTLING THAT UPROAR. IS THIS HOW WE PAY HER BACK?!
WORRIED

I love the placenta essence my older sister gave me.

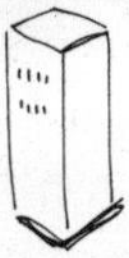

My skin has become so dewy... ♡

It worked so well on me, I've recommended it to my friends.

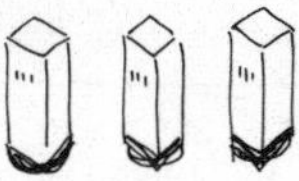

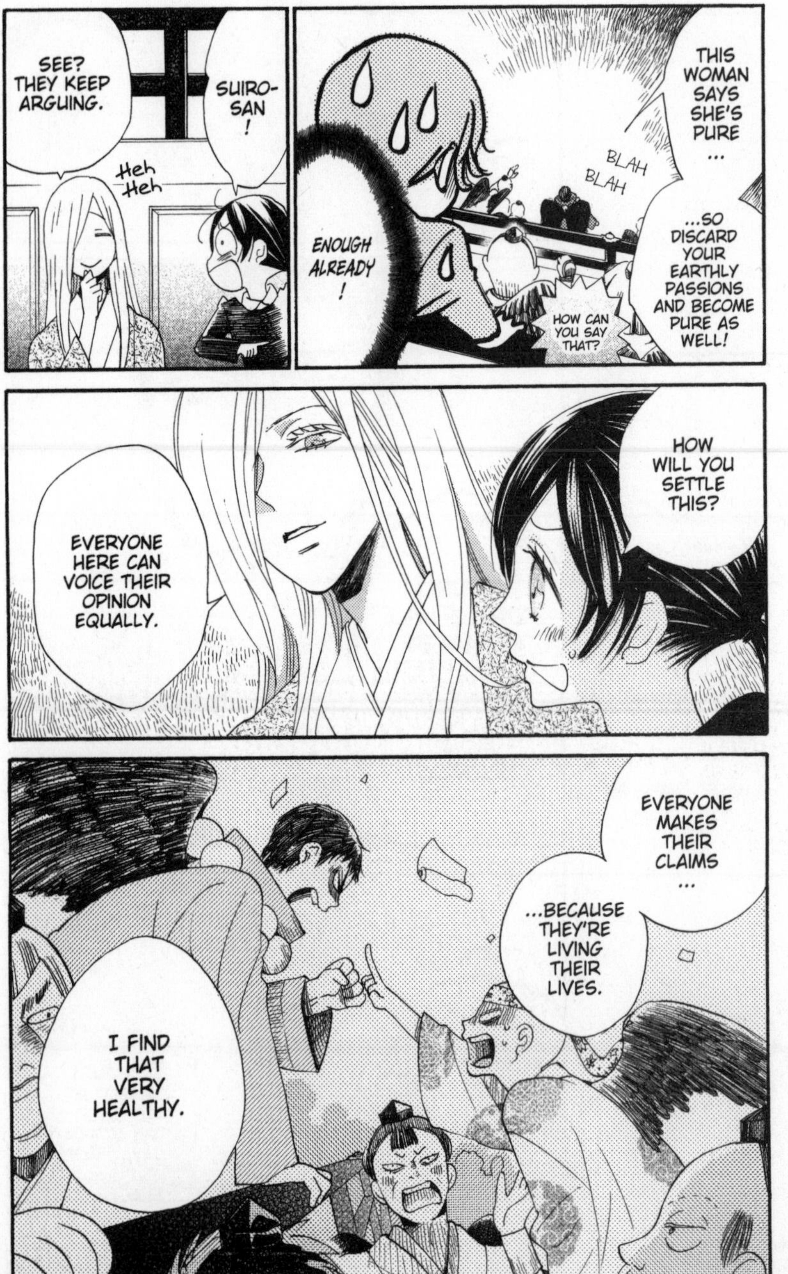
THIS WOMAN SAYS SHE'S PURE...
BLAH BLAH
...SO DISCARD YOUR EARTHLY PASSIONS AND BECOME PURE AS WELL!
HOW CAN YOU SAY THAT?
ENOUGH ALREADY!
SUIRO-SAN!
SEE? THEY KEEP ARGUING.
Heh Heh
HOW WILL YOU SETTLE THIS?
EVERYONE HERE CAN VOICE THEIR OPINION EQUALLY.
EVERYONE MAKES THEIR CLAIMS...
...BECAUSE THEY'RE LIVING THEIR LIVES.
I FIND THAT VERY HEALTHY.

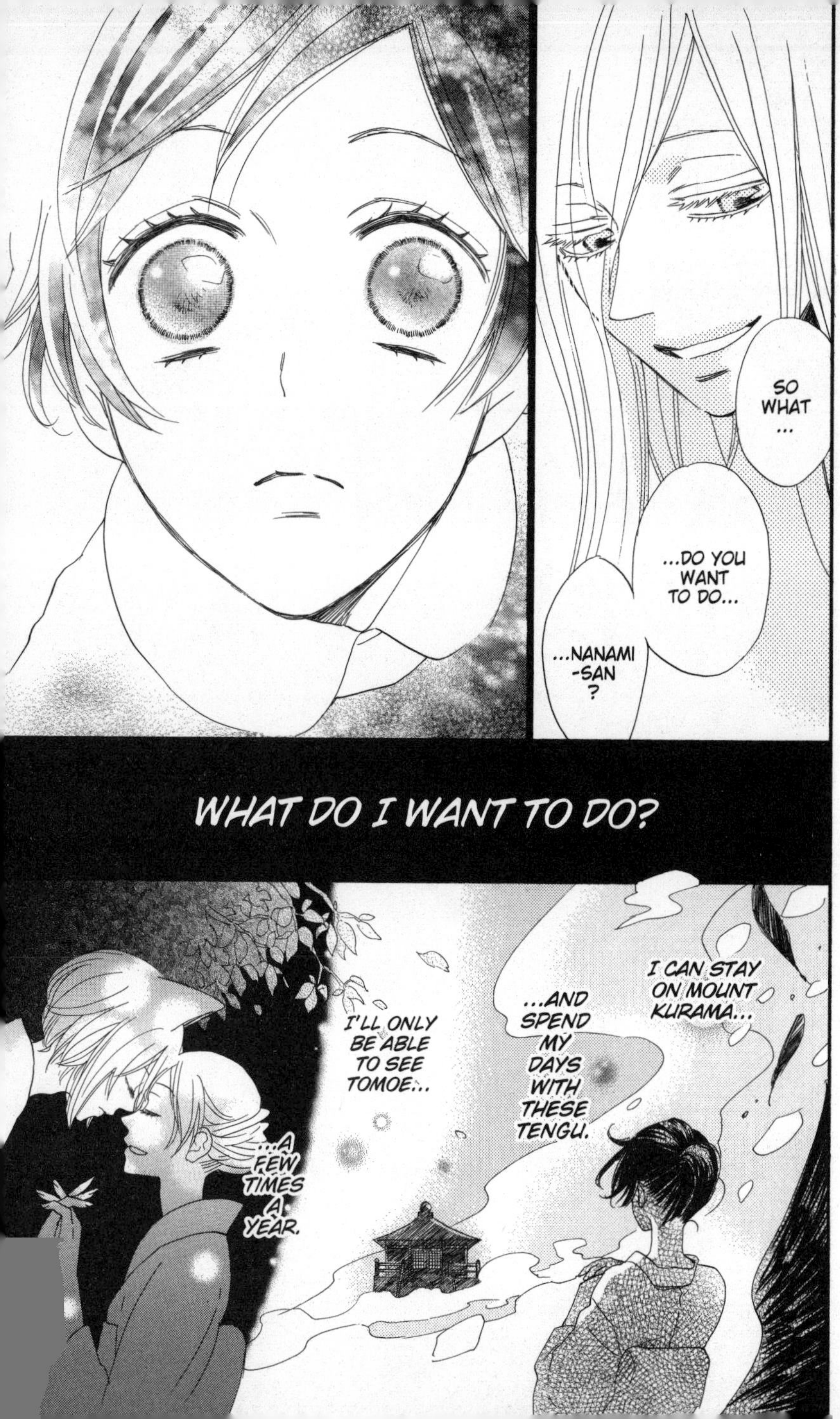
SO WHAT ...
...DO YOU WANT TO DO...
...NANAMI -SAN ?
WHAT DO I WANT TO DO?
I CAN STAY ON MOUNT KURAMA...
...AND SPEND MY DAYS WITH THESE TENGU.
I'LL ONLY BE ABLE TO SEE TOMOE...
...A FEW TIMES A YEAR.

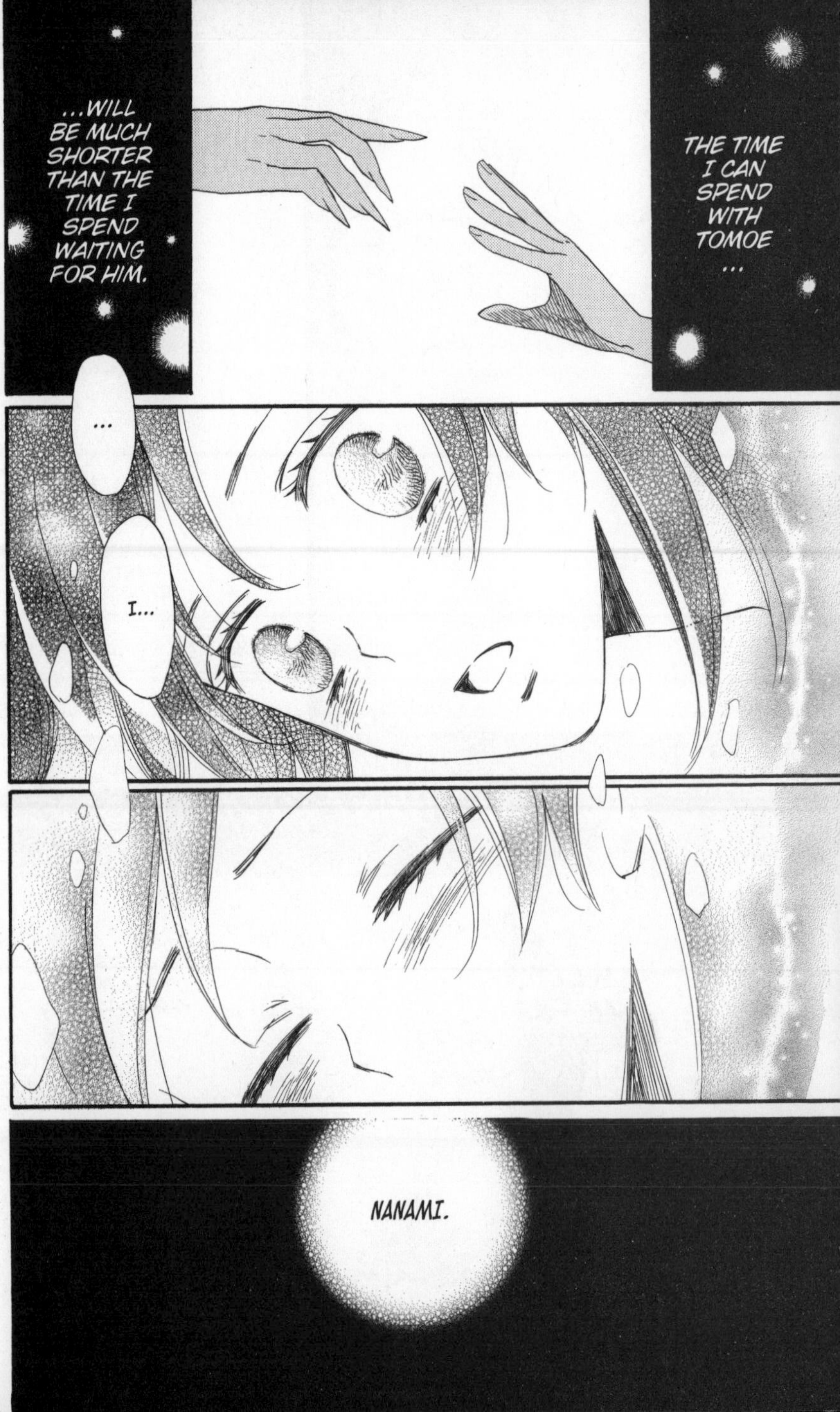
THE TIME I CAN SPEND WITH TOMOE ...
...WILL BE MUCH SHORTER THAN THE TIME I SPEND WAITING FOR HIM.
...
I...
NANAMI.

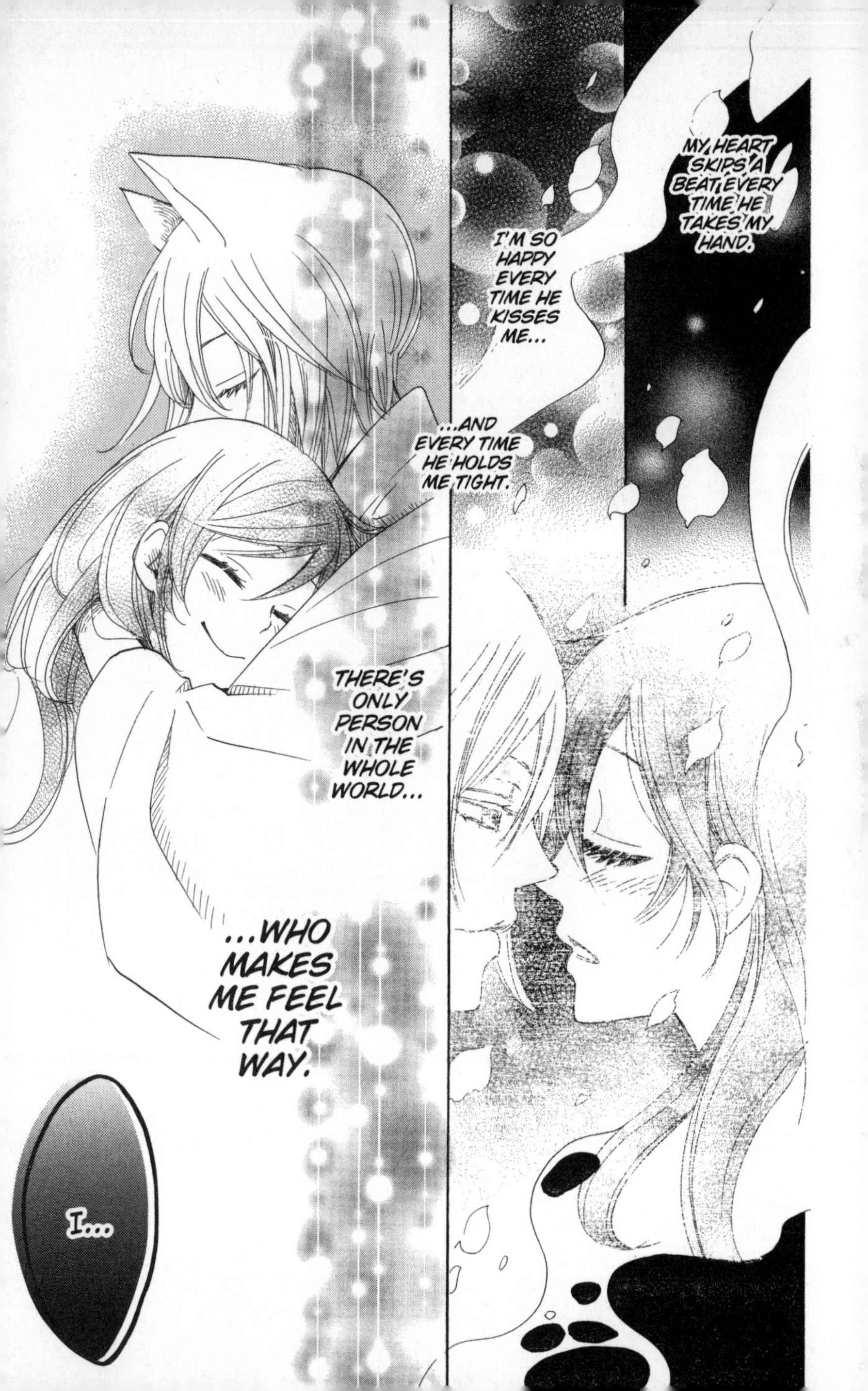
MY HEART SKIPS A BEAT EVERY TIME HE TAKES MY HAND.
I'M SO HAPPY EVERY TIME HE KISSES ME...
...AND EVERY TIME HE HOLDS ME TIGHT.
THERE'S ONLY PERSON IN THE WHOLE WORLD...
...WHO MAKES ME FEEL THAT WAY.
I...

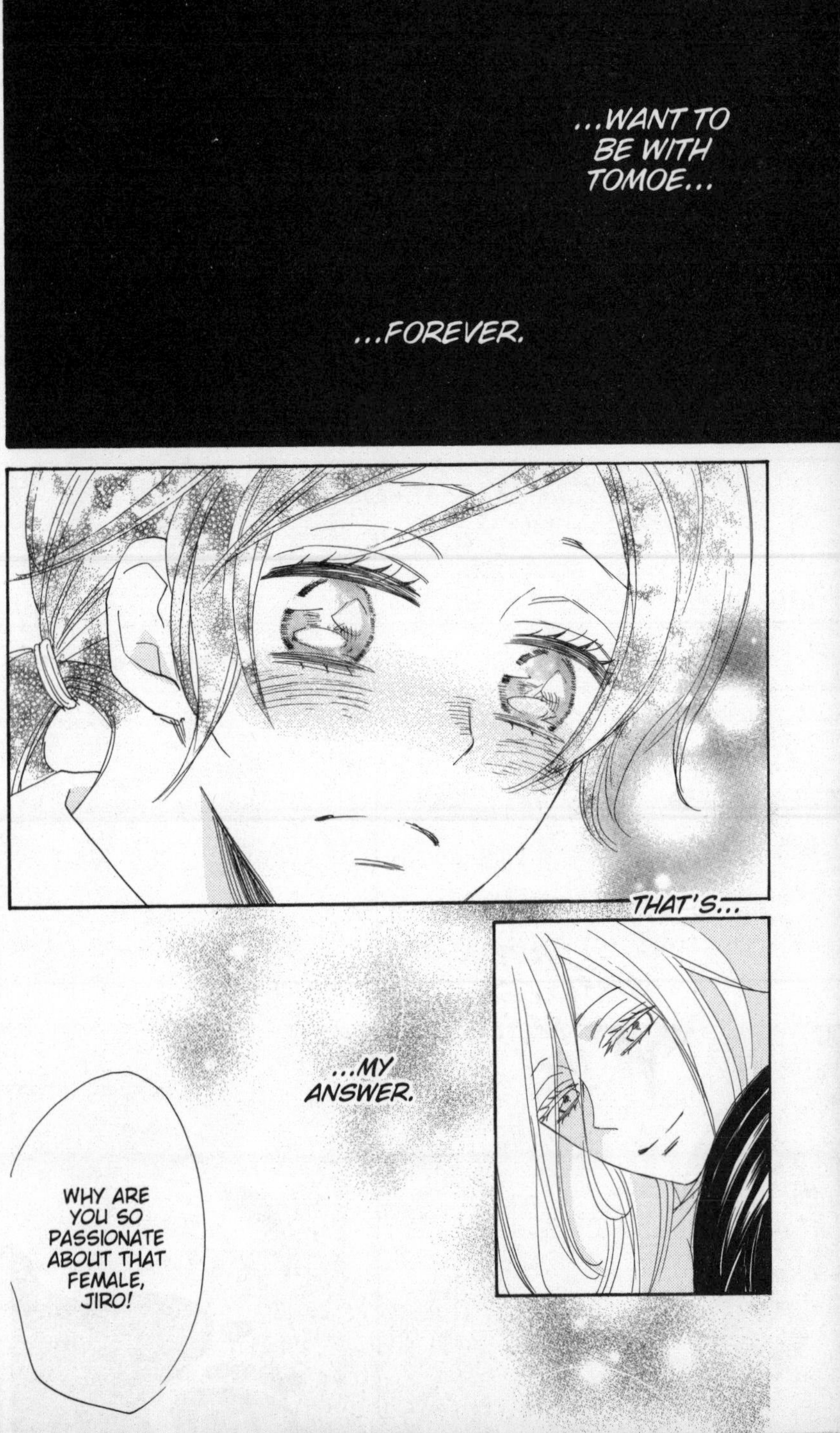
...WANT TO BE WITH TOMOE...
...FOREVER.
THAT'S...
...MY ANSWER.
WHY ARE YOU SO PASSIONATE ABOUT THAT FEMALE, JIRO!

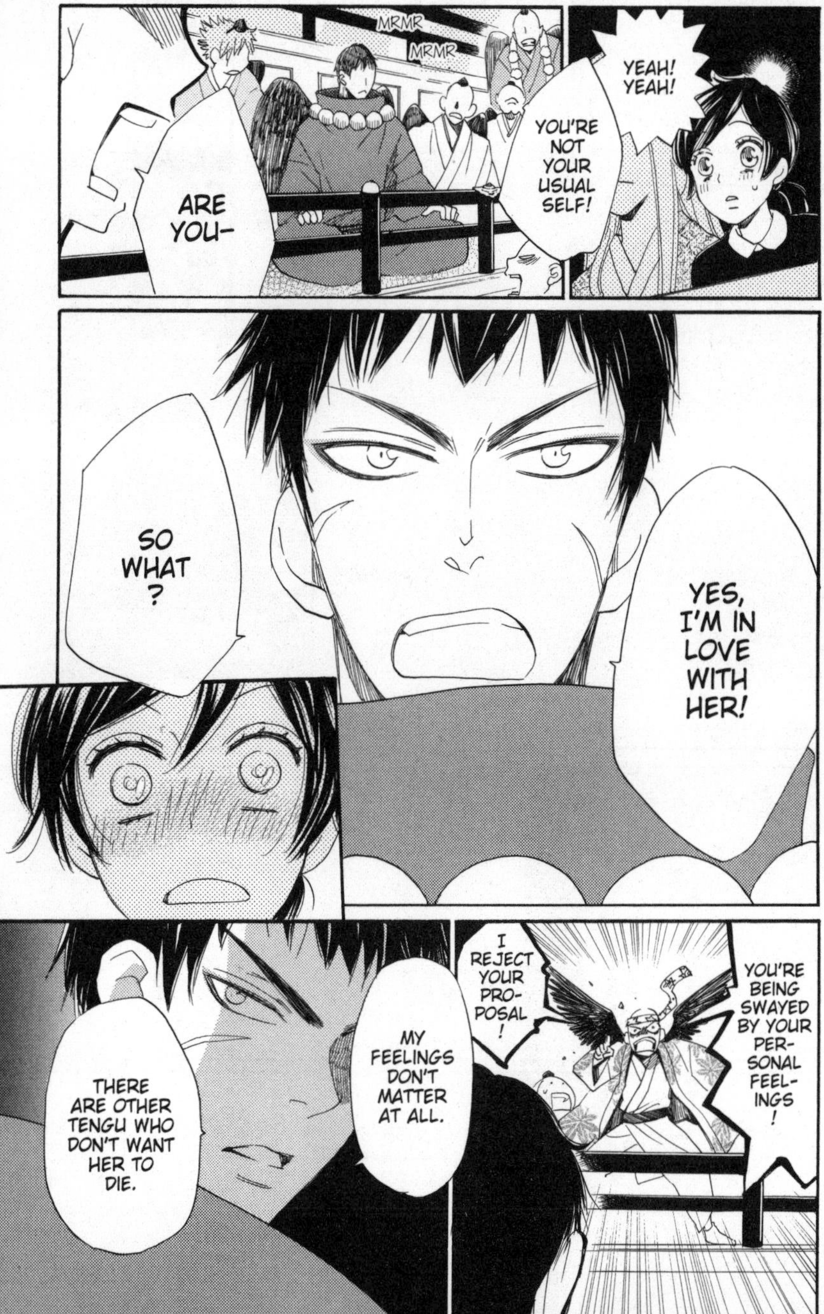
YEAH! YEAH!
YOU'RE NOT YOUR USUAL SELF!
MRMR
MRMR
ARE YOU-
YES, I'M IN LOVE WITH HER!
SO WHAT?
YOU'RE BEING SWAYED BY YOUR PERSONAL FEELINGS!
I REJECT YOUR PROPOSAL!
MY FEELINGS DON'T MATTER AT ALL.
THERE ARE OTHER TENGU WHO DON'T WANT HER TO DIE.

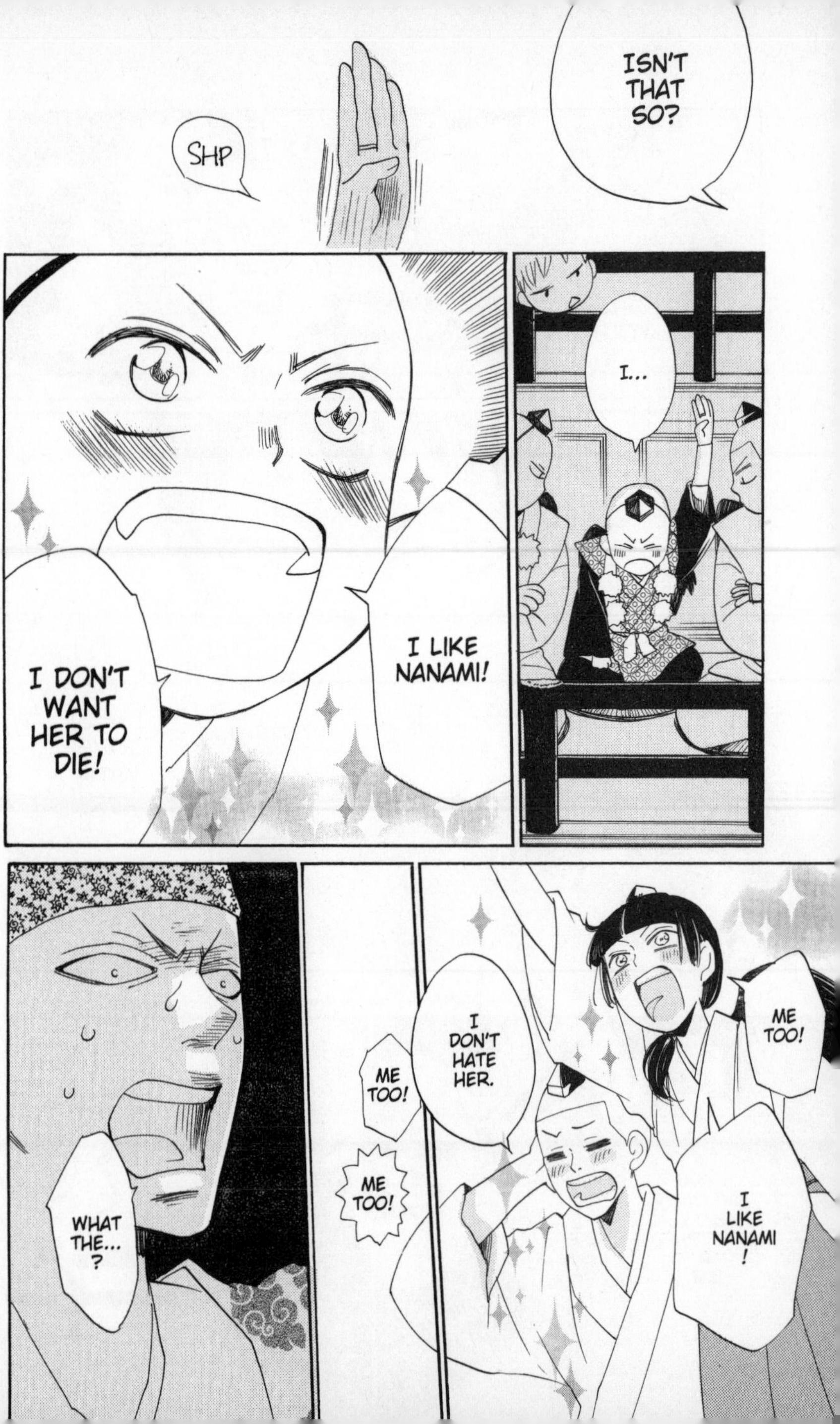
ISN'T THAT SO?
SHP
I...
I LIKE NANAMI!
I DON'T WANT HER TO DIE!
ME TOO!
I DON'T HATE HER.
ME TOO!
I LIKE NANAMI!
ME TOO!
WHAT THE...?

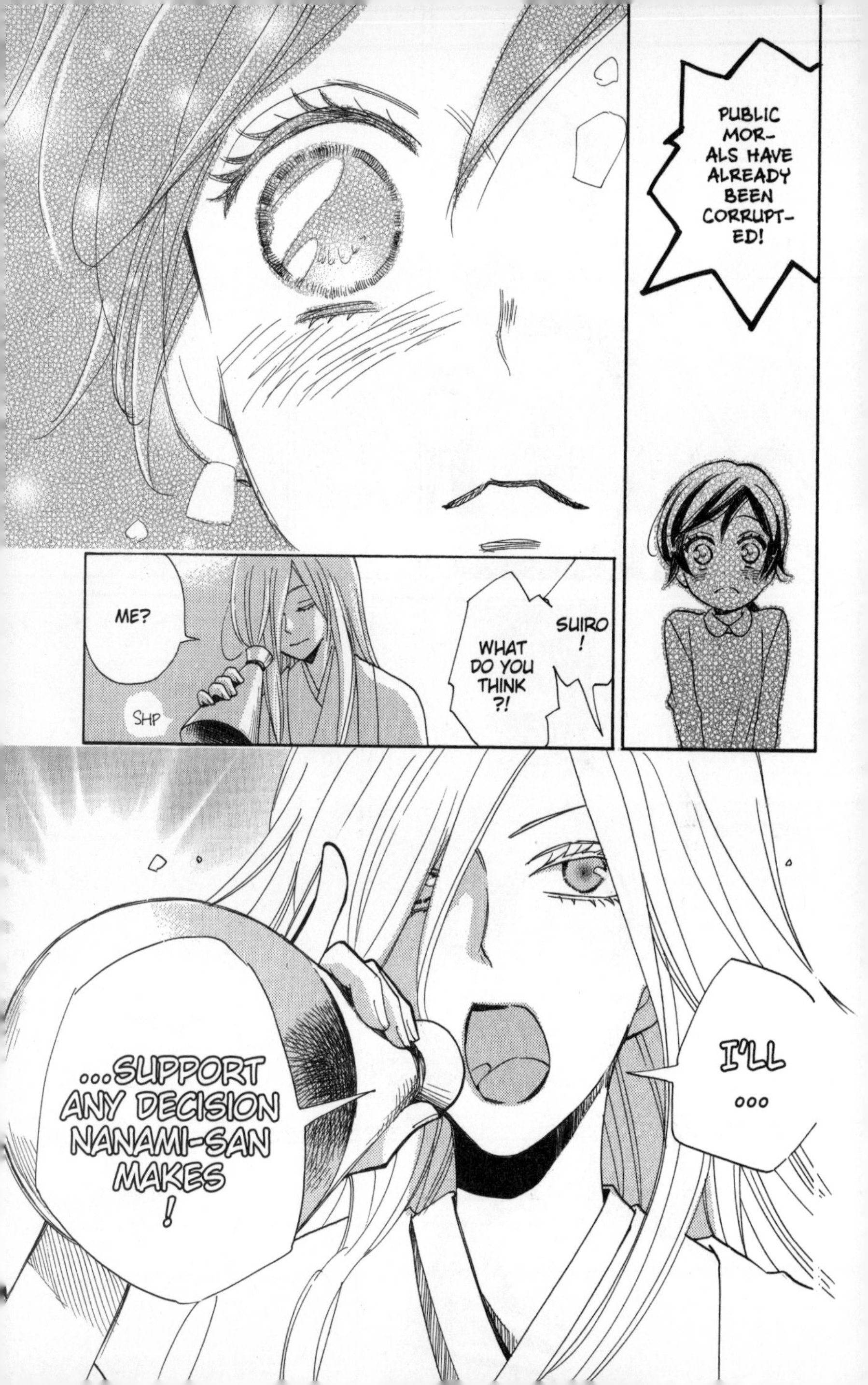
PUBLIC MOR-ALS HAVE ALREADY BEEN CORRUPT-ED!
SUIRO!
WHAT DO YOU THINK?!
ME?
SHP
I'LL...
...SUPPORT ANY DECISION NANAMI-SAN MAKES!

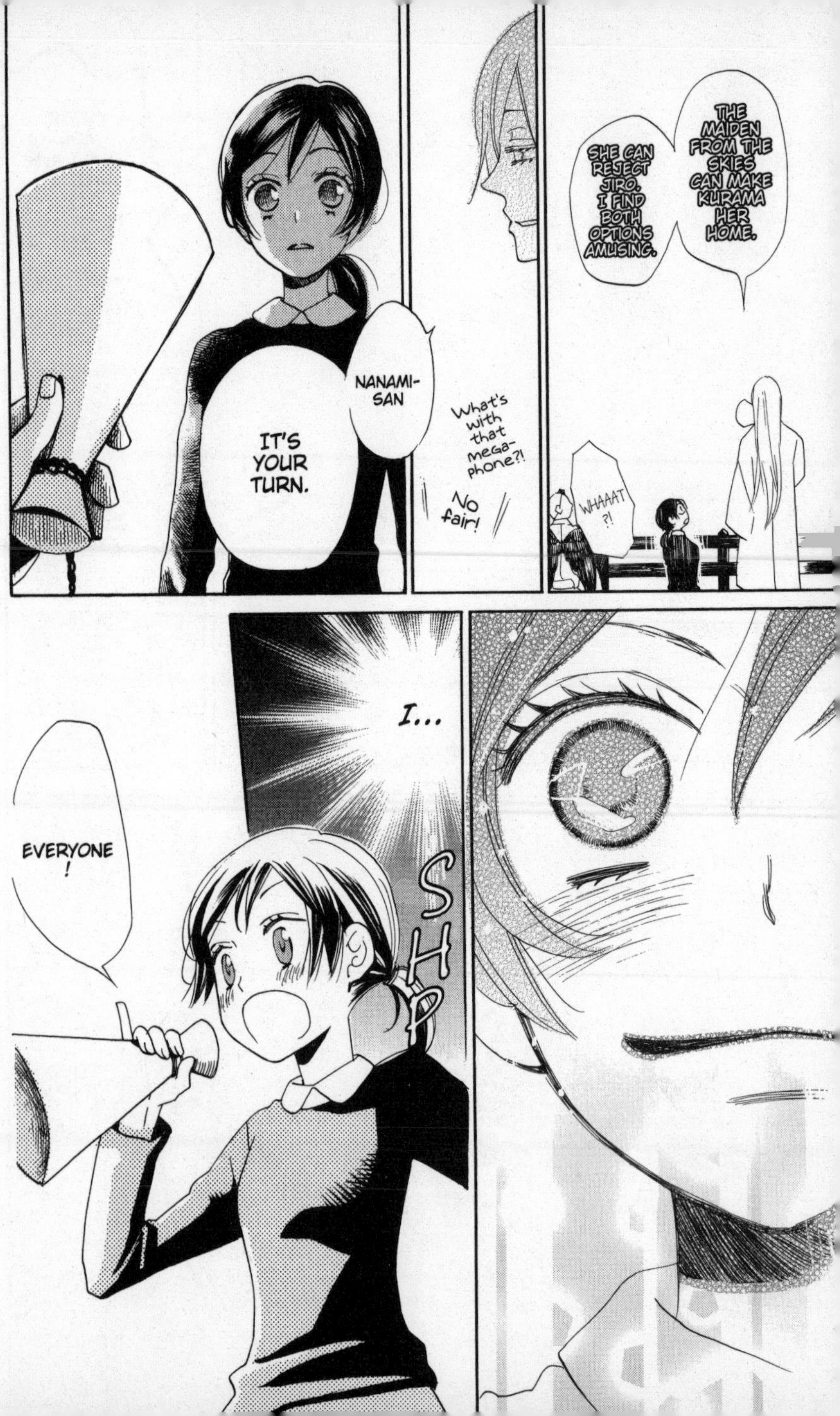
THE MAIDEN FROM THE SKIES CAN MAKE KURAMA HER HOME.
SHE CAN REJECT JIRO. I FIND BOTH OPTIONS AMUSING.
WHAAAT?!
What's with that mega-phone?!
No fair!
NANAMI-SAN
IT'S YOUR TURN.
I...
SHP
EVERYONE!

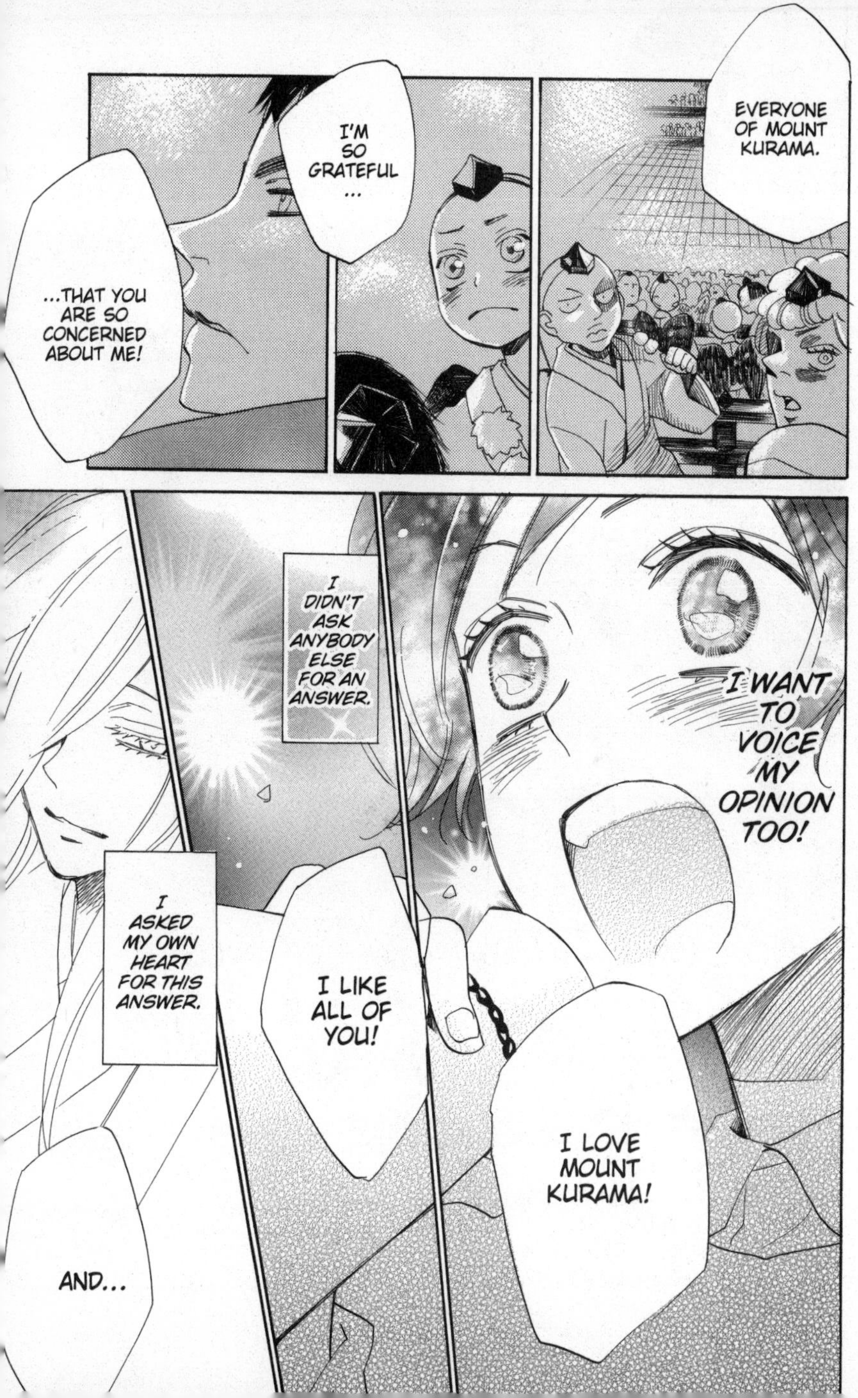
EVERYONE OF MOUNT KURAMA.
I'M SO GRATEFUL ...
...THAT YOU ARE SO CONCERNED ABOUT ME!
I WANT TO VOICE MY OPINION TOO!
I DIDN'T ASK ANYBODY ELSE FOR AN ANSWER.
I ASKED MY OWN HEART FOR THIS ANSWER.
I LIKE ALL OF YOU!
I LOVE MOUNT KURAMA!
AND...

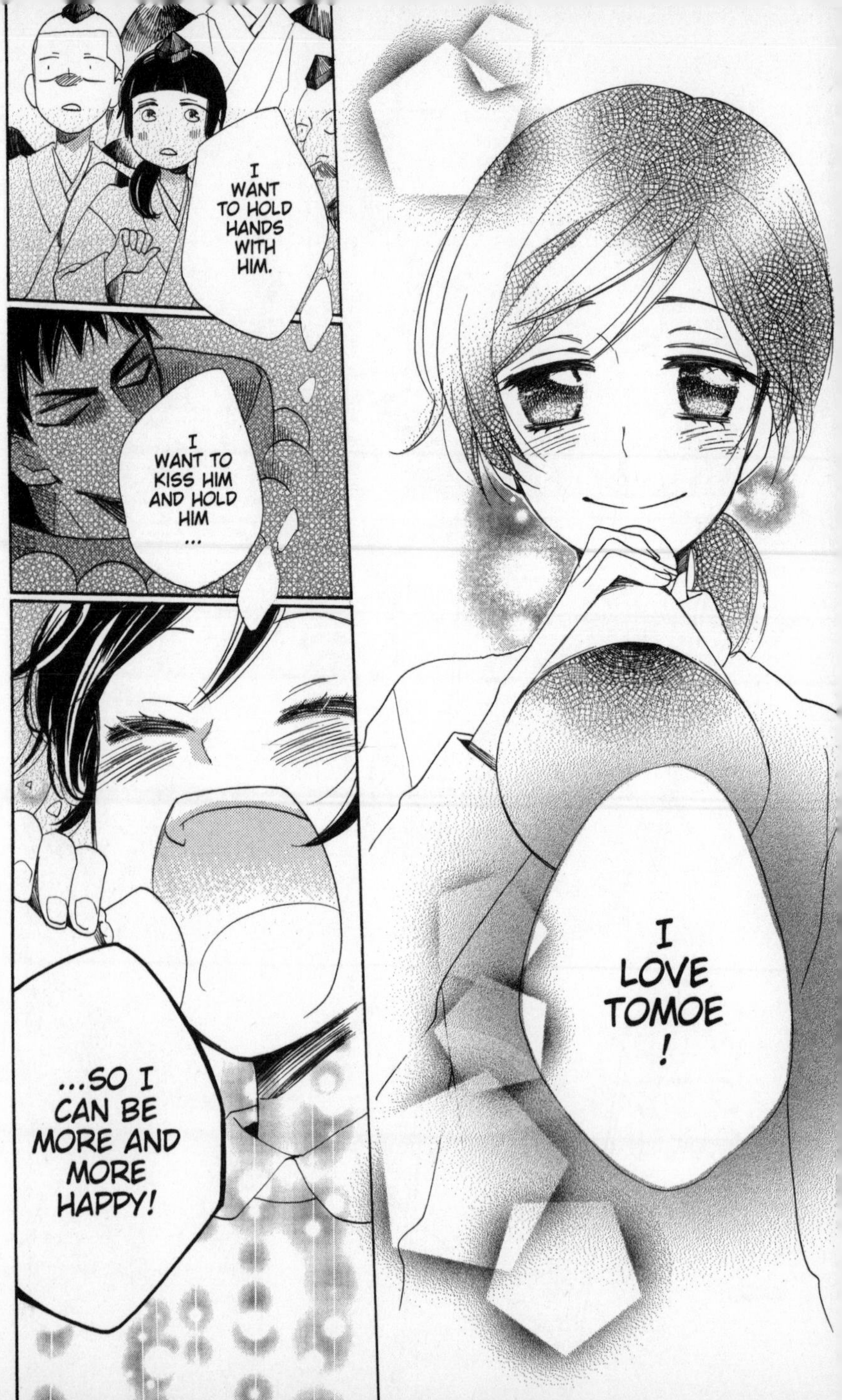
I LOVE TOMOE!
I WANT TO HOLD HANDS WITH HIM.
I WANT TO KISS HIM AND HOLD HIM...
...SO I CAN BE MORE AND MORE HAPPY!

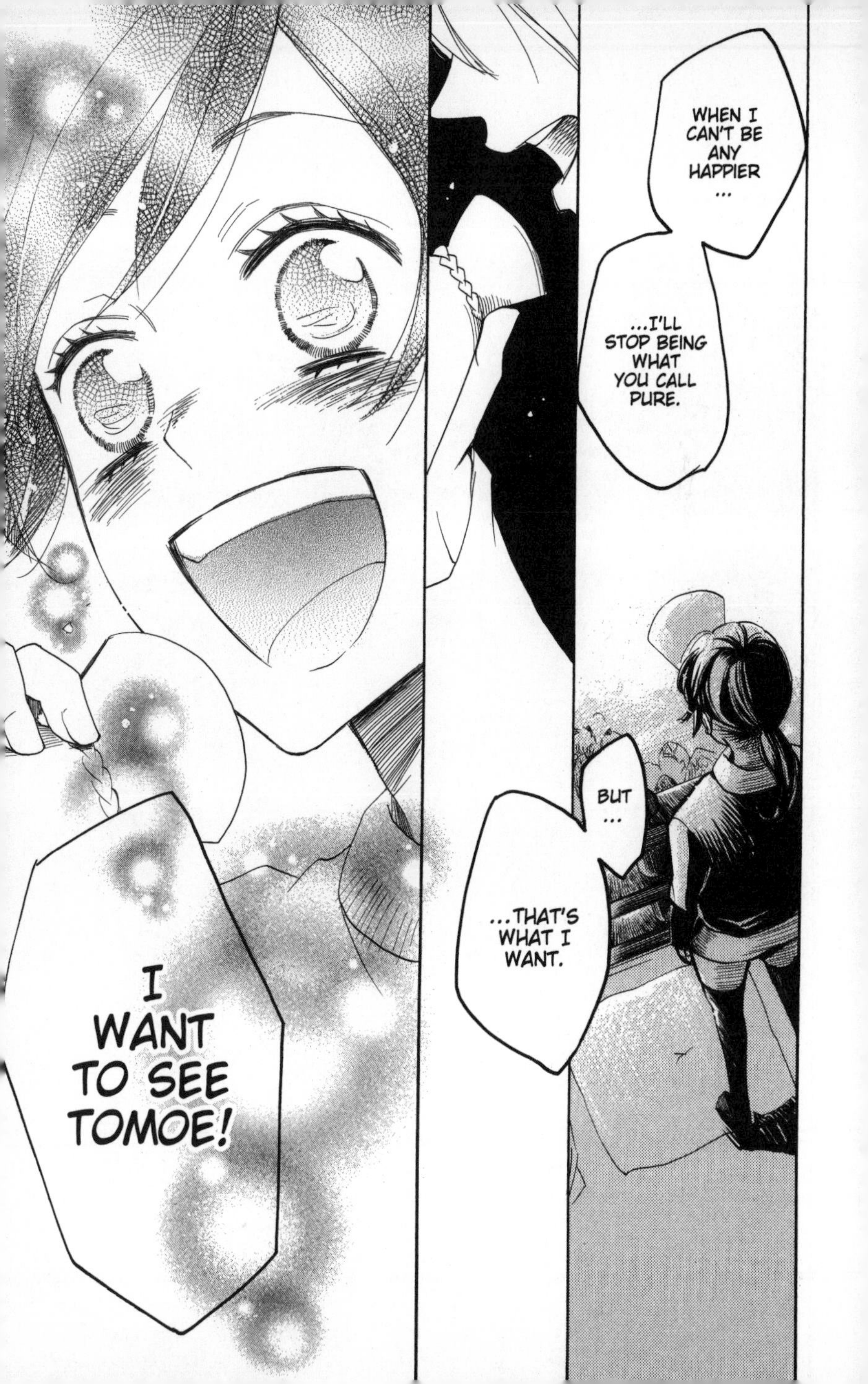
WHEN I CAN'T BE ANY HAPPIER ...
...I'LL STOP BEING WHAT YOU CALL PURE.
BUT ...
...THAT'S WHAT I WANT.
I WANT TO SEE TOMOE!

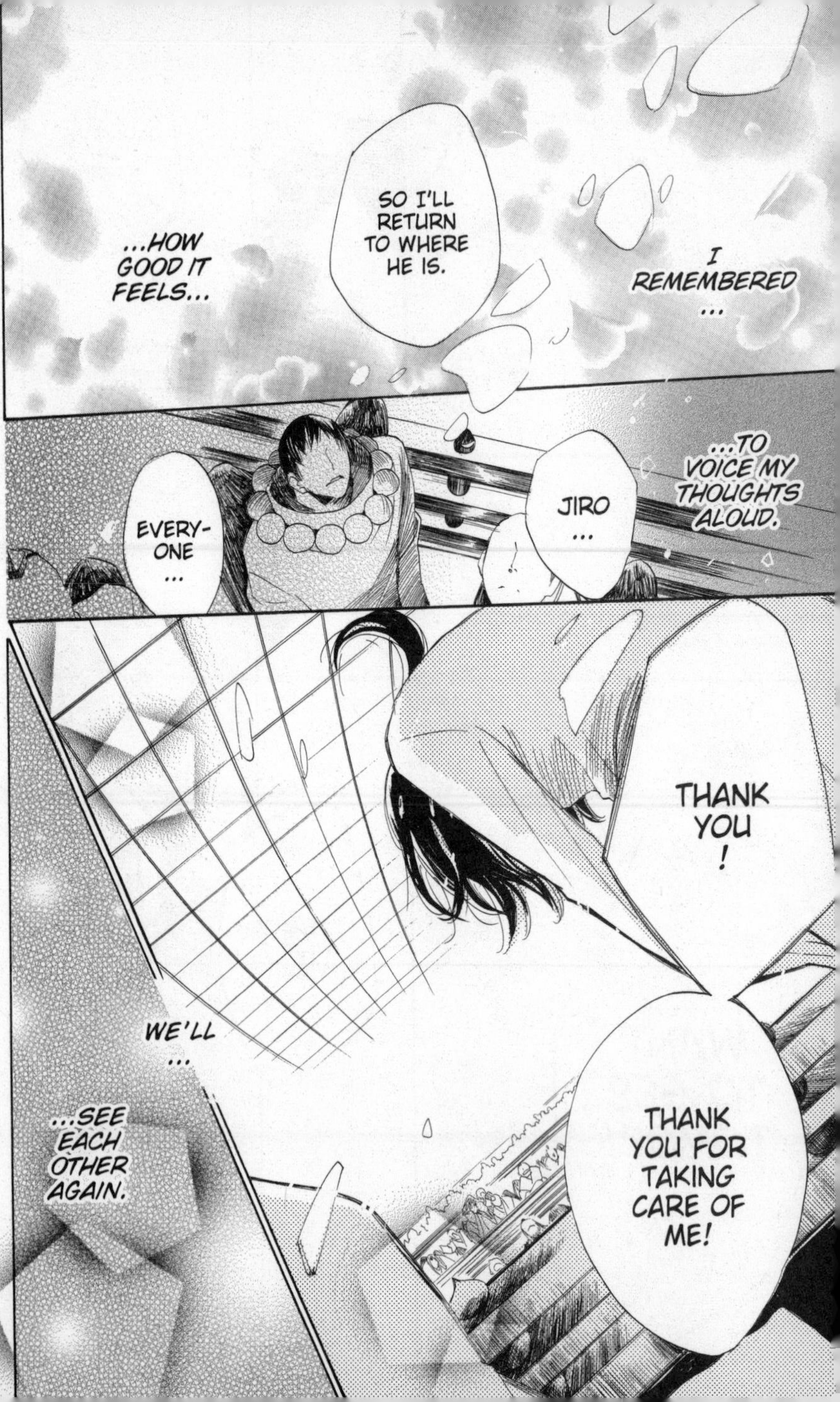
I REMEMBERED ...
SO I'LL RETURN TO WHERE HE IS.
...HOW GOOD IT FEELS...
...TO VOICE MY THOUGHTS ALOUD.
JIRO ...
EVERY-ONE ...
THANK YOU!
THANK YOU FOR TAKING CARE OF ME!
WE'LL ...
...SEE EACH OTHER AGAIN.

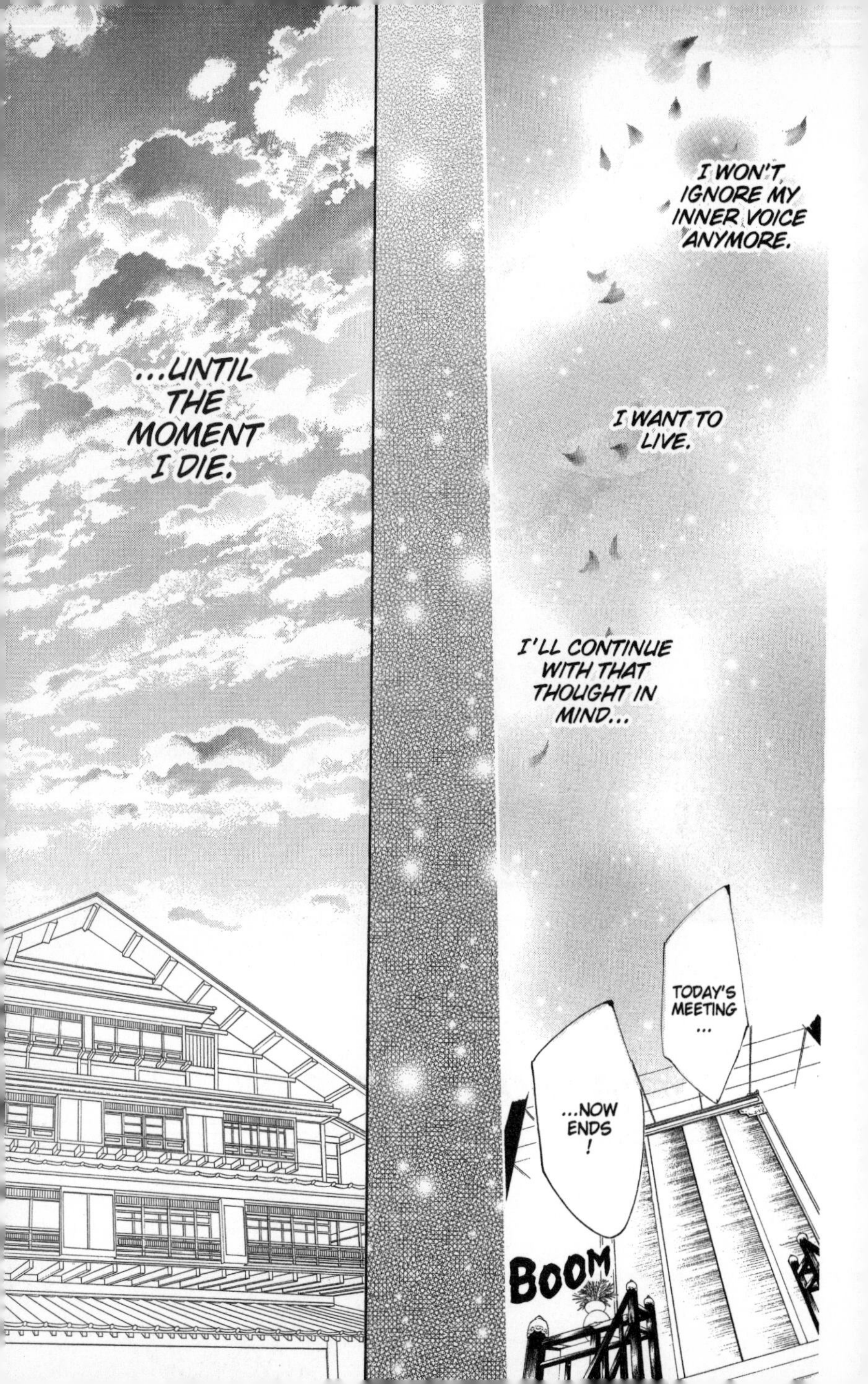
I WON'T IGNORE MY INNER VOICE ANYMORE.
I WANT TO LIVE.
I'LL CONTINUE WITH THAT THOUGHT IN MIND...
TODAY'S MEETING...
...NOW ENDS!
BOOM
...UNTIL THE MOMENT I DIE.

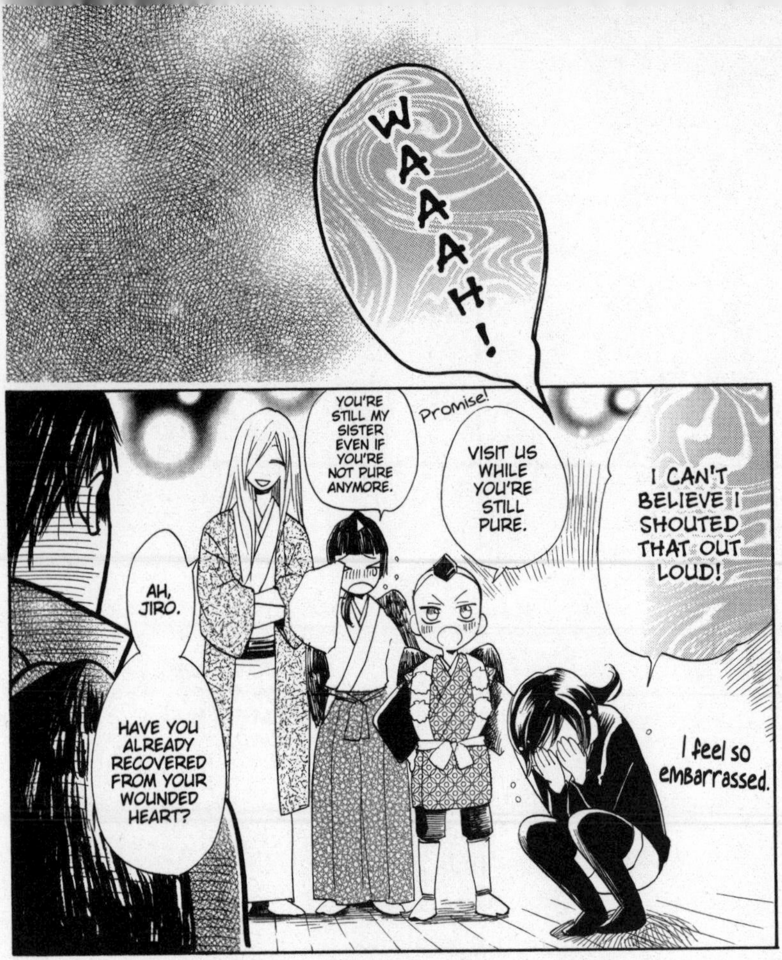
WAAAH!
I CAN'T BELIEVE I SHOUTED THAT OUT LOUD!
I feel so embarrassed.
VISIT US WHILE YOU'RE STILL PURE.
Promise!
YOU'RE STILL MY SISTER EVEN IF YOU'RE NOT PURE ANYMORE.
AH, JIRO.
HAVE YOU ALREADY RECOVERED FROM YOUR WOUNDED HEART?

IT'S TIME TO MOVE ON.

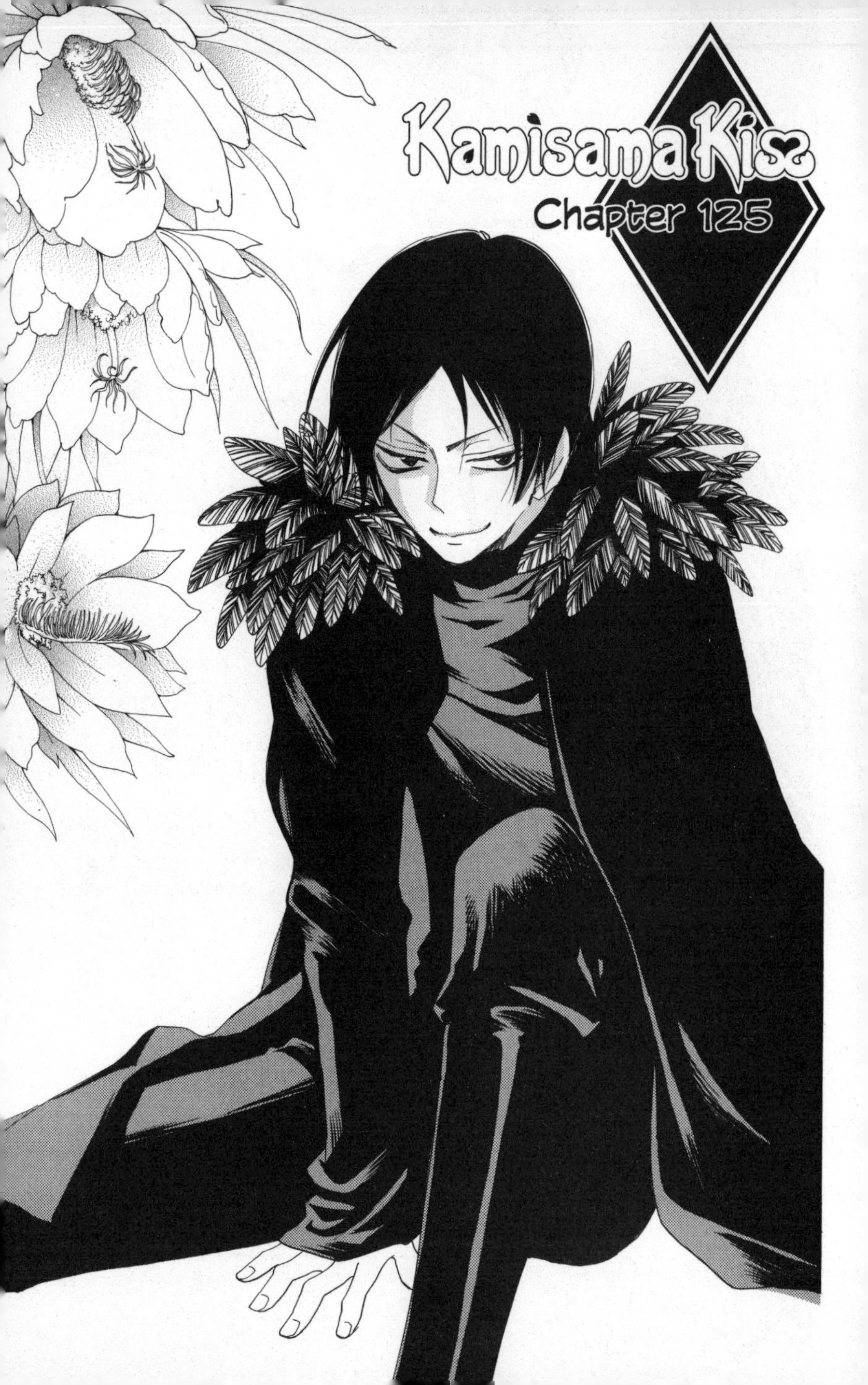
Kamisama Kiss
Chapter 125

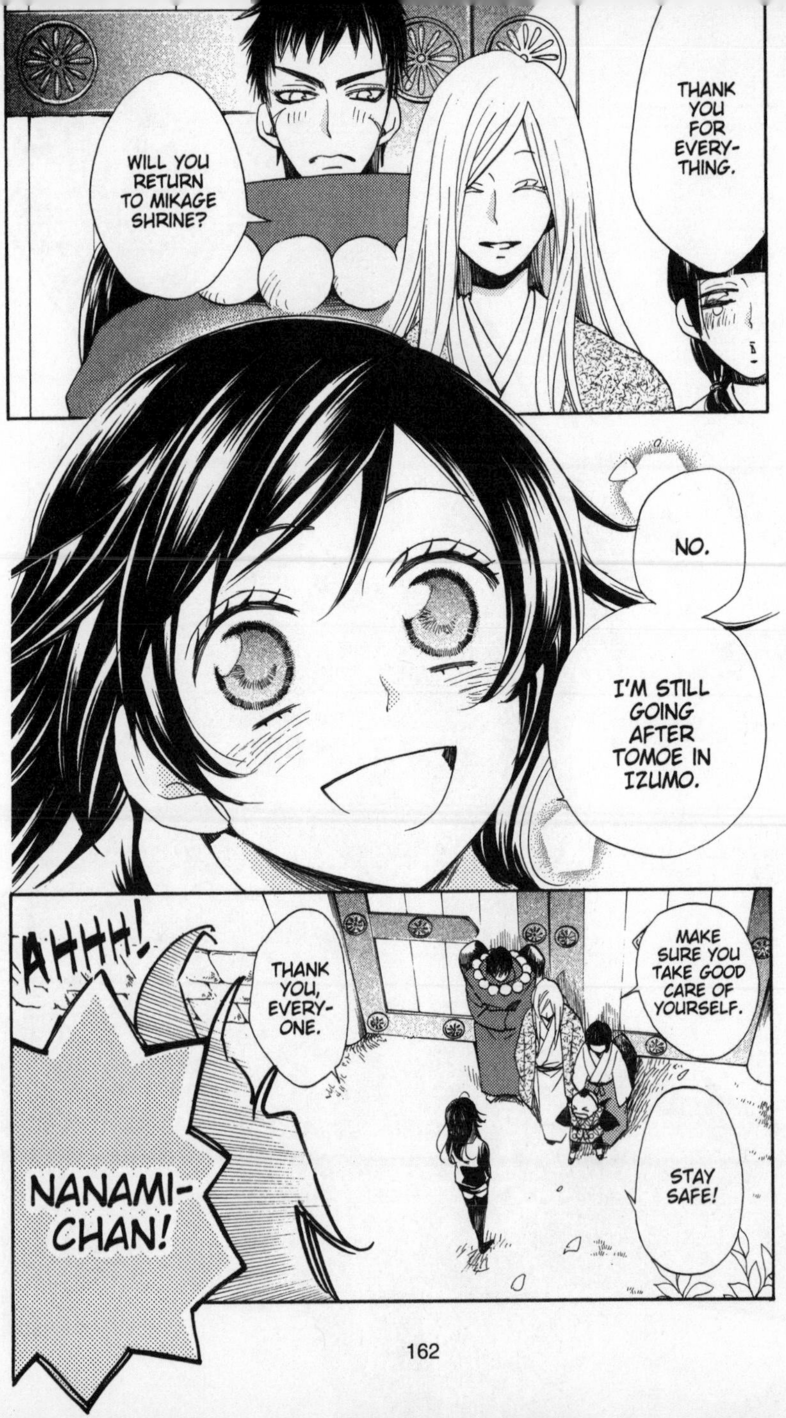
THANK YOU FOR EVERY-THING.
WILL YOU RETURN TO MIKAGE SHRINE?
NO.
I'M STILL GOING AFTER TOMOE IN IZUMO.
MAKE SURE YOU TAKE GOOD CARE OF YOURSELF.
STAY SAFE!
THANK YOU, EVERY-ONE.
AHHH!
NANAMI-CHAN!

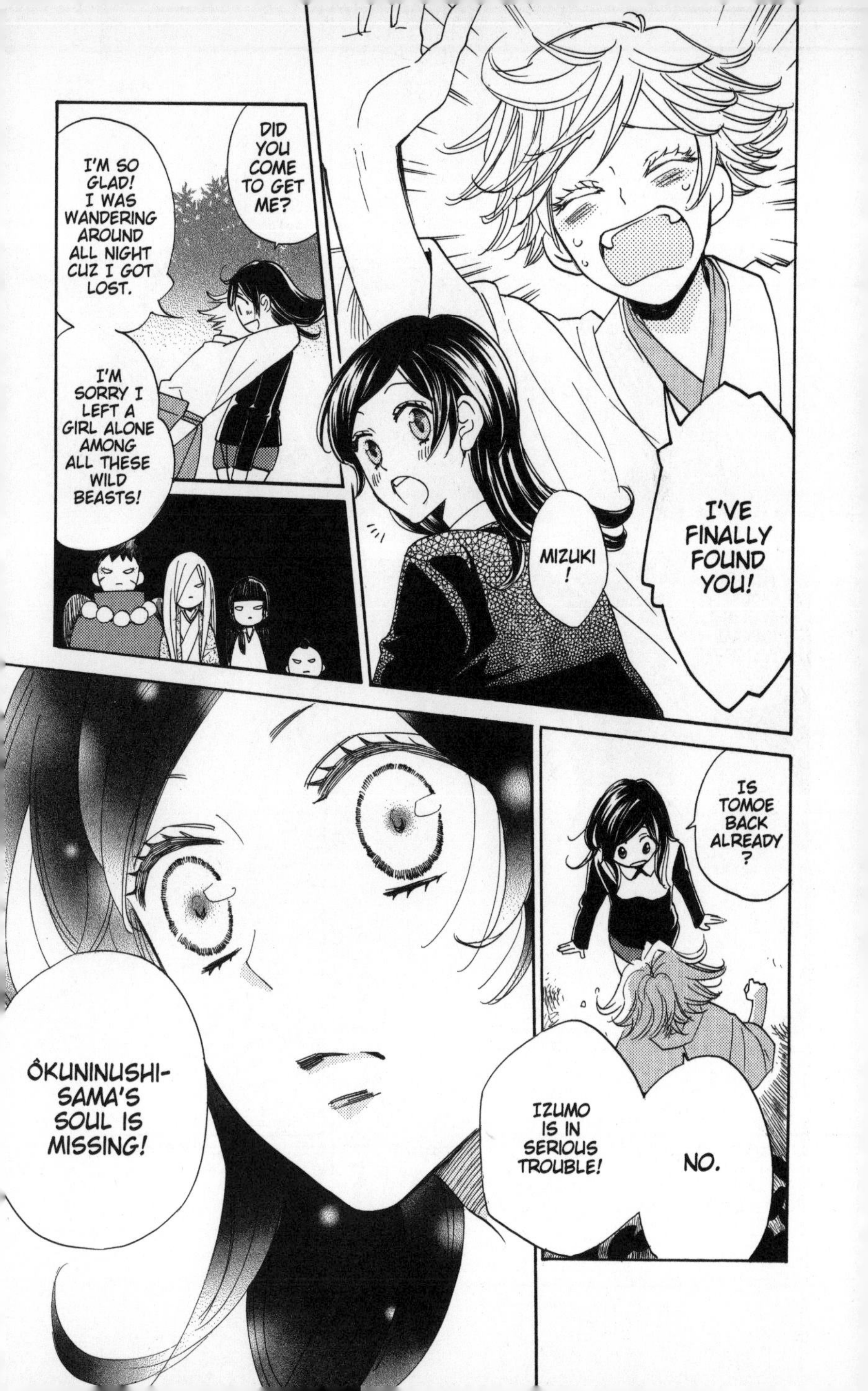
I'VE FINALLY FOUND YOU!
MIZUKI!
DID YOU COME TO GET ME?
I'M SO GLAD! I WAS WANDERING AROUND ALL NIGHT CUZ I GOT LOST.
I'M SORRY I LEFT A GIRL ALONE AMONG ALL THESE WILD BEASTS!
IS TOMOE BACK ALREADY?
NO.
IZUMO IS IN SERIOUS TROUBLE!
ÔKUNINUSHI-SAMA'S SOUL IS MISSING!

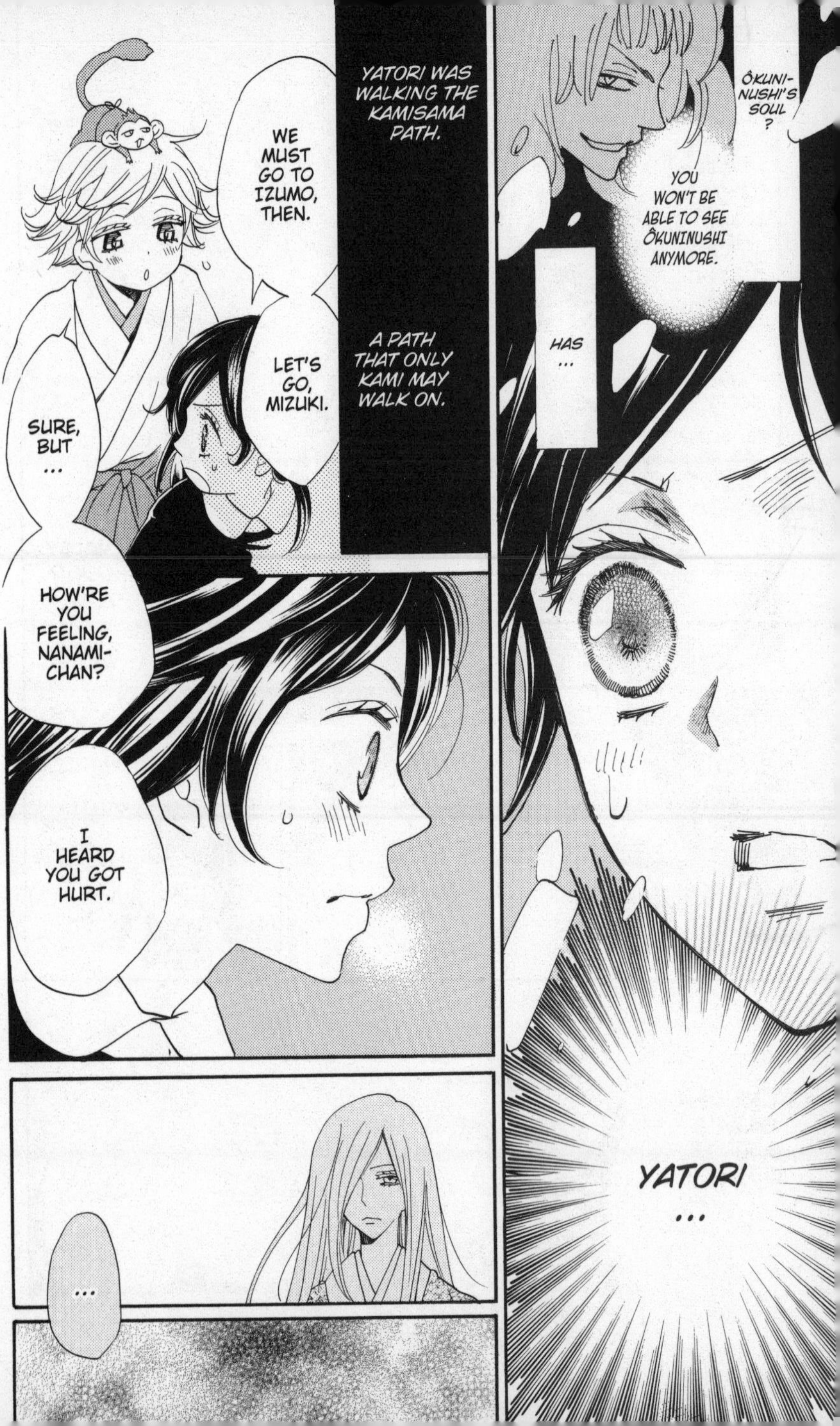
ÔKUNINUSHI'S SOUL?
YOU WON'T BE ABLE TO SEE ÔKUNINUSHI ANYMORE.
HAS ...
YATORI ...
YATORI WAS WALKING THE KAMISAMA PATH.
A PATH THAT ONLY KAMI MAY WALK ON.
WE MUST GO TO IZUMO, THEN.
LET'S GO, MIZUKI.
SURE, BUT ...
HOW'RE YOU FEELING, NANAMI-CHAN?
I HEARD YOU GOT HURT.
...

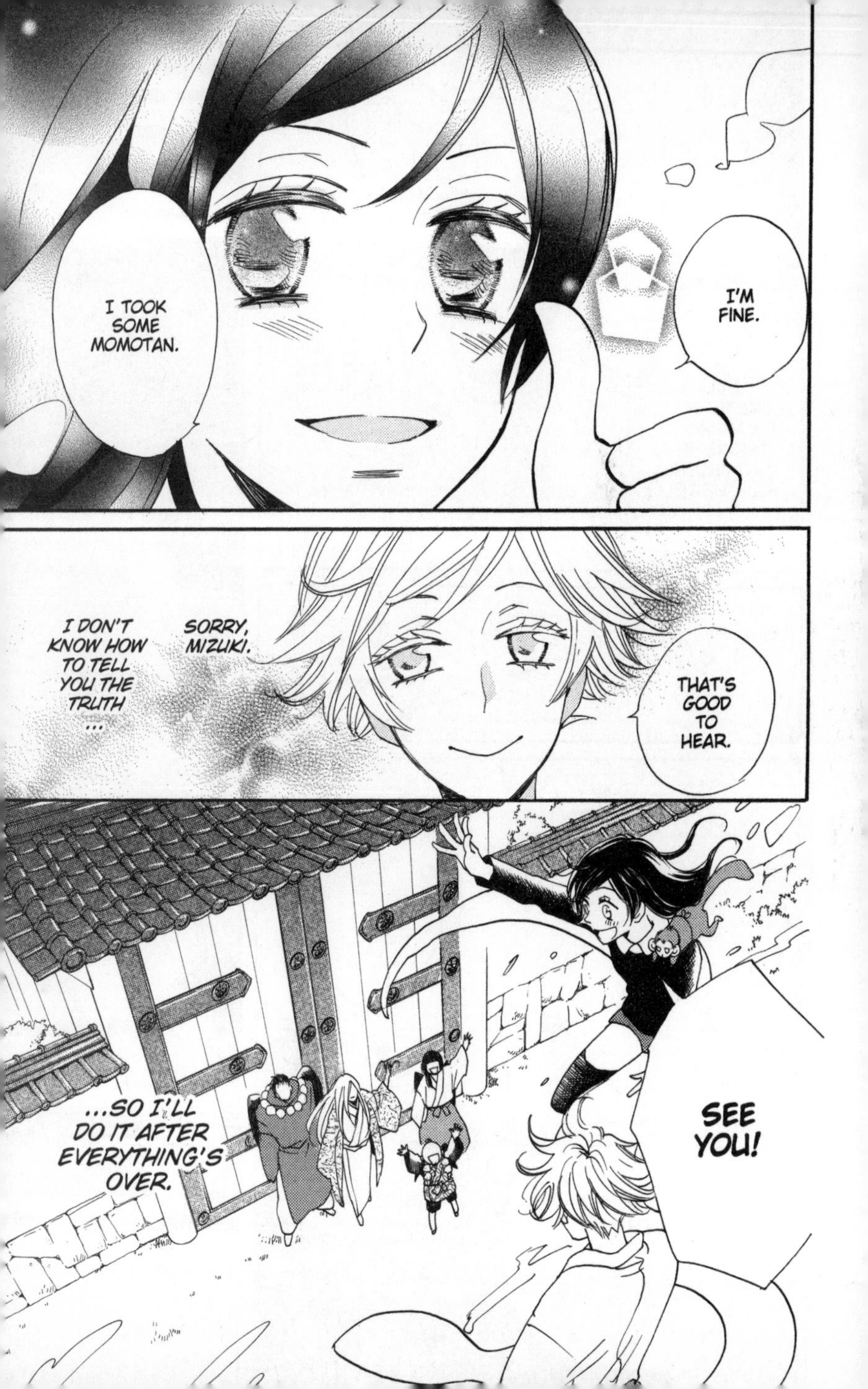
I'M FINE.
I TOOK SOME MOMOTAN.
THAT'S GOOD TO HEAR.
SORRY, MIZUKI.
I DON'T KNOW HOW TO TELL YOU THE TRUTH ...
SEE YOU!
...SO I'LL DO IT AFTER EVERYTHING'S OVER.

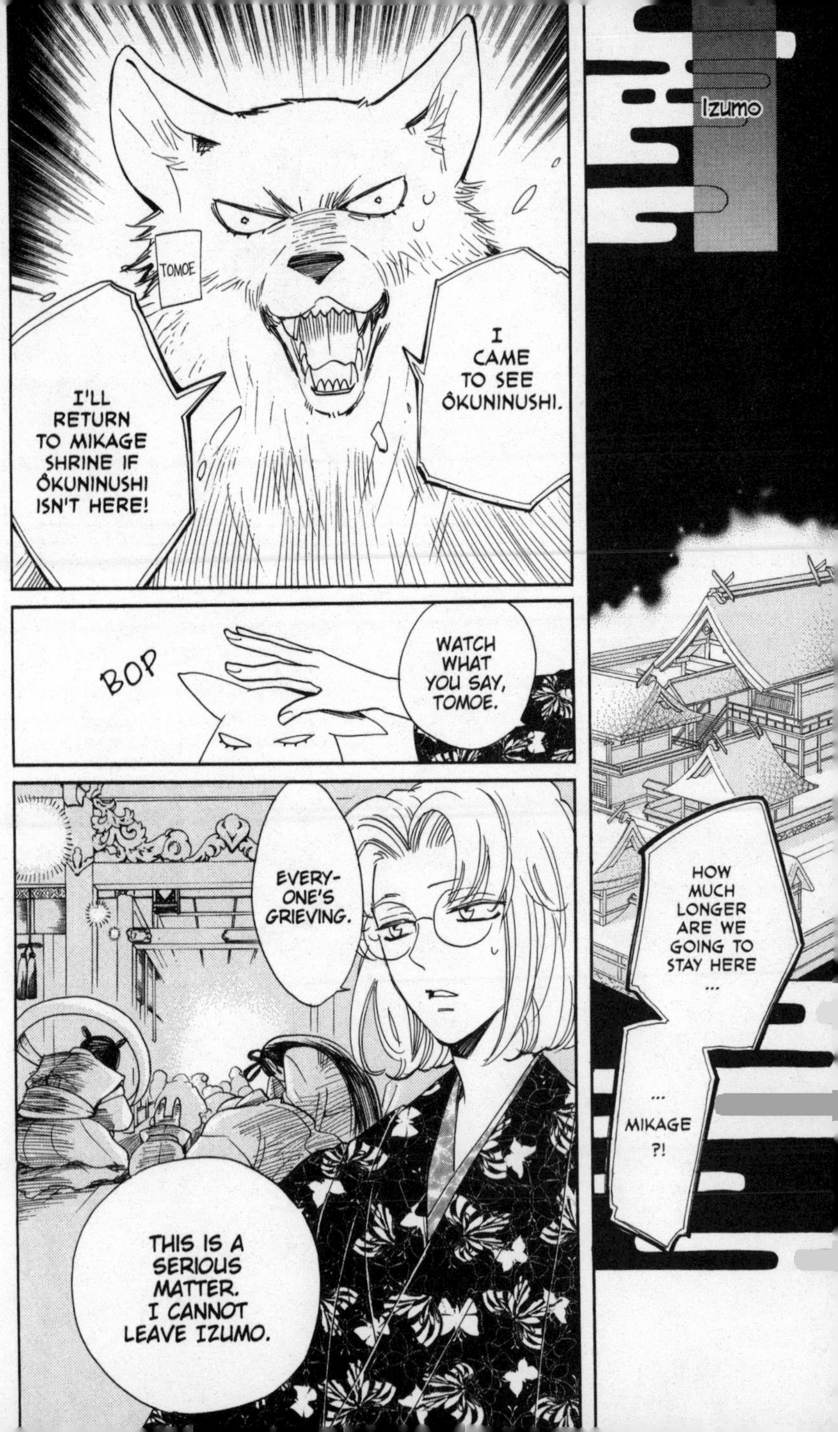
Izumo
HOW MUCH LONGER ARE WE GOING TO STAY HERE ...
... MIKAGE ?!
I CAME TO SEE ÔKUNINUSHI.
TOMOE
I'LL RETURN TO MIKAGE SHRINE IF ÔKUNINUSHI ISN'T HERE!
WATCH WHAT YOU SAY, TOMOE.
BOP
EVERY-ONE'S GRIEVING.
THIS IS A SERIOUS MATTER. I CANNOT LEAVE IZUMO.

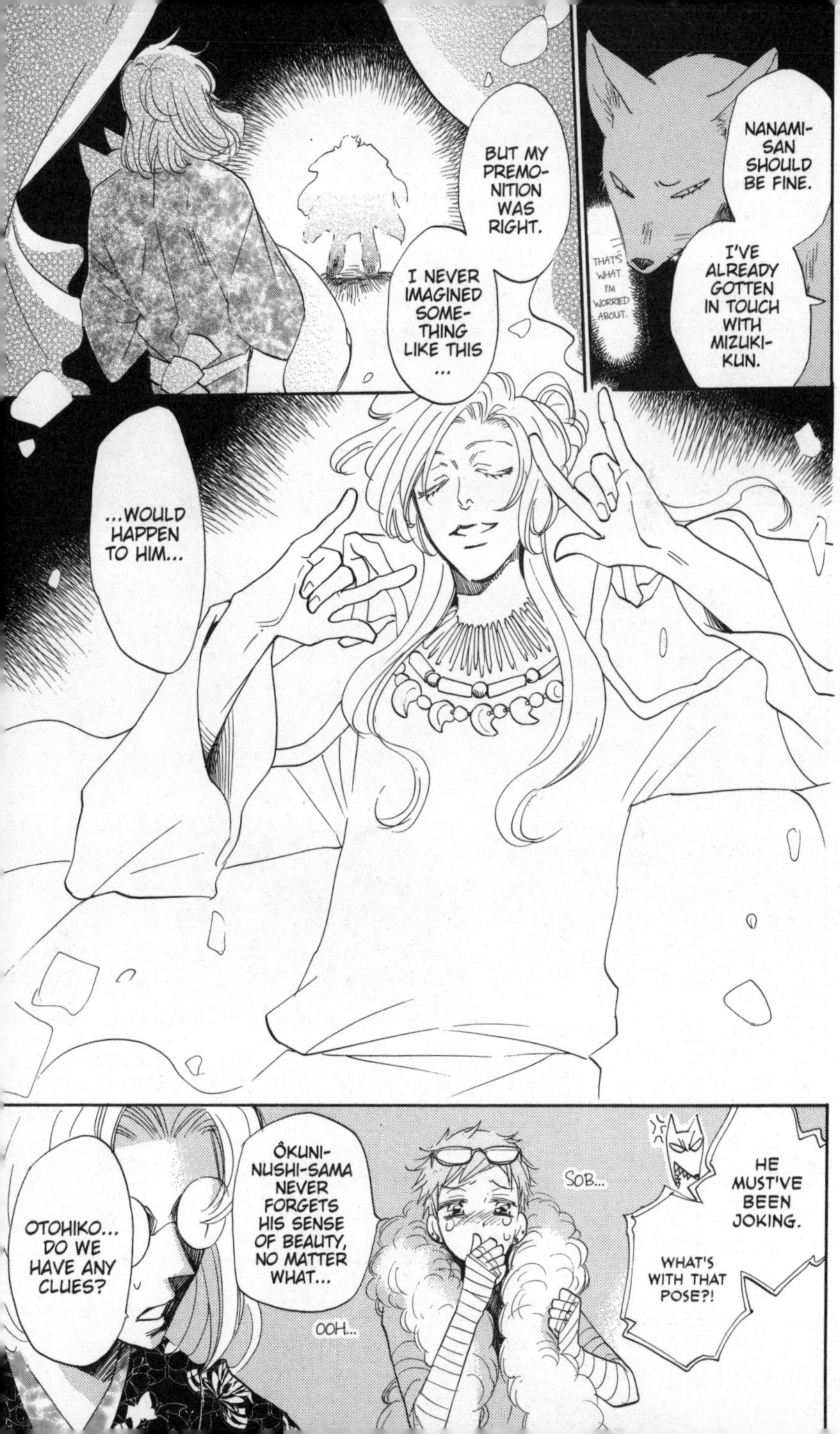
NANAMI-SAN SHOULD BE FINE.
I'VE ALREADY GOTTEN IN TOUCH WITH MIZUKI-KUN.
THAT'S WHAT I'M WORRIED ABOUT.
BUT MY PREMONITION WAS RIGHT.
I NEVER IMAGINED SOMETHING LIKE THIS...
...WOULD HAPPEN TO HIM...
HE MUST'VE BEEN JOKING.
WHAT'S WITH THAT POSE?!
SOB...
ÔKUNI-NUSHI-SAMA NEVER FORGETS HIS SENSE OF BEAUTY, NO MATTER WHAT...
OOH...
OTOHIKO... DO WE HAVE ANY CLUES?

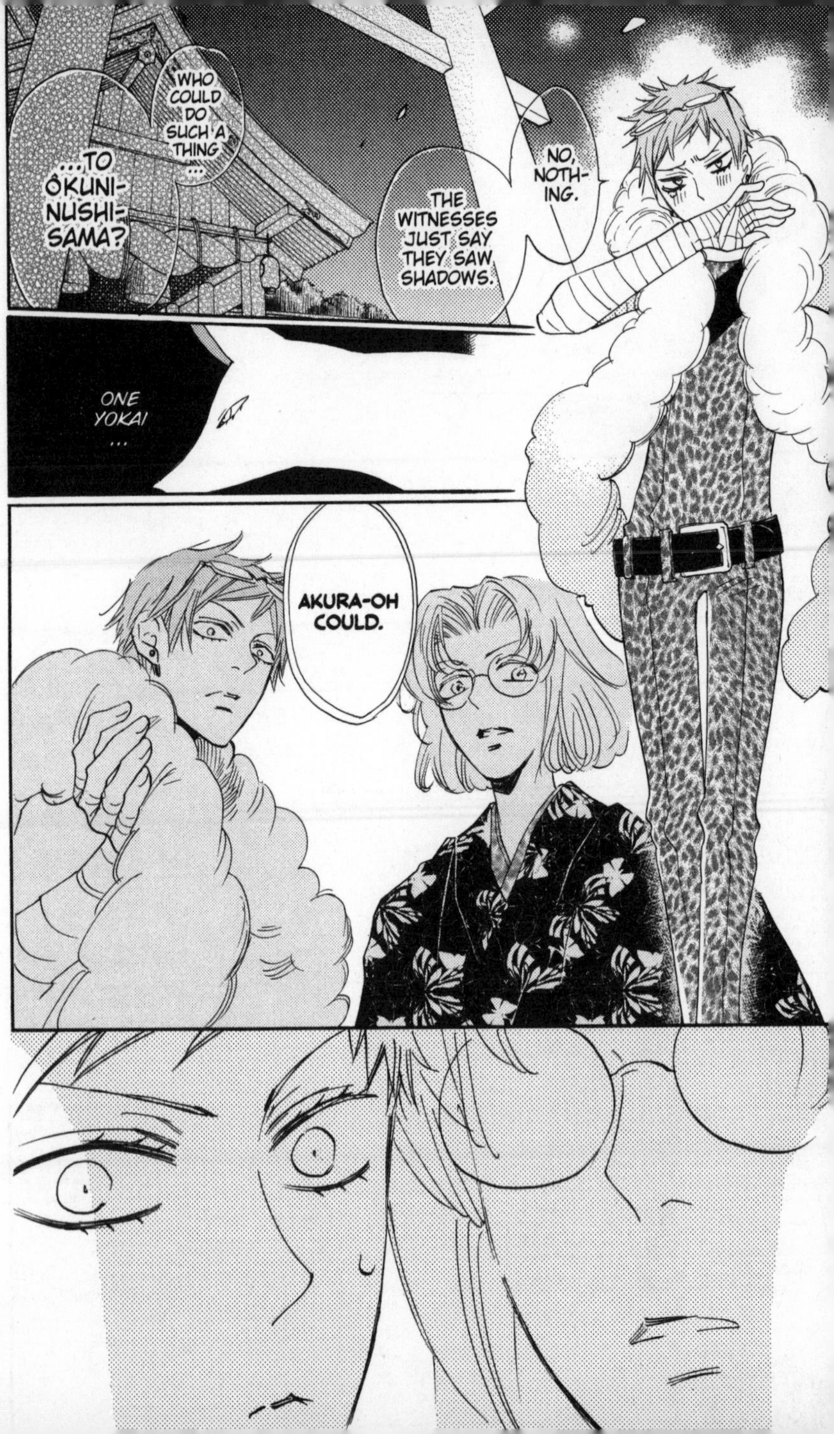
NO, NOTHING.
THE WITNESSES JUST SAY THEY SAW SHADOWS.
WHO COULD DO SUCH A THING...
...TO OKUNINUSHI-SAMA?
ONE YOKAI...
AKURA-OH COULD.

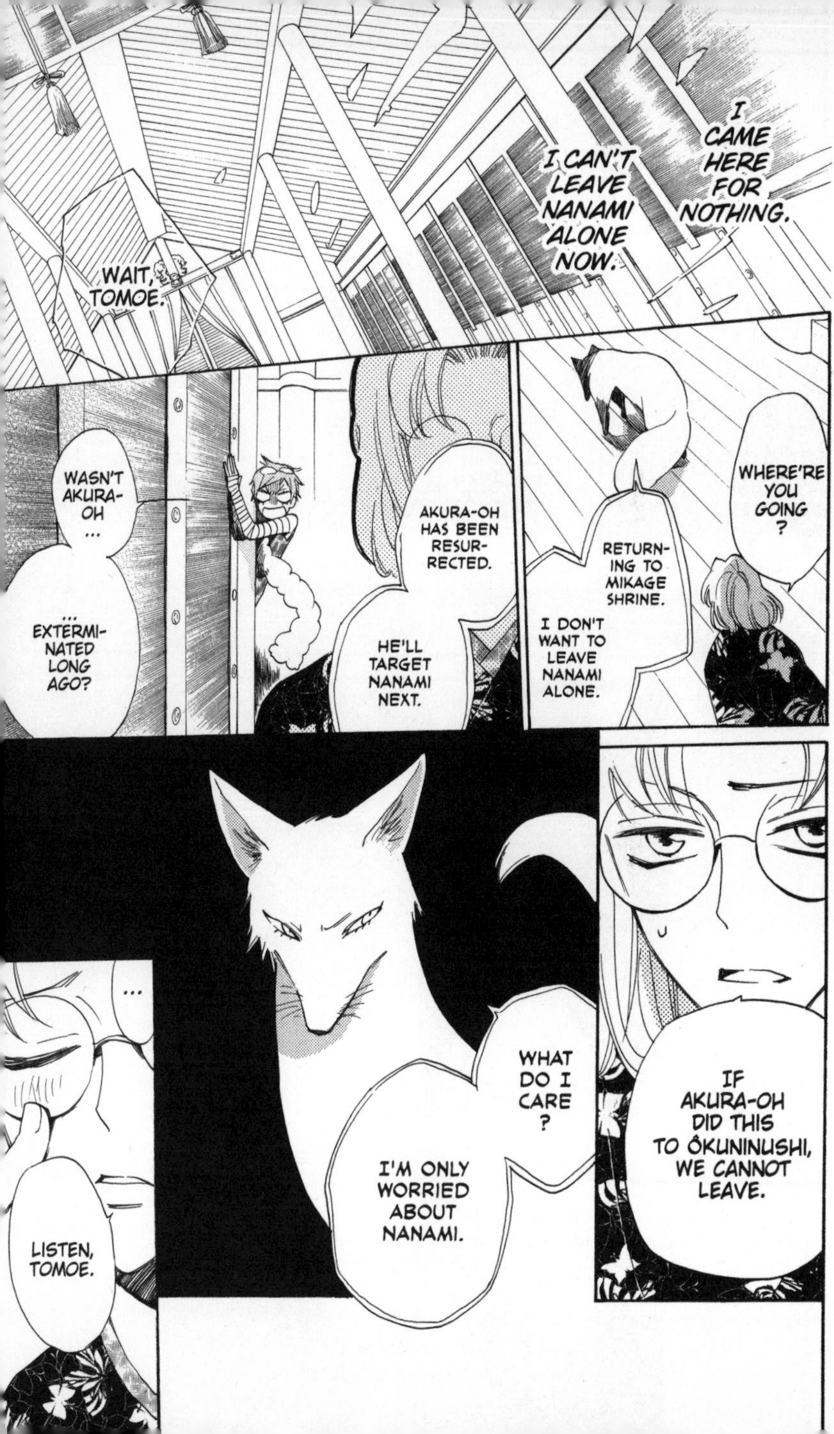
I CAME HERE FOR NOTHING.
I CAN'T LEAVE NANAMI ALONE NOW.
WAIT, TOMOE.
WHERE'RE YOU GOING?
RETURNING TO MIKAGE SHRINE.
I DON'T WANT TO LEAVE NANAMI ALONE.
AKURA-OH HAS BEEN RESURRECTED.
HE'LL TARGET NANAMI NEXT.
WASN'T AKURA-OH...
...EXTERMINATED LONG AGO?
IF AKURA-OH DID THIS TO ÔKUNINUSHI, WE CANNOT LEAVE.
WHAT DO I CARE?
I'M ONLY WORRIED ABOUT NANAMI.
...
LISTEN, TOMOE.

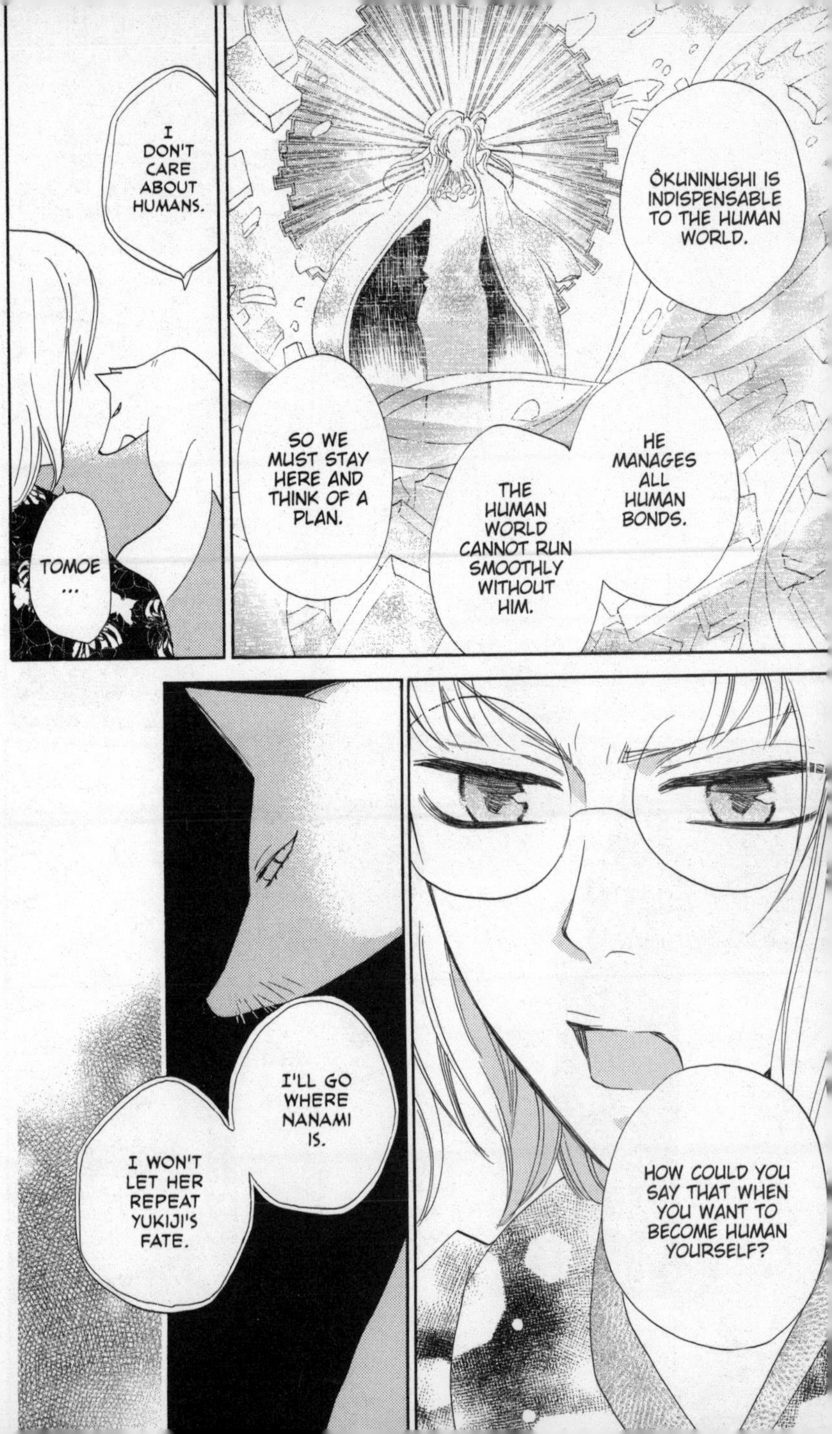
ÔKUNINUSHI IS INDISPENSABLE TO THE HUMAN WORLD.
HE MANAGES ALL HUMAN BONDS.
THE HUMAN WORLD CANNOT RUN SMOOTHLY WITHOUT HIM.
SO WE MUST STAY HERE AND THINK OF A PLAN.
I DON'T CARE ABOUT HUMANS.
TOMOE ...
HOW COULD YOU SAY THAT WHEN YOU WANT TO BECOME HUMAN YOURSELF?
I'LL GO WHERE NANAMI IS.
I WON'T LET HER REPEAT YUKIJI'S FATE.

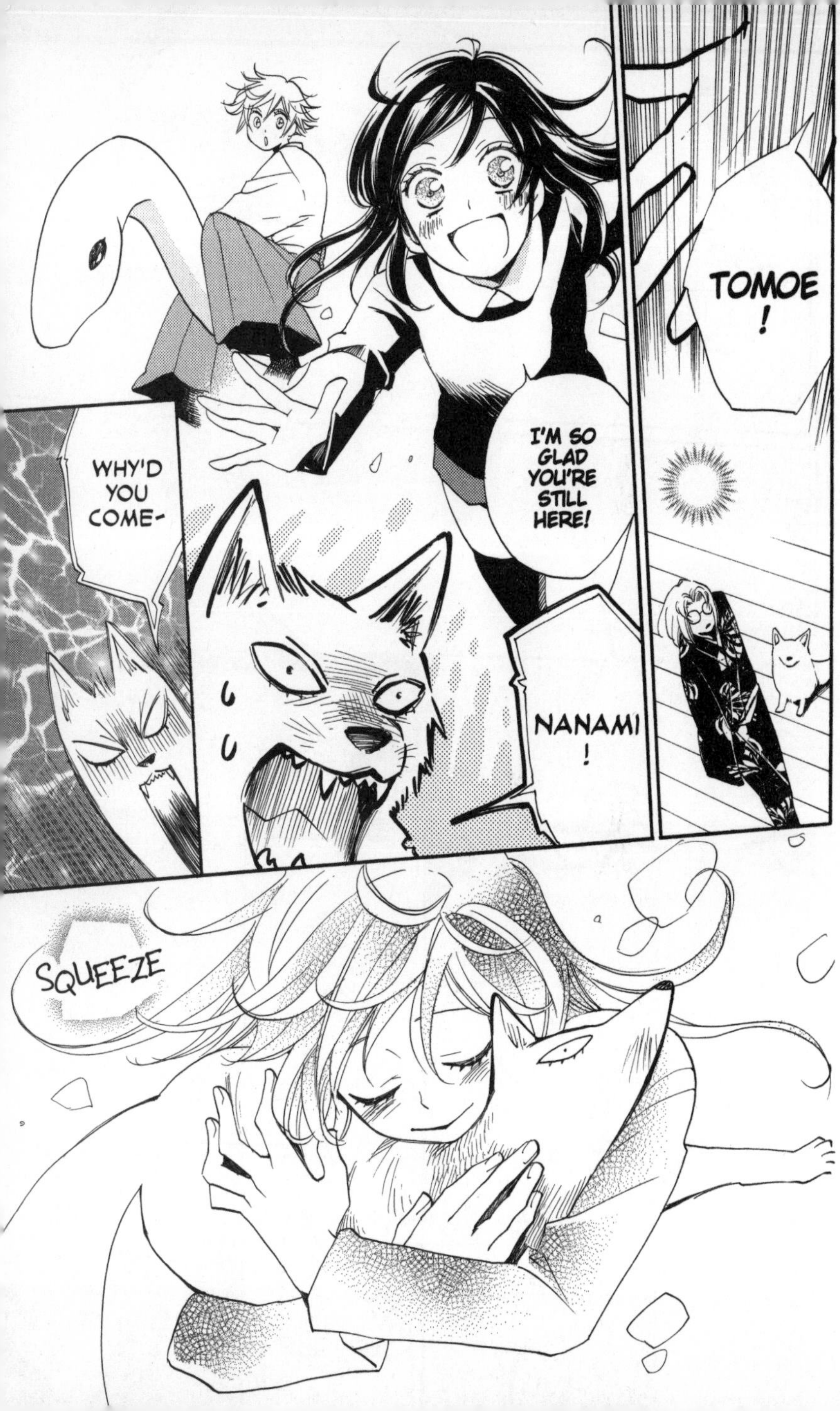
TOMOE!
I'M SO GLAD YOU'RE STILL HERE!
NANAMI!
WHY'D YOU COME-
SQUEEZE

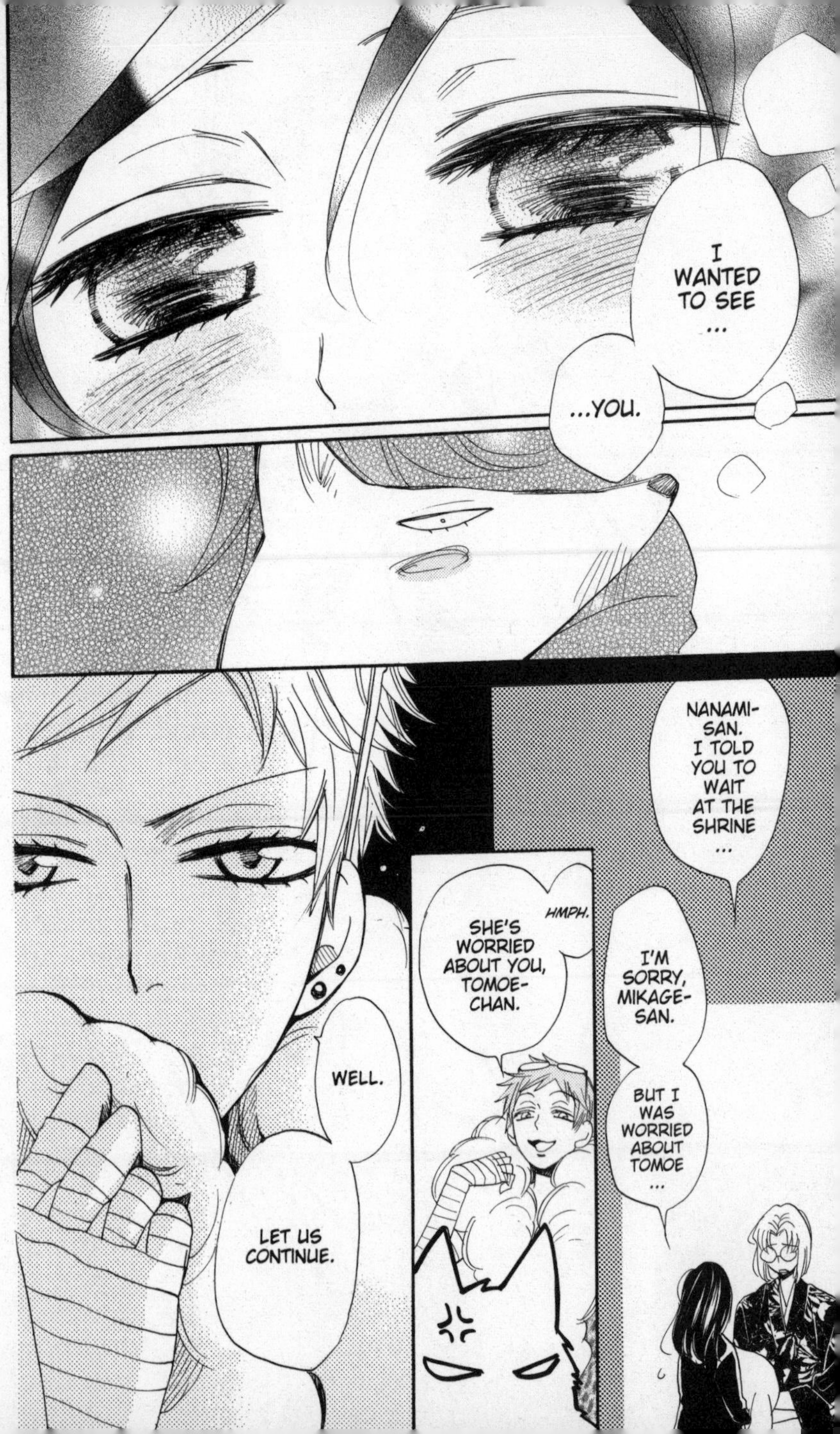
I WANTED TO SEE ...
...YOU.
NANAMI-SAN. I TOLD YOU TO WAIT AT THE SHRINE ...
I'M SORRY, MIKAGE-SAN.
BUT I WAS WORRIED ABOUT TOMOE ...
HMPH.
SHE'S WORRIED ABOUT YOU, TOMOE-CHAN.
WELL.
LET US CONTINUE.

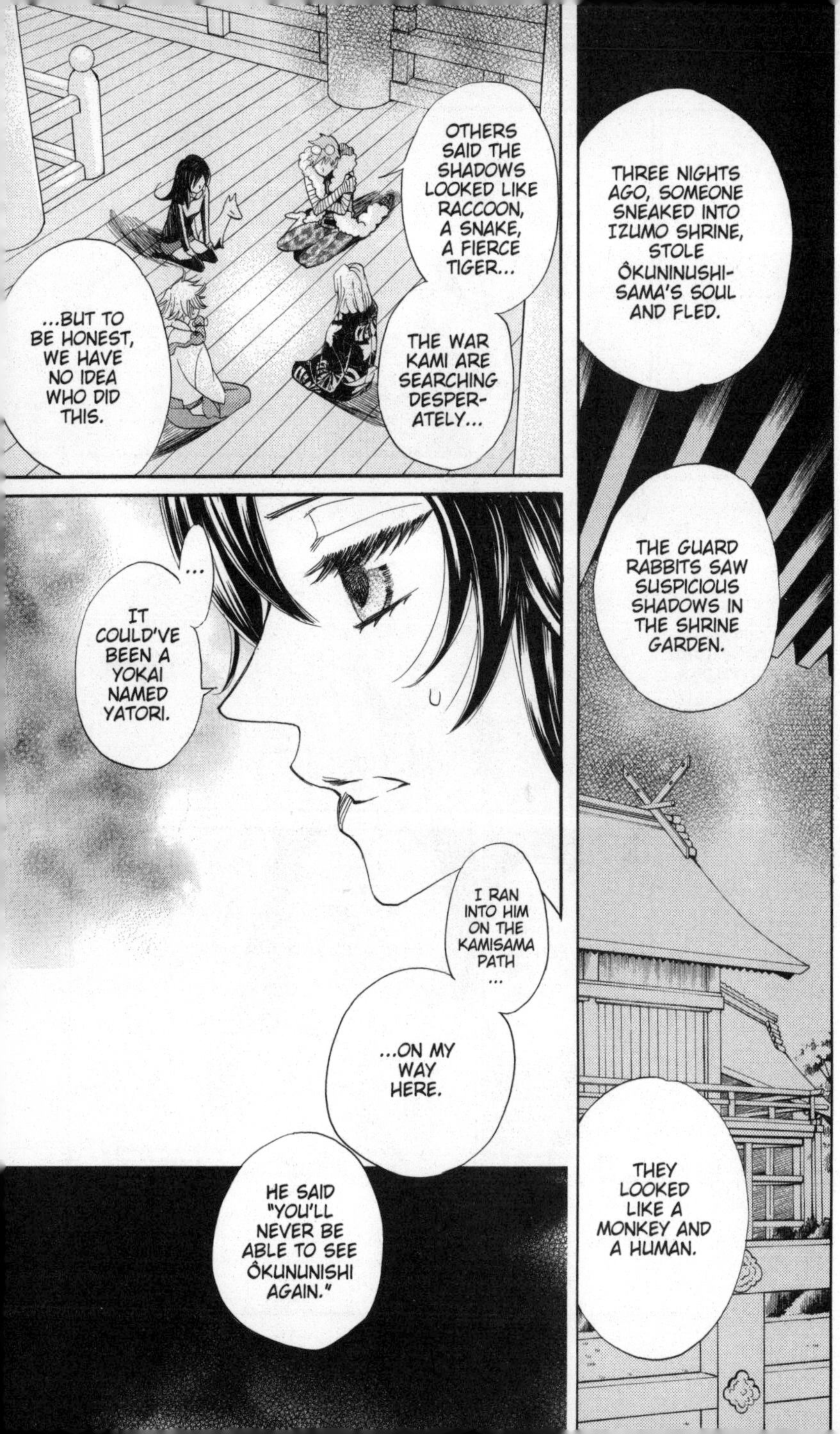
THREE NIGHTS AGO, SOMEONE SNEAKED INTO IZUMO SHRINE, STOLE ÔKUNINUSHI-SAMA'S SOUL AND FLED.
THE GUARD RABBITS SAW SUSPICIOUS SHADOWS IN THE SHRINE GARDEN.
THEY LOOKED LIKE A MONKEY AND A HUMAN.
OTHERS SAID THE SHADOWS LOOKED LIKE RACCOON, A SNAKE, A FIERCE TIGER...
THE WAR KAMI ARE SEARCHING DESPER-ATELY...
...BUT TO BE HONEST, WE HAVE NO IDEA WHO DID THIS.
...
IT COULD'VE BEEN A YOKAI NAMED YATORI.
I RAN INTO HIM ON THE KAMISAMA PATH...
...ON MY WAY HERE.
HE SAID "YOU'LL NEVER BE ABLE TO SEE ÔKUNUNISHI AGAIN."

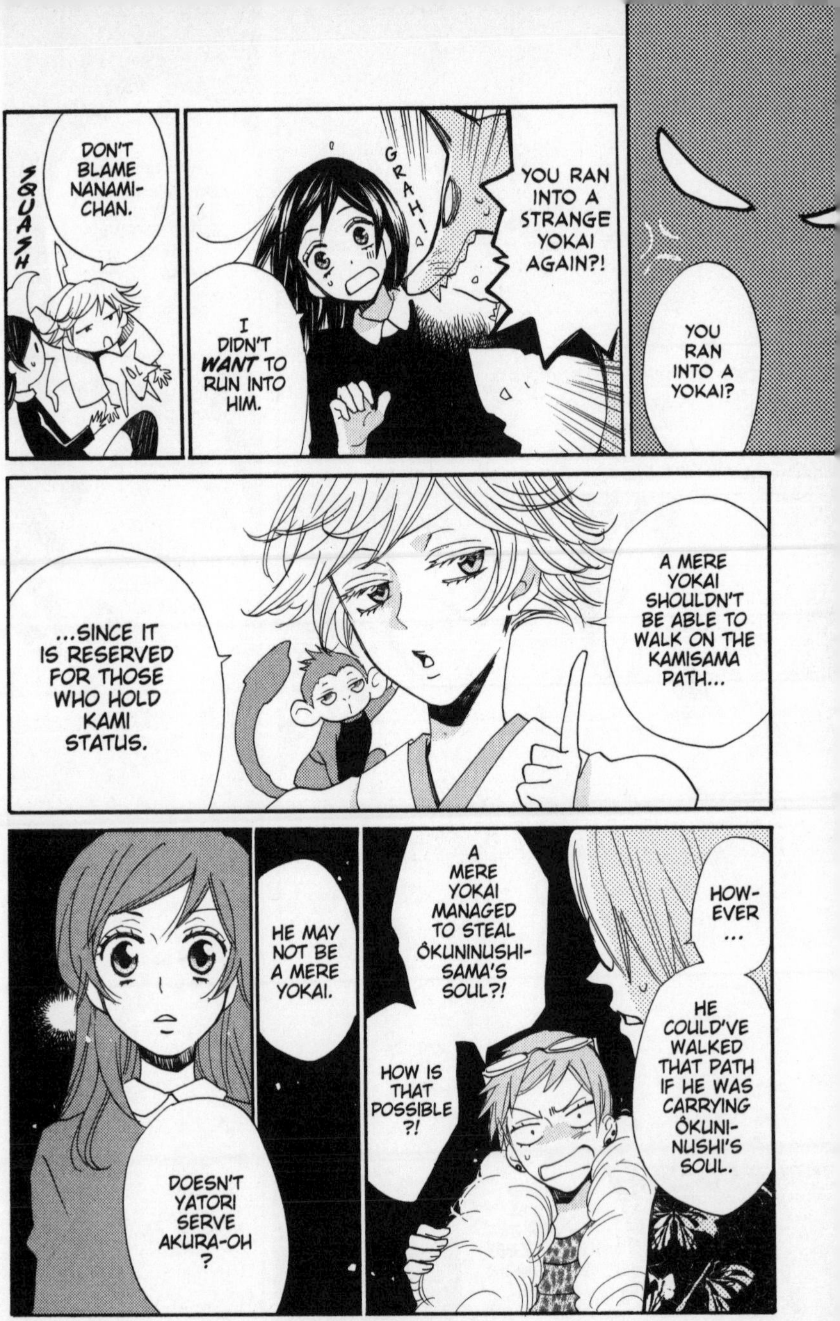
YOU RAN INTO A YOKAI?
YOU RAN INTO A STRANGE YOKAI AGAIN?!
GRAH!
I DIDN'T *WANT* TO RUN INTO HIM.
SQUASH
DON'T BLAME NANAMI-CHAN.
A MERE YOKAI SHOULDN'T BE ABLE TO WALK ON THE KAMISAMA PATH...
...SINCE IT IS RESERVED FOR THOSE WHO HOLD KAMI STATUS.
HOW-EVER...
HE COULD'VE WALKED THAT PATH IF HE WAS CARRYING ÔKUNI-NUSHI'S SOUL.
A MERE YOKAI MANAGED TO STEAL ÔKUNINUSHI-SAMA'S SOUL?!
HOW IS THAT POSSIBLE?!
HE MAY NOT BE A MERE YOKAI.
DOESN'T YATORI SERVE AKURA-OH?

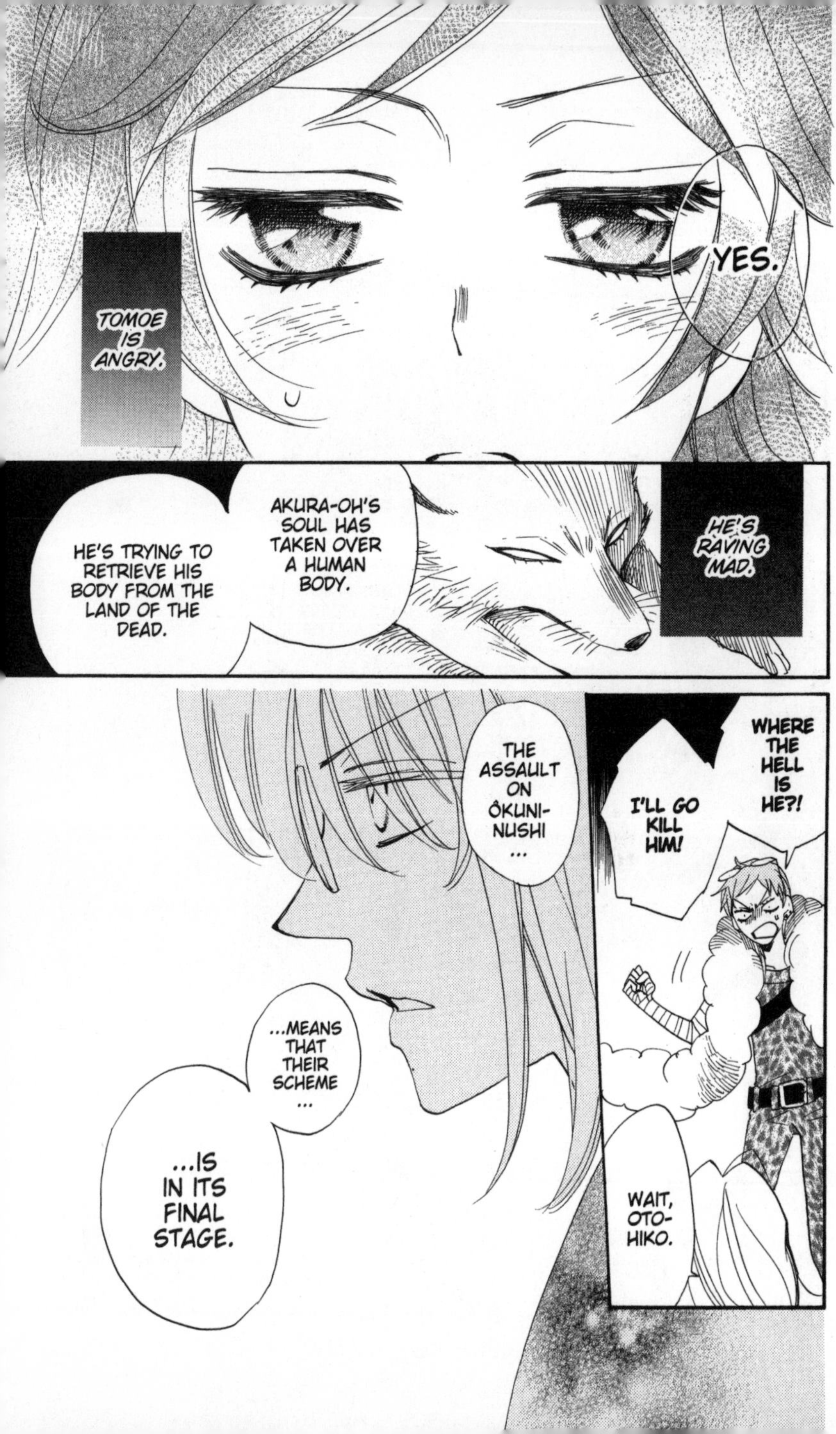
YES.
TOMOE IS ANGRY.
HE'S RAVING MAD.
AKURA-OH'S SOUL HAS TAKEN OVER A HUMAN BODY.
HE'S TRYING TO RETRIEVE HIS BODY FROM THE LAND OF THE DEAD.
WHERE THE HELL IS HE?!
I'LL GO KILL HIM!
WAIT, OTO-HIKO.
THE ASSAULT ON ÔKUNI-NUSHI...
...MEANS THAT THEIR SCHEME...
...IS IN ITS FINAL STAGE.

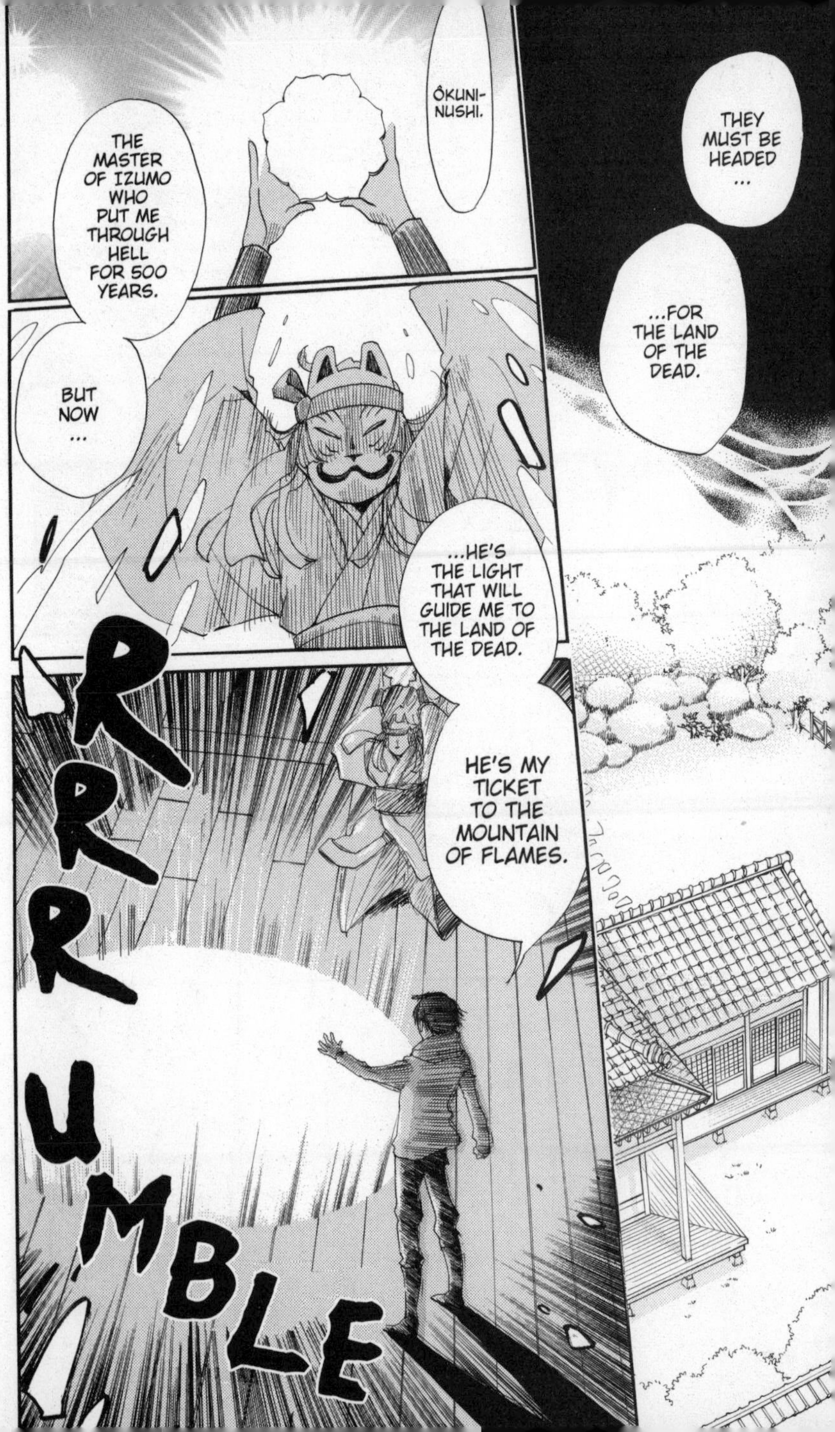
THEY MUST BE HEADED...
...FOR THE LAND OF THE DEAD.
ÔKUNI-NUSHI.
THE MASTER OF IZUMO WHO PUT ME THROUGH HELL FOR 500 YEARS.
BUT NOW...
...HE'S THE LIGHT THAT WILL GUIDE ME TO THE LAND OF THE DEAD.
HE'S MY TICKET TO THE MOUNTAIN OF FLAMES.
RRRUMBLE

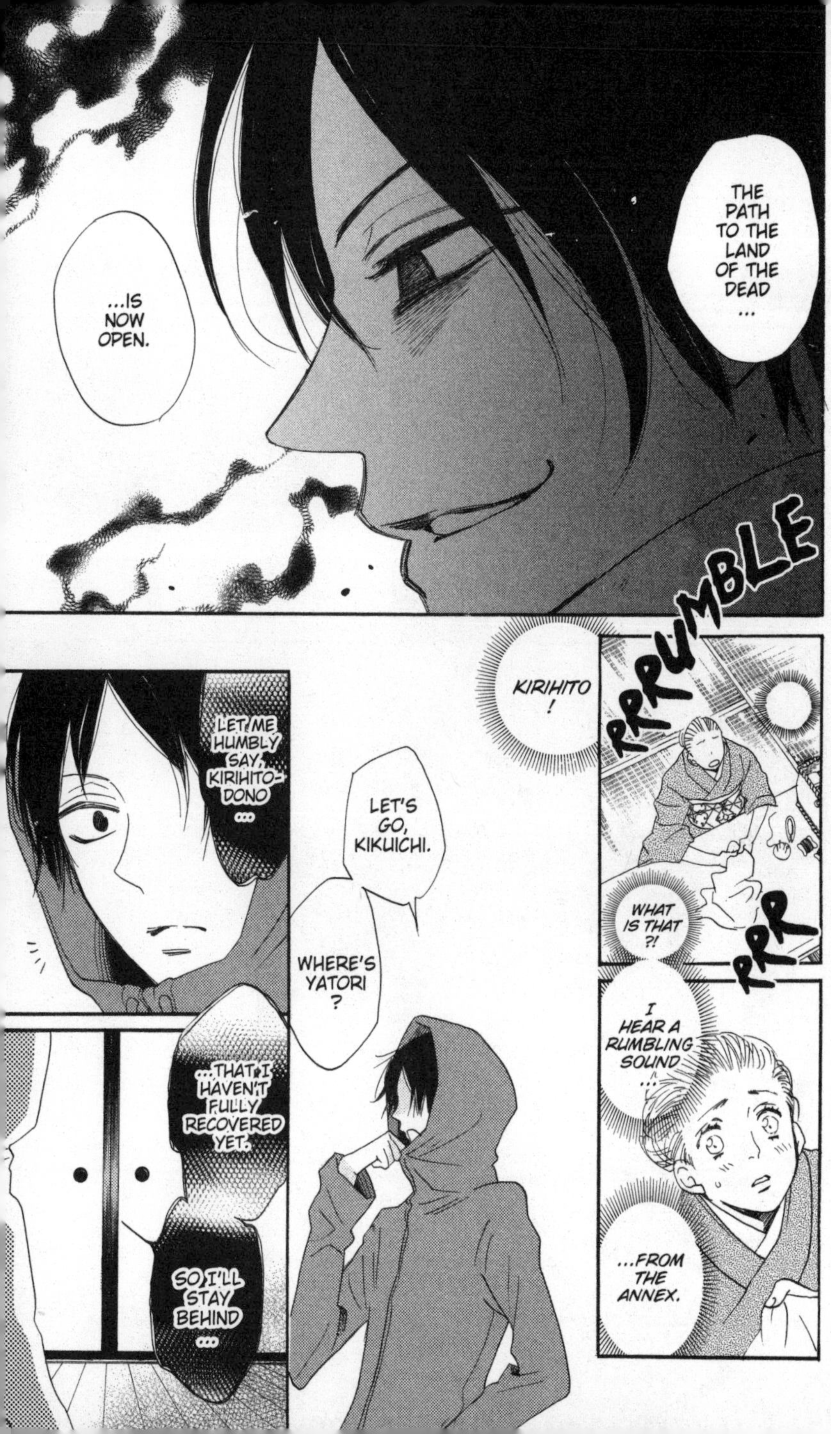
THE PATH TO THE LAND OF THE DEAD...
...IS NOW OPEN.
RRRUMBLE
KIRIHITO!
WHAT IS THAT?!
RRR
I HEAR A RUMBLING SOUND...
...FROM THE ANNEX.
LET'S GO, KIKUICHI.
WHERE'S YATORI?
LET ME HUMBLY SAY, KIRIHITO-DONO...
...THAT I HAVEN'T FULLY RECOVERED YET.
SO I'LL STAY BEHIND...

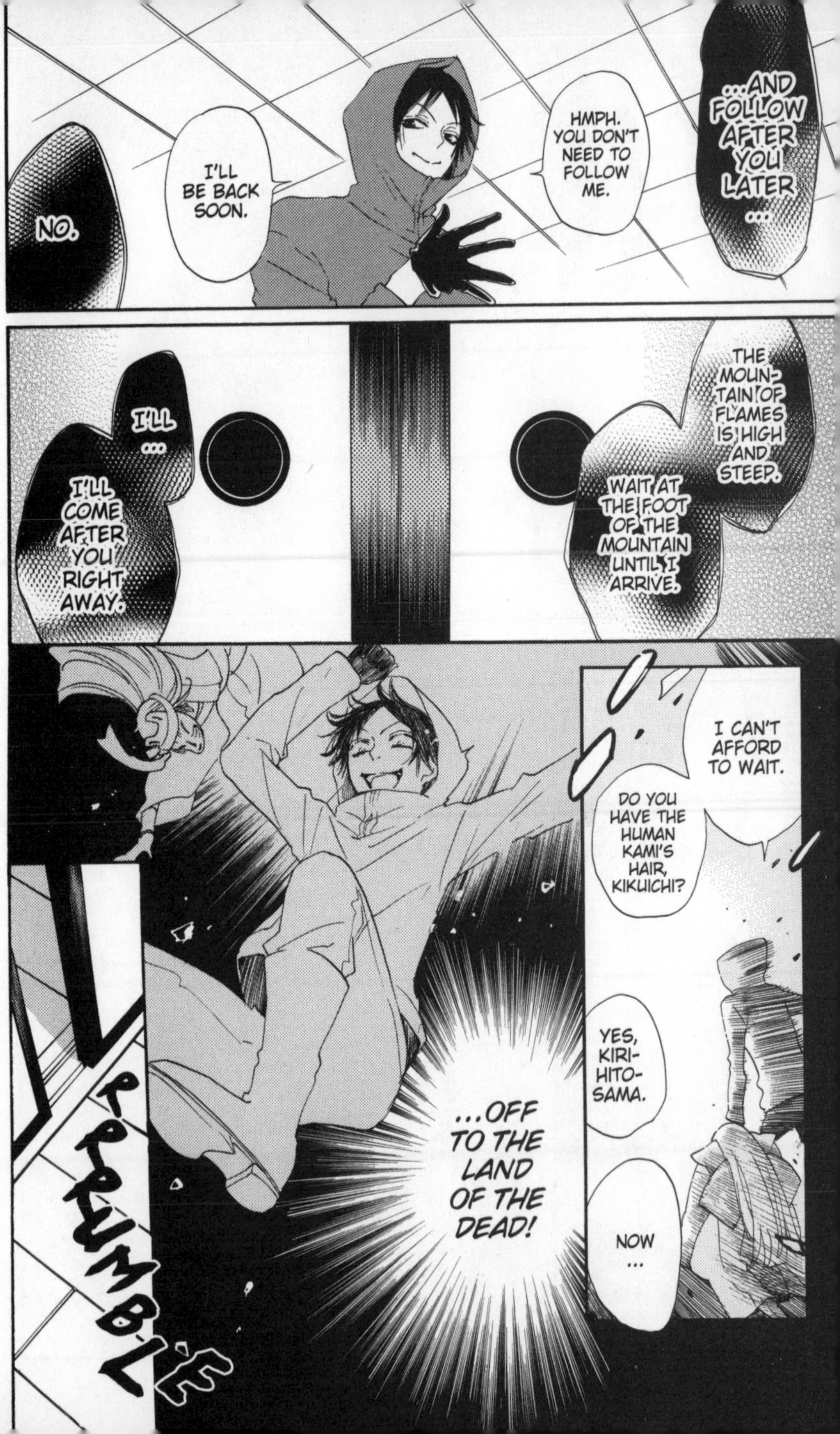
...AND FOLLOW AFTER YOU LATER ...
HMPH. YOU DON'T NEED TO FOLLOW ME.
I'LL BE BACK SOON.
NO.
THE MOUN-TAIN OF FLAMES IS HIGH AND STEEP.
WAIT AT THE FOOT OF THE MOUNTAIN UNTIL I ARRIVE.
I'LL ...
I'LL COME AFTER YOU RIGHT AWAY.
I CAN'T AFFORD TO WAIT.
DO YOU HAVE THE HUMAN KAMI'S HAIR, KIKUICHI?
YES, KIRI-HITO-SAMA.
NOW ...
...OFF TO THE LAND OF THE DEAD!
RRUMBLE

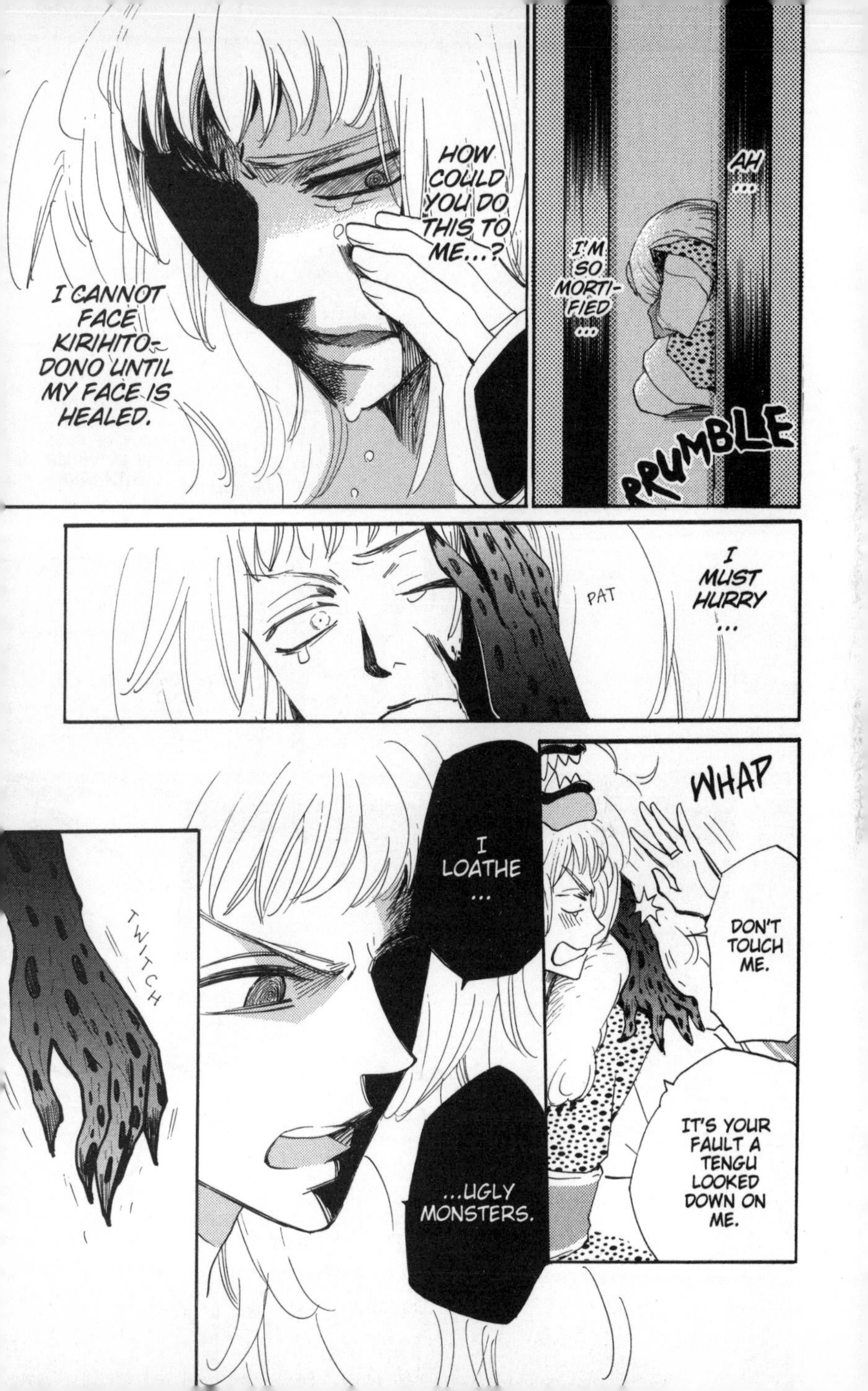
AH...
I'M SO MORTIFIED...
RRUMBLE
HOW COULD YOU DO THIS TO ME...?
I CANNOT FACE KIRIHITO-DONO UNTIL MY FACE IS HEALED.
I MUST HURRY...
PAT
WHAP
DON'T TOUCH ME.
IT'S YOUR FAULT A TENGU LOOKED DOWN ON ME.
I LOATHE...
...UGLY MONSTERS.
TWITCH

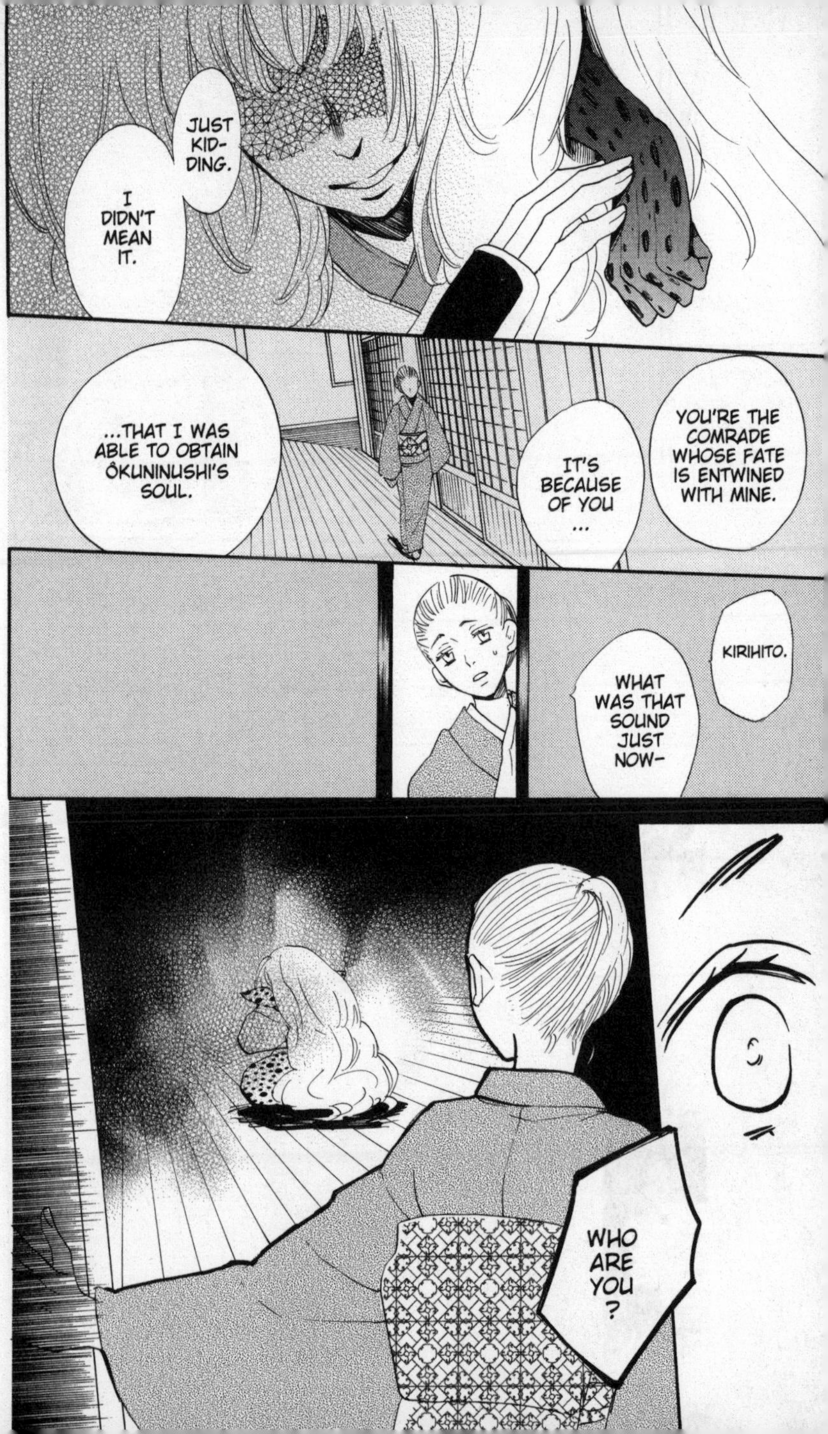
JUST KID-DING.
I DIDN'T MEAN IT.
YOU'RE THE COMRADE WHOSE FATE IS ENTWINED WITH MINE.
IT'S BECAUSE OF YOU ...
...THAT I WAS ABLE TO OBTAIN ÔKUNINUSHI'S SOUL.
KIRIHITO.
WHAT WAS THAT SOUND JUST NOW-
WHO ARE YOU?

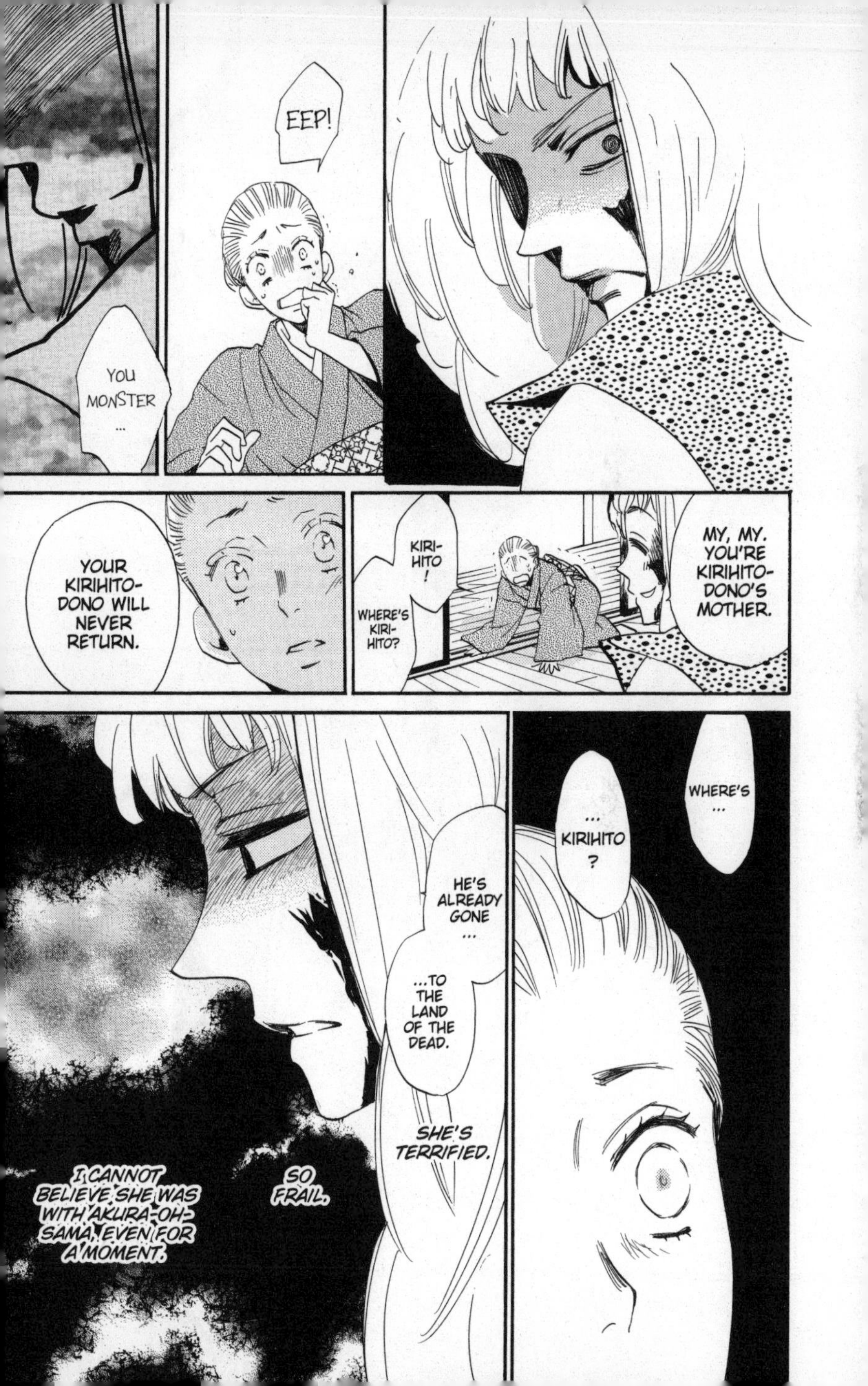
EEP!
YOU MONSTER ...
MY, MY. YOU'RE KIRIHITO-DONO'S MOTHER.
KIRIHITO!
WHERE'S KIRIHITO?
YOUR KIRIHITO-DONO WILL NEVER RETURN.
WHERE'S ...
... KIRIHITO ?
HE'S ALREADY GONE ...
...TO THE LAND OF THE DEAD.
SHE'S TERRIFIED.
SO FRAIL.
I CANNOT BELIEVE SHE WAS WITH AKURA-OH-SAMA, EVEN FOR A MOMENT.

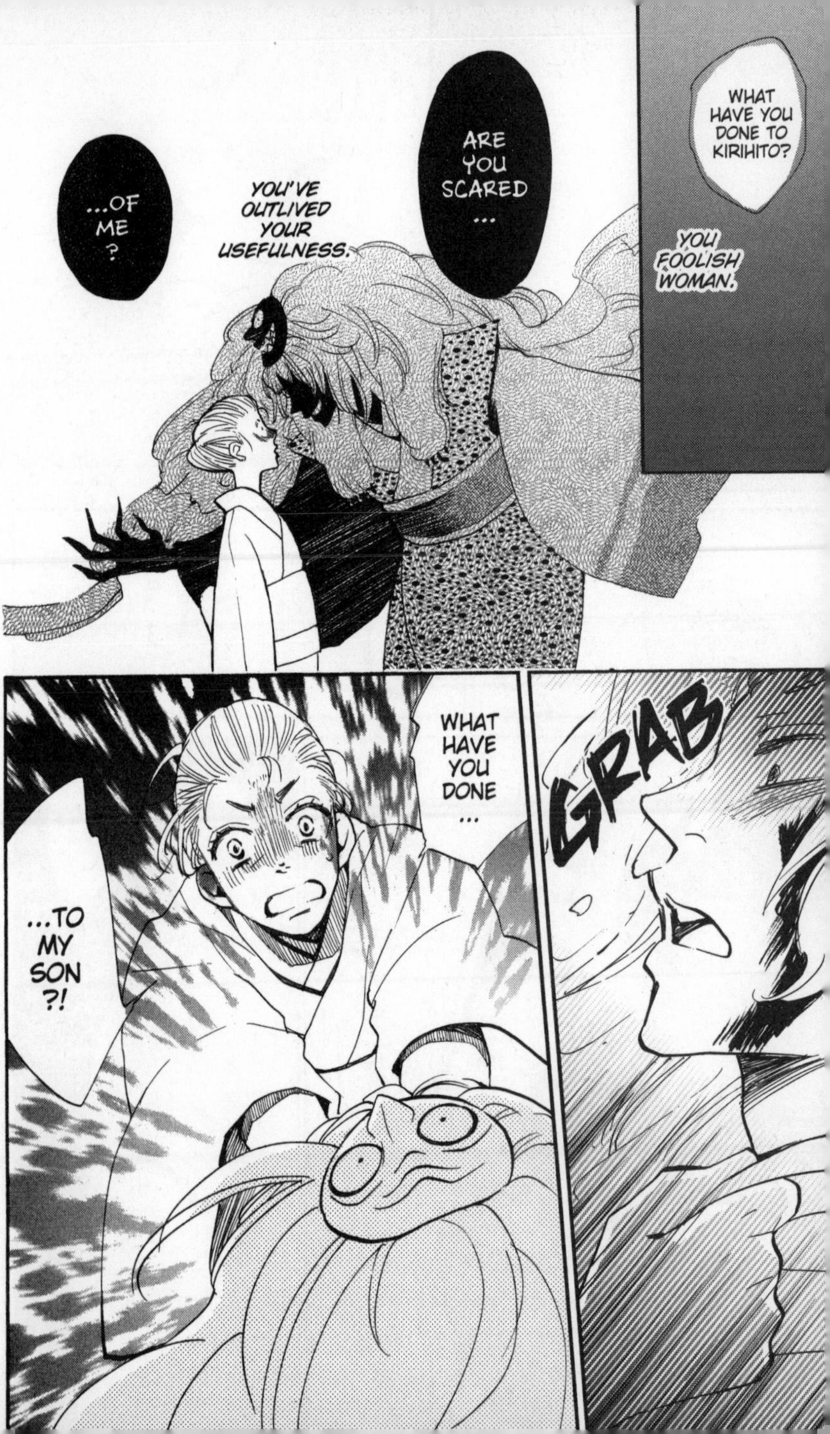
WHAT HAVE YOU DONE TO KIRIHITO?
YOU FOOLISH WOMAN.
ARE YOU SCARED...
YOU'VE OUTLIVED YOUR USEFULNESS.
...OF ME?
GRAB
WHAT HAVE YOU DONE...
...TO MY SON?!

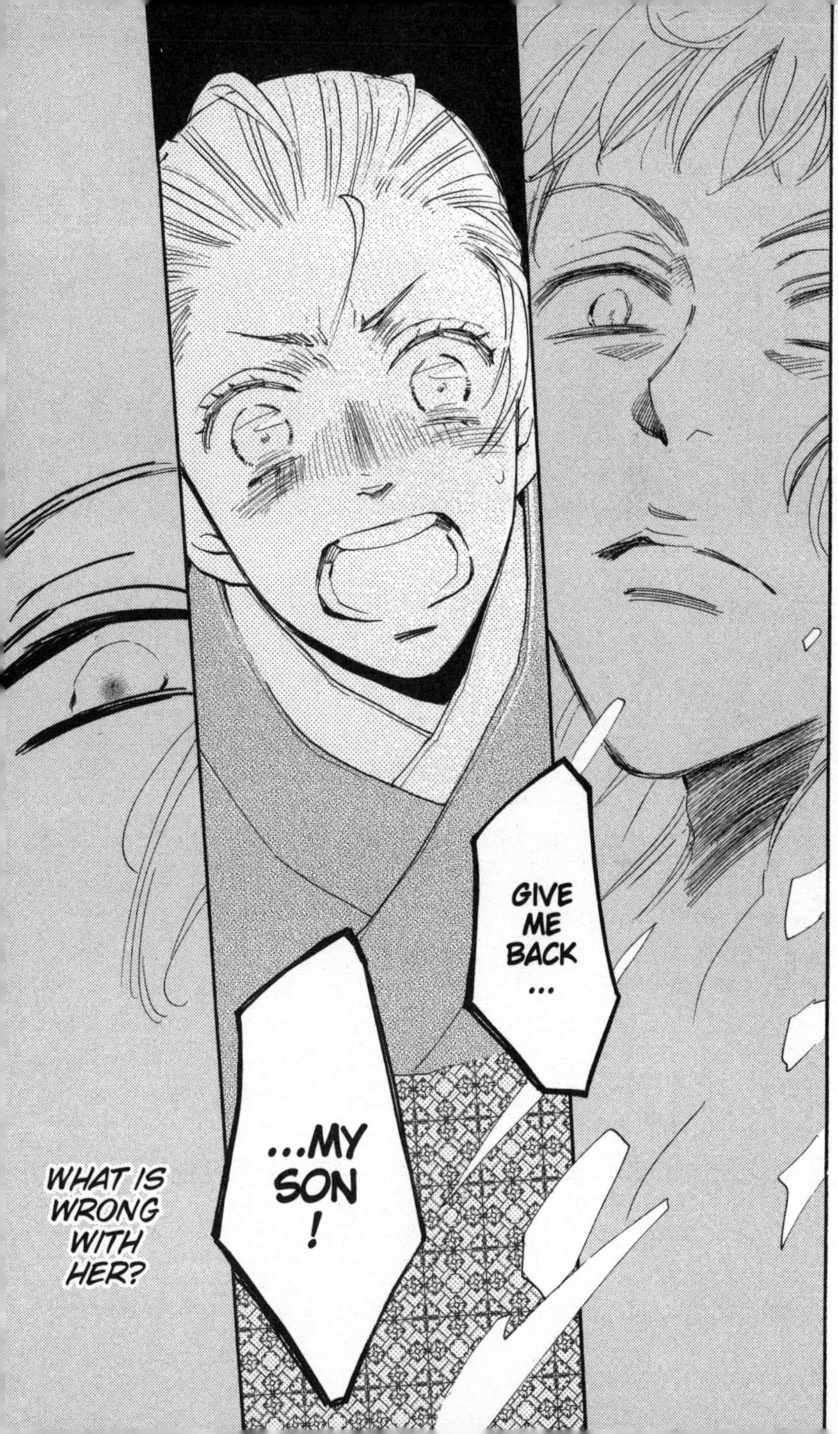
GIVE ME BACK ...
...MY SON!
WHAT IS WRONG WITH HER?

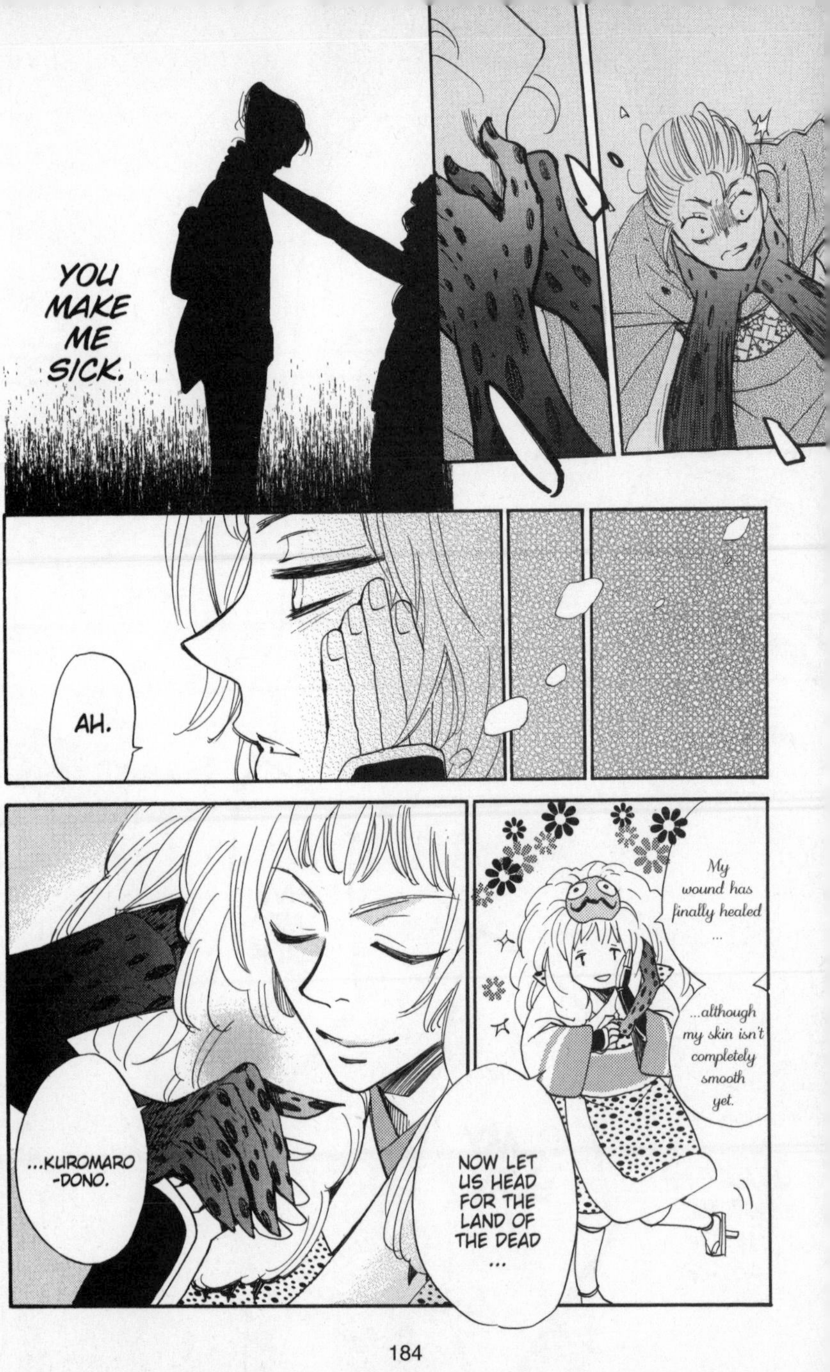
YOU MAKE ME SICK.
AH.
My wound has finally healed ...
...although my skin isn't completely smooth yet.
NOW LET US HEAD FOR THE LAND OF THE DEAD ...
...KUROMARO-DONO.

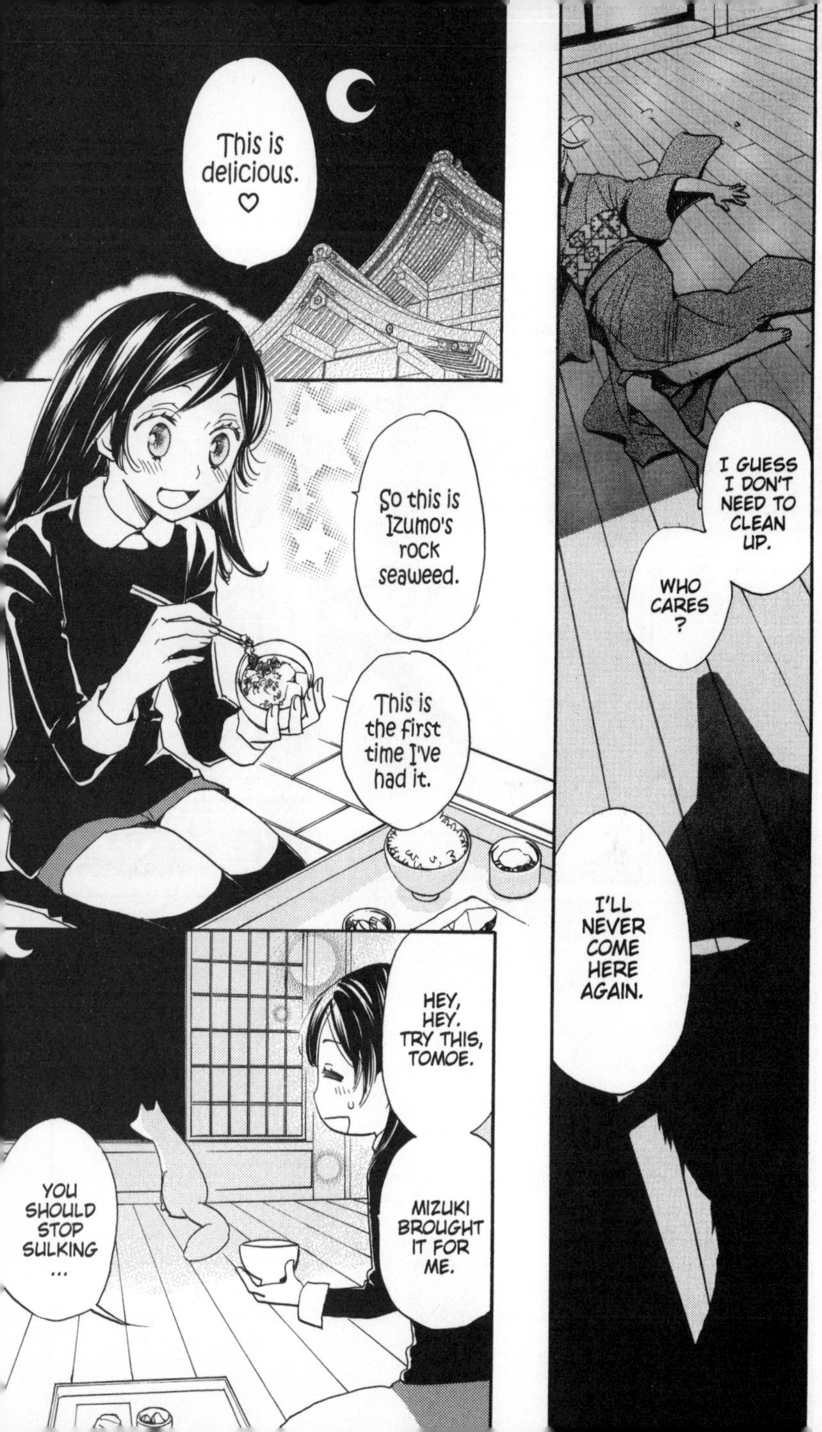
I GUESS I DON'T NEED TO CLEAN UP.
WHO CARES?
I'LL NEVER COME HERE AGAIN.
This is delicious. ♡
So this is Izumo's rock seaweed.
This is the first time I've had it.
HEY, HEY. TRY THIS, TOMOE.
MIZUKI BROUGHT IT FOR ME.
YOU SHOULD STOP SULKING...

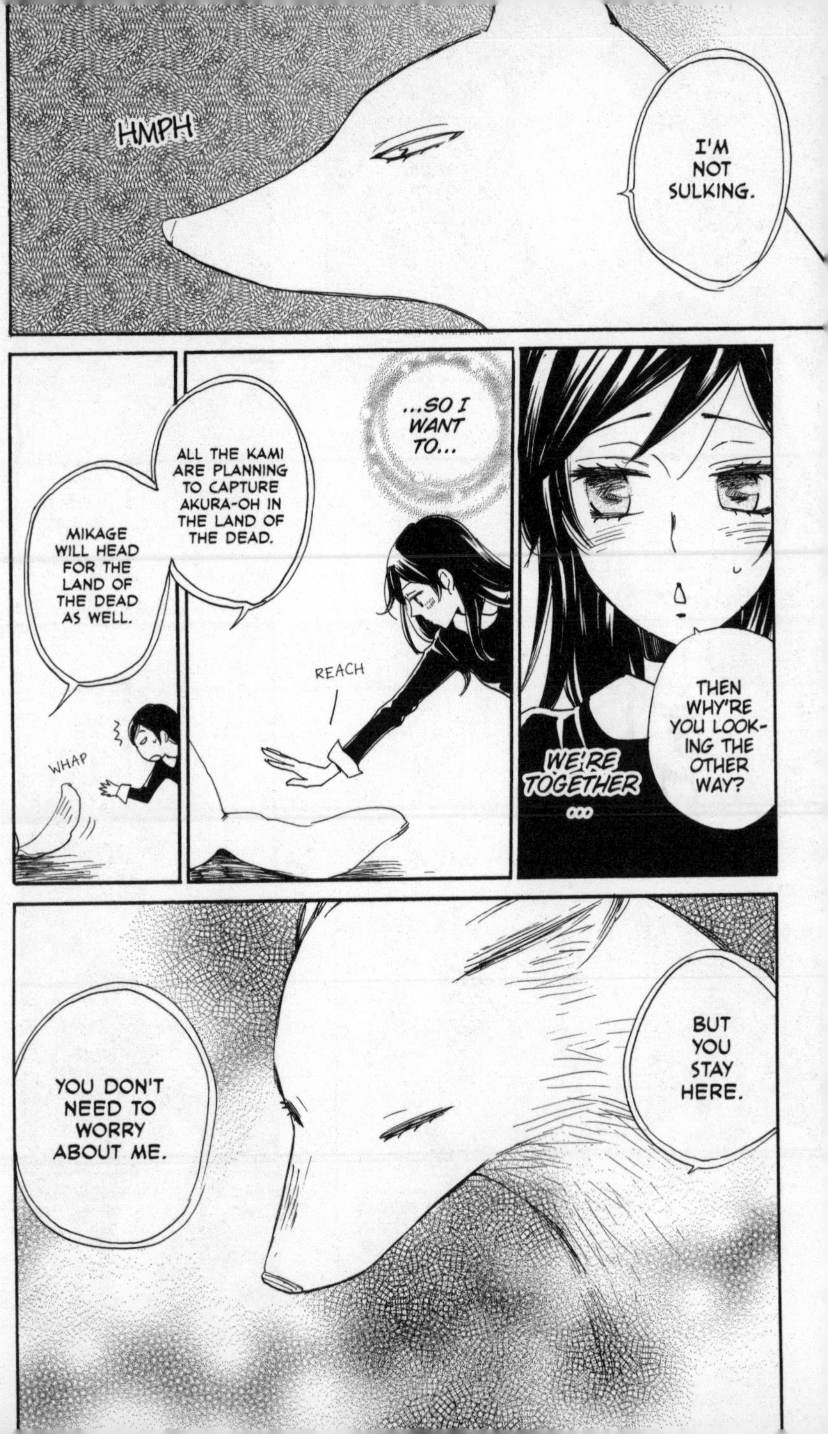
I'M NOT SULKING.
HMPH
THEN WHY'RE YOU LOOKING THE OTHER WAY?
WE'RE TOGETHER...
...SO I WANT TO...
ALL THE KAMI ARE PLANNING TO CAPTURE AKURA-OH IN THE LAND OF THE DEAD.
REACH
MIKAGE WILL HEAD FOR THE LAND OF THE DEAD AS WELL.
WHAP
BUT YOU STAY HERE.
YOU DON'T NEED TO WORRY ABOUT ME.

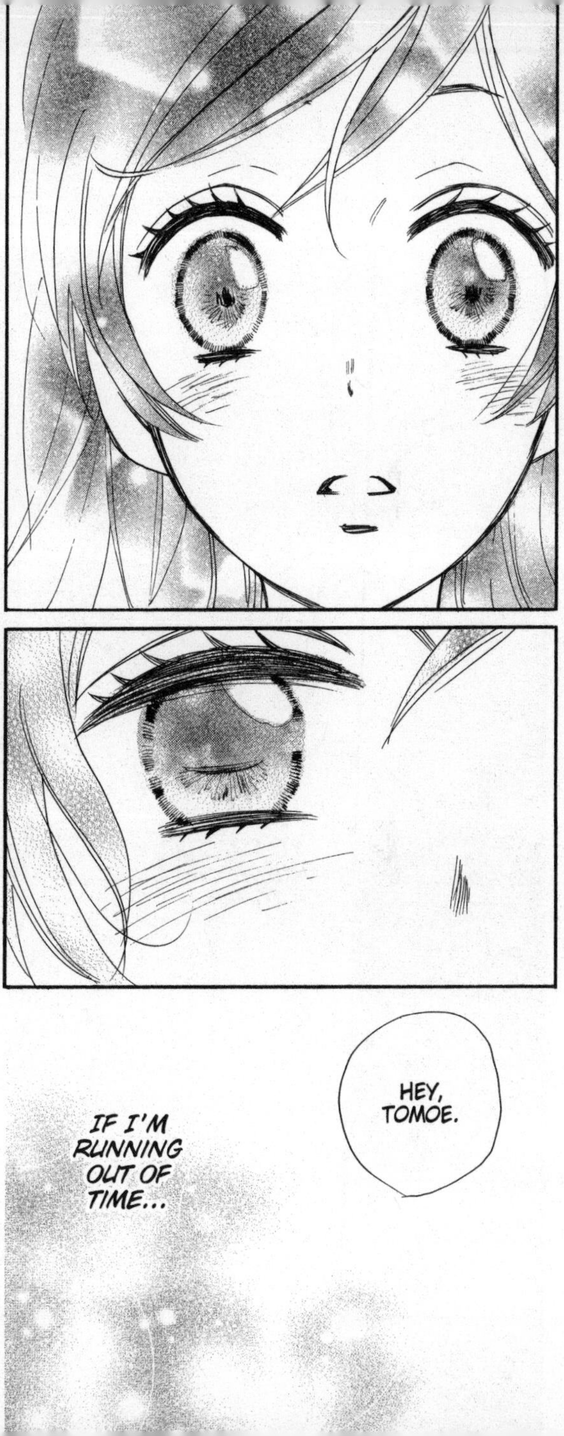
HEY, TOMOE.
IF I'M RUNNING OUT OF TIME...

Julietta Suzuki
c/o Shojo Beat
VIZ Media, LLC
P.O. Box 77010
San Francisco
CA 94107

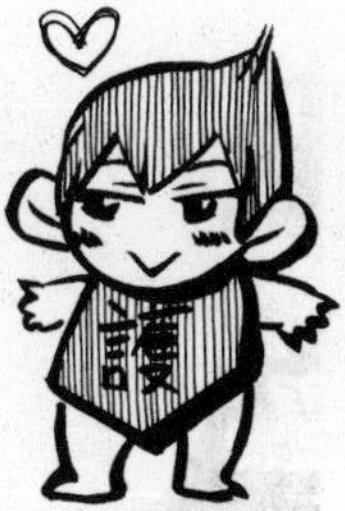

Thank you!

*My BLOG
http://suzuju.jugem.jp/

*Twitter
@hiyokosweet

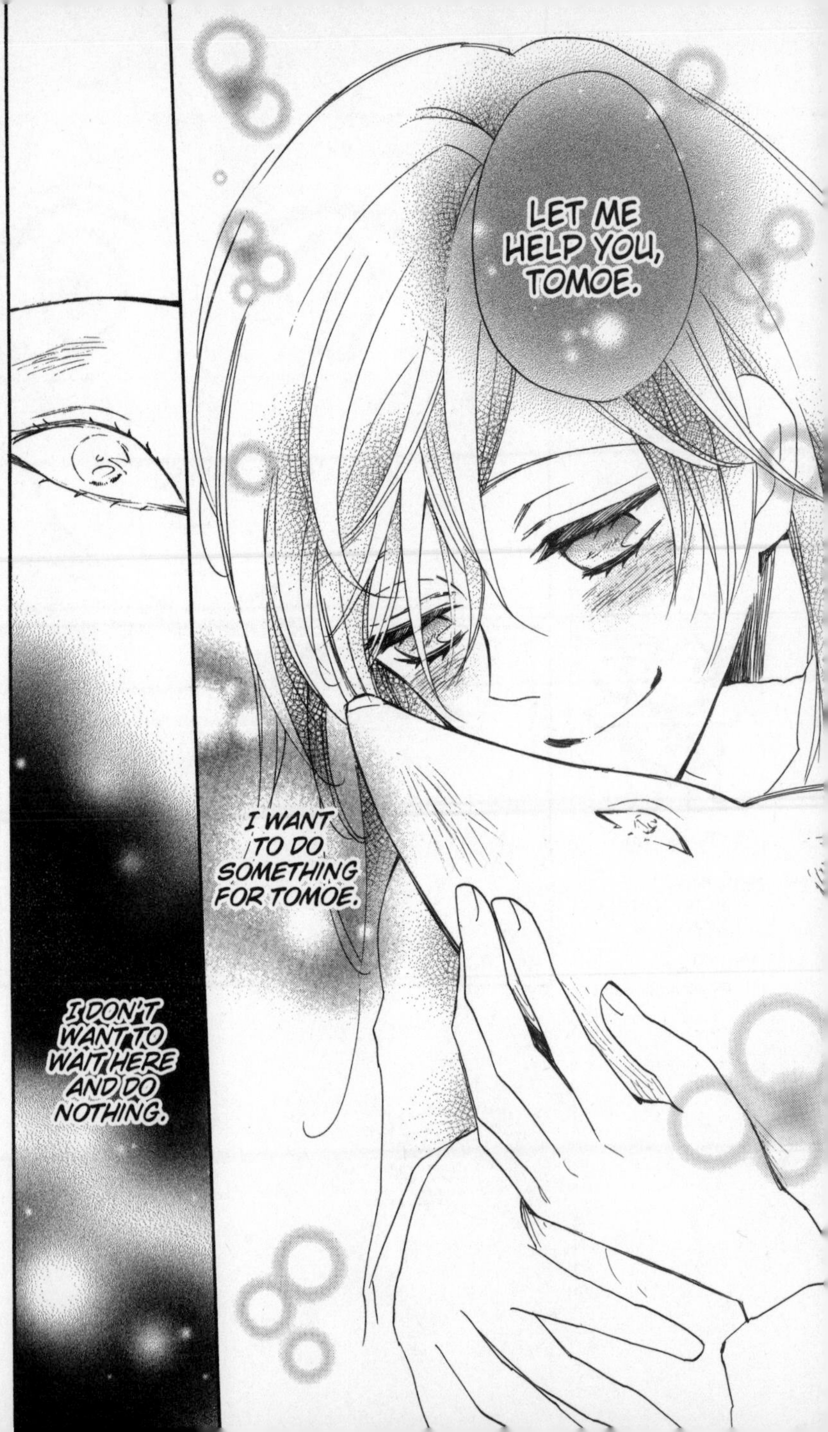
LET ME HELP YOU, TOMOE.
I WANT TO DO SOMETHING FOR TOMOE.
I DON'T WANT TO WAIT HERE AND DO NOTHING.

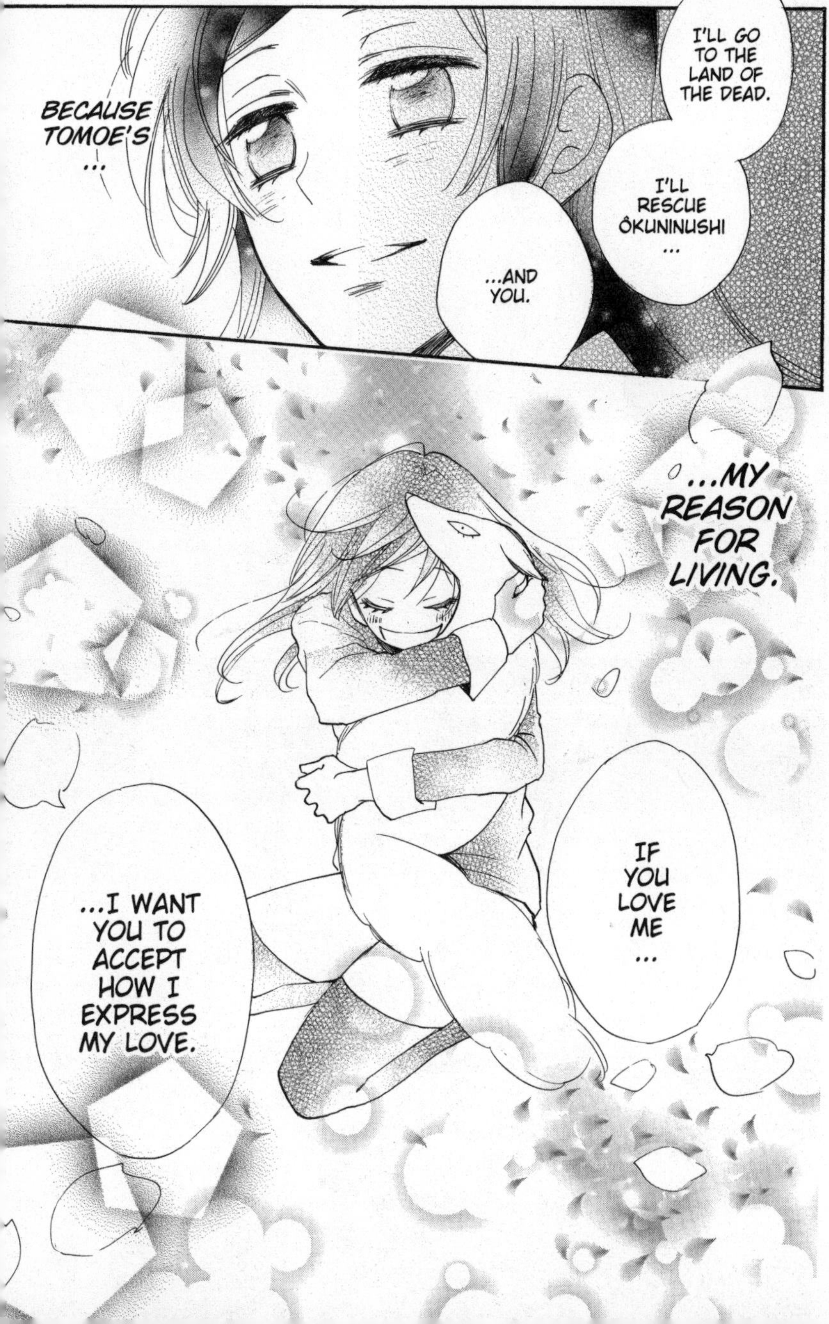
I'LL GO TO THE LAND OF THE DEAD.
I'LL RESCUE ÔKUNINUSHI ...
...AND YOU.
BECAUSE TOMOE'S ...
...MY REASON FOR LIVING.
IF YOU LOVE ME ...
...I WANT YOU TO ACCEPT HOW I EXPRESS MY LOVE.

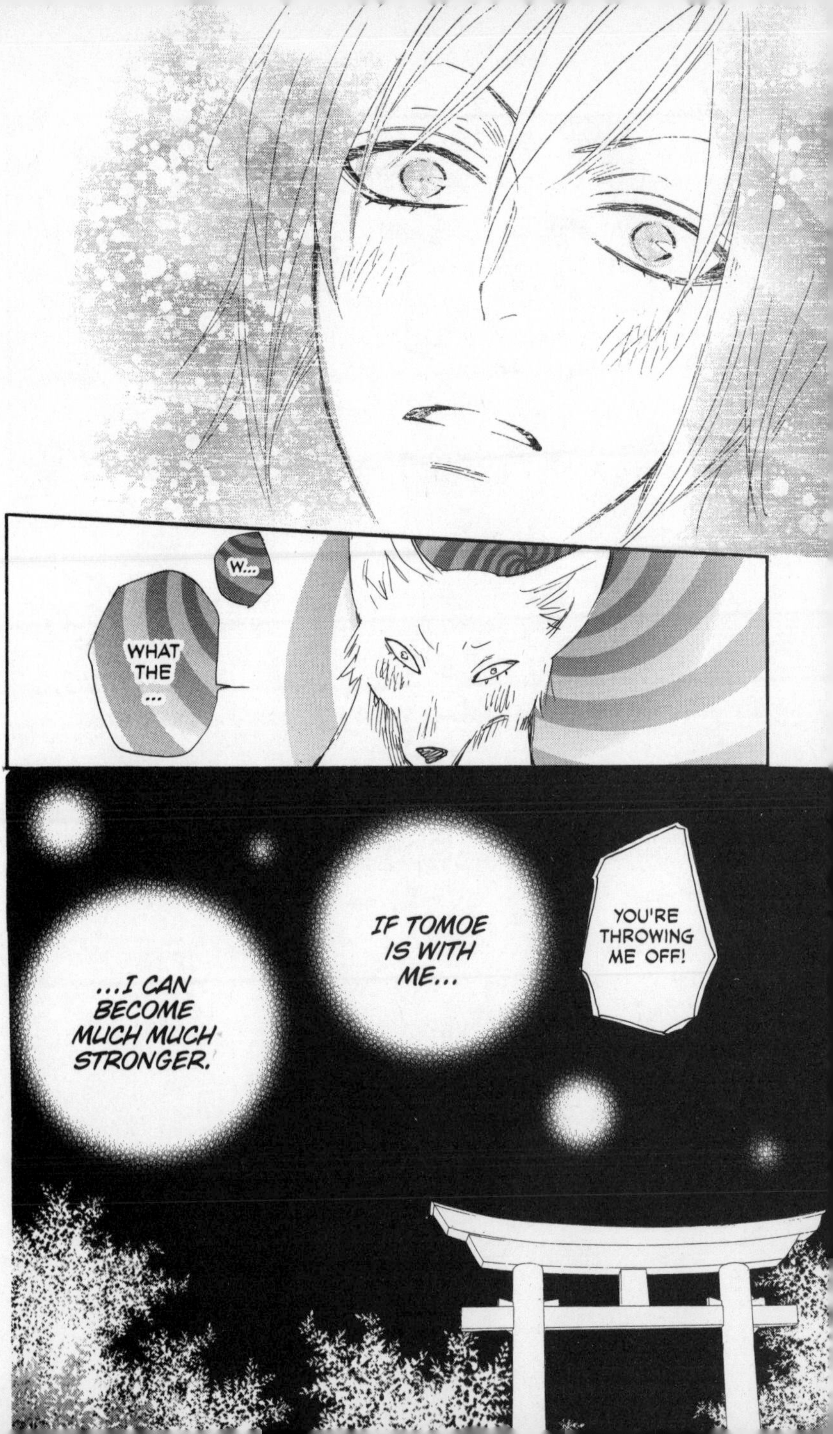
W...
WHAT THE ...
YOU'RE THROWING ME OFF!
IF TOMOE IS WITH ME...
...I CAN BECOME MUCH MUCH STRONGER.

The Otherworld

Ayakashi is an archaic term for yokai.

Kami are Shinto deities or spirits. The word can be used for a range of creatures, from nature spirits to strong and dangerous gods.

Komainu are a pair of guardian statues placed at the gate of a shrine, usually carved of stone. Depending on the shrine, they can be lions, foxes or cows.

Onibi-warashi are like will-o'-the-wisps.

Shikigami are spirits that are summoned and employed by onmyoji (yin-yang sorcerers).

Shinshi are birds, beasts, insects or fish that have a special relationship with a kami.

Tengu are a type of yokai. They are sometimes associated with excess pride.

Tochigami (or *jinushigami*) are deities of a specific area of land.

Yokai are demons, monsters or goblins.

Honorifics

-chan is a diminutive most often used with babies, children or teenage girls.

-dono roughly means "my lord," although not in the aristocratic sense.

-kun is used by persons of superior rank to their juniors. It can sometimes have a familiar connotation.

-san is a standard honorific similar to Mr., Mrs., Miss or Ms.

-sama is used with people of much higher rank.

Notes

Page 39, panel 3: Izumo
A city in Shimane prefecture, and home to Izumo Oyashiro shrine, one of the most sacred sites in Shinto. Ôkuninushi (Daikokuten) is the kami enshrined in Izumo Oyashiro.

Page 44, panel 2: Yogiri-guruma
It literally means "night fog carriage."

Page 55, panel 2: Ofuda
A strip of paper or small wooden tablet that acts as a spell.

Page 92, panel 1: Mount Kurama
A sacred mountain in Kyoto and the birthplace of the Reiki philosophy. In folklore it is the home of the tengu king Sojobo.

Julietta Suzuki's debut manga *Hoshi ni Naru Hi* (The Day One Becomes a Star) appeared in the 2004 *Hana to Yume Plus*. Her other books include *Akuma to Dolce* (The Devil and Sweets) and *Karakuri Odette*. Born in December in Fukuoka Prefecture, she enjoys having movies play in the background while she works on her manga.

KAMISAMA KISS
VOL. 21
Shojo Beat Edition

STORY AND ART BY
Julietta Suzuki

English Translation & Adaptation/Tomo Kimura
Touch-up Art & Lettering/Joanna Estep
Design/Yukiko Whitley
Editor/Pancha Diaz

KAMISAMA HAJIMEMASHITA by Julietta Suzuki
© Julietta Suzuki 2015
All rights reserved.
First published in Japan in 2015 by HAKUSENSHA, Inc., Tokyo.
English language translation rights arranged with
HAKUSENSHA, Inc., Tokyo.

Printed in the U.S.A.

Published by VIZ Media, LLC
P.O. Box 77010
San Francisco, CA 94107

10 9 8 7 6 5 4 3 2 1
First printing, June 2016

www.viz.com
www.shojobeat.com

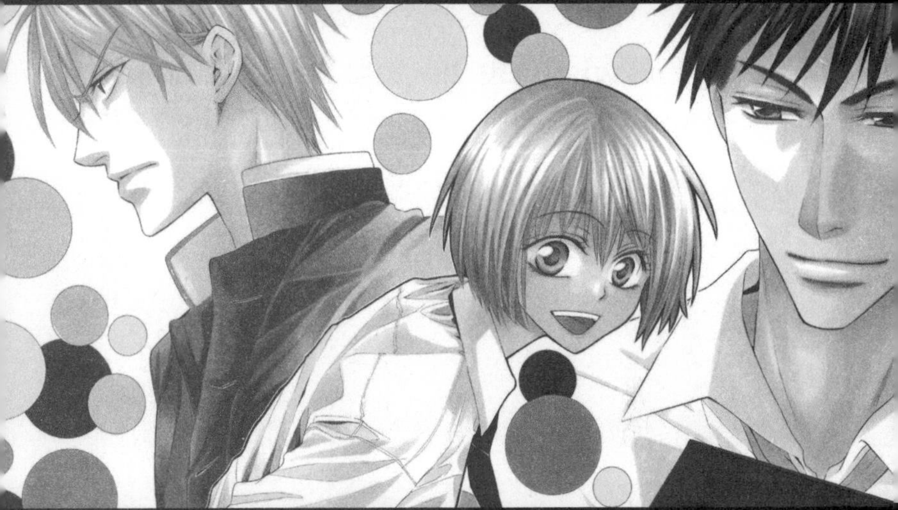

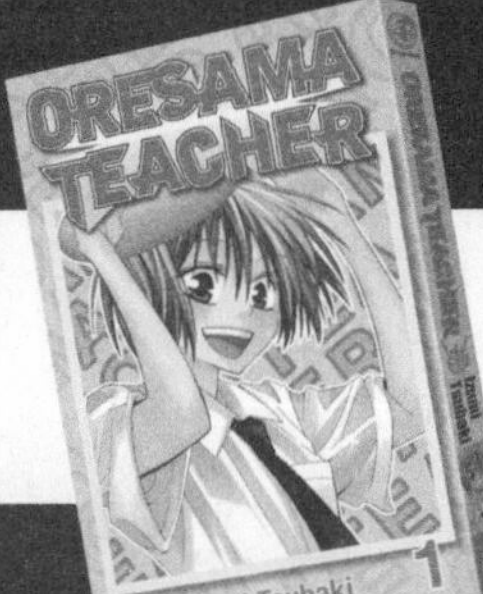
ORESAMA TEACHER
Izumi Tsubaki
1

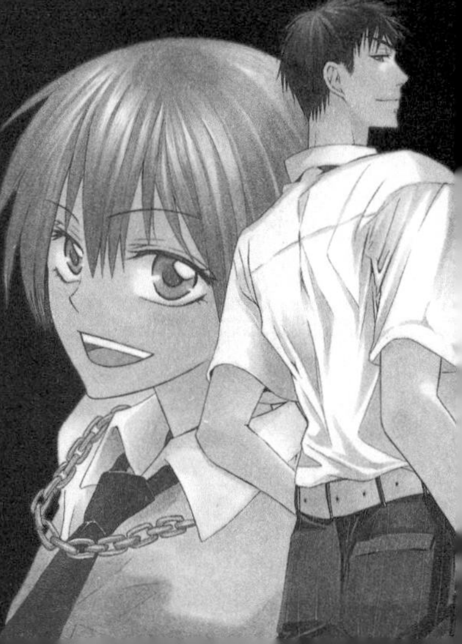